REPUBLICS OF KNOWLEDGE

Republics of Knowledge

NATIONS OF THE FUTURE IN LATIN AMERICA

NICOLA MILLER

PRINCETON UNIVERSITY PRESS

PRINCETON & OXFORD

Published by Princeton University Press
41 William Street, Princeton, New Jersey 08540
99 Banbury Road, Oxford OX2 6JX

press.princeton.edu

First paperback printing, 2025
Paperback ISBN 9780691271347

The Library of Congress has cataloged the cloth edition as follows:

Names: Miller, Nicola, author.
Title: Republics of knowledge : nations of the future Latin America / Nicola Miller.
Description: Princeton : Princeton University Press, 2020. | Includes bibliographical
    references and index.
Identifiers: LCCN 2020009287 (print) | LCCN 2020009288 (ebook) |
    ISBN 9780691176758 (hardback) | ISBN 9780691185835 (ebook)
Subjects: LCSH: Political science—Philosophy. | Knowledge, Theory of. |
    Nationalism—Latin America.
Classification: LCC B65 .M55 2020 (print) | LCC B65 (ebook) | DDC 980–dc23
LC record available at https://lccn.loc.gov/2020009287
LC ebook record available at https://lccn.loc.gov/2020009288

British Library Cataloging-in-Publication Data is available

Editorial: Ben Tate, Hannah Paul, and Josh Drake
Production Editorial: Kathleen Cioffi
Jacket/Cover Design: Chris Ferrante
Production: Danielle Amatucci
Publicity: Alyssa Sanford and Amy Stewart

Jacket/Cover art: Elena Izcue (Lima, 1889–1970), study of pre-Hispanic design.
Watercolor on paper, 11.3 × 21.5 cm. Lima Art Museum. Donated by Elba de
Izcue Jordán / ARCHI / Digital Archive of Peruvian Art

This book has been composed in Arno

Printed in the United States of America

CONTENTS

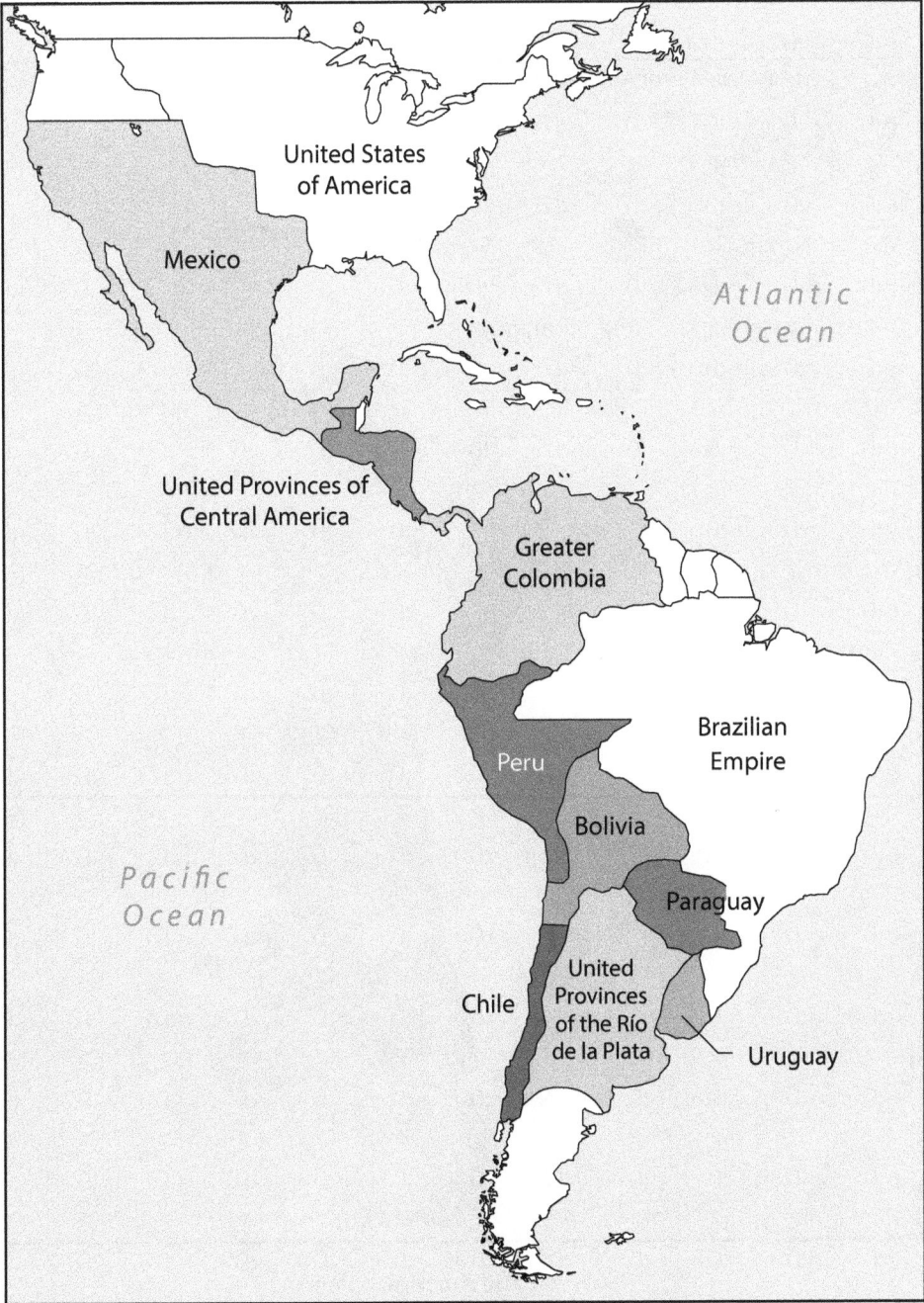

MAP 1. Latin America, *c.* 1830

United States of America

Mexico

Cuba

Haiti/Dominican Republic

Puerto Rico

Honduras

Guatemala

Nicaragua

El Salvador

Costa Rica

Venezuela

Colombia

Ecuador

Atlantic Ocean

Peru

Brazil

Bolivia

Paraguay

Pacific Ocean

Chile

Argentina

Uruguay

MAP 2. Latin America, *c.* 1900

REPUBLICS OF KNOWLEDGE

Introduction

PICTURE YOURSELF as a scientific explorer in the Age of Revolution, setting out in the 1820s to brave the high passes of the southern Andes. Travelling overland from the Argentine coast, you might well have broken your journey at Mendoza, a small city a day's horse-ride away from the cordillera. Here, more than a thousand kilometres from the cosmopolitan port of Buenos Aires, you'd probably have been surprised to find a place thriving on the benefits of the latest knowledge in agronomy, philosophy and education.

Your trip across the 'gloomy brown' desert would have been long and nerve-wracking.[1] It took at least two weeks by stage-coach, a month by oxen and cart; the roads were rough and lawless.[2] What a relief, then, to be strolling at sunset along Mendoza's tree-lined Alameda, refreshed by a gentle breeze lifting the hot, dry air, awed by the granite-under-snow soaring above.[3] Gazing out over the well-irrigated orchards and market gardens, you'd have spotted some vineyards, too, but the wine industry for which the area is now famous was still half a century away. Wandering the paved streets, you could have counted seven churches and nearly as many schools,[4] including the Colegio de la Santísima Trinidad (College of the Most Holy Trinity), one of independent Argentina's first state secondary schools. You'd have seen a large hospital, a public library and a theatre, all in the low-lying buildings that in those days were the only defence against earthquakes.[5] You might have noticed the absence of church bells, most of which had been melted down to make 'cannons, ammunition and bayonets' during the war.[6] But you would have heard music, strains of Bach and Rossini mingling with Peruvian *tristes*, the songs of mourning for the Inca emperor.[7] In the main square, wandering over to join a cluster of people listening to the news read aloud, you'd have picked up stories from local papers that were among the first to appear in South America. The three publications available reflected the fault-lines of this post-independence era: a liberal weekly, promoting social reform through modern subjects such as political economy, geography and education; an official register, containing decrees and regulations both governmental and civil; and a Catholic paper denouncing the governor's anticlerical reforms.[8] None of these experiences would have been commonplace for a traveller to the interior in the early 1820s, when Mendoza was unusual in its variety of cultural life. Ten years earlier—or, indeed, ten years later—it would have struck any visitor as a very different place.

Mendoza's ephemeral 'age of enlightenment', as one historian of the city ruefully dubbed it, can be dated virtually to the day.[9] It began on 7 September 1814, when the arrival of General José de San Martín (1778–1850) brought the struggle for independence right into the heart of a city that had hitherto been distant from the main events. Three thousand Chilean patriots arrived a month later, fleeing defeat by the Spanish at the Battle of Rancagua (1–2 October). San Martín had requested the post of governor, having identified Mendoza as the best base of operations for his planned military campaign to liberate Chile. It is easy to see why he chose it. The local economy might have been designed to supply an army, producing leather for saddlery and tack, cloth for uniforms, food, and saltpetre to make gunpowder. Political conditions were right: Mendoza had declared in favour of the May Revolution of 1810, which deposed the Spanish viceroy, initiated self-government in Buenos Aires and triggered the war that led to independence in 1816.[10] Mendoza's location, at the intersection of lands later known as the Republics of Chile and Argentina, had made it a hub for goods, people and information. Chinese silk and Bengal cotton were hauled over the mountains from the Chilean port of Valparaíso; the 'herb of Paraguay', brought by gauchos, went the other way to fill the maté-pots of Santiago.[11] People of many kinds passed through Mendoza, so San Martín had no difficulty finding an Argentine engineer to run a gunpowder factory, or a Chilean friar with the expertise to take charge of the arsenal and ordnance.[12] Nor was there any shortage of manual labour: the local economy had relied on African slaves since the early 1700s, after most of the enslaved indigenous people had been taken by landowners to work in other parts of Chile. An estimated two-thirds of Mendoza's Black people, whom San Martín famously declared to be the best foot soldiers, were 'liberated' to join the Army of the Andes when it left in 1817, constituting about half of the whole force. During the previous two years they had continued to work the mines and fields for the war effort, while taking every opportunity to deploy the new liberal principles to improve their lot.[13]

The war economy brought both practical and philosophical enlightenment to Mendoza and its surroundings. Out in the rural areas, a long tradition of innovative irrigation, dating back to pre-Inca days, was moved on again by the latest techniques. The town benefited from improvements in public health: a military hospital, dispensaries, smallpox vaccination and sanitation. Education had been a priority in Mendoza since the Jesuits arrived in 1608, but at the municipal secondary school opened in 1818 the curriculum, shorn of scholasticism, introduced students to both academic and applied knowledge, including the nation-making skill of drawing (see chapter 4). Lay teachers were trained to take elementary education into the countryside. San Martín ordered the town's first printing press so that news of the war could be spread as quickly and accurately as possible. The mobilisation generated a spirit of common endeavour which made a benign environment for civil associational life. By the 1820s, Mendoza had been transformed. James Thomson, missionary of the London Bible Society, who had travelled widely in South America promoting Lancasterian schools as a sweetener for Protestantism, arrived in Mendoza in 1822 to find both a sympathetic governor and a pool of citizens keen to found a society that encouraged primary instruction for all children.[14] The scars of war were all around, of course. Death, fear and political reaction cast long shadows over social reform. In the main square, someone would probably have pointed a visitor to the spot where the Chilean brothers Carrera, conspirators against San Martín, had been executed by firing squad. Still, Mendoza was something of an oasis, a place where there were at least signs of the modern knowledge order envisaged by independence leaders. Even the music sounded better: the bands of the Liberating Army had improved their skills and expanded their repertory as they tramped back and forth across the Andes.[15]

For these crucial ten years or so after independence, Mendoza can be seen as a republic of knowledge in microcosm. If San Martín's arrival symbolised the beginning of this experience, then a sign of the end was the departure, in February 1824, of the young reformist intellectual Juan Crisóstomo Lafinur. The multitalented Lafinur, a poet, dramatist and composer, had spent three years in Mendoza, during which time he co-founded the theatre, edited the official periodical and entertained the locals with concerts featuring his own music. As master of philosophy at the secondary college, he had also been teaching the secular liberalism that had finished his career in Buenos Aires. The success of his Catholic opponents in forcing him into exile in Chile indicated the enduring strength of political forces marshalled against any experiments in modern ways. In the early 1820s, conditions in Mendoza were

emblematic both of the drive to reform unleashed by the wars of independence and of the various forces acting as a brake. In this respect, as in so many
others, the changes brought by independence appeared to be dramatic, and in
the long run turned out to be, but they were slow to work their way into the
interstices of society.

Republics of Knowledge

The term 'republic of knowledge' is intended to evoke three ideas that guide
this book. First, it conceives of knowledge as having a reality and an organisation along the lines of a republic or series of republics. In this sense the phrase
deliberately echoes the well-studied early modern Republic of Letters (a virtual community of intellectuals, based on networks of correspondence reaching across the globe, active from the mid-sixteenth to the late eighteenth centuries), while indicating some significant differences. Second, the term
highlights the fact that the sovereign states created in Spanish America were
founded on promises of enlightenment for all the people; hence access to
knowledge was intrinsic to the legitimacy of the new republics. Third, it suggests the potential for nations to be interpreted as communities of shared
knowledge.

The image of knowledge as a republic alludes to a transnational ideal based
on principles of openness, free exchange, absence of privilege and a sense of
the common good. The republic of knowledge aspires to be sovereign, in the
sense of being governed by its own values and, it follows, secular, meaning
outside the control of any religious authority (rather than non-religious or
anti-religious). Like the Republic of Letters, it could only fulfil its purpose of
advancing knowledge through the exchange of ideas by being a community
'not of those who shared beliefs but of those who differed'.[16] Like the Republic
of Letters, the republic of knowledge is sustained by a mix of formal institutions, voluntary associational life, voyages of both body and mind, rites of
exchange, and rituals of belonging. But while the Republic of Letters was a
network of learned individuals, membership of which required certain credentials, the modern republic of knowledge is constituted as rightfully open to all.

During the wars of independence in Spanish America, republics of knowledge in this first sense of open exchange converged and to an extent overlapped with the second sense of knowledge as foundational to a modern republic. On battlefields across the region, one of the most precious pieces of
equipment was the *imprenta volante* (portable—literally flying—printing

press). About half a metre long, sturdily built yet light enough to be trans-ported on the back of a mule, these European-made gadgets of gleaming wood and bronze were easily operated with a single lever. Reports of the campaigns, proclamations of victory and rallying calls to hastily designed flags, as well as military orders and policy edicts, were cranked out onto single sheets of scarce paper, snatched from the miniature press and borne away to be read—often out loud—wherever people gathered.[17] These new nations of the 1810s and 1820s were born in smudgy print.

The idea for this book took shape when I discovered so many references in the primary sources to new kinds of knowledge and the benefits they could bring. Advocates of independence played astutely on the burgeoning popular interest in ideas and information, stoking the Black Legend with claims that the Spanish rulers had deliberately kept the Americas in ignorance of modern science and philosophy in order to sustain their 'tyranny' and prevent Ameri-cans from coming to 'the awareness [*el conocimiento*] of their own dignity'.[18] In the fight to retain control of American lands, the Spanish authorities lent substance to these claims by calling for the destruction of recently developed industries, such as cloth factories in Quito and vineyards in Chile, and closing new educational institutions and libraries founded by provisional govern-ments. Independence leaders made compelling offers to go out and get 'all the knowledge that we lack: [. . .] Chemists, Mineralogists, books, all kinds of instruments for the sciences and the arts, a Chemical Laboratory, and a colony of craftsmen'.[19] The new knowledge was to be secular and open to public scru-tiny. No longer channelled down the secret passages of Jesuit compounds, it was already out on the streets, being shouted aloud from the new printed matter. Periodicals and newspapers multiplied, even if few lasted more than one or two months, and all the incoming governments made sure to publish one. References to the importance of knowledge came up in popular songs and street theatre. An embrace of modern knowledge was both a founding justification for the new political communities emerging in the Americas and a necessary condition of an inspirational future.

Knowledge, especially of a science or an industrial process, conferred citizenship rights on foreigners in many parts of independent Latin Amer-ica.[20] All the republican constitutions contained clauses protecting freedom of the press; some also guaranteed free speech and free association. Most of them—unlike the US Constitution—contained a commitment to promote public education; some of them specifically deferred making literacy a re-quirement for citizenship for ten to twenty years, in an optimistic prediction of how long it would take to implement the policy.[21] A few went further still, making it a constitutional stipulation to advance the general enlightenment of the population.[22] The connection between knowledge and the nation was embedded at the outset and echoed down the generations. It is striking how often nineteenth-century disputes over policy were couched in terms of a conflict about what kind of knowledge was legitimate and whose claims to knowledge had the higher status. The causes of a meat shortage, the demarcation of a border, the correct response to a foreign power—all were conducted as battles of knowledge, each side deploying an arsenal of references, metaphors and citations to rout their opponents.[23] At the centenaries of independence, the governments of Latin America showcased their commitment to knowledge as a key element in their strategies for the twentieth century. Their critics, especially students and workers, targeted universities as sites for national regeneration through decolonisation (the University Reform Movement). In the twenty-first century, now that access to knowledge has risen to the top of the political agenda everywhere, Ecuador was the first country in the world to establish a Ministry of Knowledge and Human Talent.[24] Colombia, after decades of civil war, in 2017 introduced mobile libraries into the zones of bitterest conflict, in a pioneering initiative to revive hope and stimulate economic development.[25] While US presidents enshrine their legacies in archival vaults, Latin American presidents build public centres of culture.

The term 'republic of knowledge' stands for an ideal political community in which republican values—autonomy, equality, liberty, justice—are invested and realised in equitable access to knowledge for everyone. This ideal was embedded in the political discourse of the Spanish American republics, where all the people were in principle citizens, so that even when schools could not be built to educate them governments produced countless political catechisms to instruct everyone in republican rights and duties. As is well known, in practice most people were excluded from citizenship, under both liberal and conservative regimes, until well into the twentieth century. Yet what has always struck me as remarkable about the course of modern Latin American history, and in need of explanation, is the continual return, despite all the obstacles, to the cause of making knowledge and culture more accessible. The question of public knowledge has continued to matter greatly in Latin America, as was inversely (perversely) confirmed by the burning of books under the military dictatorships of the 1970s.[26] This book explores the period between independence and its centenaries to find out why.

What Is Knowledge?

There are many kinds of knowledge, of course, and many ways of knowing. The English language is unusual in its catch-all noun, which defers any differentiations—practical or theoretical, formal or informal, pure or applied—to the secondary, adjectival place. Likewise, English has only the verb 'to know'. In contrast, there are two words for 'knowledge' in Spanish (*el conocimiento / el saber*) and Portuguese (*o conhecimento / o saber*), as in other modern European languages. These distinctions vary between languages and are hard to capture in English, precisely because the corresponding vocabulary is lacking, but in broad terms they differentiate knowledge acquired through immediate experience of the material world (such as sensation, perception or personal acquaintance) from more abstract types of cognition (concepts, ideas and theories). In Spanish and Portuguese, moreover, both of the nouns for 'knowledge' tend to be used in the plural form, especially *los/os saberes*. 'Ignorance', however, always seems to be a substantive singular.

At the time of Latin American independence, there was no common equivalent to the generic term 'knowledge'. The singular noun *el conocimiento* was used primarily in the sense of awareness of something, with the implication of its being brought out into the open. In early draft constitutions, it often referred to practices of accountability—for example, in the stipulation that the legislature should 'publish an annual statement and account of income and expenditure of funds for the knowledge [*conocimiento*] of all'.[27] This phrase is adapted from the US Constitution, significantly with the emphasis on making the information *known to everyone* rather than merely making it available.[28] There are rare examples of a usage of *conocimiento* closer to the modern sense of a body of information socially endorsed as true, but to convey that meaning it assumed the plural form. The Constitution of El Salvador (1824), for example, included the caveat that 'in eight years' time, when practice and more knowledge [*más conocimientos*] have laid bare the disadvantages and advantages of the present Constitution, a Constituent Congress can be convened to examine it fully in order to reform it'.[29] *Saber* appeared occasionally as a verb, in the sense of 'to know how to'—especially common was *saber leer y escribir* (to be able to read and write)—but not at this stage (that I have seen) as a noun. Plural forms—*ciencias, saberes, conocimientos*—remain the norm in Spanish rather than the singular, generic 'science' or 'knowledge' of English.

It follows that to use the English term 'knowledge' in a history of *los saberes* and *los conocimientos* of Latin America is potentially hazardous. At the very least, it risks imposing a conception of knowledge derived from one particular set of historical circumstances onto societies with quite different histories. At worst, given the current dominance of English as an international scholarly language, it may be seen to condone the claims to objectivity and universal validity made by the Anglo-American academy, some sectors of which often seem oblivious to the economic and political advantages that have shaped their international lead in research and technological development. My aims are precisely the opposite: to question any such claims to easy transferability of knowledge and to analyse how it is that certain forms of knowledge come to acquire greater legitimacy and status than others, both locally and globally. I use the generic term 'knowledge' not to prioritise any particular type of knowledge over any other, but to prompt the necessary questions about how different kinds of knowledge came to be valued or despised or ignored in any particular context. Typologies of knowledge may highlight variety, but they also embed into the analysis certain assumptions from one context that may not be appropriate in another. They often rely on the binary divides that are prevalent in modern European thought—formal or informal; abstract or concrete; pure or applied—and that have been criticised by many thinkers from Latin America. The generic term makes it possible to keep open a global, comparative framework that is both truer to the historical record—in that many connections and exchanges were made both within and between different societies—and allows us to avoid working on the basis that different cultures are incommensurable. It also avoids the essentialist assumption that particular kinds of knowledge are unique to specific groups—for example, 'creole' or 'indigenous' knowledge. My working definition of knowledge is information that the holder believes to be verifiable by criteria that command social acceptance. For the purposes of this book, knowledge is the outcome of a process of interpretation that involves a human mind making a claim to a demonstrable truth. The crux of the matter is how and why some such claims are socially accepted while others are not, with all the attendant consequences for asymmetries of power.

Nations as Republics of Knowledge

It is easy to see why Benedict Anderson, looking to the Americas for a new way of thinking about nationalism, came up with the term 'imagined communities'. After independence, new governments sat precariously in former viceregal capitals, trying to extend control over racially divided populations spread over vast territories. Their economies, which had been geared to the needs of the colonial power, were further weakened by the destruction or ne-glect of mines and livestock during the wars. Formal sovereignty was quickly compromised by informal imperialism, as Britain, France and, from the mid-century onwards, the United States competed to take advantage of the end of Iberian rule. Entrenched regional and corporate interests, not least the Catho-lic Church, stood ready to defend their privileges. Despite the rapid creation of flags, anthems and shields, many people argued that these countries were little more than figments of the imagination. Building a state, let alone a nation, was a formidable task. Yet the great Cuban intellectual José Martí made a valid point when he argued, in 1891, that the nations of Spanish America had in fact made remarkable progress in a relatively short time, especially when compared with the European nations that had taken centuries of war and social unrest to achieve stability.[30] In Spanish America, state-building and the creation of col-lective identities intersected and were negotiated in the realm of public knowl-edge, which was central to the success or otherwise of national integration. On that basis, I will explore the idea that these nations—and possibly all modern nations—are best understood as communities of shared knowledge rather than as imagined communities.

The book is in two parts. The first, 'Landscapes of Knowledge', explores a variety of approaches to the history of knowledge, all of them designed to bring together questions often treated separately (in histories of education, art or science). I'm hoping to avoid academic silos by drawing on a variety of disciplines to frame the questions, rather than merely to adjust the answers. This entails thinking about institutions and practices of knowledge (usually the preserve of sociology) alongside ideas, images and discourses (the con-cerns of intellectual history or cultural studies). It involves looking beyond the famous public intellectuals, whose lives and works have been widely studied, to highlight the contributions to knowledge of many other kinds of people. It means paying attention to the variety of locations, both geographical and so-cial, in which knowledge was exchanged—from fashionable salons in the capi-tal city, where society women exercised their discreet influence on policymak-ers, to small-town squares, where travelling theatre companies acted out the heroic deeds of struggles against the Spanish. In the second part of the book, 'Knowledge for Nation-Making', I aim to illustrate how and why knowledge and its circulation mattered in public debates, in policy-making and in the formation of collective identities.

The book draws on evidence from independence in the 1810s to the cente-nary celebrations of the 1910s, when governments made much of their achievements in making knowledge more accessible and restated the founding commitments to public knowledge as a key constituent of a modern nation. The 1920s saw a series of changes that made me close there. The Mexican Revolution (1910–20) highlighted the tensions between the liberal republican discourse of rights for all and the harsh practices of exclusion and authoritarianism; its reverberations throughout Latin America, along with the new possibilities raised by the Soviet Revolution, gave a new urgency to the questions of what the majority of the population knew, as well as what was known—or not known—about them. At the same time, and not coincidentally, there were increasingly aggressive moves by the United States to colonise knowledge production throughout the Americas. Besides the promotion of its own financial, commercial and management practices, there was effectively a US takeover of scientific exchange within the Americas, as what had been congresses organised by and for Latin Americans became events orchestrated to serve the Pan-American Union, resulting in a dramatic drop in attendance.[31] In the knowledge economy itself, the introduction of radio and cinema redefined the possibilities for information and ideas to circulate.

There are many more areas of knowledge to explore than was possible in this project. In part 2, below, I look at philosophy of language, geography, political economy, civil engineering and philosophy of education, because they emerged as especially relevant to debates about nation-making, but there could equally well have been chapters on law, political thought, history, medicine, mining engineering, ethnography and theology. I chose to focus on institutions that I felt shaped the landscapes of knowledge throughout Latin America, mainly national libraries and universities, but in some places, at some times, others were equally if not more important, notably official bodies for gathering statistics, certain secondary colleges or particular museums. And I came to suspect that actually informal settings such as travelling shows, agricultural fairs or improvised lecture halls were the real unexplored hinterland of knowledge circulation. Nor have I dwelt on the institutional roles of the Catholic Church and the religious orders, because as discussed in chapter 2, some clerics were more receptive to modern science and philosophy than their secular peers, and I argue that the fundamental epistemological questions at stake blurred the divide between church and state. My greatest regret is that I have only touched upon the history of struggles by indigenous peoples to secure recognition for their knowledge, because without the requisite languages and ethnographic training I did not feel qualified to undertake this work, which in itself raises serious questions about how historians can access the world of ideas that exists beyond written texts.

My evidence is drawn mainly from three case studies: Argentina, Chile and Peru. It seemed necessary to look in some depth at particular examples of knowledge orders in different societies, but they are intended to be indicative of a range of possibilities, not in any sense representative. These three were chosen because Argentina and Chile had many features in common at the time of independence, while their diverging histories over the course of the following century should prove telling. Evidence for Peru's extensive connections with both Argentina and Chile made it a good choice for the third example, which was confirmed by thinking about how its differences from Argentina and Chile—above all in having a far higher proportion of indigenous peoples in its population—would stimulate comparative thinking. Moreover, all three countries compared themselves with each other throughout the nineteenth century. But they also made connections and comparisons with various other Latin American countries, notably Mexico, Brazil, Uruguay, Colombia and Ecuador, so I will follow the sources to trace these transnational connections and thereby open windows onto the history of knowledge in other parts of Latin America. The question of nomenclature is always tricky, but in general I will refer to 'Spanish America' when comparing the three case studies and to 'Latin America' when making observations I have reason to think are more widely applicable. As outlined above, the founding commitment to public knowledge was evident in primary sources from all over the region (including the Empire of Brazil). Although the specific conclusions about my case studies will not necessarily apply even to other Spanish American republics, I hope that this book's variations on the general theme of knowledge in relation to the making of nation-states will resonate with historians of anywhere in the modern world. The book aims to be suggestive rather than comprehensive in approach.

Latin America is usually regarded as an exception to general theories, notably of colonialism, nationalism and liberalism. Yet it was in that part of the world, not in Europe, that the Age of Revolution brought the founding of a second wave of modern republics (1808–26), as the outcome of uprisings that certainly *evolved into* wars of anti-colonial liberation, even if they did not all start out as such. It was in Latin America that pioneering attempts were made to apply liberal principles in societies with inherited caste divisions and corporate institutions. It was there that some of the richest debates about the vexed relationship between collective identities and contract-based individualism took place. Anderson was right that these countries were the ultimate test-cases of viable nation-statehood, because they were constituted without any obvious differences of race or language to differentiate one from another. His main point stands despite all the problems that historians of the Americas have identified with the specifics of his interpretation.[32] What was meant by a 'nation' was debated throughout Europe and the Americas during the nineteenth century; it was not so much the idea itself that was 'European' as the one-state, one-culture model that acquired the status of ideal type there. The differently constituted nation-states of Latin America have been grappling for two centuries with questions that have more recently become troubling throughout the world. To what extent could modern political systems based on secular rights and freedoms coexist with widespread religiosity and racially based social hierarchies? How could the defence of sovereignty be combined with openness to investment and ideas from elsewhere? What role could the circulation of knowledge play in supporting cohesive social identities and participatory democratic life? Latin America has a unique reserve of historical experience which challenges historians of all areas of the world (including core European countries) to rethink their approaches to the history of knowledge.

PART I

Landscapes of Knowledge

1

Public Libraries, Modern Nations

Siempre imaginé que el Paraíso sería algún tipo de biblioteca
(I have always imagined that Paradise would be some kind of library)

—JORGE LUIS BORGES[1]

BORGES WAS BY NO MEANS the first Latin American to imagine the history of the future contained in a library. In the midst of the wars of independence (1808–26), when legitimacy was precarious and literacy confined to a privileged few, the Liberators took time out from their military campaigns to attend to the creation of major public libraries. Often the first institutions to be founded, these libraries were located close to the centre of political power in the cities that became the capitals of the newly sovereign states. Individuals of varied political views saw them as both symbol and source of the 'universal enlightenment' that General José de San Martín serenely declared to be 'more powerful than our armies' for protecting the embryonic political communities.[2] San Martín himself waived some of his expenses on condition that they went to the new library in Santiago de Chile, and one of his first acts as Protector of Peru was to found the Biblioteca Nacional.[3] Simón Bolívar, who declared 'morality and enlightenment' to be the 'twin poles of a Republic', instigated a public library in Caracas in 1814 and later intervened to ensure that Lima's library was restored after sackings by royalist troops in 1823 and again in 1824.[4] In Bolivia, Generals Antonio José de Sucre and Andrés de Santa Cruz created the Biblioteca Pública de Chuquisaca (now the capital, Sucre). In Bogotá, Francisco de Paula Santander moved the existing Royal Public Library— the only one in Spanish America, opened in 1777—into better premises, added materials from the famous botanical expedition led by José Celestino Mutis

TABLE 1. The Founding of National Libraries in Latin America

Foundation date of library	Country	Date of independence*	Name of library
1810	Brazil	1822 (1821–24)	Real Biblioteca de Rio de Janeiro, opened to the public 1814; renamed Biblioteca Imperial e Pública 1822; renamed Biblioteca Nacional 1876
1812	Argentina	1816 (1810–18)	Biblioteca Pública de Buenos Aires; renamed Biblioteca Nacional de Argentina 1884
1813	Chile	1810 (1810–18)	Biblioteca Nacional de Chile
1815	Uruguay	1825 (1811–30)	Biblioteca Pública de Montevideo; renamed Biblioteca Nacional de Uruguay 1938
1821	Peru	1821 (1811–24)	Biblioteca Nacional del Perú
1825	Colombia	1810 (1810–19)	Real Biblioteca Pública, founded 1777; renamed Biblioteca Nacional de Colombia 1825
1825	Bolivia	1825 (1809–25)	Biblioteca Pública de Chuquisaca; renamed Biblioteca Nacional de Bolivia 1872
1830	Ecuador	1809 (1820–22)	Biblioteca Pública de Quito, founded 1792; renamed Biblioteca Nacional del Ecuador 1830
1833	Mexico	1810 (1810–21)	Biblioteca Nacional de México
1833	Venezuela	1810 (1810–23)	Biblioteca Nacional de Venezuela
1870	El Salvador	1821; independent republic 1840	Biblioteca Nacional Salvadoreña
1879	Guatemala	1821; independent republic 1847	Biblioteca Nacional de Guatemala
1880	Honduras	1821; independent republic 1838	Biblioteca Nacional de Honduras
1882	Nicaragua	1821; independent republic 1838	Biblioteca Nacional de Nicaragua
1887	Paraguay	1811	Biblioteca Nacional del Paraguay
1888	Costa Rica	1821; independent republic 1838	Biblioteca Nacional de Costa Rica
1901	Cuba	1868; 1902** (1868–78 and 1895–98)	Biblioteca Nacional de Cuba
1941	Panama	1821; independent republic 1903	Biblioteca Nacional de Panamá

* These are the dates officially commemorated on national independence days. In most countries, the wars lasted several years: the most widely accepted dates are indicated in brackets.

** 1868 is the official date; 1902 was the date of formal constitutional sovereignty after US occupation (1898–1902).

(1732–1808), and duly baptised it the Biblioteca Nacional de Colombia.[5] The Uruguayan General José Artigas, who has been inaccurately caricatured as a wild man of the plains with scant regard for ideas, urged his troops to be 'as learned as [they were] brave' and sanctioned the founding of the Biblioteca Pública de Montevideo as conducive to 'public happiness'.[6] At the inauguration ceremony in 1816 the schoolchildren of Montevideo sung of 'opening the doors / to enlightenment' after 'three centuries' of living 'in the shadows'.[7] As Don Quijote had argued, in a passage frequently cited by independence leaders, arms and letters were at heart collaborators rather than rivals.[8] By the end of the wars of independence, a state-supported library, intended for public use, with a remit to build up a national collection, had been founded in nearly all of the new countries (see table 1).

Over the following century, despite periods of official neglect and persistent underfunding, the national libraries were recurrently invoked as a source—sometimes the only credible one—of institutional continuity. As institutions 'born with the *patria* itself',[9] they fulfilled a central role in social self-definition as touchstones of what was meant by *lo público* and—the distinctions are revealing in themselves—*lo nacional*. They became the sites of legendary knowledge endeavours: the library in Buenos Aires provided a home for the periodical *La Abeja Argentina*, a cornucopia of new discoveries in both sciences and humanities;[10] the members of Andrés Bello's commission to draft Chile's Civil Code, which was imitated throughout the Americas, did their research in the Biblioteca Nacional;[11] Peru's influential Sociedad Geográfica de Lima started out in offices on the top floor of its national library.[12] Many of them have also been sites of national disaster, both natural (an earthquake devastated Ecuador's library in 1859; a fire destroyed Peru's in 1943) and manmade (the libraries of Uruguay, Colombia and Peru were all used as barracks during nineteenth-century wars). Their place in national life continues to be celebrated: foundation days have long featured annually in the press; special anniversaries have customarily been gala occasions, attended by local dignitaries and foreign guests.[13] Borges is only the most internationally famous of a long list of distinguished Latin American literati who have served as directors of their national libraries. As symbols of the fundamental role of knowledge in battles for sovereignty, the national libraries were microcosms of public policies, social attitudes towards knowledge, and conceptions of nationhood. The initial holdings—a mix of sequestrations from religious orders, contributions from private collectors and donations from members of the public—mirrored the range of interests and ideas jostling for position in the new polities. Would the public good prevail over corporate power? Could a few slim volumes of enlightenment philosophy cast a long enough shadow over the massive tomes of canon law and scholastic theology? Who actually ventured into the dim reading rooms in former monasteries or colonial courts, and what did they do there?

Founding Visions

The independence-era public libraries were founded on enlightenment principles of applied learning as the route to a good society, by which was meant a society of learning (*letras*), industry (*artes*) and political rights (*derechos*). Within this common framework, there were marked variations in emphasis, reflecting specific configurations of power and knowledge in different locations. In Buenos Aires, the library was envisaged as a secular 'school of knowledge' (*escuela de los conocimientos*) for the creation of 'enlightened ideas' (*las luces*); in Chile, as a repository of freedom and utility; in Peru, as a centre of the enlightened spirit that would conserve popular political rights.[14]

The very names of these new libraries indicated the diversity of views about the desirable balance between the *public* mission of education (creating citizen readers) and the *national* role of conservation (preserving heritage). In Buenos Aires, Montevideo and Chuquisaca, they started out as *public* and were not officially designated as national until 1884, 1938 and 1872, respectively. The emphasis on the public was not confined to the republics of Spanish America: the independent Empire of Brazil, which was exceptional in benefiting from the contents of the Biblioteca Real of Lisbon, brought over by the Portuguese royal family after 1808, also embedded a public element in designating its prestigious institution the Biblioteca Imperial e Pública da Corte. In most other countries, including Chile and Peru, the library was founded as the *national* library. Of course, what was meant by either national or public in any of these new countries, whether republican or monarchical in constitution, was both changing and contested. In the mid-nineteenth century, Peru's main library was commonly referred to as the Biblioteca Nacional de Lima, in a small but telling sign of both the aspirations and the limitations of nationhood at that time. Primarily a *limeño* project, the idea of a unified nation had little or no resonance in many parts of Peru's territory. In each of the countries, the libraries were prisms through which such wider social concerns were refracted. Their varying emphases on general education, specialist research and conservation had implications for conceptions of citizenship, inclusivity and identity in the new political communities. A comparison of Argentina, Chile and Peru will illustrate what I mean.

The most manifestly *public* of the independence-era libraries, at least in the sense of popular involvement in its creation, was the first of them, the Biblioteca Pública de Buenos Aires (BPBA). The BPBA was founded in September 1810, shortly after the Revolución de Mayo (May Revolution) had established a provisional creole government, and it opened to readers in 1812, four years before independence was achieved as the United Provinces of the River Plate. The library was proposed by the secular intellectual Mariano Moreno (1778–1811) as part of a wider strategy to foster public debate through print culture. In his far-reaching vision, the BPBA would be linked to periodical publishing (the esteemed *Gazeta de Buenos Aires*, 1810–21), translation (Rousseau's *The Social Contract*, 1810) and support for local writers. Moreno memorably evoked the library as a space open to all, where creative encounters could take place between the learned and the curious, with the books standing by as arbiters, 'on hand to settle [any] dispute'.[15] Moreno, who was himself from a relatively modest background, wanted the library to operate independently not only of the Catholic Church but also of any institution of formal education. He therefore astutely sought to strengthen the library's legitimacy as a genuinely popular undertaking by encouraging public contributions to the collections.[16]

Moreno correctly anticipated that a call for donations would meet with an enthusiastic response in the particular circumstances of Buenos Aires, where—unlike in the rest of the region—fighting began not after 1808 because of Napoleon's invasion of Iberia, but in 1806, against a British invasion. The *porteños* (inhabitants of Buenos Aires) twice expelled the invaders, but not before they had seen the Colegio de San Carlos, the jewel of their few colonial institutions of learning, turned into a barracks for British troops. They probably also knew that the British had seized a portfolio of maps of the Pacific Ocean from the Compañía de las Filipinas, a Spanish government trading agency and therefore technically classifiable as a 'public' body, the property of which it was possible to justify including as the spoils of war.[17] These maps, shipped to London along with the more publicised booty of silver from the Argentine treasury, ultimately proved to be worth far more than five tons of pesos to the British as their empire expanded into the Pacific.[18] When debates about sovereignty began after the French overthrow of Fernando VII, *porteños* had recently been on the receiving end of a ruthless act of imperial knowledge theft that highlighted only too well the importance of information in the exercise of power. At the same time, their confidence had been dramatically boosted by the successful defence of their city against the world's leading imperial power. They had good reason to believe that a secure foundation of knowledge would make a difference to the future.

The lists of donations to the library, published in the *Gazeta de Buenos Ayres*, were almost as long as those on other pages registering contributions to the war effort.[19] Most came from the well-heeled, but the records specify fourteen donations worth less than 10 pesos, for example, from 'Don Antonio Camargo, porter at the Secretaria del Superior Gobierno', who gave 2 pesos (out of a monthly salary of perhaps 30 pesos), and Doña Manuela de Castro, who sent 'various pieces of wood for the shelves worth 8 pesos'.[20] Most people gave money; some gave books or furniture; a few handed over whole collections of papers, artefacts and drawings for the librarians to sift. Unsurprisingly, the desirability of the gifts varied: however public-spirited you felt, in a place where the pleasure of the text was hard to come by, it was easier to part with a 'stern *Tractatus* of law or theology' (which the library probably already had) than to relinquish a favourite 'sentimental novel (*novela lacrimosa*), such as Mme Cottin's *Matilde*'.[21] But most of the modern books in the library came from members of the public. The Irish-born physician Miguel O'Gorman generously presented his medical tomes; English merchants gave commercial handbooks and surveys of political economy; José Miralla, a former pupil of the first librarian, sent from Havana a complete edition of the classics by state-of-the-art Italian printer Giambattista Bodoni. Bartolomé Muñoz, a priest attached to the army of the Banda Oriental (the eastern territory that is now Uruguay), sent 'several useful dictionaries, a collection of plans and engravings of European and American cities, including Montevideo and Córdoba, and a series of his own drawings and paintings of birds and mammals of the River Plate'.[22] Later, public subscription enabled the purchase of distinguished French botanist Aimé Bonpland's private collection when he abandoned Buenos Aires for fieldwork in the interior.[23] Thus, although books from public donations constituted a relatively small proportion (probably about a quarter) of a collection registered in 1823 at 17,229 volumes,[24] their significance outweighed their numbers. In substance, as printed books in modern European languages they stood out among the long lines of vast parchment tomes in Latin; in symbolic terms, they were markers of a potential civil society. Such was the interest in the library that the public clamour for it to open prevailed over the pleas of the first librarian for more time to arrange the thousands of books into a respectable order on the shelves.[25] Moreno, appointed as Protector of the new institution, sadly did not live to defend its founding radicalism; he died at sea en route to London in early 1811, before the BPBA had even opened. The first two librarians, both painstaking clerics, reasserted a more orthodox approach to running a library, drafting a long list of regulations to ensure that any creative encounters took place in the strictest silence.[26] The BPBA's early experience of public involvement was both an inspiration and a warning for founders of libraries elsewhere.[27]

In Santiago, the national library was planned in tandem with the Instituto Nacional, the upper-level institution designed to teach useful knowledge (*conocimientos útiles*) and thereby to create citizens well versed in modern techniques of agriculture, mining and artisanal industry.[28] Indeed, the foundation of the library was announced at the inauguration of the institute, in 1813. The government's call for donations was patriotic, rather than public, in emphasis, and it was more explicitly oriented towards economic development— even listing the specific texts required for courses at the Instituto Nacional— than Moreno's evocation of enlightenment as a general good. The founders, Francisco Antonio Pérez (1764–1828), Agustín Manuel Eyzaguirre (1768–1837) and Juan Egaña (1768–1836), announced 'a patriotic subscription' on the basis that 'the first step that all peoples take to become wise is to establish great libraries', but Chile's library was not yet 'worthy of a people that marches protected by Providence along all the paths of glory'. Thus, in order to ensure that 'everyone understood the interest that each citizen had in the well-being of the others, and that Chile made up a single family', they invited contributions of 'books and models of machines for the [industrial] arts'.[29] In response, a steady stream of donations came in, not only from Santiago but also from other parts of Chile, and there is evidence that they continued—albeit sporadically— throughout the Spanish occupation of 1814–17, even though the library was shut.[30] The decision of the royalist troops to close the public library lent substance to the claims of independence supporters that to remain part of Spain was to remain ignorant of modern science. To defend the library was to defend the future of a sovereign Chile. After independence had been secured, in 1818, official papers relating to the library emphasised its 'utility' as a resource for stimulating 'national prosperity'.[31] Throughout the nineteenth century, Chilean statesmen continued to invoke the decree of 1823 that characterised the Biblioteca Nacional de Chile (BNCh) as a shared resource of up-to-date information 'for the instruction of all citizens'.[32] The idea was that a vine-grower anxious to cure a new plant disease, or a manufacturer hoping to go into olive oil production, or a building worker interested in learning more about the principles of construction would all find their needs met in the BNCh.[33] Unlike in Buenos Aires, practical enlightenment was embedded at the outset.

In Lima, the establishment of 'a Biblioteca Nacional in this Capital for the use of everyone who wishes to come to it' was decreed by San Martín on 28 August 1821, one month to the day after the proclamation of independence.[34] The library was envisaged as a beacon of enlightenment, able to dispel the 'dense atmosphere' of ignorance that Spanish rule had left hanging over Peru like the notorious *garúa* (sea mist) of Lima. The library's presence alone would act as the stimulus for the 'natural human impulse towards perfectibility' to rise from 'the ruins of tyranny'.[35] Given the long and distinguished history of research and scholarship at the Universidad Mayor de San Marcos, it is striking that San Martín chose to depict Peru as 'the centre of [Spanish] despotism and arbitrariness', where 'all the resources of enlightenment' were scarce.[36] The vehemence of the anti-Spanish rhetoric—which runs through the discourse of the early 1820s—can partly be explained by the fact that although independence had been declared, it took three more years to be won, in December 1824. In the course of the fighting, two royalist attacks on the new library reinforced its role as a symbol of resistance to imperial despotism. Yet there is also an epistemological point to be made here. It was the 'study of the sciences relative to the rights of man' that San Martín claimed Peru had been denied by Spanish policy; for the Protector and his ministers this was the 'useful knowledge' that it was the particular duty of an independent government to make immediately available to 'all classes of the state'.[37] If 'the advances made by human reason over the preceding centuries' were accessible to the next generation, the Liberator maintained, then 'the principles that conserve public and private rights would spread, law and tolerance would triumph and philosophy, the principle of all liberty, the consolation of all ills and the origin of all noble actions, would ascend the throne'.[38] And the first director, the pro-republican canon Mariano José de Arce, agreed, citing Isaiah in Latin—'those that walked in darkness have seen a great light'—to support his own view that 'our political regeneration [was] due to the lights of right reason, and to philosophy'.[39] Thus, in the foundation of the national library, there became lodged in the Peruvian state a perceived connection that was to prove lasting between access to knowledge and the conservation of political rights. 'Useful knowledge' was conceived very differently in Lima and in Santiago.

The initial holdings of the national libraries spoke volumes about the extent to which continuity with the colonial past was inescapable despite commitment to another future. While most of the holdings were formed from a combination of state requisitions from religious orders, private gifts or purchases from individual bibliophiles and donations from members of the public, the interest lies in the extent to which the proportions of these three elements varied from country to country. The libraries left behind by the Jesuits, after their expulsion from all Spanish territories in 1767, were a notable component of all three: about one-third in Buenos Aires, over half in Santiago and more than three-quarters in Lima. Given the obduracy of the Black Legend stereotype of Jesuits as obscurantist pedants, it is worth emphasising the range and variety of their materials, which included manuscripts, maps and scientific instruments as well as books.[40] In many ways, the Jesuit worlds of learning were microcosms of the wider knowledge ecosystem, in their eclectic mix of theology, classical traditions of the Americas, linguistic and ethnographic scholarship, jurisprudence, philosophy—both European and Asian—and modern science.[41] The problem was that these collections had not been kept up to date or were poorly preserved, or both.[42]

In Buenos Aires, the stocking of the shelves of the public library prefigured the recurrent battles over resources between the port city and the interior that shaped the history of Argentina during the nineteenth century and have continued to this day. About 2,500 Jesuit books were confiscated from Córdoba, in retaliation for a royalist uprising, although wily locals found various ways of retaining some of them for the university library. Books were also hauled in from other Jesuit sites throughout the River Plate.[43] The other main contributions, apart from the public donations, were the private library of a late-colonial bishop, Manuel de Azamor y Ramírez; the holdings of the main secondary school, the Colegio de San Carlos; and the personal collection of its rector, Luis José Chorroarín, who became the first librarian of the BPBA. In Santiago, over 8,200 Jesuit books, more than half the initial holdings, were transferred from the Universidad de San Felipe, where they had been held, apparently without much care being taken of them, since the expulsion. The rest of the collection was assembled from wherever there were books to be found, in a move parallel to the merging of all the educational institutions of Santiago, apart from the university, into the new Instituto Nacional. To supplement the public donations, Bernardo O'Higgins (1778–1842), the liberator of Chile and its first head of state (1817–23), commandeered books from the Convictorio de San Carlos, Santiago's leading secondary school; from the booty of a shipwrecked Spanish frigate;[44] and from the courts of justice (Tribunales).[45] In Lima, the core of the new library, some ten thousand books, was the magnificent Jesuit collection dating back to 1568, which contained many rare early works, not least because the Jesuits had introduced printing in 1584. After the Order was expelled, ownership of their Peruvian library was transferred to the Universidad de San Marcos, although the books themselves remained in the building of the Jesuit College, where the national library was installed in 1822.[46] Donations from the general public were not sought, but the collection was increased to 11,256 volumes by gifts from independence leaders Hipólito Unánue, Manuel Pérez de Tudela, Francisco Xavier Mariátegui, José Joaquín de Olmedo and—famously—San Martín. The Liberator gave around six hundred books from his personal library.[47] It is well known that many of them were products of the French Enlightenment, but it is less often noted that they featured serious works of *practical* enlightenment. The *philosophes* were certainly there, but so were major studies of modern agricultural and industrial methods, such as the *Encyclopédie*'s sixteen volumes on *Arts et métiers*; the *Encyclopédie méthodique*'s edition on *Manufactures*; and the *Colección general de máquinas* (1783), a compilation of mechanical advances by Spaniard Miguel Suárez y Núñez.[48] There were also works in Spanish on mining from Mexico, where specialist training had been introduced in 1792.[49] Overall, the establishment of national public libraries came at significant cost to the colonial institutions of learning—above all, the universities. What Benedict Anderson referred to as 'the wiring of the old state' was still in place,[50] but new circuits had been devised to circumvent some of its default connections.

The sites of national libraries are saturated with symbolism. The BPBA opened in 1812 in a former Jesuit complex near the Plaza de Mayo, then, as now, the centre of political power in Buenos Aires. From this cluster of church, college and procurator's office, the Jesuits had dispensed the only classical education available in Buenos Aires, along with remedies prepared in the city's first pharmacy, as well as run their prosperous missions in the interior. After the expulsion, a reforming Bourbon viceroy installed Buenos Aires's first printing press (1780), a Protomedicato (College of Royal Physicians) to teach modern medicine (1779) and an Escuela Naútica (School of Navigation) (1779). To locate the public library on this site, which became known as the Manzana de las Luces (literally, the Block of Lights, or Enlightenment Block),[51] was to insert it into a historical tradition of advances in knowledge. It was also to make a bold statement of deconsecration by occupation: from then on, knowledge was to be secular and accessible instead of ecclesiastical and concealed (beneath the gleaming marble and mahogany of the Jesuit halls ran a network of secret tunnels). Yet the initial current of radicalism ran dry and the BPBA was to remain in its cramped and forlorn, if austerely beautiful, premises in the Manzana de las Luces until 1901. The Chilean library started out in the stolid splendour of the colonial Customs House, then was moved in 1834 into the former Jesuit site near the cathedral, placing it next to the Museo Nacional de Historia Natural, which, under the direction of Claudio Gay, was developing into a notable research centre. The National Library of Peru was unusual in remaining on its original site, the former Jesuit College in the heart of old Lima, for 185 years—the special significance of which will be explained below.

The Public and the National, from the 1830s to the 1920s

As in other fields of nation-making, it soon became evident that the meaning of 'public' in relation to libraries was, in practice, constrained in various ways. A severe lack of resources was part of the problem, because the founding enthusiasm for the libraries was followed by decades of erratic state funding and inadequate accommodation. It was not until the twentieth century that the national libraries had enough staff to open in the evenings and thereby make them accessible to anyone who worked during the day.[52] But other factors were involved, notably a fundamental tension between two visions of the library: as a resource for public education or as a repository for national culture. To an extent, this echoes the conflict experienced in libraries down the ages, between conserving the books and permitting them to be read, with the attendant risk of damage. National libraries throughout Europe were also struggling with this problem, but most of them solved it by formally restricting access to their collections, a policy that went largely uncontested during the nineteenth century. This was not an option for the Latin American libraries, which were founded to be *public*. What is particularly noteworthy is that even though these libraries were used by only tiny minorities of the populations, there were fierce battles to defend the *right* to public access, in relation to opening hours, availability of the books and, above all, lending. Concern about the libraries was by no means confined to intellectuals.

The evidence on library usage is sketchy until the late nineteenth century, when consistent records began to be kept. Even then, some registers show numbers of visits, others numbers of individual readers, so it is hard to make comparisons. In Buenos Aires, isolated figures from 1823 show an impressive 3,284 visits, of which 2,174 were from Buenos Aires itself, 677 from other provinces and 426 from abroad.[53] When consistent records were begun in 1872, there were fewer than three thousand visits, even though the population of the city of Buenos Aires had quadrupled. By 1881, the peak year, there were 7,715; the numbers later declined, a fact the then director attributed to improvements in other libraries, especially the municipal lending library.[54] In both Chile and Peru, it was estimated that there were twenty to thirty readers a day in the 1850s, which would mean more than seven thousand visits a year.[55] By the end of the nineteenth century, the BNCh recorded more than a hundred readers every day.[56] Most of the accounts of what it was like inside these libraries were written by intellectuals, whose complaints about noisy reading rooms imply that the majority of readers were there for purposes other than pursuing scholarship. Chilean writer Benjamín Vicuña Mackenna loved many things about the reading rooms at the British Museum, but above all he luxuriated in the 'deep silence' that was such a contrast to what he had experienced in the BNCh.[57] Memoirs and travelogues suggest that visitors to their national library went there to keep up with the newspapers and periodicals, to consult encyclopedias or reference works or to read recently published works of fiction, especially by eminent foreign authors—Alexandre Dumas (père) being a particular favourite. [58] Textbooks were more readily available, and borrowable, from collections in schools and colleges; they were also serialised in periodicals.

Throughout the nineteenth century, newspapers reported incidents that showed a degree of public concern about policy in 'their' libraries. For example, in Chile in 1834 a new rule prohibiting readers from direct access to the books provoked protests, as did a restriction on bringing in packages or one's own books. In response, Andrés Bello sternly pointed out that direct access to the shelves was not allowed in the British Museum, either.[59] When opening hours were eventually extended beyond working hours, to coincide with the independence centenary, it was at least partly in response to public pressure, especially from teachers' and workers' organisations, many of which by then had their own libraries (see chapter 10). In Buenos Aires, there were intermittent protests over the regulations stipulating that books were on no account to be taken out of the library. When a political battle over lending was fought, in the 1870s, it was resolved by paving the way for a network of new 'popular libraries' dedicated to a loan service. The enduring public interest in the national libraries makes them barometers of the volatile atmosphere created by the combination of republicanism, with its pressures to extend popular sovereignty and political rights, and nation-building, with its imperatives to foster political and cultural unity. Let us see how the relationship between the public and the national played out differently in the libraries of my three case studies.

Argentina

The first director to advocate a national role for the BPBA was Vicente Quesada, who did a great deal to modernise the library during his decade-long tenure (1871–79): overseeing a new reading room; making a start on a subject catalogue; introducing statistical record-keeping; and cultivating international exchanges to ensure the distribution of Argentine publications.[60] His main legacy, however, was to play down the public remit of the library in order to assert a national role for it. He did so in a political context in which the constitutional status of Buenos Aires was still unresolved after a period of secession from the other provinces (1854–61). Although Buenos Aires province rejoined the federation in 1861, matters were not settled until the 1880s, when the city of Buenos Aires was formally established as the capital of the Argentine nation and various organisations were duly transferred from provincial to national jurisdiction. It was as part of this process that the BPBA was renamed the Biblioteca Nacional Argentina in 1884. Before then, one consequence of the divided authorities in Buenos Aires, which functioned as the de facto but not de jure capital, was that an alternative Biblioteca Nacional was established in 1870 by Domingo F. Sarmiento, President of the United Provinces of the River Plate, as part of a whole network of nation-building educational institutions. Located at the heart of government, in the Casa de Gobierno itself, this second library was given a generous subvention 'for book purchases, binding, and distribution [of Argentine publications] to the Governments of Europe and the Provinces'.[61] Such a role might have been deemed more appropriate for the BPBA, but it remained under the jurisdiction of Buenos Aires province. Other provincial authorities remained reluctant to comply with the laws requiring them to deposit copies of periodicals and official publications in the BPBA, making it well-nigh impossible for that institution to play a role which was in any meaningful sense national. The uneasy coexistence of these two libraries from 1870 to 1884 was a perfect symbol of Argentina's wider constitutional anomaly.

Quesada, who had spent much of his intellectual career in the Argentine interior, founding newspapers and periodicals to develop networks of communication throughout the territory, envisaged the BPBA as the repository of a culture he identified as both Argentine and national. He aimed to establish it as the historical archive of the whole country and as a centre for scientific research of all kinds. In 1877, in support of his campaign, Quesada sought leave of absence to conduct comparative research on the libraries of Europe and the

Americas. The report of his trip is highly revealing about changing conceptions of the relationship between knowledge and nationalism in the 1870s, when a new emphasis on defining a 'national' culture can be observed in Argentine public discourse. Quesada seems to have undertaken his journey around Europe, which he conducted at break-neck speed—not even pausing to see inside the British Library's famed rotunda reading room—mainly in order to lend credibility to the arguments he wished to make to Argentine officials who idealised European models. He actually based large sections of his report upon an extensive survey carried out three years earlier by the Brazilian bibliographer Benjamin Franklin Ramiz Galvão.[62] Quesada sought to play on the political rivalry between Brazil and Argentina by pointedly noting the contrast between the imperial government's generous funding of Ramiz Galvão's investigation and his own meagre grant, implying that the emperor appreciated the importance of libraries to a nation's reputation far more than did the republican liberals in Buenos Aires. Critical of most of the practices of European librarians, Quesada reserved his unqualified praise for the Germans, who did what he wished to do in Argentina—namely, to differentiate clearly between research libraries and libraries for public education. The main theme of his report was the detrimental effect of public access. He marshalled evidence both statistical and anecdotal to argue that unrestricted public handling of the books could result only in what Borges later characterised as 'a library of attrition' (*una biblioteca de desgaste*), in which the collection became eroded by damage: spines broken, pages torn or items stolen, the books sacrificed to the creation of citizen readers.[63] The implication of Quesada's argument was that the public good and the national interest were not compatible.

In a famous response to Quesada's report, Sarmiento, who had already introduced laws to mandate the creation of local lending libraries in every Argentine town, argued that Quesada posited a false alternative between a research library in the capital and libraries for the people throughout the country.[64] In practice, however, there was increasing differentiation of purpose as library provision expanded. Sarmiento's 'national' library was renamed the Biblioteca Nacional de Maestros in 1884 and thereafter functioned mainly as a repository of books for teachers, although it continued to acquire material—such as British patent acts—arguably more suitable for the national library.[65] Ultimately Quesada's vision of a national library of conservation and research prevailed at the BPBA, having been embraced by Paul Groussac during his long term as director (1885–1929) and then consolidated by Borges (director, 1955–73) to make it one of the most influential in Latin

America. Yet there have been directors who regretted the change from public to national, arguing that it broke the founding connection with democracy.[66] It was certainly the case that throughout the twentieth century the Biblioteca Nacional de la República Argentina (BNA) remained isolated from the wider network of public libraries throughout Argentina, in contrast to the situation in Chile. In 2017, the incoming director, Alberto Manguel, who sees a national library as 'a storehouse of every kind of manifestation of justice', still found this to be a problem.[67]

Chile

By the 1870s, the BNCh was in the strongest institutional position of these three national libraries, mainly because it was the only one of them that consistently enjoyed the financial and legal support of the state. When a new cultural infrastructure was created in the 1840s, the BNCh was fully integrated into it, to the extent that from 1852 until 1886 directors of the library automatically went on to become dean of the Faculty of Philosophy and Humanities at the University of Chile.[68] It also had the advantage of a highly able second director, Francisco García Huidobro, who held the post from 1825 until his death in 1852. One of García Huidobro's triumphs was to secure a law of deposit, covering all publications in Chile, in 1834. Despite the difficulties of ensuring full compliance, as is evident in the correspondence of successive directors, the BNCh could at least normally be sure of receiving official publications.[69] A one-off government grant in 1846 enabled the BNCh to expand substantially its holdings of modern European works by purchasing the eight thousand volumes owned by Mariano Egaña, author of the 1833 Constitution. A purpose-built reading room for this collection, designed by the neoclassical French architect Claude François Brunet de Baines, was opened to the public in 1856, with a catalogue published in 1860.[70] Relatively secure government funding enabled the BNCh not only to purchase other major collections but also to attract bequests from intellectuals anxious to ensure that their laboriously acquired bibliographic treasures would be cared for appropriately. Significant gifts were made by Andrés Bello (over 1,500 works, described as a microcosm of elite creole culture); Claudio Gay (eight hundred volumes of material which had contributed to his thirty-volume *Historia física y política de Chile*, 1844–71); and José Ignacio Eyzaguirre, a priest and historian, who left his library of 4,122 mostly religious works in 1878.[71] In the 1920s, the BNCh was further enriched by the private collections of the leading historians Diego

Barros Arana and José Toribio Medina, and it has continued to attract bequests from prominent scholars, in one manifestation of the general trend
towards concentrating national resources in Santiago. Notoriously, the late
nineteenth-century expansion of Chile's national library was also achieved at
the expense of Peru's, books from which were seized by Chilean troops occupying Lima during the War of the Pacific (1879–83).

Chile commemorated the centenary of its declaration of independence in
1813, which was also the anniversary of the foundation of the library, by commissioning a purpose-built building, to be erected on the site of a former con-
vent. Much was made of the *national* credentials of the 'palace of books', as it
was popularly known: official statements and articles in the press all proclaimed that it was built by a Chilean architect (Gustavo García del Postigo,
whose design had been chosen over two French proposals), with Chilean
workers and Chilean materials. It was one of the first buildings in the country
to incorporate modern techniques of reinforcement against earthquakes, a
provision which may in itself mark the centrality of the library to the national
self-image, given recent work on the significance of earthquakes in the history
of Chilean identity.[72] It was a building of which Chile could be justifiably
proud, declared poet Ángel Cruchaga in 1922, one that showed to the world
that 'in our land there is a fervent cult of learning', a building that 'gave the lie
to all the pessimists who think that everything Chilean is so deficient and poor
that we are shamed before other nations'.[73] As the foundation stone was laid,
President Barros Luco pointedly highlighted the contrast between the bright
prospects for learning celebrated that day and 'the severity of the silence and
strict seclusion [that had] reigned for two centuries'.[74] The magnificent neoclassical library, with Art Deco touches, opened in 1925, the same year that a
revised constitution formally separated church and state. It remains there, on
Santiago's main thoroughfare, the Alameda, to this day, with the Archivo Nacional right next door. In contrast to Argentina's BPBA, the BNCh played a
central role in Chile's cultural infrastructure, purchasing and distributing material to local libraries throughout the country. It also increasingly took the
lead in coordinating the country's state cultural institutions, particularly after
the creation of the Dirección de Bibliotecas, Archivos y Museos (DIBAM) in
1929, to an extent that is unusual anywhere in the world. More recently, the
BNCh has become an internationally acclaimed digital pioneer, notably in the
virtual library Memoria Chilena, which was designed to make available online
'the cultural heritage of Chile, contributing to the recovery, preservation and
strengthening of our historical memory'.[75]

Peru

The significance of Peru's library to its national identity has been heightened by the fact that it was twice reduced to virtually nothing. The first time was during the War of the Pacific, when the building was used as a barracks by Chilean troops and had its contents ransacked. The restoration of the library, in the same place and in the same design, was widely represented as an analogy for the revival of the nation, predestined to rise triumphant from defeat to blaze a trail to future glory. Although the general public had played no role in the founding of the Biblioteca Nacional del Perú (BNP), they were closely involved in 1884, when an estimated 8,315 of its 27,824 missing books were returned by members of the public who had spotted its telltale stamp on volumes they chanced upon in taverns and markets.[76] Such was the symbolic weight of 1884 that after the second tragedy to befall Peru's national library, the fire of 1943, in which nearly everything was lost, regeneration came literally out of the ashes when it was decided to reconstruct the building on the same ground.[77] A portion of the necessary funds was raised by a special tax on sales of jewellery and other luxury goods, drawing on a tradition dating back to 1830 of Peruvian government initiatives to finance the national library through dedicated taxation.[78] Before the fire, the impact of which was felt throughout the subcontinent,[79] Peru's library had been among the top three in Latin America, rivalling those of Mexico and Brazil, and it still contains remarkable bibliographic treasures.[80]

The enduring role of the library as a talisman of Peru's national identity is illustrated in the history of the books seized by Chilean occupying forces during the War of the Pacific. At the time, the Chilean authorities did not scruple to hide what they had taken: an inventory was published in the *Diario Oficial* of August 1881 and an official report drawn up by prominent scientist Ignacio Domeyko.[81] The haul consisted of seventy boxes and eighty packages, containing mostly books, but also specimens of natural history, equipment for teaching chemistry, and anatomical models from the university medical school. Yet the BNP was reopened remarkably quickly, on Independence Day in 1884, mainly because of the work of Ricardo Palma, who was persuaded by his friend President Miguel Iglesias to mobilise his international contacts to restore the collections. Palma was soon successful in securing the return of a substantial proportion of the books through the good offices of Chilean president Domingo Santa María, whom he had befriended while in exile in Santiago during the early 1860s. He then spent many years working to recoup books with their distinctive seal "Biblioteca de Lima" and also attracted donations from all over the Americas and Spain. Palma wrote an account of his labours which was widely published in the Peruvian press on the day of the library's reopening. In recounting his story, Palma deployed all the literary skill that had brought him fame as *the* chronicler of what he called 'Peruvian traditions' (actually, scenes of life in Lima). Casting himself as the 'begging librarian', like one of the popular archetypes in his stories, he vividly told—and retold—the tale of snatching priceless incunabula from the hands of soldiers and rescuing leather-bound tomes from being bartered for liquor.[82] Palma compared the Chilean general Pedro Lagos, who had given the order to set up quarters in the BNP, to 'Amron, general of the Caliph Omar, arsonist of the Library of Alexandria',[83] which is a disputed, not to say discredited, attribution of blame for whatever may have happened at Alexandria. Palma presumably deployed the slur in order to represent the occupying Chileans as culturally alien, even barbarous, and to boost the idea, which was at that time gaining ground in Peru, that their own country had a long history of civilisation. If anything, Palma was too successful in promoting the national significance of the restored library, because the site itself became sacred and he failed in all his efforts to secure a new building for the centenary celebrations, as had been granted in Chile. It was not until the 1980s that the decision was taken to raise funds for a purpose-built library—through a levy on the departure tax paid by anyone leaving on an international flight—which opened in 2006. A year later, Michelle Bachelet's government in Chile officially returned to the BNP 3,788 of the books taken in 1881. The handover received extensive coverage in both the Peruvian and Chilean media. The Chileans emphasised that they had given back every item identified in public institutions, but insisted that 'a democratic state' could do nothing about any materials in private collections, which Peruvian experts estimated to be far greater in number than those returned. Of great symbolic significance in Peru was the return of 37 books from San Martín's original donation which, even though they are now too fragile to be consulted by the public, reanimated the Liberator's founding dream by their very presence.[84] In 2017 the stairway of the BNP was adorned with poster-sized photographs of leading scholars and writers from all over the Americas endorsing the recently launched campaign for the return of all the books lost from the library down the years.

As the focus shifted in the late nineteenth century towards national priorities of conservation and heritage, alternative initiatives were taken in all three countries to fulfil the founding promise of genuinely public access to libraries.

Sarmiento pioneered *bibliotecas populares* (popular libraries) in Chile, during the 1840s,[85] then rolled out the policy as president of Argentina a quarter of a century later. The Law for Protection of Popular Libraries (1870) revived Moreno's idea of 'a common effort between government and citizens to guarantee the development of libraries' by promising state funds to match any private contributions raised to open a local lending library.[86] Significantly, these were designated not as public libraries but as 'popular libraries', or libraries for the people. This decision was an early instance of the displacement of the public (implying constitutional rights that can be exercised) by the popular (implying an identity and a benefit conferred) that was to become so significant in twentieth-century Latin American history. Unsurprisingly, given that the crafting of a popular identity was at stake, there was a great deal of controversy over what should be included on lists of recommended reading for these libraries.[87] The final version included biographies of Argentine heroes, Mignet's biography of Franklin, Sainte-Beuve's *Gallery of Famous Women*, general histories of the Americas, and encyclopedias and reference works of all kinds: on political economy, scientific inventions, Castilian grammar, agricultural techniques, domestic hygiene and social etiquette. It was a microcosm of the nation-building policy of Argentine governments in the late nineteenth century.[88]

The efforts of the Commission for Popular Libraries notwithstanding, during the late nineteenth century many of Argentina's most successful community libraries—where people could actually read the books rather than gaze at them in glass-fronted cabinets—were created by workers' organisations, not by the state, which did not seize the initiative again until the 1920s. Most of the country's extensive network of municipal libraries was created from 1920 (when there were forty-six, thirty of them in the city of Buenos Aires) to 1945 (when there were nearly two hundred distributed across the country).[89] In 1921, after more than a decade of campaigning, the government finally agreed to install cabinet libraries in public squares and parks for people to read on the spot on weekends and holidays.[90] As will be illustrated in chapter 10, state popular libraries in Peru, even more than in Argentina, were the side products of libraries created by workers' organisations. In Chile, the role of labour unions and parties in founding libraries mattered even more, because state attempts to encourage the habit of reading were directed through the schools and the BNCh until the 1920s, when policy shifted towards building separate municipal libraries, although it was not until the 1990s that a network of state-funded *bibliotecas públicas* was established throughout the country.

The Libraries at the Independence Centenaries

By the time of the centenary celebrations, all three national libraries had fulfilled Walter Benjamin's idea of collection as emancipation, in their case emancipation from European claims to a monopoly on knowledge. In no small part
their success was due to the dedication and talent of those librarians who embraced their roles as 'interpreters of fate', rather than being content to serve as
its guardians.[91] Labouring away, often for many years, with minimal support
staff, they painstakingly drew up catalogues, persevered in trying to fill gaps in
the collections, and kept up an endless flow of correspondence to maintain
exchange agreements with their often unresponsive counterparts in Europe.
Acquisitions policy in all three countries had prioritised two main areas: first,
periodicals, which were more important than books as a conduit of new
knowledge, especially from elsewhere in Latin America, and, second, history
of the Americas. By the time of its centenary, the BNA had built up a periodical
section 'superior to many in Europe and the United States'.[92] A catalogue from
1935 of nineteenth-century periodicals in the BNA shows more than two hundred from other Latin American countries, as well as 350 from Europe and
over one hundred from the United States.[93] In both Peru and Chile, major
collections on all aspects of life in the Americas were created. In Chile, the
Americas collections contained many rare works, many of them originally
owned by itinerant intellectual Benjamín Vicuña Mackenna, whose personal
library of over a thousand items, in nine languages, was purchased in 1861.[94] In
Peru, if in the mid-1850s it could be alleged that the national library lacked the
necessary material to write a complete history of Lima,[95] by the 1870s that was
far from the case. During that decade, when Civilista governments brought
relative stability, holdings were nearly doubled, to over 56,000, in 1880. Although historians of the library have focused on the long tenure of librarian
Francisco de Paula González Vigil, an excommunicated former cleric, who was
director from 1836 to 1839 and then from 1845 until his death in 1875, much of
the credit for the rapid expansion seems to be due to his deputy and successor
Colonel Manuel de Odriozola, himself a prodigious collector and publisher
of historical documents.[96] After the destruction during the War of the Pacific,
restoring the Salón America to its former glory was one of the main tasks
Ricardo Palma set himself.[97]

These acquisitions of material on the Americas as a whole were complemented by extensive national bibliographical endeavours. By the start of the
twentieth century, Chile had long been publishing annual lists of all new works

of Chilean literature (since 1862) and of the Chilean press (since 1886).[98] Argentina pioneered the establishment of national bibliographic offices in 1909, soon followed by Peru and Brazil. The increasing emphasis on the role of these libraries as repositories of national culture dovetailed with an international drive towards professionalising library services during the late nineteenth century. Latin Americans were involved in the movement for international coordination of bibliography and documentation launched in Brussels in 1895.[99] Brazil's training course for librarians, 'Biblioteconomía', which started in 1911 in the Biblioteca Nacional itself, was the first in the Americas and only the third in the world.[100] As a result of professionalisation, the book was resacralised as a cultural artefact worthy of preservation in itself, after decades of being viewed as a tool of knowledge.[101] This shift is detectable in the furious strictures of Manuel González Prada, director of the BNP from 1914 to 1918, against his predecessor Ricardo Palma's habit of scribbling in the margins of the books.[102]

In many respects, though, what was most instructive about these libraries was their unusual experience of sustaining the dual remit of being both public and national, which few other libraries anywhere in the world had tried to do. Some of the issues at stake became clear in Paul Groussac's introduction to the catalogue he published in 1893. Librarians have long been familiar with the inherent tension between classifying books on principles drawn from the philosophy of knowledge and arranging them for the convenience of readers. It is all too easy to create the nightmare library conjured up by Umberto Eco, in which catalogues are 'split up to the maximum degree', with different spellings in all of them.[103] Groussac pointed out the drawbacks of organising the BNA 'on the basis of an exact classification of the sciences', as had been repeatedly recommended by government commissions. The positivist division of subjects, into the abstract, the concrete and a blend of the two, gave little help, he noted, to a browsing reader likely to be bewildered by finding astronomy alongside psychology on the principle that they both fell into the third category.[104] Most cataloguing systems were far too complicated, he concluded, especially the current vogue for adapting Linnaeus's botanical system to bibliography. It was inappropriate to impose nature's organic order onto the world of books, where there was 'not necessarily any correlation of parts' and 'heterogeneous productions' were the norm.[105] Groussac himself retained the broad subject divisions established by Quesada: sciences and [industrial] arts; history and geography; law; literature; and theology. He did make the significant addition of social sciences, which he placed with law, reflecting the late nineteenth-century rise in Argentine work on 'the social question', much of which was done by lawyers as well as medical doctors.[106] Groussac was working to develop principles of cataloguing that would enable readers to browse, on the assumption that members of the public would want to trace their own itineraries over the landscape of knowledge.[107]

Conclusion

The histories of the national libraries are revealing about the key questions of who could participate in public debate, how knowledge was conceived and classified, and why access to it continued to be paraded as an official priority. The significance of the libraries as symbols of the founding promise of popular sovereignty was evident at the celebrations for the centenaries of independence. Governments played on it for their own political purposes, but precisely because the libraries were deemed to be measures of national reputation, advocates of greater access to knowledge were sometimes able to manipulate the situation to their advantage. In Argentina, even after the library's name was changed from public to national and its role as a resource for a specialist community of scholars was being established, it was hailed as 'democratic in its origin and destiny [...] born from the people and developed for the people', echoing the rhetoric of the Revolución de Mayo.[108] When the Chilean government commissioned a new, purpose-built library in 1913, it was at least partly in order to counter a pervasive sense of national crisis, by lending concrete form to official claims that in Chile the public good and the national interest were institutionally at one. In Peru, the library became symbolic of the nation's capacity to emerge triumphant from defeat. In order for the refoundation myth to take hold, invocation of the public was deemed to be crucial in order to strengthen the national: in the 1880s and again in the 2010s, in the form of seeking out and returning books; in the 1940s and again in the 1980s, by hypothecated taxation. In most other Latin American countries, similar tales can be told. The Biblioteca Nacional de México, for example, was founded first in 1833, then again in 1846, just before US troops invaded at the start of the Mexican-American War, then twice more in 1856 and 1857, in the brief interval between the overthrow of Santa Anna and the War of Reform, thus echoing successive attempts to establish secure republican government despite internal divisions and foreign invasions. The foundation date now officially recognised by the library is 1867, thereby aligning it with the 'Restored Republic' constituted after liberal troops defeated the French-imposed Second Mexican

Empire, in what was widely viewed in Mexico as a second war of independence. Libraries were sites of contestation, where clashes took place between different conceptions of the public, the national and the desirable balance between the two. The national libraries of Latin America are palimpsests of national histories, living records of how knowledge is erased and revived.

One vivid illustration is the history of how Argentina's current national library was built. A decision was taken in 1961 to commission a purpose-built structure. The chosen site was saturated with political significance. It was where Perón's official residence, the Unzué Palace, had stood, in the wealthy suburb of Recoleta. Evita died there, and it had been demolished in 1958 as part of a military government's ill-fated attempt to bulldoze Peronism out of popular memory. Ghosts are not so easily exorcised, however: the memory of Evita was restored to the landscaped grounds between the library and the Avenida del Libertador in 1999, when a monument to her was inaugurated by President Carlos Menem in one of the his very last public acts before leaving office. The library eventually opened in its modernist temple in 1992, after repeated delays and a two-year suspension of work during the military dictatorship of 1976–83. Categorised as an example of brutalism and deplored by devotees of neoclassical elegance, the design, by Argentine architect Clorindo Testa, aimed to revive the democratic impetus of the library's main founder, Mariano Moreno, after whom it was renamed. It is, as its detractors lament, made of metal, glass and reinforced concrete, but more sympathetic observers have noted that the design invites an interactive encounter with the surrounding parks and landscaped gardens. The building extends several floors below ground level, in order to create storage space for an expanding collection, away from the light. The reading rooms are raised and offer panoramic views of the city and the River Plate that would be breathtaking if only there were a budget to get the windows cleaned. Thus the intellectual role of the library as a stimulus to learning was physically separated from its conservation role in relation to national history and memory. There is a publicly accessible plaza and esplanade, echoing the open frontage of a *quinta*, or country-style house.[109] Reading was envisaged by these architects, as by Moreno, as an activity closely connected to the surrounding society.

Like a nation, a public library is at once a repository of memory, a record of the present and a recipe for the future. It is this orientation towards the future that distinguishes libraries from the museums, censuses and maps that many historians, taking their cue from Benedict Anderson, have analysed as microcosms of national identity. In Latin America, the founding of public libraries simultaneously with new political communities, apparently so boldly modern a move, speaks volumes about the peculiar constellation of radical and conservative forces that impelled creole nation-making. The libraries, like the nations, were willed into existence by powerful individuals, but there was a necessary popular element, too, not only in rhetoric but also, even if intermittently, in practice. The histories of the libraries, like those of the nations, cannot be told as a narrative of steady progress: there were periods of both advance (often uneven) and decline, both in the fabric of the institutions and in their degree of inclusiveness. Yet the libraries of Latin America, even in imperial Brazil, stood apart from the elite projects of Europe in their founding commitment to public access, the consequences of which were felt in the histories of the new nations.

2

Repertoires of Knowledge

PUBLIC INSTITUTIONS, practical knowledge, popular enlightenment—the prescription for a virtuous and prosperous community was the same everywhere. The periodicals of the 1810s and 1820s were full of *artes, industrias y ciencias* (arts and crafts, manufacturing industries, and scientific subjects) and *conocimientos útiles* (useful knowledge). The lexicon changed: terms such as 'popular', 'public' and 'sovereign' displaced colonial categories remarkably quickly.[1] New institutions were created and old ones—depicted by the new rulers as the bastions of the colonial order—subjected to a volley of reforming decrees. 'We intend to reform all the institutions of learning in [Lima],' declared Bernardo Monteagudo, San Martín's leading minister of state.[2] There were innovative aspects to some of these initiatives, especially in higher education. Buenos Aires presented a unique opportunity to create institutions of learning tailored to republican nation-building, because it was the one new seat of government without either a university (Córdoba had successfully resisted late-colonial attempts to found one) or a tradition of education by the lay orders. In a pioneering move, the Universidad de Buenos Aires (UBA), opened in 1821 (see table 2) was given responsibility for the whole education system, a policy emulated in Chile two decades later, when the Universidad de San Felipe was reorganised and inaugurated as the Universidad de Chile (1843). In Santiago, the Instituto Nacional, which was founded jointly with the Biblioteca Nacional in 1813, adopted a relatively open admissions policy, which helped to make possible a degree of social mobility through educational achievement, at least from the mid-nineteenth century onwards. New subjects for an industrial age—drawing, modern languages, political economy—were introduced to break the mould of a structure of knowledge dating back to the medieval universities, with their four faculties of arts (meaning the study of language, mathematics and music), law, medicine and theology. The rulers of

TABLE 2. The Founding of Universities in Spanish America, c. 1550–1950

1551	Universidad Mayor de San Marcos, Lima (Peru)
1551	Universidad Mayor de México, Mexico City
1558	Universidad de Santo Tomás de Aquino, Santo Domingo (Dominican Republic)
1580	Universidad de Santo Tomás, Bogotá (Colombia)
1613	Universidad de Córdoba (Argentina)
1620	Universidad de San Gregorio Magno, Quito (Ecuador)
1623	Pontificia Universidad Javeriana, Bogotá (Colombia)
1624	Universidad de San Francisco Xavier, Chuquisaca (Bolivia)
1624	Universidad de Mérida de Yucatán (Mexico)
1676	Universidad de San Carlos de Borremeo, Guatemala City
1677	Universidad de San Cristóbal de Huamanga, Ayacucho (Peru)
1692	Universidad de San Antonio Abad, Cuzco (Peru)
1721	Universidad de Caracas (Venezuela)
1728	Universidad de la Habana (Cuba)
1738	Universidad de San Felipe (Santiago, Chile)
1792	Universidad de Guadalajara
1812	Universidad de Nicaragua, León
1821	Universidad de Buenos Aires (Argentina)
1827	Universidad del Cauca, Popayán (Colombia)
1828	Universidad de San Agustín, Arequipa (Peru)
1841	Universidad de El Salvador
1843	Universidad de Chile
1847	Universidad de Honduras, Tegucigalpa
1849	Universidad de la República, Montevideo (Uruguay)
1888	Pontificia Universidad Católica de Chile (Santiago)
1889	Universidad Nacional de Asunción (Paraguay)
1905	Universidad Nacional de La Plata (Argentina)
1910	Universidad Nacional de México
1917	Pontificia Universidad Católica del Perú (Lima)
1919	Universidad de Concepción (Chile)
1920	Universidade Federal do Rio de Janeiro (from Real Academia de Artilharia, Fortificação e Desenho, founded in 1792)
1934	Universidade de São Paulo
1935	Universidad de Panamá, Panama City
1940	Universidad de Costa Rica, San José
1941	Pontificia Universidade Católica de Rio de Janeiro
1943	Tecnológico de Monterrey (Mexico)
1948	Universidad de los Andes, Bogotá (Colombia)

Note: Modern country name in parentheses.

the independence era envisaged a comprehensive new knowledge order: secular in orientation, scientific in method, social in purpose—and accountable to the state.

Yet the radical impulse of these early plans could not be sustained. At the elementary level, various imaginative proposals from the 1810s to the 1820s for a state curriculum to stimulate creativity for an industrial age gave way to the prosaic Lancasterian system of pupils drilling each other in the basics of literacy, not least because there were so few trained teachers.[3] Despite the independence generation's enthusiasm for practical enlightenment, public technical education reached only a tiny proportion of the population before the 1920s. At higher levels, little applied science was taught, apart from medicine. Practical skills, such as engineering or architecture, were passed on through apprenticeships, acquired on the job (often in the military) or imported. Throughout the nineteenth century, nearly all those who graduated from Spanish American universities did so in law.

The well-known political and economic difficulties of the half century after independence certainly play a major part in explaining why the founding ambitions to create a modern educational system were not realised during those years, but in my view they do not fully account for it. As conditions became more stable, from the 1840s in Chile and from the 1860s in Argentina and Peru, there were periods when the universities had able, reforming rectors who achieved significant advances, some of which were internationally ahead of the curve. For example, UBA introduced a degree in engineering (1865) long before the University of Oxford did (1908). Yet across Spanish America the same criticisms of public educational establishments, particularly the universities, echoed down the generations: Catholic dogma stifling scientific debate, intrusive religious ritual, outdated curricula, teaching by rote, and irrelevant imported theories. Indeed, such were the main grievances behind the student-led University Reform Movement of 1918, which was an outcome of three decades of public debate about the role of the university that began in the 1890s, especially in Argentina, Peru and Mexico. Histories of knowledge in Spanish America during the century after independence have a curiously schizophrenic aspect. If we look at only the history of the universities, we see mainly sterility; if we look at the works of specific individuals, generations or groups, we find great creativity. Why is this so?

I found some clues in an exchange published in a Buenos Aires periodical of 1819, in which a seasoned medical doctor, Cosme Argerich (1758–1820), cautioned a radical young philosopher, Juan Crisóstomo Lafinur (1797–1824), against trespassing on territory best left to theology.[4] Both men were prominent figures in the new republic. Argerich, by then in his seventies, was among the most esteemed physicians of his day. Having introduced smallpox vaccination and modern medical training to the viceroyalty of the River Plate, he became renowned for his work tending injured troops during the British invasions of Buenos Aires in 1806–7. After participating in the Revolución de Mayo, he was appointed official surgeon to San Martín's Liberating Army in Upper Peru. Lafinur, at the age of just twenty-two, was the first person in the River Plate to teach philosophy in Spanish instead of Latin. His time as a student at the University of Córdoba had coincided with Gregorio Funes's short-lived period of reform, notably his attempt to establish philosophy as a subject independent of theology. Like many of his generation, Lafinur abandoned his studies to fight for independence. On arrival in Buenos Aires in 1818 he won a competition for the philosophy post at the prestigious secondary school the Colegio de la Unión del Sud. The course he taught there caused a scandal that spoke volumes about what was at stake in trying to change the knowledge order. Lafinur introduced the ideas of a contemporary group of secular French philosophers (the Idéologues, discussed in detail below) in order to justify departing from scholasticism. The shock of Lafinur's intervention lay in what he omitted: his lectures did not mention the divine origins of human intelligence, instead locating humankind in nature and investigating social life and knowledge as natural phenomena.[5] After intemperate protests from prominent Catholics, Lafinur was denounced for impiety. Such was the vehemence of the attacks against him that in 1821 he left Buenos Aires for Mendoza, where—as recounted in the introduction—a similar pattern repeated itself, prompting him to seek exile in Chile. Tragically, he died from an accident soon thereafter.

In a letter couched as a defence of Lafinur against his theological enemies, Argerich claimed to have been teaching the same modern thought, that of the French Idéologues, for which Lafinur had been attacked. Argerich himself had avoided censure, he maintained, by being very explicit about the limits of philosophy. He invoked Aristotle's aphorism, cited by Aquinas: 'Nothing is in the intellect that was not first in the senses',[6] which was to become one of the most quoted phrases in nineteenth-century Latin American discourse, albeit for a variety of purposes. Argerich deployed it to 'prescribe exactly the limits to which philosophy can reach' and to draw the conclusion that 'the Supreme Author of nature placed on human reason, just as on the sea, circumscribed limits that will never be overcome'.[7] Understanding the correct remit of philosophy—that is, those matters that could be understood directly through human senses—was a question, he averred, of 'good taste' (*buen gusto*). All other questions about the nature of existence were best reserved, he concluded, for the interpreters of Holy Scripture.[8] In response, Lafinur refused to accept that any such problems were outside the scope of philosophy, precisely because, he claimed, he wanted to use modern philosophical ideas to contribute to theological debates. Even if philosophy could not prove the existence of the immaterial soul a priori (through innate rationalism, following Descartes), it could do so a posteriori (through empirical knowledge subjected to critical reflection).[9] The exposition of his philosophical case is not fully clear, but what comes through forcefully is the argument that he believed in God but did not wish to constrain the scope of human reason.

This exchange between Argerich and Lafinur, both of whom were committed to introducing modern methodologies, highlights the epistemological crisis created by the wars of independence, alongside other varieties of crisis (legal, political, economic and social) that have received more attention from historians. Along with the collapse of political authority—first the dethroning of the Iberian monarchs, then colonial rule itself—came a general questioning of where legitimate authority lay. The constitutions of Spanish America were justified in terms of modern republicanism and liberalism, yet in all cases the Catholic Church was established, even though none of the independent states was recognised by the papacy until 1835. How was the authority of divine revelation to be reconciled with the various new forms of human revelation: science, individual expression, history? The question was not what do we know but *how* do we know, or even how can anybody know? Was anything to be taken as a given, or did it all have to be made anew? Such were the fractures in the landscapes of knowledge throughout the nineteenth century: What was the extent of reason's right to roam? What were the sources of legitimate knowledge (divine revelation, Cartesian rationality, scientific method, or some combination thereof)? How could liberty be conserved and licence avoided?

It is not easy to chart these epistemological conflicts in Spanish America by adopting any of the conventional methods of focusing on institutions, intellectuals or bodies of ideas (isms). The universities were themselves sites where the battles were fought; neither the isms nor the individuals configured their ideas in predictable ways. There were clergy, both secular and regular, who championed modern scientific practice; there were lay intellectuals who insisted that the Gospel was the source of all true knowledge. The divide has been suggestively characterised as between a 'theological' and a 'critical-rational' mode of thought,[10] but even that doesn't quite capture it. Everyone thought they were being rational, but there was a variety of conceptions of reason and its role; there were many understandings of what it was to be 'critical'—ranging from public scrutiny to the art of judicious imitation. Most people agreed that reasoning based on observation and experimentation had its place. But there were sharp disagreements over the extent of its remit. On the other hand, hardly anybody argued that modern science alone was the answer.

In this chapter, I aim to shed light on the divisions in nineteenth-century Spanish American history through the perspective of repertoires of knowledge. This approach draws upon Geoffrey Lloyd's argument that for intellectual exchange to take place in a society, there must be a basic level of agreement about the ideals of inquiry.[11] There must also be a critical mass of shared terms and reference points for communication to take place. In what follows, I explore the fundamental assumptions, the stock of common references and the conventional cultural practices that made public debate possible and policed the borders of the unsayable. This method makes it easier to appreciate the rationale of positions and arguments that make little sense if analysed in terms of conventional binaries such as the sacred and the secular, or clusters of ideas such as scholasticism and the enlightenment or liberalism and conservatism. Three reportoires featured prominently in Spanish American landscapes of knowledge: (1) the ideal of a natural laboratory; (2) shared references to classical Greece and Rome; and (3) the practice of rhetoric, or the art of speaking and writing well. Here I will explore in depth two influential examples from Argentina, both of which illustrate the working of all three of these repertoires.

Diego Alcorta's Philosophy Course (1827–42)

My first illustration is the philosophy course taught by a young doctor of medicine, Diego Alcorta (1801–1842), at UBA from 1827 until his death in 1842.[12] There is no doubting the impact of this course: many of the luminaries of mid-nineteenth-century Argentine public life testified to its deep and lasting influence on their intellectual and personal development.[13] It also fulfilled the role of fostering sociability and networks: a deep bond was felt both within and between the cohorts of Alcorta's students, not least because it was one of the few courses to be offered without interruption during Juan Manuel de Rosas's dictatorship (1829–52), when the university was barely able to function, especially after 1838, for lack of funds.[14] The syllabus drew upon the

French Idéologues and was subsequently dismissed as mere propagation of their ideas.[15] Yet on closer examination it can tell us a great deal about the knowledge environment of its time.

The Idéologues were a circle of Parisian intellectuals who, from 1795 to about 1820, sought to establish the philosophical principles for governing a secular post-revolutionary republic. The term 'ideology' referred to the 'science of ideas' they worked to promote by adapting enlightenment ideas for practical government and by building institutions, such as the Institut de France, to cultivate a knowledge elite to serve the state. The role of intellectuals went beyond contributing expertise, in their view, to encompass the development of new forms of knowledge to regenerate society.[16] It is not hard to see why these philosophers seemed relevant to many Argentine intellectuals during the 1810s and 1820s. Among the most frequently cited in the documents of the Revolución de Mayo and the press were Condorcet, Destutt de Tracy and Volney, but more minor figures (Cabanis, Lakanal, Daunou) and the Christian spiritualists Laromiguière and Degerando were also read, translated and discussed.[17] As with most groups of intellectuals seen as unified, there was in fact a wide range of positions taken among them. They all tended to reject a priori knowledge in favour of empirical knowledge, but those who resonated most in Argentina argued that knowledge from the senses had to be complemented by knowledge from critical reflection. Expert analysis has shown that Alcorta did not closely follow the ideas of the French Idéologues,[18] but he shared some of their concerns and his teaching relied on a certain familiarity with their approach.

Alcorta's course was taught over two years and divided into three parts: (1) 'Study of human understanding, or Metaphysics'; (2) 'Understanding applied to reasoning and language, or Method, Logic and Language'; and (3) 'Rules to adorn the expression of our reasonings, or Rhetoric'. Thus, he retained the conventional scholastic categories, noting in his introduction that by starting with metaphysics he had merely changed the order in which they were taught, because scholastics began with logic on the basis that you need to learn the rules of reasoning before you can reason rightly. Despite these headings, much of the first part of Alcorta's course was actually about anatomy or physiology; much of the second part was about the social use of language; and much of the third part, which took up the whole of the second year, was about style and good taste. He thereby set up a smokescreen for the far more radical challenge he was posing to scholasticism: to ground the production of knowledge in human reason instead of faith in God—that is, in philosophy not theology. It was no coincidence that Alcorta's opening sally emphasised his decision to teach 'Philosophy' in general, not the more specific domains of 'the Science of Understanding, Ideology, Psychology, [or] General Theory of the Sciences'.[19] He defined philosophy as the study of human understanding in both abstract and concrete forms—that is, the history of knowledge and of how it has been created ('el origen, deducción y generación de las ideas'). Crucially, he then emphasised that nature was 'our first instructor', perhaps partly in a bid to make it harder for orthodox theologians to discredit him for 'impiety', as they had done with his two predecessors, including Lafinur.

Yet in invoking nature as the source of human knowledge, Alcorta was also touching upon one of the few shared assumptions at the time of independence—namely, the idea of the Americas as a natural laboratory for human perfectibility. The biblical concept of providential nature had been adapted during the colonial period by lay intellectuals eager to promote their territories as Edenic microcosms of proverbial richness, both scientific and commercial. These ideas gained greater purchase with the explorations of Alexander von Humboldt, whose own concept of a benign and harmonious cosmos was formed during his 6,000-mile journey through the Americas (1799–1804). [20] During and after the wars of independence, nature thus conceived provided a basis for grounding new political communities in terms that appealed to advocates of both revealed and empirical knowledge. Images of the natural world, both textual and visual, could be found everywhere—from the most elevated of proclamations to the most ephemeral of papers circulating in taverns—and along the full spectrum of political opinion, from monarchists to radical republicans. Nature was the ground upon which arguments for independence could be made.[21] No natural law obliged provinces ruled by Spain in Europe and America to stay together, argued Father Camilo Henríquez: indeed 'nature itself has formed them to live separately'.[22] The imagery of a natural laboratory supplied the route to a self-grounding polity, enabling revolutionaries to move on from natural law arguments, which could be deployed in support of the status quo. It also opened up a space, as Alcorta wished to do, for the intervention of free will. Nature left human beings to their own devices, he argued, beyond the 'satisfaction of our primary needs'. Under the mild observation that it was 'more natural' to start by observing 'what happens, when we think', Alcorta smuggled in the far bolder claims that knowledge was derived from scientific practice rather than being revealed or innate, that epistemology mattered more than metaphysics and that free will had a concrete foundation in nature. [23]

Alcorta likewise followed the conventions of his time in hailing the ancient Greeks as 'our models in everything'.[24] Classical references—written, spoken, engraved—were everywhere, sprinkled like drops of holy water onto the ground of the new republics. During the wars of independence, classical references became increasingly useful as tools for thinking. They provided a way out of the dilemma faced by any state emerging from colonialism: where to locate national origins, or how to ensure that antiquity stays in the past. To draw on the colonial period was out of bounds when staking a claim to independence and difference from Spain; but to draw on the pre-colonial era was to risk not being accepted as modern.[25] It was far more effective to posit a direct connection between their modern nation and the ancient world, unmediated by any traditions—European or American—from the intervening centuries. Alcorta recommended his students translate passages from classical authors to identify the elements of their style, but his point was explicitly to encourage the imitation of principles rather than the mere copying of practices. Fully aware that the methods of observation he advocated as a source for knowledge ran the risk of encouraging the uncritical adoption of ideas, he invoked 'an ancient axiom' to remind his students to keep their critical faculties engaged: 'I respect Plato, my master, but I respect the truth even more'.[26] This distinction, a preoccupation of many other intellectuals at the time, initiates a long debate about mimesis in the intellectual history of Latin America (discussed further in chapter 4).

The whole second year of Alcorta's course was devoted to rhetoric, which he saw as the main means of achieving the ideal synthesis of nature and culture that was the true destiny of the Americas. In focusing on rhetoric, he followed his philosophy teacher Juan Lafinur, whose short-lived course in Buenos Aires had caused such a stir back in 1819–20. Alcorta was among the students tested at the famous public examinations, when Lafinur's protégés were required to display their mastery of rhetorical skill, using categories adopted from the Spanish version of Edinburgh professor Hugh Blair's *Lectures on Rhetoric and Belles Lettres* (1797).[27] Alcorta had therefore witnessed Lafinur's capacity to refashion oral examinations, which long remained the main method of assessment in higher education, into a public tribunal to discuss the status of arts and sciences. After his students had performed their pieces, Lafinur, a handsome figure in the frock-coat of a European Romantic poet, had made a passionate speech criticising Rousseau for his early claim that organised knowledge was corrupting. In so doing, he enacted the ideal of criticism as public scrutiny that some individuals of the independence generation sought to instil in the new political communities. Modern content syncretised with ancient forms.

Yet a decade later, in a significant departure from Blair and other European manuals of rhetoric, Alcorta argued that figurative language was *natural*: 'far from being an invention of the schools or the fruit of study, we see that the most uneducated of men [*los hombres más rudos*] use them in their speech as often as the most educated [*los más instruídos*]'. Eloquence was 'a talent given by nature but it needs to be guided by taste', like the land which 'produces only thistles and thorns in the absence of cultivation'.[28] In the context of a republic, a good speaker had to be able to communicate in a variety of public situations: 'popular assemblies, the forum, the pulpit'.[29] The ideal style—'plain, frank and natural', 'without the slightest glimmer of arrogance'—could only be achieved through an understanding of the principles of rhetoric so ingrained as to be indetectable. The knack (*el tino*) of speaking well was to appear to do so without artifice.[30] Thus would true quality of thought be revealed through use of language.

Alcorta's own education was in itself testimony of the new opportunities created during the transition from colony to republic, even if it was only a very small number of individuals who benefited. Born in 1801 in Buenos Aires, his background was not privileged, but he was one of Argentina's very first scholarship boys, winning one of the grants offered by the Directorate of Juan Martín de Pueyrredón to attend the Colegio de la Unión del Sur, a secondary school opened in 1818 as a reformed version of the formerly Jesuit Colegio de San Carlos. There Alcorta was fortunate to coincide with both Lafinur's short-lived philosophy course and a new, scientifically oriented course in mathematics given by young Argentine physicist Avelino Díaz. He then enrolled as a medical student at the recently opened UBA, where medicine was one of the few early degrees to be rigorous and well taught. Having graduated in 1827, Alcorta was appointed through an open competition to the chair of ideology at UBA, a post which he combined with political work as a deputy in the government of Buenos Aires province (1832–34), where he helped to draft a liberal, democratic constitution and opposed granting extraordinary powers to Rosas.

By the time he took up his teaching post at UBA in 1827, Alcorta had had ample opportunity for close observation of reformist initiatives, both in education and politics. Hence the stated aim of his course: to establish a firm foundation for reliable knowledge for practical application. He preferred to focus on avoiding 'errors of method' and 'empty, meaningless words' than to hazard any grand conclusions about 'Nature, and its mysteries, the essence of things and the most obscure causes'. Perhaps Alcorta had in mind Argentina's

two failed centralist constitutions of 1819 and 1826, both of which were theoretically coherent but unworkable in practice, given their disregard for the
claims of the interior provinces. In the context of his country's trajectory since
independence, it is easy to appreciate Alcorta's view that it was crucial to get
the foundations right: 'we will have attained a great deal if we can prepare the
intelligence for specialist knowledge with [general] ideas that are clear and
methodical.'[31] Alcorta emphasised that thinking was a physical and emotional
process as well as an intellectual one ('sentir, conocer, obrar') and saw all fields
of knowledge as interrelated. The analogy he drew was with learning a mechanical art, where first you learn about the tools, then how to use them, then
you try to 'establish the rules to give the work the brilliance desired'—that is,
moving from the practical to the theoretical, rather than the other way around.
It was this sense of groundedness that was the main feature recalled by one of
his first and most distinguished students, Juan B. Alberdi: 'What a feel for the
practical! What a good sense of how to stay on the terrain of what is intelligible
and useful!'[32] By going back to first principles, Alcorta's course aimed at no
less than creating new foundations for knowledge in the new republic.

Marcos Sastre's *El Tempe argentino* (1858)

One of the most successful books anywhere in Latin America during the nineteenth century, although it is rarely read today, was Sastre's *El Tempe argentino*.[33] Marcos Sastre (1809–1887) is best known nowadays for founding one
of the earliest bookshops in Buenos Aires, the Librería Argentina, where the
celebrated Generation of 1837 gathered together first in a literary salon and
then as the overtly political Asociación de Mayo.[34] What is less well known is
that when the French blockade of Buenos Aires (1838–40) made it impossible
to continue importing books, Sastre departed, not for his birthplace, Montevideo, or for Chile, like many of his contemporaries, but for the Argentine
countryside. He spent eight years upriver, near the town now called Tigre,
tending sheep, cultivating fruit trees and exploring the islands formed by the
deposits of the River Paraná as its accumulating might advanced upon the
Atlantic. Sastre was not the first author to wax lyrical about the Paraná, but
unlike any previous works his surprise bestseller was acclaimed for both its
literary and scientific qualities. It consisted of nearly two hundred pages of
lyrical description of the riverscape, flora, fauna and inhabitants of the delta,
which Sastre represented as the Argentine equivalent of the Vale of Tempe in
ancient Thessaly. The text is part poem in prose, part study in natural history

and part manifesto for economic development. How are we to interpret the remarkable appeal of this work, which in its day outsold Sarmiento's *Facundo*?

As the editor of a 1921 edition remarked, the vast expanse of the Paraná Delta was sharply different in contour from the steep, narrow gorge in northern Greece, through which the River Perseus wound its way down from snow-capped Mount Olympus to the Gulf of Salonica.[35] Yet, as Sastre made clear, he was not making a literal, geographical comparison, but a literary, metaphorical one, with social intent. Although he duly included a footnote indicating his sources,[36] Sastre was relying on a general awareness of the 'leaf-fringed legend' (Keats) of Tempe as the haunt of Apollo, his beloved Daphne and the Muses. His explicit aim was to associate the Paraná with the purity and fertility of the ancient *locus amoenus*, drawing parallels between these two idyllic places where nature provided all that humankind could require—crystalline waters, shady glades, sheltering rocks—without the need for labour. He urged Argentines to embrace their own delta as a place of peace, harmony and beauty, where modern humans could live trusting in the beneficence of nature, like the ancient gods in Tempe. Here was the true liberty of the Americas, a positive freedom arising from people living freely in religion and in nature, rather than a negative liberty sustained by the constraints of law. The Paraná Delta was Argentina's glorious future in microcosm.

Sastre pointedly contrasted the beauty of 'our islands' with the Romantic 'picturesque' beloved of European travellers; for him, the delta's beauty was not aesthetic (that is, created by human perception) but providential (given by God). Indeed, the vast estuary was the ultimate in providential nature, where humans had no need to fertilise or irrigate the land because nature had already done so.[37] The beauty of the Paraná lay in its bounty: 'in the luxury of its eternal verdure, in the purity of its air and its waters, in the numerousness and the grace of its channels and little streams, in the fertility of its land, in the abundance and sweetness of its fruits'.[38] The difference of scale between the two valleys suited Sastre's purposes perfectly well, because his argument was that modern Argentina could realise on a grand scale what could exist only in miniature in ancient Greece. Like the Vale of Tempe, where laurels were gathered to crown those victorious in the Pythian games, the Paraná Delta—and by extension Argentina—could become 'the homeland of the laurel and the myrtle, emblems of glory and love'.[39]

One chapter, 'El Camauti', which was published separately and to great acclaim in 1846, encapsulates Sastre's whole endeavour. Launching his argument

from three epigraphs, by Plutarch, Virgil and Latreille (a French entomolo-
gist), evoking the beehive as a model for human society, Sastre made an alternative case for 'the *camuati* wasps of America', which he pronounced 'far more
admirable than' the bees of Europe.[40] The choice of authors to assign epi-
graphic status is significant: Sastre claimed a direct line from the ancients, as
well as the support of modern scientific methods, bypassing the obvious reference point of Mandeville's *Fable of the Bees* (1714). Invoking both an ancient
and a modern precedent was a common device in Latin American essays from
the mid-nineteenth century onwards, indicating a conviction that all previous
knowledge would be surpassed in the Americas. The Guaraní word *camuati*
referred both to the insect and to the edifice it builds, which Sastre argued was
superior to the beehive because while bees needed a hole in a rock or other
structure in which to build, the *camuati* wasp, 'more ingenious and audacious,
confident of its skill and industry', needed only a thin branch to start weaving
a hanging home. The resulting structure was a natural republic, 'made up only
of hardworking citizens who with their industry and labour contribute to form
a shelter, a source of nourishment and a common defence'. The beehive, in
contrast, was 'an elective monarchy', which had 'the fatal flaw (like many European societies) of fostering a privileged class of citizens who live without
working'.[41] Plato's ideal republic had been inspired by the beehive of the Old
World, Sastre conceded, but that was before 'the Evangelist came to dispel the
great errors of human politics'. In the New World, there already existed an
example of the *camuati* model of a peaceful republic combined with religious
inspiration, in the Jesuit-run Guaraní settlements.[42] Modern scholarship on
the *reducciones* was just starting at this time and Sastre included select extracts
in later editions of his book.

El Tempe argentino was a disquisition on knowledge as much as a work of
natural history or agriculture. Sastre attended UBA for only a short time in
1830, so he probably did not take Alcorta's course himself, but he would have
been familiar with the ideas from discussions in his bookshop.[43] He had evidently taken to heart the importance then attached to literary style, but as a
committed advocate of scientific practice he also took care to establish his
credentials as a student of natural history. His text followed the conventions
of providing detailed descriptions of natural phenomena, supported by a
scholarly apparatus of notes and references. He included his own drawings of
botanical specimens, several of which he had discovered; in later editions, he
added an appendix of favourable reactions to his scientific findings by European natural scientists. As inspector-general of Buenos Aires schools, just a

year after *El Tempe argentino*, he published an article arguing that unless Argentines quickly caught up with developments in science and industry, in a few years they would see 'our nationality lost, our industries absorbed, our race annihilated', which he saw already happening to the French in Canada and Louisiana and to the Spanish in New Mexico.[44] Science was necessary, he argued, because it told humankind the most efficient means of obtaining the desired results. For him, civilisation was best defined as 'economy of effort' and he regarded any 'useless expenditure of effort' as a sign of being uncivilised. Such arguments were not uncommon, as one way of refuting claims from Europe (or Europeanised Spanish Americans) that the inhabitants of the region were by nature idle and therefore uncivilised. Sastre criticised the cultivators of the delta for not following scientific principles but instead working with practices generalised from other conditions, which meant that they wasted their labour working a land that did not need it because of its natural abundance.[45] But—and here Sastre articulated a widely held view in mid-nineteenth-century Latin America—science would lead humanity astray without religion, which in turn entailed a sense of awe towards nature, a greater awareness of all that was not known or understood, a recognition that modern science was 'full of ignorance'.[46] A lyrical chapter evoking night-time on the islands of the Paraná was the backdrop to further discussion of the need to be sceptical about the pretensions of modern science to total knowledge of the natural world. Progress entailed not only accumulation of data but advancement of understanding, which Sastre saw as 'also the faith of the Gospel' (137).[47]

Sastre's *El Tempe argentino* developed a critique both of European science, especially as it has been applied to the Americas, and of what he identified as an increasing Argentine tendency to absorb it uncritically. In challenging the consensus among geologists that deltas took thousands of years to form, he argued that learned men often contravened their own methodology of observation: 'Such is the hallucination that a pre-established theory sometimes produces in the mind of the sage (*sabio*), that during their observations they see only those phenomena that serve to confirm it.'[48] Sastre himself deployed a combination of observation, local knowledge and deductive reasoning to draw his own conclusions. Many of the rules and advice in agriculture textbooks should be abandoned, he argued, in favour of working from the first principles of agronomy, together with the study of the specific conditions of 'our land'.[49] One of the few existing works by which Sastre set some store was the *Manual de agricultura* (1819) by Argentine-born Tomás Grigera, which he claimed to be updating.[50] His references were eclectic, perhaps strategically so: eighteenth-century authorities were called upon to support his arguments as often as nineteenth-century ones, thereby enacting a denial of the inevitability of scientific progress. Europeans, mostly Frenchmen, were called upon not for their theories but for calculations, such as the 342,000 eggs produced by an average carp, according to one 'M. Petit', cited in turn from Saint-Pierre.[51] Even Humboldt figured only as the estimator of how many eggs and how much oil could be extracted from turtles by the Indians of the Orinoco in one week.[52] Sastre's main point was that the Americas produced new evidence, and therefore scientists needed to pose new questions. They had to be prepared to learn from nature and to approach it with Christian humility. Thus Sastre's book was a blend of all the main features of the landscape of knowledge in mid-nineteenth-century Argentina: care for linguistic style, application without reification of scientific method and acknowledgement of Catholic doctrine, all harnessed in the cause of understanding the conditions of the Americas.

Conclusion

For all their political and economic differences, for much of the nineteenth century creole elites disputed claims to authority on the common ground of the following assumptions: (a) that American nature had the potential to realise the perfection of humankind; (b) that the ancient classical world was a valid source of origin myths; and (c) that speaking and writing well mattered, not only socially but also morally. It was through these shared elements of the knowledge order that a basis was created—however precarious at times—for communication and debate, both within Spanish American societies and between them.

The imagery of the natural laboratory was useful in so many ways. Chapter 7 explores how it inflected nation-making discourses and practices related to the land. Beyond the nation, the Americas were imagined as a testing ground for relations between nature and culture: a vision of organic harmony underpins all the many varieties of Americanismo, from the Panama Congress of 1826 to the deliberations at the first Latin American Scientific Congress of 1898. In 1826, as Spanish Americans discussed a possible confederation of American states, the Peruvian delegate Manuel de Vidaurre echoed Rousseau's axioms on the superiority of a state of nature in order to support claims that the peoples of the Americas were destined to realise the dream of human perfectibility. 'The inhabitants of those parts of the Americas that were Span-ish,' he declared, 'restored to the state of nature, free and independent, in per-fect possession of all their rights, [...] are more perfect than in the days after creation'. To their existing advantage of naturalness they could now add experi-ence: 'Today, in complete control of all their faculties, they can distinguish the just from the unjust, the useful and agreeable from the pernicious and the annoying, the safe from the dangerous'. [53] The Spanish American republics were ready, in short, to assume their world-historical role of regenerating ci-vilisation: as beacons of liberty, toleration and equality at home—where the former 'oppressed African' would 'start to become rational in the realisation that nothing distinguished him from other men'—they would advance the cause of peace and open exchange abroad. [54] At the end of the century, at the inauguration of the first Latin American Scientific Congress, it was proclaimed that what the republics fundamentally had in common was their shared ten-dency towards 'greater human perfection, in the midst of the beauties of our prodigious American nature', even though they were coming together on 'the neutral terrain of science'. [55] By this time there were claims, rare at first but more common from the early twentieth century onwards, that it was the in-digenous peoples, not the creoles, who knew how to reconcile nature and culture. [56] Even after Darwin's *On the Origin of Species* (1859) had shattered the Humboldtian model of a harmonious natural world, by representing nature as a battle zone and arguing that atavism or even extinction could occur, the image of the natural laboratory persisted. Building on the fact that Darwin had carried out much of his research in the region, American nature was reinter-preted as a testing ground for science (as well as political philosophy): its 'monumentality' was held to pose challenges to 'reason, method and technol-ogy', [57] not only bringing European knowledge up against its limits but also inviting a redrawing of the frontiers of what can be known. On the basis of the shared ideal of inquiry about how to release the natural potential of the Amer-icas for greatness, thinkers in Spanish America began to explore the potential for different ways of knowing from those created and validated in certain Eu-ropean seats of learning.

Motifs of ancient history, philosophy, literature, art and mythology consti-tuted perhaps the most significant set of shared references in a wide variety of public commentaries on nationhood in Latin America. The classical past was, as is well known, the dominant frame of reference of the Age of Revolution: governments throughout Europe and in the United States deployed classical references to emphasise their own modernity. The Greek liberation struggle of the 1820s, during which ancient glories were revived in the cause of modern freedom, had a particular, often overlooked, resonance in Buenos Aires, where liberal reforms were attempted with great rapidity. But images of ancient Greece and Rome mattered throughout Latin America, where there was a second frame of reference to the classical world. Multiple classical traditions had developed in the colonial period, when many works were produced, both ecclesiastical and lay, which reworked classical and humanist conventions for a variety of purposes, some of which upheld the existing order, others of which questioned it. Under the Hapsburg monarchy, for example, there were works which brought together the classical and the biblical in the service of the Christian humanist project. Yet classical learning was also mobilised to display—and account for—the marvels of the New World; or to negotiate differences between Spanish and indigenous codes of representation. Above all, scholars drew upon classical references to contest European ideas about the Americas,[58] which were often startling in their inaccuracy. Although intellectuals of the independence generation rarely drew upon the works of colonial scholars, there was an element of continuity in the official commemorations of independence organised by new states. Independence-era claims of ancestral origin in the pre-Columbian civilisations were rendered in classical form, echoing the festivals of the colonial era.[59] Fragments of classical antiquity, which would have been recognisable to anyone with even a few years of education, enabled those who rebelled against the status quo to frame their arguments in terms that those who upheld it had to acknowledge. In sum, classical references were tools for interpreting the present and imagining the future,[60] unburdened by the colonial past.

This was so not only among the intellectuals, for whom the ancients were life-long interlocutors, as they were for their counterparts in Europe, but also in wider society, as the study of popular poetry shows.[61] These references were mainly, at least at first, to classical Greece and Rome. Later in the nineteenth century, there were also evocations of ancient Egypt, Assyria and Mesopotamia, many of which were deployed, along with images of medieval Byzantium, to challenge the prominence of classical images. Of course, biblical references were often used, but those were more divisive, as were evocations of indigenous pasts. The classics were the common pool. It may seem surprising given that classical languages and texts were little taught in universities—the classics did not become a scholarly discipline in Latin America, as happened in the United States. Famously, independence leaders declared Latin and Greek irrelevant to societies in need of 'useful knowledge'.[62] But there were many ways to encounter the classics. Above all, Latin was heard at church, in the liturgy and the sermons. One of the consequences of the continuing dominance of the religious orders in both secondary and elementary education until the late nineteenth century was that Latin continued to be taught, especially at secondary level. In the military academies, recruits were taught the history of ancient battles.[63] The architecture, statuary and monuments built even in small squares of quiet provincial towns were all in neoclassical style. Newspapers, magazines and song sheets often bore a classical motif. Fragments of Latin were cited in etiquette manuals, in political catechisms, on the flyleaves of school textbooks, on the covers of almanacs. Well into the twentieth century, the official national histories of Latin America came draped in classical garb. Yet the countermove to fashion a secular spirituality in José Enrique Rodó's influential essay *Ariel* (1900), which championed Hellenic ideals of virtue and beauty to defend Latin America against vulgar materialism, also depended on the resonance of images of the classical world.

The potent mix of continuity and change in both ideals of inquiry and references was also evident in practices of knowledge. This chapter has focused on the importance attached to speaking and writing well. Rhetoric, which had been taught in the Iberian Americas as a central component of scholastic philosophy since the sixteenth century, remained an important part of the syllabus of most educational institutions for a hundred years or so after independence (oratory for the rich, recitation for the poor).[64] It was far more than a colonial hangover. The new states urgently required people who were able to speak well in public, to formulate constitutions and laws, and to convey government edicts in clear, compelling prose. At this time, command of language was seen—both by scholastics and by devotees of the *Encyclopédie*—as intrinsic to quality of thought. The disciplining of speech and writing through rhetoric was seen as a weapon against the spontaneous eloquence of demagogues.[65] Thus, the post-independence emphasis on *el arte de hablar* and *el arte de escribir* was geared towards a modernising strategy. Likewise, drama, which was a crucial element in the curriculum of the Jesuits, who themselves had borrowed from strong indigenous traditions,[66] continued to be seen as a valuable training in confident public speaking and civilised sociability well into the republican period. Public performance was one way to lend substance and immediacy to republics that were hard to imagine. The new politics were *staged*: theatrical productions of suitably patriotic fervour toured the land; theatrical images permeated public debates; theatrical etiquette informed educational rituals and ceremonies. There were both radical and reactionary

aspects to the periodic revivals of rhetoric, oratory and drama. It was possible
to do as Lafinur had done and turn a rhetorical performance into a public
tribune. In the Cuzco of the 1870s, for example, the oral examinations of Trinidad Enríquez, the first woman to study for a law degree, became 'the public
space' of the city as crowds turned to up to witness her brilliant intellect in
action.[67] Yet rhetoric was also about control; it was a means of containing pas-
sion or uninhibited expression. It established guidelines for what was appropriate in the range of new public situations brought about by independence.
Its rules were designed to achieve not only clarity but also 'suitability' (*conveniencia*), that was, conforming to morality and good taste (*buen gusto*). Good
style, in both speaking and writing, carried connotations of purity, order and
harmony. No wonder, then, that there were so many treatises on style published in Latin America during the half century after independence.[68] The
requirement of good taste was long to remain a barrier to the kind of public
scrutiny and critical debate that some of the intellectuals of independence era
had wanted to establish.

Knowledge for the new political communities was initially envisaged as
practical, evidence-based, socially oriented and interconnected across different subjects and levels of learning. The plans of the independence era for new
institutions of higher education were radical and innovative. Over the next half
century, however, the ideals of practical enlightenment were reduced to narrow professional training; scientific methods struggled to extend their remit
into fields jealously guarded by the guardians of Catholic orthodoxy; imported
theories were often privileged over homegrown investigations; knowledge
developed in silos. In consequence, while there were pockets of innovation in
the universities, much of the work of critical inquiry was carried out elsewhere—in periodicals, museums or private associations—by generalist intellectuals who ranged far beyond the subject in which they were formally trained
(usually law), or by complete autodidacts.

By the late nineteenth century, the universities were being widely criticised
for having grafted a positivist commitment to progress through empirical
knowledge onto teaching and assessment methods deemed to be out of date
and unfit for purpose. Yet the founding ideals of early republican institutions
of higher education had not disappeared. Indeed, they re-emerged in force
during the late nineteenth century in vigorous debates about the role of universities, which antedated the University Reform Movement itself by more
than twenty years. The Universidad Nacional de La Plata (UNLP), opened in
1905, was explicitly designed to be 'a modern university', different in all

respects from the 'academicist' form epitomised by Córdoba and acquired by UBA.[69] Argentina's third university was located in the new city of La Plata, founded in 1882 to be the capital of Buenos Aires province after the city of Buenos Aires was separated to become the capital of the Argentine nation in 1880. The founding vision was to revive the old idea of the university as the 'natural environment' of a general education in all branches of knowledge (as well as a specialism) and to combine it both with original research and what we would now call outreach (*extensión universitaria*) into the local and national community. The founder, the minister of justice and public instruction, Joaquín González (1863–1923), who had taken a doctorate in jurisprudence at Córdoba, criticised existing universities, both in the Old World and the New, for scarcely advancing beyond a long-outdated conception of knowledge as 'Law, Medicine, Exact Sciences and Mathematics, and Philosophy', so that Oxford, he pointed out, had been the last university in Europe to admit the science of education into its curriculum. Most universities were dedicated to 'abstract speculation, decorative titles' and reproducing the ruling class. Argentina was in prime position to innovate, he argued, proposing the UNLP as an institution for those who thought about national prosperity 'in its scientific and economic aspect', rather than 'solely from the literary point of view'.[70] In his conception *conocimientos útiles* was to mean something more than the pragmatic utility of a professional qualification: he envisaged universities as creating the critical capacities for greater intellectual autonomy, both individual and national. Similar ambitions motivated the renaming and reform of the Universidad Nacional de México in 1910.[71] The model pioneered by these two institutions provided inspiration for extensive reforms to universities across Latin America, including Brazil, after the student movements of 1918. These ideals had been kept alive at least partly because, for all the sharp divides among nation builders over both the substance of knowledge and its social role, the shared assumptions, references and practices explored in this chapter made it possible for opponents to engage with each other's arguments in the multiple sites of encounter between scientific method and Catholic doctrine.

3

Writing in the Dark

A MARKET FOR KNOWLEDGE

IN CHILE, printing was born with the republic, as any visitor to the national library is reminded by the handsome wooden frame of the country's first full-size press, standing proudly in its own room just off the foyer.[1] Brought from Boston in late 1811, it was soon set in motion to print the country's first periodical, *La Aurora de Chile* (The dawn of Chile, 1812–13). Printing had a far longer history in most Spanish American countries, especially Peru and Mexico, where it dated back to the sixteenth century. Yet all the new political communities were baptised in print, because the independence wars generated both quantitative and qualitative changes in publishing. There was a rapid increase in the volume of material—a veritable explosion of periodicals and pamphlets, proclamations and manifestos—and a marked change in its orientation, away from a learned readership and towards a broader general public.[2] The idea of the public, which became ubiquitous during these years, certainly did not include all inhabitants but was nonetheless premised on making knowledge more accessible. The great journals that championed the cause of independence not only established a founding tradition of speaking truth to power but also stimulated a demand for new ideas and discoveries, as well as for news and information. Press freedom was deemed a basic republic right. For the independent governments, the printing press was the great propagator of modern ways of doing things, a means of sustaining the momentum of the promised popular enlightenment in the interval before plans for public education could be implemented. Most of them ensured funds were available for a regular official publication, such as *El Araucano* (1830–77), a twice-weekly newspaper edited for many years by Andrés Bello in Chile, or the Argentine daily *La Gaceta Mercantil* (1823–52), which was financed by both unitarian and federalist governments, as was the English-language *British Packet and Argentine News* (1826–59).

After independence, however, as in other areas of the knowledge environment, the founding impetus for a print revolution waned. The volume of periodicals declined overall after independence, and despite some local fluctuations it was not until the 1870s that the level of the 1810s was restored.[3] Without state funding or a wealthy private backer, periodicals found it hard to keep going before the last quarter of the nineteenth century, when production costs began to decline sufficiently to recoup them through sales and advertising. Books were mainly imported from Europe and intellectuals repeatedly expressed despair at the lack of a readership for their own writing. Both the distribution and the production of printed matter presented formidable challenges during these years. Before the introduction of steamships (the 1840s) and of railways and telegraphy (the 1850s), it was expensive and slow to distribute material beyond the place of publication. A good deal of printed matter was carried between port cities, but inland circuits of exchange were harder to sustain: a newspaper from Buenos Aires took up to wend its way to Mendoza and several weeks more to be transported by mules over the Andes to Chile.[4] In times of conflict, travel was even more gruelling and dangerous: books and periodicals were often entrusted to priests, as they were the only people generally granted safe conduct. The legal climate for publishing was also adverse. Nearly everyone paid lip-service to freedom to publish, but the press was one of the key arenas in which the battles between liberty and morality were fought and new norms of political and social behaviour were tested and contested. There was some state censorship (usually reactive), almost certainly a significant level of self-censorship and even more partisanship. Perhaps the most severe obstacles to publication were economic. Production costs were high, because printing presses, typeface, ink and paper all had to be imported. A few early visionaries had advocated investing in local supplies, but they were not heeded. In Buenos Aires, for example, Juan Luis de Aguirre y Tejada argued in 1812 that the isolation of Europe during the Napoleonic Wars presented the Americas with a marvellous opportunity to establish its own printing industry, forging typeface 'from our abundant, high quality lead' and building paper factories to reduce the exorbitant costs of importation.[5] His dream was partially realised during the 1860s and 1870s, when local production of printing materials started in Argentina, but substantial quantities continued to be imported.[6] In this respect, there is some force to the often drawn contrast between developments in Latin America and in the United States, where factories began to produce paper, ink and typeface in the

TABLE 3. Literacy Rates in Latin America, 1900 and 1950, with Selected
Comparisons

	1900	1950
Argentina	51	88
Brazil	35	49
Chile	44	79
Colombia	34	62
Mexico	24	61
Venezuela	28	51
Bolivia	?	32
Ecuador	?	58
Peru	?	48
Uruguay	?	83
France	84	97
Italy	52	88
Spain	41	83
United States	90	98

Sources: For the first six Latin American countries listed above: Pablo Astorga, Ame R.
Bergés and Valpy Fitzgerald, 'The Standard of Living in Latin America during the
Twentieth Century', Economic History Review, 58:4, Nov. 2005, 765–96. Their data defined
literacy consistently as the percentage of the population aged fifteen or over and able to
read and write a simple statement about everyday life. For Bolivia, Ecuador, Peru, Uruguay
and comparative figures: UNESCO, Progress of Literacy in Various Countries: A Preliminary
Statistical Survey of Available Census Data Since 1900, 1953, available at https://unesdoc
.unesco.org/ark:/48223/pf0000002898. These figures were derived from varying
definitions of literacy, so they should be taken as no more than indicative. Earlier literacy
statistics tend to refer to the capital cities only and are rarely reliable or comparable.

early nineteenth century,[7] thereby lowering costs and making it profitable to
sell high quantities of printed matter at low prices to a population rapidly acquiring literacy (see table 3).

It is hard to establish an accurate picture of literacy rates or schooling in
Latin America for most of the nineteenth century, because the patchy data
available remains unreliable until well into the twentieth century. It is clear
that only tiny percentages of the populations received higher education, a proportion that did not rise appreciably until after the Second World War, and
that the numbers were not much higher for secondary education. Primary
school enrolment in Argentina was on a par with that in southern European
countries (at around 10% of the total population) by the early twentieth
century; Mexico began to catch up during the 1920s, after the revolution.[8] Such
data, though, may have captured only short periods of schooling, just one or
two years, and whether that sufficed to instil lasting literacy probably

depended upon what an individual went on to do. In any case, literacy in itself is only the beginning of the story. The evidence accumulated by historians who have studied the circulation of ideas and information before mass literacy, both in Latin America and in other areas of the world, suggests that the ways in to the world of print were many and varied.[9] The figure of the individual standing in a public place, reading aloud to a huddle of people, is a common sight in sketches and paintings. The Lancasterian method of schooling, in which the older children taught the younger ones what they had just learnt themselves, in itself created a predisposition and a capacity to pass on basic skills. Boys taught their sisters; children taught their nannies. Carlos Forment has identified various instances in mid-nineteenth-century Peru which point to the limitations of the tale told by the statistics. Slaves who accompanied their masters' sons to university, and who were often far more eloquent than the enrolled students, were taught to read and write to render their help of maximum use. The social ritual of attending court sessions was another way in which women and others excluded from formal education picked up a knowledge of reading. Indigenous people learnt to read and write in the army.[10] A leader such as the Argentine *caudillo* Rosas would surely not have paid for publications directed at the gauchos had he not assumed that their contents would be made known.[11] It is reasonable to assume that many people who were not themselves literate knew someone who was, certainly in the capital cities and most likely in other urban areas.

By the mid-century there was more of a market for knowledge goods than either the laments of intellectuals or literacy rates might lead us to expect. Indeed, the printing, publishing and bookselling industries of Latin America were among the most entrepreneurial of the nineteenth century. As soon as political and economic conditions offered even a glimmer of hope for success, someone would launch a new periodical. If most of these publications were ephemeral, that is hardly surprising, given the scarce resources for production and the unsettled conditions for distribution. What is far more remarkable is the fact that new ones kept emerging to take the place of those that folded. To be sure, many of them were vehicles for political factionalism, or even the set-tling of personal scores, especially in the first half of the century, but even so most of them sought to enhance their appeal by including articles on science, history and literature as well as commercial, social and political information. There were exceptional publications that established themselves over the lon-ger term—for example, the *Mercurio de Valparaíso*, founded in 1827, which evolved into a magnificent compendium of general knowledge, keeping its

readers informed of all the latest scientific discoveries and inventions, alongside curiosities from around the world. Taking full advantage of being based
in the main South American port of the early to mid-nineteenth century, by
the 1860s it had become a transnational publication both in content (with
contributors from France, England, Germany, the United States, Peru, Bolivia
and Central America) and in distribution (seventeen agents in Chile and eight
in Argentina, Bolivia, Peru, Panama and London).[12] Titles of such scope and
ambition became all the more significant to the circulation of knowledge precisely because many of their rivals did not last beyond a few issues. Although
for a long time most newspapers and journals were published in the capital
cities, especially the ports, a notable minority was sold not only in other parts
of the country but also abroad. Periodicals were the main means of disseminating ideas and information in print until well into the twentieth century in Latin
America. They ranged from the specialised to the general to the popular, from
scientific to satirical; many of them, including rather august journals, gave
pride of place to material that can only have been intended to expand their
readership, such as *folletines* (serialised melodramas) or the ubiquitous *variedades* (varieties) sections presented as a cabinet of curiosities in print. Even
those periodicals that did not aim to make a profit aspired to financial viability
and so were driven at least partly by market stimuli.

One promising way to gauge the scope of the book trade in nineteenth-
century Latin America is to look beyond the genres of work that have attracted
most attention: histories, novels and philosophical essays, which indeed struggled to sell even a couple of hundred copies. Booksellers' catalogues show that
there was an array of other books available: catechisms, devotional works and
almanacs; manuals on etiquette and handbooks of technical skills; guides to
travel, local customs or household management; miscellanies, dictionaries and
encyclopaedias; textbooks for literacy, grammar, foreign-language learning;
national exhibition catalogues and illustrated volumes portraying patriotic
heroes. Many of these deserve to be called popular successes by any definition.
And by no means all of these books were imported. Of the nearly eight hundred books listed in the catalogue of one of Argentina's leading booksellers,
Carlos Casavalle, in 1870, over half were published in Buenos Aires and a further 21 per cent in other Latin American countries (mostly Chile and Uruguay), with imports from Europe accounting for the remaining 23 per cent of
the stock.[13] Given that in the mid-1830s the first bookshop of Buenos Aires
stocked mainly books imported from France and Spain,[14] market conditions
had evidently undergone dramatic changes. Argentina was in the vanguard

here, but comparable shifts in the balance between imported and home-produced books can be detected, usually a little later, in other countries of the region. Moreover, the flurry of cheap pamphlets and *hojas sueltas* (single sheets of paper) that bore poems, songs and cartoons around the taverns, barber-shops and popular theatres is further evidence of a nascent popular market for knowledge goods from the outset of republican life. Much of this unbound material has not survived, so it is hard to estimate its extent, but the frequent references to such items in the massive bibliographical compilations made later in the nineteenth century suggest that it was plentiful.

The sheer diversity of printed matter available alerts us to a degree of local entrepreneurial activity in publishing, which came in successive waves during the nineteenth century. This chapter explores four strategies adopted by Spanish American publishers to create a market for knowledge goods in conditions of restricted literacy. One was to make extensive use of illustration, which became possible in the 1820s, when lithography arrived; another was to produce all kinds of teach-yourself manuals and reference works, reflecting the changing social conditions of the mid-century; a third was to attract more readers by diversifying into a range of cultural activities; and the last, which became a feature of the book trade from the 1870s onwards, was to promote publications on the Americas by authors from the Americas. Towards the end of the chapter, in a fifth section, I pick up again on the significance of illustration in creating a market for knowledge goods beyond the well educated.

The Lithographic Revolution of the 1820s: Bacle & Co. of Buenos Aires

A highly visual culture prevailed during Iberian colonial rule, as a necessary complement to the privileging of writing famously analysed by Angel Rama in *The Lettered City* (1984).[15] In societies where the mastery of letters was jealously guarded by the powerful, a degree of social consent was manufactured by ceremony, performance and iconography, which in turn were occasionally subverted to express opposition. New knowledge, too, came in visual form: Alexander von Humboldt, travelling through remote parts of Venezuela at the very beginning of the nineteenth century, recalled villagers clustering around magic lanterns to see the 'sights of the great European cities, the Tuileries palace and the statue of the Great Elector in Berlin'.[16] Champions of independence made haste to commission the visual trappings of a new state: flags and shields were designed long before the final victory. Public commemorations

of independence began to be staged on the very first anniversary, often mod-
elled on the public *fiestas* of the colonial era. In the cascade of printed matter
of the 1810s, images featured as much as the wood-block technology would
allow: a tiny drawing of a national shield; a smudgy classical figure; a swift
caricature. There was a receptive public for the lithographers who arrived in
the 1820s to transform the possibilities for printing illustrations.

The history of the company founded by Swiss lithographer César Hipólito
Bacle (1794–1838) and his artist wife Andrea Macaire (1796–1855), who migrated to Buenos Aires in the mid-1820s, shows how and why illustration was
so important in creating a market for printed goods. In 1828, the Bacles advertised their new 'establishment of lithography and painting', the first of its kind
in Buenos Aires. They hoped to make a living by entering two emerging markets: first, for 'portraits of all kinds', demand which had already been created by
a range of artists, including voyagers from Europe and Argentines trained at the
University Drawing School; and, second, for the accoutrements of commercial
and social transaction: 'bills of exchange, [lists of] current prices, circulars,
cards, etc.', all of which could be made more stylish by the use of lithographic
techniques.[17] Although the historiography has focused on César's skills as both
printer and engraver, Andrea's artistic talent was clearly vital to the success of
the enterprise. To add to the hundreds if not thousands of portrait miniatures
for which she became well known, it has recently been discovered that she drew
many of the fine engravings produced by the company. She also gave other
women the possibility of earning a living by teaching them to do the same.[18]

The Bacles, a couple of wide cultural and scientific interests, ran their printworks as 'an informal *tertulia* [cultural discussion group]'. Centrally located,
close to the Plaza de Mayo, they attracted a transnational crowd of individuals
interested in the power of images—architects, artists, cartographers and
illustrators—who helped them to identify every possible commercial opportunity. Initially they published mainly reference works targeted at traders and
merchants: maps of Buenos Aires and Montevideo, plans of the ports, and a
guide to the markings on the British packets that brought the mail down the
coast from Rio de Janeiro. They launched a pioneering *Boletín del Comercio*
(Commercial bulletin) in 1830, which listed import and export prices, shipping
costs and ship movements, customs duties and the coinage of various countries. This information was distilled from imported newspapers, merchant
houses and private correspondence. The journal closed two years later not
because of a lack of sales but because the Bacles refused to accede to Rosas's
demand that all foreigners make a public commitment to stay in Buenos Aires.

One venture that nearly broke the business was a gigantic illustrated register—over a metre high—of cattle markings. The first government of Buenos Aires province had identified an urgent need for such a publication, but Bacle's hefty product, which was comprehensive in scope but lacking in any principle of classification, was so expensive and difficult to use that the Rosas administration only reluctantly purchased fifty copies at a discount when told that Bacle would otherwise go bust.[19] Although Bacle & Co. had been given the official title of State Lithographic Works in 1829, it was evident that Rosas could not be relied upon to follow through on purchases of anything but the propaganda portraits he commissioned. After that disaster, the Bacles diversified their range, producing goods of varying quality for different target audiences. Some of their publications were distinctly upmarket. For example, the Bacles produced a collection of *Engravings of Buenos Aires* (1833) to exploit a gap in the market created when European publishers deemed the lavish 'customs and costumes' albums so fashionable in Europe too expensive for the South American market. Bacle made his own engravings, which were small, restrained and mildly subversive: dignified images of labourers with Black countenances sitting alongside a somewhat scurrilous rendering of 'The Beggar', who was manifestly white.[20] Bacle made a feature of the fact that his images had been drawn from life, unlike the European volumes, which were often drawn by artists who had never set foot in whichever part of the world they were supposed to be depicting. An even more upmarket publication, indeed the *pièce de résistance* of the Bacles' endeavours, was the *Museo Americano* (1835–36), a 'Book of All the World', which promised to include 'everything that was worthy of a second glance'.[21] Echoing in style similar publications in Madrid, London and Paris, it became renowned for the superior quality of its design and illustrations and was intended as a luxury item.

Yet the Bacles were clearly aiming for a wider audience, as indicated by the range of their products. Their popular series of *Trajes y costumbres de la Provincia de Buenos Aires* were published in small booklets of six illustrations to make them more affordable.

Later, they explored the idea of printing their *Fastos* (Annals) on different qualities of paper, ranging from 'superfine' to 'vellum' to 'Chinese paper', in order to offer a range of prices, although the prospectus does not seem to have been well received and the bound collections never appeared, only a succession of loose portraits.[22] Their staple income came from selling vast quantities of sheet music and flyers of all kinds. Although Bacle complained incessantly of lack of funds, the business was doing well enough by 1836 to establish a book-publishing house, the Imprenta del Comercio. Shortly afterwards, the couple was induced to go to Chile, to work for the government there. Bacle's decision to encourage other talented Argentines to follow him to Santiago was one that cost him first his liberty, when Rosas found out, and then his life (he died early, in 1838, soon after a six-month spell in prison).[23]

The Bacles' enterprise was central to the circulation of illustrated matter and commercial information throughout the River Plate. The company not only published the first illustrated periodicals in Argentina but also showed ceaseless inventiveness in trying to stimulate demand for other lithographed products. Their experiences show both the opportunities and the limitations of early market conditions for knowledge goods.

As they found with their register of cattle markings, there was no market for really expensive books, however 'useful', and the Rosas government was an unreliable source of patronage. The only way to stay in business was to strive for a high turnover of low-priced printed matter. The Bacles did supply portraits and other visual propaganda to Rosas, but they also pioneered two other strategies for keeping afloat: first, publication in instalments by public subscription, which enabled demand to be tested by advertisement before costs had been incurred; and, second, cross-subsidy of books from sales of an assortment of other goods. Cross-subsidy was widely used among the lithographers who arrived in Latin America from Europe and the United States from the 1820s to the 1840s and set up businesses, usually in the port cities. They produced anything that could benefit from the techniques of illustration: sheet music, playing cards, postcards, visiting cards with miniature portraits, commercial and social stationery, even the identity cards required to vote in elections—the more ornate the better, to prevent fraud. They printed thousands of *viñetas* (loose-leaf sketches or cartoons) for sale to periodicals and newspapers.[24] It was not an easy market, but in most places the worst pressures were political not economic. Commercial printing could not have survived at this time through the written word alone: visual images were crucial to making it viable.

Publishing for Autodidacts:
Almanacs, Manuals, Guidebooks

From the mid-century onwards, publishers were able to seek out new opportunities as production costs fell and mechanisms of distribution improved. Imports of printing materials became less expensive as trans-oceanic shipping was revolutionised by steam. From 1840 onwards, the Pacific Steam

Navigation Company ploughed up and down the coast from Valparaíso to Callao, linking a host of smaller towns on the way.[25] The telegraph and then the railways speeded up the circulation of knowledge in the interior. The range of sites of knowledge production increased as communications expanded, becoming less reliant on the capital cities. More economic activity resulted in the emergence of various middling sorts, anxious to accrue social status by showing themselves to be well informed on certain required topics. Pablo Whipple, a historian from Chile, has emphasised the importance attached by republican governments to fostering a moral order completely different from that of the colonial administration. In the competing republican conceptions of what it meant to be one of the 'decent people' (*gente decente*), which 'did not necessarily mean to be part of the elite, although it was certainly the elite that dictated the cultural values of decency',[26] the acquisition of a set repertoire of general knowledge had become a key element by the mid-nineteenth century. Autodidacticism flourished in the gap between the rhetorical commitment to popular education and the limited provision of state schools until late in the nineteenth century. A whole range of publications were designed to meet these longings for cultural capital among aspirant groups.

Historians have paid a good deal of attention to the manuals of etiquette and decorum that were distributed across Latin America from the mid-nineteenth century onwards, most of which were adaptations or echoes of the Venezuelan Manuel Antonio Carreño's *Manual de urbanidad y buenas maneras* (1853). It is increasingly evident that these secular catechisms were intended not only for the upper classes, as used to be thought, but for a far wider range of people who wanted to learn how to negotiate the changing social conditions around them.[27] Similar arguments apply to the countless teach-yourself manuals that sold in their thousands throughout Latin America in the second half of the nineteenth century. These pocket-sized books gave detailed instructions on a whole variety of practical skills and processes of industrial arts and crafts. One oft-raided source of extracts was the twelve-volume *Secretos raros de artes y oficios*, first published in Madrid in 1825 and reproduced many times, especially as abridged editions. One version from 1873 covered painting, engraving, paper-making, selecting pencils for drawing, decorating porcelain and—most poignantly of all—writing in the dark.[28]

The enduring popularity of almanacs—yearly compilations of important dates and statistical data—gives historians a clue about what knowledge was widely deemed to be essential in any particular society. Many countries had bestselling almanacs during the eighteenth and nineteenth centuries (for example, *Old Moore's Almanack*, from 1697 onwards, in Britain and Ireland; Benjamin Franklin's *Poor Richard's Almanack*, 1732–58, in Philadelphia; or *Barbanera*, starting in 1762 in Italy). In Latin America the invariable contents were the Catholic calendar and the movements of time and tide. Most of them also listed shipping movements; later, railway timetables. There are a few isolated editions of almanacs published during the early republican period—Bacle produced one in 1836, for example—and even the late colonial years,[29] but consistent annual publication dates from the mid-nineteenth century onwards. Beyond the common features, there was a great diversity of additional information, targeted at different consumers. Popular almanacs might include an agricultural calendar, showing 'month by month, which plants to grow', in which particular climatic conditions.[30] The far more upmarket volume published by the pioneering Argentine Editorial Peuser from 1888 onwards boasted of including 'the most distinguished figures in American letters and the most prestigious illustrators'.[31] There were almanacs for specific places, often compiled by the main newspapers, providing information about where to buy everything from bricks to sewing machines to pelota equipment.[32] Some aimed to conquer a transnational market across Spanish America.[33] Most were designed 'to instruct and entertain at the same time',[34] such as the almanac of commerce and jokes from Lima.[35]

Promoters of national consciousness also borrowed the astronomical term 'ephemerides', used for the daily plotting of the movements of the spheres, to refer to events in patriotic history, listing them by the day on which they occurred. Everyone was familiar with these day-by-day records of events because they were frequently adopted by the Catholic Church, which, as one Peruvian bibliographer noted, was always 'so careful to employ the most effective means for realising its purposes'.[36] Ephemerides had additional advantages for nationalists: such an inherently ahistorical approach to history conjured up a sense of continuity without making any claims about causality, enabling the multiple chronologies of different societies within the national territories to be momentarily aligned. They also offered a comprehensible way of integrating the secular and the sacred. Newspapers often headed their main column with a saint of the day set alongside a patriotic hero whose birth or death fell on that date, aiming to create an everyday association in the minds of their readers between the glories of the *patria* and the virtues of Christianity. Ephemerides were used extensively to instil national awareness in the state education programmes rolled out during the mid-twentieth century.[37] They continue to feature in the press and in schools to this day.

As Spanish American countries began to feature national ephemerides during the late nineteenth century, the same device was directed towards creating the sense of a common history across the continent. The *Efémerides americanas* published in Rosario, Argentina, in 1879, became a bestseller, with a second edition taken up by a Spanish publisher.[38] Its author, Pedro Rivas, followed the by then conventional practice of citing an ancient model (Ovid's *Fasti*) alongside a modern one (*Les Fastes, ou les usages de Iannie*, 1779, by French poet Antoine-Marin Lemierre, who was best known for reviving the legend of William Tell). Yet Rivas introduced several new features to make his book attractive to a contemporary Spanish American readership. The work contained four thousand articles on notable events from all over the region. It included an alphabetical index, which was very unusual at the time. A reviewer acclaimed Rivas's 'clear and uncomplicated style', his 'methodical' approach and his tone of impartiality, even in relation to recent affairs.[39] A remarkable amount of information could be gleaned from Rivas's book, which reinvented a traditional format to create a handbook of knowledge about the societies of the Americas in relation to each other.

Entrepreneurs of Culture: The Figure of the Bookseller-Publisher

By the second half of the century, the book trade was sufficiently established to make possible a new cultural figure who dominated the scene for several decades: the bookseller-publisher. These grand entrepreneurs of culture had a finger in every pie—bookshops, book publishing, periodical publishing— and accrued huge influence through their decision to promote work about the Americas, especially, as time went on, by intellectuals based in the Americas. Some of them were immigrants: for example, José Santos Tornero (1808–1894), who arrived in Valparaíso from Spain in 1834, went on to own the newspaper *El Mercurio de Valparaíso* and its associated bookshop and publishing house, and achieved commercial success by making a point of being nonpartisan;[40] or Carlos Prince (1836–1919), who arrived in Lima in 1862, from Paris via the United States and Valparaíso, founded El Universo—publisher of Ricardo Palma and Antonio Raimondi—and also contributed a great deal to the history of bibliography in Peru.

A key figure was the Uruguayan-born Carlos Casavalle (1826?–1905), owner of the Imprenta y Librería de Mayo in Buenos Aires, who cultivated contacts with authors, publishers, printers and booksellers throughout South America and

Europe in his quest to build up a stock of all works in print relating to the Americas. The well-preserved collection of his correspondence is a rich source for the state of the book trade in South America during the late nineteenth century. Everyone in the world of learning wrote to him asking him to stock their books—a medical manual from Leipzig,[41] Ricardo Palma's *Tradiciones peruanas*[42]—publish their manuscripts, persuade government bodies to buy their work,[43] induce newspaper editors to review it,[44] send bibliographical references,[45] supply books for educational libraries and textbooks for all levels of education, [46] track down rare books from Europe,[47] and donate to restock the Biblioteca Nacional del Perú.[48] The catalogue of his bookshop, which listed works printed in 'the South-American Republics' as well as 'ancient and modern foreign books on America to be found on sale in the bookshop', was distributed for free and became a reference work in its own right.[49] Casavalle's bibliographical expertise is evident in his catalogue annotations: he could even spot when hitherto unpublished historical documents were made available.[50] The distinguished Spanish scholar Manuel Torres Campos went to some lengths to procure a copy to use for his famous bibliography of nineteenth-century work on law and politics.[51]

Like Bacle, Casavalle appreciated the importance of location, opening his bookshop in 1861 just a few blocks from the Plaza de Mayo. There, in the midst of all the other cultural institutions clustered together in the Manzana de las Luces—schools, churches, archives, other booksellers, music stores and, by no means least as a site of cultural exchange, 'the Post Office barbershop'—it was possible to establish the Librería de Mayo as a prime venue for cultural events.[52] Like Bacle, too, Casavalle took great care over the design and presentation of certain prestigious publications, insisting on the highest quality of paper and typography, producing handsome editions of major texts such as Esteban Echeverría's complete works, or Antonio Zinny's history of the governors of Argentine provinces, books that in themselves acted as ambassadors for his enterprise.[53] Argentina was recognised for the high quality of its publishing industry at the 1876 World Fair in Philadelphia. Inspired by his time in Paraná as official printer to the confederation in 1860, Casavalle started a series of publications, both periodicals and books, on the nature and history of Argentina. Writers from all over Spanish America wanted him to publish their works, but Casavalle gave priority to developing Argentine science and letters.

Casavalle's entrepreneurial activity was made possible by the opportunities opened up by political and infrastructural developments in the 1850s. Improvements in transportation and communications converged with the secession of Buenos Aires province (1854–61) to create an alternative centre of gravity at the

inland river port of Paraná, where the capital of the confederation was established. Although it had only a small population of traders and clerks, Paraná, as
the capital, attracted various 'well-known learned figures from abroad', including the French-born mining engineer turned palaeontologist Auguste Bravard,
the Chilean political thinker Francisco Bilbao and the German-born zoologist
Hermann Burmeister, who went on to play a prominent role in Argentine scientific life.[54] In one of his earliest ventures, Casavalle supported the publication
of the *Revista del Paraná* (1861), edited by Vicente Quesada, to showcase Argentine intellectual life outside Buenos Aires and to connect it to wider Spanish
American networks. Exceptionally for the time, it had a print run of a thousand
copies.[55] Contrary to the Buenos Aires press depiction of provincial leaders as
uncouth caudillos in the style of Sarmiento's Juan Quiroga, many of the governors were men who cared for literature and history. Quesada's own extensive
network of correspondents, from whom he solicited information about the
history and traditions of each of the Argentine provinces, supports his claim
that there were 'lovers of knowledge' throughout the republic.[56] In its brief
existence, which was brought to an end by the reversion of the capital to Buenos
Aires, the *Revista del Paraná* established an impressive list of correspondents
from abroad: Vicente Fidel López in Montevideo; Benjamín Vicuña Mackenna
in Santiago; Ricardo Palma, exiled in Valparaíso; Juan Ramón Múñoz, director
of *Revista de Sud America*, in Valparaíso; and, in Paris, Juan Bautista Alberdi,
who encouraged Quesada to target European readers too and show them that
culture in Argentina was not confined to Buenos Aires.[57]

The Invention of the Latin American Author

One widely used tactic in boosting the market for work by Latin Americans
was the creation of the persona of the named author during the 1870s and
1880s. Before then, many authors wrote anonymously, using a pseudonym or
only their initials.[58] Books were usually listed by title, with the author's name
coming afterwards if it appeared at all—for example, *Vida pública del General
San Martín, por el Dr D. Juan M. Gutiérrez.*[59] Such decisions sometimes arose
out of the need to evade censorship or political repercussions. Yet it was also
the case that mechanisms of publicity were not yet sufficiently effective for
most authors to compel interest by their name alone, even someone like
Gutiérrez, who wrote prolifically and would now be deemed a major figure. In
the 1870 edition of his catalogue, Casavalle registered the onset of change
when he singled out the Chilean writer José Victorino Lastarria as someone

WRITING IN THE DARK   73

who had 'the prerogative of attracting attention' to anything he published.[60] Chile was one of the first countries in the Americas to pass an intellectual property law, even though in practice individual authors remained dependent on informal means of enforcement, such as public denunciation of infringements (as is still, after all, often the case today). The historian Diego Barros Arana's indictment of plagiarism in 1853 testified to the changing conditions of named authorship.[61] In the absence of accessible legal sanction, the opportunity to publicise a distinctive persona became all the more important to authors seeking to defend their rights and reputations.

The tensions around authorship are vividly illustrated by the publishing history of Vicente Quesada's bestselling memoirs, published in 1888 and, in a different edition by another publisher, in 1889. The material first appeared, as was common, as articles in a periodical, in this case the *Nueva Revista de Buenos Aires*, which Quesada had founded and jointly edited with his son, Ernesto.[62] Personal reminiscences were a novelty genre at this time and Quesada felt compelled to lend credibility to his reflections by publishing them under the title 'Memorias de un viejo' (Memoirs of an old man), even though he was only fifty years old and in good health. He may also have been making an implied criticism of the growing cult of youth. According to Quesada, the first book edition of these articles was published without his permission, when editor F. M. Chavez Paz poached them to launch a pioneering series of Latin American works patronised by Bartolomé Mitre, who duly supplied a prologue introducing the new book series rather than Quesada's own work.[63] In order to distract attention from his act of piracy, Paz conjured up a mysterious author, living in magnificent seclusion, 'in the depths of our Mediterranean provinces', yet still in touch, 'in spite of the distance', with contemporary intellectual developments.[64] The well-established publisher Jacobo Peuser, seeing how well the book was selling, alerted Quesada and offered to work with him to publish a third, expanded edition. Quesada was not averse, however, to playing with—and profiting from—the enigmatic persona created for him by Paz: he retained the fig-leaf pseudonym Victor Gálvez; signed off 'Villa Olvido' (Villa Oblivion); mocked literary conventions; and made a rhetorical appeal to readers to hear the truth, while continuing to dissemble in his text.

One frequently used device for attracting attention to books by lesser-known authors was to include a prologue, written by someone whose name was already publicly known, to endorse the contents or, more commonly, the writer. These short pieces, artfully crafted to highlight the views of their august signatories, became virtually a genre in their own right. They often said little about the actual work that followed. Their characteristic tone was to celebrate the qualities of their protégés, sound moral character being as important to a writer's worth as good style. In the years before book reviews were established as regular features in periodicals and newspapers, the endorsement of a prologue was one of the few clues available as to whether any particular title was worth buying, especially given that books were sold with their pages uncut. The writing—and commissioning—of prologues was central to the process of legitimising new knowledge. Certain intellectuals, such as Juan María Gutiérrez (1809–1878) in Argentina, Diego Barros Arana (1830–1907) in Chile and Manuel Atanasio Fuentes (1820–1889) in Peru, accumulated great power as gatekeepers. Often they used these powers of patronage to encourage the publication of books on the Americas by American-born authors.

By the 1870s authors were employing a variety of strategies to promote their work: Antonio Zinny went on a book tour, travelling round Buenos Aires province, reading extracts from his pioneering history of the Argentine provinces since independence. He assured his publisher Casavalle that his work was 'received with the greatest enthusiasm and a vehement desire to see the next volume [. . . by] priests, estate owners, municipalities, school boards and private individuals'.[65] The prolific Chilean writer Benjamín Vicuña Mackenna made a bibliographic study of himself, compiling and publishing long lists of both his own publications and of his collection of works on the Americas, thereby 'turn[ing] himself over to the public [. . .] without scruple or reticence' in order to establish himself as a site of knowledge accumulation.[66] It was testimony to his success that soon a leading French publisher, who knew the South American book market well, expressed confidence that a moderately priced, illustrated edition of Vicuña Mackenna's complete works would sell not only in Chile but also in neighbouring countries.[67]

The sections of 'bibliography' introduced by most general *revistas* from the mid-century onwards corroborate the evidence from publishers' and booksellers' catalogues that there was a gradual transition over the second half of the nineteenth century from a majority of works published abroad, mostly in Europe, to a majority of works published in Latin America. These surveys of the latest books ranged from listings, with no opinion ventured as to quality, to short summaries, which conventionally avoided direct criticism of the work (although ad hominem attacks on the author were by no means rare), to extended critical responses to the arguments. In Chile the state-funded *Anales de la Universidad de Chile* provided a regular source of book reviews from 1843 onwards, supported by a range of other periodicals. Many of these sections of

'bibliography' featured locally published books on local subjects. Travel literature by Europeans had long found a ready market, but by the 1870s the records of travels around their countries by Argentines, Chileans and Peruvians—
natural scientists, military officers, journalists and politicians—became at least
as widely known as the often fanciful accounts of European visitors. Travelogues by Latin Americans were often serialised in newspapers first and then
ran to several editions. Although scholarly attention has tended to focus on
their impressions of Europe and the United States, which certainly did sell,
there were also many commercially successful accounts of journeys exploring
national territories or other countries of Latin America. Many of these expeditions had a scientific remit and were sponsored by states newly attuned to the
potential of geography as a tool of nation-building (see chapter 7). They also
arose from wars of conquest of indigenous lands in both Argentina and Chile:
a voyage to Patagonia seems to have become a rite of passage for anyone aspiring to a role in public life.[68]

Beyond works of scientific endeavour, publishers both responded to and
stimulated interest in all things both national and American by producing
cheap editions of works included in the canons of poetry and historiography
that began to be created in the 1850s.[69] In Argentina, during the early twentieth
century, José Ingenieros (1877–1925) launched a series of key works of 'Argentine culture', published at cost price for 'educational ends and not as a commercial undertaking'. He publicised his rejection of subsidies or guaranteed
government orders on the back covers, but the initiative would not have been
feasible at all had there not been an audience for these works.[70] In Chile, commercial publishing was more dominated by imported books; even so, in 1917
Portuguese immigrant Carlos George Nascimento decided, on the basis of the
successful bookshop established by his uncle back in 1875, that it would be
worth his while to found a publishing house to promote Chilean scholarship
and literature. It was never easy, but Editorial Nascimento published the first
editions of Gabriela Mistral's poetry collection *Desolación* (1924) and Pablo
Neruda's *Residencia en la Tierra* (1933), among the six thousand titles, mainly
by Chilean authors, that it brought out before closing in 1986.[71]

The *Cronistas visuales* (Chroniclers in Images)

The vanguard role of illustration in expanding demand for printed matter is
highlighted by the emergence, during the 1860s and 1870s, of another new
professional role, that of the visual chronicler. The career of Luis Fernando

Rojas (1857–1942), a brilliant graphic artist from Chile, is a representative example. Rojas, who has been dubbed the first 'people's illustrator',[72] became very famous in his lifetime but was then largely forgotten until recently, when Chilean designer Carola Ureta Marín and Pedro Alvarez Caselli drew attention to his significance.[73] During the 1880s and 1890s there was hardly a newspaper or periodical in late nineteenth-century Santiago or Valparaíso that did not carry one of his drawings, emblazoned with his large and distinctive initials. He also worked with leading Chilean historians—Diego Barros Arana, the great biographer Pedro Pablo Figueroa and José Toribio Medina—to illustrate their works on the history of not only Chile but also other countries in the Americas. Later, he illustrated government-approved school textbooks. Rojas was no political radical—in 1917 he published colourful pamphlets of patriotic pictures to be distributed among workers and soldiers to counteract communist ideas—but in the wide range of his stylistically realist scenes of everyday life in various parts of the country he made visible something of the social diversity of Chile. Indeed Rojas virtually drew the republic in the late nineteenth century, before techniques of photographic reproduction displaced graphic drawing from its prime position as a means of printable representation. He produced a huge range of drawings chronicling Chilean life, past and present, and virtually carved out single-handedly the new role of *cronista visual*. His success showed that it was possible, though not easy, to earn a living as a professional illustrator several decades earlier than as a professional journalist.

Rojas was able to do so partly because of changes in the cultural infrastructure of Chile during the late 1860s and 1870s. His training was a mix of the formal and informal, reflecting both the achievements and the limitations of the educational network established by the reforms of the 1840s. From a poor provincial background, he had only a few years of elementary schooling, but when his widowed mother took him to Santiago he was able to benefit from the open admission policy implemented by Diego Barros Arana as rector of the Instituto Nacional (1863–72). Rojas thrived there not least because drawing, for which he showed prodigious talent, had been made a central element in the revised curriculum. He went on to start a course at the Academy of Painting in 1874, but discontinued his studies after a row with an uninspiring teacher from Italy, Giovanni Mochi, whose dogmatic insistence on a formal classical style he had the temerity to question.[74] Rojas's decision cost him the chance of a lucrative career in fine art, which was enjoying a golden age at that time as economic boom times enabled the wealthy to commission portraits and landscapes. He was initially able to scrape by on the income from copying drawings from novels, but what transformed his options was his own initiative to persuade a lithographer to teach him the technique of drawing on metal. Once he had mastered the basics of lithography, Rojas was in a position to take advantage of new technical possibilities opened up by a greater range of imported printing materials: more flexible presses, cheaper varieties of paper and brighter inks. Rojas made his reputation by securing the commission to do the illustrations for the periodical publication accompanying Chile's National Exhibition of 1875.[75] However, there was another crucial factor that made his later success possible: the War of the Pacific (1879–1884), in which Chile fought Peru and Bolivia over nitrate-rich territory in the Atacama Desert.

Rojas was appointed Chile's official illustrator of the war, producing sketches, plans and engravings to accompany newspaper reports and official accounts. So far as we know, he did not travel to the battle areas in the north of the country but used letters and eyewitness accounts from soldiers as sources for his illustrations. His drawings would have gone into the homes of many a Chilean patriot, not least because of his collaboration with the popular satirist Juan Rafael Allende (1848–1909), whose illustrated magazine *El Padre Cobo*, relentless in its caricaturing of the Peruvian and Bolivian enemies, achieved a high circulation during the war. On his own initiative, Rojas also produced a portrait of the naval commander Arturo Prat, who was killed, aged thirty-one, soon after the start of the war, attempting to board a Peruvian ship at the Battle of Iquique (May 1879). As he had anticipated, Rojas's soulful depiction of the tragic young hero sold well among the patriotic multitude (ten thousand copies) and contributed to creating a legend that inspired many young Chileans to enlist. After the war, he did the illustrations for the album compiled by Benjamín Vicuña Mackenna to commemorate Chile's victory.[76] The military granted him the honorary title Veteran of '79 and a tomb in the military pantheon.

The War of the Pacific was only the fourth war to be photographed anywhere in the world, after the Crimean War (1853–56), the US Civil War (1861–65) and the War of the Triple Alliance, 1865–70 (Argentina, Brazil and Uruguay against Paraguay). Both of these two Latin American wars stimulated demand in the capital cities not only for news reports but also for images, information and ideas. New products were created to meet the demand, many of which relied on illustration for their success. Photography, which could not be satisfactorily reproduced until the technique of photo-engraving arrived in the early twentieth century, did not displace drawing and painting but instead was used as a resource for it. Some of the famous paintings of these wars were done from photographs.[77] Later, albums of photographs of the War of the Pacific sold well, including images of injured soldiers (*los mutilados*) to emphasise their bravery and sacrifice.[78] In Chile, the War of the Pacific stimulated the circulation of loose-leaf sheets of popular poetry (*lira popular*), ornamented with woodcut prints, that had first emerged during Chile's conflict with Spain in 1866. Over the next three decades, huge quantities of these were sold, carried into remote areas of the country by travelling poets, who were usually also musicians.[79] Verse, song and visual imagery combined to create an alternative world of popular patriotism.

The strategies for creating a popular market—illustration, popular enlightenment and national content—came together with spectacular success in certain illustrated magazines of the early twentieth century, which became key cultural reference points in Latin American countries. The main examples from my three case studies are *Caras y Caretas* (Buenos Aires, 1898–1939); *Sucesos* (Valparaíso, 1902–32); *Variedades* (Lima, 1908–31) and, the most enduring of all, *Zig-Zag* (Santiago, 1905–64). These landmark publications introduced major innovations in production and design, used colloquial language and slang, enjoyed a high circulation (at its peak *Caras y Caretas* sold a hundred thousand copies a week in a country of five million people), and lasted over three decades. Part of their appeal lay in the variety of topics covered, spanning news, gossip, sport, political analysis, stories, poems and songs. But the secret of their success lay in the sheer exuberance of their visual display. The pioneer, *Caras y Caretas*, was founded to give the public what the daily newspapers at that stage could not: namely, 'a visual depiction of current affairs' (*el aspecto gráfico de la actualidad*).[80] This was an era in which improvements in technologies of both production and reproduction made photography ubiquitous: itinerant box-camera operators toured beaches and fairgrounds, races and festivals—wherever crowds gathered. Schoolchildren, union members and newly recruited soldiers all posed for group portraits; photographs were visible in the press, on posters and on noticeboards. These magazines catered to the popular interest in photography, but they also included more familiar graphic techniques—cartoons, caricatures, sketches, watercolours, tinted engravings—so that 'even people who could not read approached [their] pages with curiosity, even devotion'.[81] Readers encountered material from various areas of their country, not just the capital city. Eustaquio Pellicer (1857–1937), founder of *Caras y Caretas*, spent three years travelling around Argentina as a reporter for *La Nación* in order to meet the people he hoped would become his readers. And the illustrations, many of them in colour, enabled the magazines to emanate a humour that was irreverent but not savage, taking pleasure in the absurdities of life rather than raging against them. In these magazines the nation was presented as a kaleidoscope of colourful fragments that could be endlessly combined and recombined in attractive patterns.

In Peru, one transformative figure was Manuel Moral y Vega (1865–1913), who arrived in Lima from Portugal in 1883, aged eighteen. Finding an international community of photographers in Lima and Callao, as there also was in Valparaíso and Santiago, Moral y Vega was inspired to become a photographer.[82] There was already an active market for illustrated magazines in early twentieth-century Lima, but they were mainly targeted at the elites. Moral y Vega revolutionised journalism with photo-reportage for a wider audience, founding *Variedades* in 1908 and *La Crónica*, Peru's first tabloid newspaper, in 1912. He imported high-quality photographic equipment, travelling to Europe and the United States to do so. Moral y Vega also travelled all around Peru, contacting local photographers and artists and earning his living by setting up temporary photographic studios, which he advertised in the local press. He and his colleagues 'made photograph portraits of the whole of Peru', from the magnificence of belle époque Lima to 'the darkest corners of humble, mixed-race and indigenous Peru'.[83]

Conclusion

The documents of the book and periodical trade imply that a far wider range of people were interested in printed matter throughout the nineteenth century than can be accounted for by rates of participation in formal education. By the early twentieth century there was an extensive workers' press throughout Latin America (see chapter 10). In 1867 in Buenos Aires, at the instigation of a Chilean editor, the sale of newspapers moved from the printworks out onto the streets, when teenage boys—known as *canillitas* (thin-legged ones)—were first employed to hawk them around.[84] Other publishers paid milkmen or other delivery boys to take the papers with them. A former student of Santiago's soberly minded training centre for artisans, the Escuela de Artes y Oficios, recalled how he and his pals went to some lengths to circumvent the strict ban on reading newspapers during the 1890s. One of the servant boys, for a fee, would smuggle the papers in hidden 'between his jacket and his shirt and leave them all filthy in the washrooms, where the inspectors rarely went. Many of us gathered together to read them, one reading aloud while the others listened'. The students bought both the morning and evening papers; they knew not only all the various titles but also their political positions, the names of their proprietors and their best journalists. They 'never missed' Juan Rafael Allende's satirical publications and were entertained when sales of *La Ley*, one of the first newspapers to pursue investigative journalism, shot up after it was excommunicated by the archbishop of Santiago.[85] These students were an elite among workers, in that they were in a minority of recipients of advanced technical education, but their informed critical stance upon the different papers is testimony to the existence of a market for knowledge goods beyond the wealthy.

There is plenty of evidence of publishers being highly inventive in their strategies to stimulate demand for their products. Entrepreneurial publishers sought out potential markets and sometimes managed to exploit them with no little success. Slim volumes of poetry rarely received the attention their authors desired—even Neruda's career began with editions of one hundred—but books on history, geography, natural science and exploration often had notable commercial success. There were known bestsellers: Benjamin Franklin's autobiography, Sarmiento's biography of Lincoln, Marcos Sastre's *El Tempe argentine* (1858), Harriet Beecher Stowe's *Uncle Tom's Cabin*, Ricardo Palma's *Tradiciones*, the eighteenth-century fables of Tomás de Iriarte and Félix María de Samaniego, Alexandre Dumas's *The Three Musketeers* (1844). Illustration was fundamental to broadening the appeal of knowledge products, with every technological improvement being used to expand the market. Thus analysis of the significance of print capitalism to nation-building is strengthened by thinking about the written and the spoken or sung word as complementary, as working in tandem rather than displacing each other. While print culture has usually been analysed as a vehicle for spreading the *written* word (following Anderson's focus on nation-building novels and newspapers), in nineteenth-century Latin America many of its effects derived from its capacity to disseminate visual images.

While the history of publishing in Latin America is certainly a transnational tale (as is usually the case in any sector where technology drives change), it is not only or even primarily a trans-oceanic tale. During the 1820s, to be sure, when newly independent South America was a seductive destination for all the explorers and speculators of the world, adventurous printers from both Europe and the United States lugged their new technology across the Atlantic or the Pacific. Lithography, which transformed the scope for spreading knowledge because it made possible the printing of illustrations, was brought to Buenos Aires by a Frenchman, an Englishman and a Genevan, to Santiago by a Frenchman and to Lima by a Spaniard. Foreign publishers and traders, from London, Bordeaux, Paris, Barcelona, Leipzig, New York and elsewhere, played a part in the book markets of Latin America, the chronology of their prominence roughly following the order in which they have just been mentioned. Yet local entrepreneurs took the leading role in developing the publishing and bookselling trades of Latin America, and *localised* transnational connections were necessary to their success. Moreover, it was primarily internal factors—wars, the identification of social status with knowledge acquisition and a thirst for locally generated knowledge—that stimulated the creation of a popular market for knowledge goods that was related to but not reducible to the expansion of state education.

4

Knowledge Brokers

HOW DRAWING TEACHERS MADE
NATIONS POSSIBLE

IF THE NINETEENTH CENTURY was a century of engineers,[1] it was also, more fundamentally, the age of those who could draw. Drawing was crucial to so many areas of nation-building: the surveying of land and sea; cartography; natural history and science; architecture and town planning; civil and mechanical engineering; military strategy; artisanal industry; and the dissemination of all kinds of information, including images of national heroes (and villains) and impressions of war. It shaped the forms of national imaginings: sketching out the people, the streets and buildings, the landscape, and the flora and fauna of the various regions of the territory. The art of the miniature, which began to flourish in the 1820s, helped to make a divided social elite visible both to themselves and to other sectors of the population, because their cameo portraits were published in news sheets and on death notices posted on street corners. Photography came early to Latin America and certainly played a part in stimulating national consciousness from the 1840s onwards, but its effects were limited until the late nineteenth century by the technological difficulties of reproduction. In any case, the camera lens could not so easily—or so cheaply—caricature or satirise as the cartoonist's pen and ink; nor did the photograph naturally lend itself to the archetypes of nationalism. While drawing had been championed as the great enabler of the industrial arts in France, Spain and elsewhere in Europe from the mid-eighteenth century onwards, its significance took on a new order of magnitude in independent Spanish America. Drawing was no ornamental extra but a basic necessity for becoming a modern country.

This argument was made frequently across Latin America during the independence era, the sources for which contain a remarkable number of speeches and articles emphasising the urgent need to establish schools of drawing. Indeed, some impressive claims were made for the potential contribution of drawing to nation-making. If Diderot and d'Alembert had prescribed the mastery of hand–eye coordination for artisans in order to counter the unthinking repetition instilled by the guilds,[2] certain independence leaders in Latin America saw the generic skill of drawing as the source of all desirable capacities, qualities and virtues for the first generation of nation builders. For example, Father Francisco Castañeda, who campaigned in 1815 for a school of drawing in Buenos Aires, argued that drawing was the one great skill that would deliver the people from ignorance and barbarity, by instilling a work ethic, creating receptivity to republican laws and cultivating good taste. By learning to draw squares and circles the students would come to understand geometry; by drawing hands and eyes they would discover anatomy; by drawing buildings and forts and ships they would intuit the principles of civil, military and naval architecture; by drawing machines they would appreciate mechanics and glean the principles of invention. Their drawing practice would give them a good knowledge of ancient history and mythology, of the Bible, and of modern history, and it would lead them naturally to other desirable accomplishments in music, dance and theatre.[3] Drawing was widely seen both as indispensable to the development of industry (meaning all kinds of productive activity rather than specifically manufacturing) and as a virtuous outlet for the surplus energies of labouring men.[4] Prominent figures of the time lent their support, financial and political, to the creation of opportunities to learn to draw in state educational institutions.[5] Drawing featured prominently in the curriculum of UBA, the Instituto Nacional in Santiago and the reformed Universidad de San Marcos in Lima.

It turned out that these founding initiatives could not be consolidated in the way their champions had hoped, because of lack of resources, political instability and war. Nonetheless, drawing classes kept popping up in both public and private spheres: in secondary colleges, in the elementary schools run by religious orders, in the cramped backrooms of small-town general stores. Nearly everyone with any education learnt to draw and some famous intellectuals, including Sarmiento, spent years earning their living from those skills (in Sarmiento's case, as a surveyor). As soon as possible, from the mid-century onwards, Latin American governments began to extend state provision for artisans, engineers and artists to develop their skills in plotting line and plane. The training available in both technical drawing and fine art was criticised as inadequate on a variety of grounds, which will be explored below; for now, the point to note is that there was a great deal of public interest in learning to draw and a prevalent sense that it should be accessible beyond those who could afford a private tutor. The view that any 'lover of drawing deserves the honourable title of lover of the public good' was widely held.[6] Annual shows of student work at drawing schools were well attended. Public enthusiasm for botanical exhibits owed a lot to the sheer beauty of the delicately tinted sketches of the specimens. At the national exhibitions of the 1870s, when Latin American countries displayed their achievements across a range of endeavour, visitors saw maps, plans, diagrams, sketches, engravings, caricatures, cartoons, paintings, children's drawings and examples of fine calligraphy.[7] It is evident not only that there were many individuals highly skilled in drawing but also that there was a substantial audience for their work.

Who was teaching these skills of both execution and appreciation? Little attention has been paid to this question, mainly because of academic silos. The history of drawing has been deemed marginal to the main events of war, politics and economic development, so it has been ignored by many historians and studied only in specialist subfields of the discipline. Historians of education have focused on provision in schools; historians of science have concentrated on technical training; and historians of art have traced national artistic traditions, an approach that has been particularly misleading. Nationalist histories of art, which began to be written around the time of the centennials of independence and continued into the 1960s, routinely highlighted the autodidacticism of nineteenth-century artists, elaborating the idea of the exceptional individual springing untutored from his—or very occasionally her—native land to express the spirit of the people. More recently, research by art historians has discredited this myth, highlighting the variety of ways in which people were taught to draw, even when formal institutional training was unavailable. Throughout the nineteenth century, there were certain key individuals in Latin America who made their living from a combination of artistic teaching and practice: giving drawing lessons, painting portraits, sketching local scenes, surveying land, and designing buildings and public works, even if they were not 'artists' in the conventional sense. Drawing teachers were highly prized and sought-after individuals, embedded in networks—both local and transnational—of engineers, explorers, surveyors and cartographers, scientists, printers, artists, and politicians. It was these people who brought about transformations in ways of seeing. And they did so through their teaching methods.

This chapter illustrates how debates about how to draw were microcosms of dilemmas that affected the whole knowledge environment of Spanish American countries: whether and how to imitate European culture; what kind of education policy would make the best citizens; how to contend with the colonial past and the indigenous past and present. Given that drawing was conceived as evidence of cognitive capacity as well as manual dexterity, the history of how it was taught provides a window onto epistemological questions about the relations between humankind, science and nature. What follows will focus upon two periods of transformation in ways of seeing: the 1790s to the 1820s, and the 1880s to the 1920s. Ideas sown during the age of independence were revived in the late nineteenth century to develop policies for the twentieth century. I will suggest that it was these debates about how to teach drawing that nurtured theories of creative mimesis and integrated education, both of which questioned the binary divide of nationalism and universalism.

The 1790s to the 1820s: From Recording to Investigating

Drawing teaching that was modern—that is, supported by civil rather than religious authorities, secular in content and (at least in theory) open to all— began under late-colonial rule. The ending of the monopoly on teaching drawing in *talleres* (workshops) run by the ecclesiastical orders, where apprentices were equipped to fulfil commissions of religious paintings, frescoes, statuary and altarpieces, was partly an outcome of changes set in motion in Europe. The new drawing schools opened during the 1790s (in Lima in 1791, in Santiago in 1797 and in Buenos Aires in 1799) were the product of varied local responses to the Bourbon Reforms. These measures, implemented mainly from the 1760s onwards, were intended to reassert the Spanish Crown's authority in the Americas, especially in relation to the church and the religious orders. The Bourbon rulers also sought to promote economic development in Spain by maximising returns from the American territories, which they were anxious to prevent from emerging as competitors. The unevenness of their success prompted some creoles, especially those who had worked in Spain, to plan for industrialisation in the Americas, drawing upon the new science of political economy, in which Spanish intellectuals were strong. Such was the impetus behind Manuel de Salas's Real Academia de San Luis (1797) in Santiago, where drawing featured as a central element in a curriculum designed to educate artisans, and Manuel Belgrano's Academia de Geometría y Dibujo (1799) in the Consulado Real in Buenos Aires. The arguments of creole modernisers were strengthened by the greater visibility of science and possibilities for scientific exchange as the Americas became the destination for a whole series of voyages of scientific exploration, of which Humboldt's expeditions of 1799–1804 were only the most famous.[8] Lima's Academia de Dibujo y Pintura (1791), intended to counter a distinguished tradition of religious painting that had made Cuzco a major centre of art since the sixteenth century, was started by José del Pozo, an artist from Seville who arrived on Alessandro Malaspina's expedition to the Pacific (1789–94). The viceroy then established a teaching post in drawing at the Colegio de Medicina, founded in 1810. Colonial authorities increasingly felt the pressure to steal a march on the Catholic Church by permitting modern scientific instruction. Moreover, new economic policies, not least the effects of Spain's decree of free trade in 1778, contributed to changing local market conditions in artworks as in other goods: pious purchases of works of devotion gave way to a worldly enthusiasm for historical, natural and social images, especially portraits.

As in other areas of history, there are elements of both continuity and rupture in drawing practices between Iberian rule and independent statehood. The changes that made a secular approach to the teaching of drawing seem desirable had already begun in the late colonial period, but as the struggles for independence got under way the scope and purpose of drawing was significantly expanded. War created an urgent need for drawing skills in military planning, fortification and cartography, none of which could easily be learnt from books: good teachers were needed to demonstrate the transition from theory to practice.[9] These extended applications of drawing entailed modernising far beyond what the colonial authorities had envisaged, creating a demand for new, worldly codes of representation—images of historical events and social scenes—which helped to create the imaginaries for new political communities. Most advocates of drawing endorsed the instrumental argument that it would foster an industrial sector, but they also saw it in both ethical and aesthetic terms. At the Academy of San Luis in Santiago, Belgrano's friend Manuel de Salas championed drawing as a key to deciphering the world and equal in status to literacy and arithmetic. He argued that drawing was not just a technique to be imparted but the foundation of a complete education, encompassing both humanities and sciences, geared towards the self-realisation of the individual.[10] This theory of education became the founding ethos of the Instituto Nacional, which was created from the nucleus of Salas's own academy in 1813. From the 1790s to the 1820s an expansion in the potential of drawing was marked by the gradual displacement of the colonial term *trazador* (tracer) by the broader category of *dibujante* (drawer). The lack of an idiomatic English equivalent to the Spanish noun *dibujante* is a linguistic alert to the historical process of differentiating fine art, graphic design and technical drawing that has distracted the attention of historians from the significance of the generic skill. Drawing evolved from being a means of planning or recording to a means of investigating or imagining, in itself a nexus of knowledge and a mode of apprehending the world. The generic term *dibujante*, which remained current for several decades, was a sign that drawing had the potential to open doors to knowledge of many different kinds.

In the unsettled political conditions after independence, the claims that drawing was the key to new epistemologies and new approaches to education were overridden by the concern to instil patriotic virtue and cultivate 'good taste'. This priority helps to explain why many of the independent governments of South America opted to employ neoclassically trained drawing teachers from Europe. Neoclassicism, as the style furthest removed from the passion-drenched extravagance of the colonial baroque, was the preferred visual language of the new political elites. Think of the façade of Buenos Aires cathedral, which makes it look more like an ancient temple than a Catholic church; it was designed by two French architects and based on the Palais Bourbon in Paris. Only in Mexico had neoclassicism been taught, at the prestigious Academia de San Carlos, founded in 1781 and renamed the Academia Nacional de San Carlos in 1821. In Argentina, Chile and Brazil, explicit efforts were made to attract Europeans. The Brazilian imperial court continued the programme to bring over French artists begun in 1815, some of whom moved on to other countries, usually Argentina. In the 1820s, Bernardino Rivadavia successfully pitched Buenos Aires as a liberal haven to Italians fleeing failed revolutions. At the time, there was a tendency to write as if there had been nobody to teach drawing before the glamorous travelling artists from Europe arrived, fleeing war, political persecution or heartache at home, or simply looking for adventure. It was true that the wars of independence caused a generation gap; for instance, many of the highly qualified and experienced Royal Corps of Engineers, who had taught the first republican generations of engineers and surveyors, either returned to Spain or died during the 1810s. Moreover, there was in most places a prejudice and in some places a law against employing peninsular Spaniards. Even so, there were locally trained teachers available, at least some of whom were familiar with classical principles and secular styles. Artists from Quito, Bogotá and Cartagena, which were all important centres of art during the colonial period, were to be found in many other parts of independent South America—'the painters [. . .] are almost universally Quiteños', observed the English traveller Maria Graham.[11] Only in Lima, however, did any of them find a place in a government drawing school: Francisco Javier Cortés (1770?–1841), one of the painters on the botanical expedition of New Granadan scientist José Celestino Mutis, taught drawing through the wars of independence and into the republican period, at the Colegio Médico de San Fernando.[12]

In Chile, artists from Quito were passed over in favour of an Englishman and then a Frenchman for the chair in drawing at the Instituto Nacional. In Buenos Aires, the Swiss migrant José Guth was appointed to the directorship of the government-supported drawing school, resulting not only in the demotion of two Spaniards but also in the ousting of an Argentine-born assistant, Manuel Núñez de Ibarra (1782–1862). No one ever accused Guth of devoting too much time to his students—indeed he was dismissed from his first job for negligence—but he enjoyed the twin advantages of being 'a foreigner who was not Spanish [. . .] and of coming from Paris'.[13] He was later appointed to head the School of Drawing at UBA, even though it was located in the Faculty of Exact Sciences and Guth was neither qualified nor interested in technical drawing. Núñez de Ibarra, in contrast, was an ambitious and imaginative man, with a keen eye for a commercial opportunity. A skilled silversmith and engraver from the province of Corrientes, trained first by Franciscans and then as a craftsman's apprentice, he was one of the few artists from the interior to try his luck in Buenos Aires, moving there in 1809.[14] Eventually he won recognition as the first Argentine to produce representations of the country's eminent men: San Martín, Belgrano and Rivadavia. Before then, he had proposed a succession of schemes to modernise the local knowledge economy, notably the visionary idea of a factory to make printing moulds, instead of relying on expensive imports, but he was unable to persuade the authorities to invest in any of them. After losing his teaching post, he advertised a new, private Academia de Dibujo to teach engraving along with printing and even chemistry, but the project either never started or soon failed.[15] If Spaniards were increasingly unwelcome in independent Buenos Aires, a man from the provinces was even more so. Eventually, he returned to Corrientes, where he probably made a living as a silversmith, crafting the accoutrements of 'creole life', such as gourds for infusing maté, found in 'any averagely well-off home'. He also made official seals and, later, when the political climate changed in favour of native talent under the confederation, was commissioned to engrave the plates for banknotes printed in Corrientes.[16]

In practice, the art markets established during colonial rule persisted for several decades after independence, which meant that in both Argentina and Chile most of the artworks came south, from Peru or Bolivia. The public strictures against the detrimental effects of Quito works on the aesthetic taste of Santiago residents during the 1850s inadvertently revealed how popular they continued to be.[17] The baroque and the neoclassical coexisted, sometimes cross-fertilising each other.[18] There was little doubt, though, which one was officially endorsed: neoclassicism, European-style, was firmly established as the arbiter of good taste and the guide to patriotic virtue.

The presence of European-trained teachers meant that students at public drawing classes in Latin America typically found themselves required to learn their skill by the imported method of copying. Copying was the preferred teaching method in most European schools of drawing, from the grand academies to the free schools opened in cities to encourage the children of artisans. The drawing masters of Europe all followed the *Encyclopédie*'s prescription of taking students through a carefully graduated set of masterworks from copybooks to calibrate hand and eye before inviting them to draw from life and, eventually, from imagination.[19] The many criticisms of this method voiced in Latin America from the 1820s to the 1840s were fuelled by a paucity of materials. The finely crafted copybooks of drawings by European masters used in European schools were expensive to import and local printing technology was not able to produce copies of printed drawings until the late nineteenth century. The lack of a range of examples to copy meant that students could be reduced to spending years doing the same sketch over and over again. In Chile, José Zegers tried to improve the situation by translating a French textbook, Auguste Bouillon's *Elementos del dibujo lineal* (1844), in the hope of introducing artisans to the *principles* of drawing so that they would no longer be condemned to routine copywork. The problem was that there was no easy way to make multiple copies of the accompanying illustrations. The first edition came out without them, but this was felt to be too great an omission, so it was decided to undertake the laborious task of drawing as many collections of the illustrations as there were copies of the work.[20] Thus, copying became necessary to the very attempt to overcome the lack of knowledge of first principles of line drawing that condemned Chilean artisans to copying.

More significantly, however, the copying method raised epistemological problems that lay at the core of the problem of how the newly independent republics of Spanish America were to establish a knowledge base. How was it possible to benefit from ideas and techniques from elsewhere while at the same time ensuring fidelity to the conditions and ways of knowing in your own society? Mimesis (imitation) has so many negative connotations in contemporary post-industrial cultures nostalgic for authenticity and originality that it is often over-looked that in other times and places the practice has been seen quite differently. Whether mimesis is intrinsic to creativity or antithetical to it has long been a matter of dispute, dating back to classical Athens. Plato argued that art is thrice removed from reality, a miming of a phenomenological world which itself mimes the world of essences, rendering it suspect as a route to truth. Aristotle countered that observing and copying what others did was a natural way of learning, a practice common to both human beings and animals, a process that both per-fected and universalised elements of nature. Variations on these two themes have echoed down the centuries. During the early nineteenth century, they resurfaced in the context of elaborating the 'scientific' point of view, which by the mid-nineteenth century had assumed definitive form in a blend of accurate observa-tion and the elimination of emotion in the observer. The terms 'objectivity' and 'subjectivity' had completed their 'somersault history'.[21] In early modern scho-lastic discourse, the two words were used to denote the reverse of the 'scientific' meaning they acquired in the mid-nineteenth century. For scholastic philoso-phers, objectivity referred to how things were presented to consciousness and was therefore the outcome of a process that took place in the human mind, while subjectivity referred to things in themselves, unmediated by any form of con-sciousness. The terms were revived by Kant, who reversed their meanings to bring them closer to the current usage, although he was more interested in the relationship between the universal and the particular than in questions of scien-tific methodology. The post-Enlightenment discussion in relation to the arts, as developed first by Rousseau, then the Romantic poets, pursued the Aristotelian line to posit a greater role for the agency of the creative individual. In relation to the sciences, the classical impulse towards the perfecting of nature was revived as a scientific duty, especially in botany, where drawing remained the preferred mode of representation long after the introduction of photography, precisely because of its capacity to render the generic ideal of a plant type instead of the imperfect actual specimen. This is a long and complex history of ideas, which I've outlined briefly here because these debates about the relationship of human consciousness to the natural world shaped the intellectual context in which a renewed sense of the possibilities of mimesis emerged in the independent coun-tries of Latin America.

There were drawing teachers in Latin America who worked on the basis that imitation was actually the opposite of copying, an argument associated in

Europe with the English Romantic poet Samuel Taylor Coleridge.[22] Simple copying aims at an accurate reproduction of what is visible to the eye, a process requiring close observation and technical skill, but not necessarily any under-standing or empathy. Indeed, its success depends upon the suppression of individuality, ensuring that as little as possible intervenes between the object copied and the person copying it. Artists on botanical expeditions, for ex-ample, were reprimanded for adding aesthetic touches which compromised the verisimilitude of their drawings of the plants. Imitation, in contrast, was understood as an exercise of imagination, memory and curiosity. The distinc-tion was fundamental to the whole classification of knowledge debated during the inaugural sessions of the Sociedad de Ciencias Físicas y Matemáticas in Buenos Aires in 1822. The Spanish-born mathematician Felipe Senillosa pos-ited drawing as the nexus between arts and sciences, because 'it teaches us to imitate', which he specified as meaning 'to exercise imagination and memory' in order to discern the laws or principles of nature.[23] Drawing and architecture, he stipulated, 'although disdaining to copy nature, never cease to imitate it'.[24] Thus the process of drawing, intelligently conducted, would align the laws of geometry with the laws of perspective, to produce compositions 'of good taste' in harmony with their times.[25] From this point of view, holding the mirror up to nature meant recreating the reflection in the mind's eye: it was an act of interpretation, faithful to the laws of nature (insofar as they were known), but entailing a creative intervention by an individual.[26] Mimesis can unfurl as a colourful fan of possibilities or snap shut to preclude them. Whether it was a lofty or a lowly pursuit depended upon what was being imitated, who was doing the imitation—as Coleridge noted, any fool could imitate folly, whereas 'it asks some toil to imitate the wise'—and the epistemological assumptions underlying it. Mimesis can range from unthinking reproduction (although exact verisimilitude is actually almost impossible to achieve) to adaptive in-terpretation to creation from an understanding of first principles. It's a spec-trum, with the capacity for agency of the person drawing being affected by a variety of factors: the materials used, the range of techniques pursued, the social conventions of ornamentation to be observed and the pedagogic approach adopted. Mimesis could be celebrated, as Walter Benjamin wrote—in 1933— as the 'gift of seeing resemblances'.[27] A century earlier, in the new republics of Spanish America, there were various attempts to test the limits of what mime-sis might allow.

One example was the drawing course taught at UBA from 1828 to 1835 by Pablo Caccianiga (1798–1862), an Italian immigrant. Caccianiga was appointed to the chair at UBA in a competition, when his previous role as the professor of drawing at the Royal University of Palermo apparently carried great weight, although he also had experience of teaching in the main secondary colleges of Buenos Aires. When he took over from Guth, Caccianiga transformed the classes by shifting the focus away from copying to drawing the human figure from nature. He took students to the local hospital to make anatomical drawings from corpses and even occasionally presented them with a live (male) nude in the studio. [28] He introduced oil painting, watercolours and the art of the miniature, thereby opening up a whole series of new questions raised by the presence of colour. Caccianiga sought to stimulate 'invention' in the students, encouraging them to go beyond the faithful reproduction of nature to develop a distinctive style which he argued would one day be known as the 'Academy of Buenos Aires'.[29] Among his pupils were four of the earliest individuals to win recognition as Argentine artists: Antonio Somellera (1812–1889), Carlos Morel (1813–1894), Ignacio Baz (1826–1887) and the Chilean-born Fernando García del Molino (1813–1899).

In Chile, challenges to what became disparaged as an 'academic' approach to teaching drawing through the copying of copies arose in the 1850s, when such methods were institutionalised in the Academia de Pintura, opened in 1849. The first director, Alejandro Ciccarelli, a Neapolitan invited to work in Rio de Janeiro and then poached from there by the Chilean government, gave an inaugural lecture steeped in classical references, calling upon the young generation to dedicate themselves to painting epic patriotic canvases.[30] Many of the subsequent criticisms of the academy were ad hominem, and Ciccarelli himself seems to have been virtually a caricature of the kind of teacher who crushes the slightest sign of individual expression. Yet the rebellions of two very different students indicate the fundamental clash of worldviews at stake. Antonio Smith, who was one of Chile's earliest caricaturists and the founder of its first school of landscape painting, abruptly left the academy in 1863 in frustration at Ciccarelli's dismissal of landscape art as a servile copy of nature. Smith's own studio evolved into an informal rival source of training, frequented by aspiring artists who were reluctant to abandon the career path of a society portrait painter in the academy-approved style but were nonetheless eager for the 'piquant, the poetic and the improvised'.[31] His own work, which became very popular in the late 1860s, took an expressionist approach. Luis Fernando Rojas, one of the first popular illustrators (discussed in chapter 3), likewise suddenly broke off his studies at the academy after a confrontation with another Italian drawing master, Juan Mochi. The academy stood accused of importing an instrumentalist aesthetic that was inappropriate for Chile and in any case already outdated in Europe. An alternative case was made for imagination, spontaneity and self-expression.

The question of what constituted truth to nature—the ideal type or the imperfect specimen—took on a particular urgency in relation to American nature, which often broke the mould of European expectations or classifications. By teaching drawing as a mode of cognition, it became a means of investigating and acquiring information about the specifics of the different countries, through cartography, topography, surveying and natural history, as well as artistic representation. European forms were challenged by American contents. In the late nineteenth century, the forms, too, came under scrutiny. Again, it was through debates about teaching practice that new ways of seeing came about.

The 1890s to the 1920s: Breaking the Nationalist Mould

Debates about how to draw resurfaced during the late nineteenth century in the context of widespread questioning of what might be meant by a 'national' art, culture or education policy. Cultural practitioners of all kinds found themselves caught between the official, and to an extent public, demand for images of the national and the simultaneous pressures—not least their own motivation—to achieve recognition of their work as universally valid. Debates about how to reconcile nationalism and universalism in art were prominent in the pages of national newspapers and journals from the 1880s onwards.[32] They were mainly concerned with subject matter: Should artists working in Latin American countries concentrate on *costumbrista* images of local colour or should they take the whole world as their source? The Argentine expressionist painter Martín Malharro (1865–1911) took the argument to a new level by privileging form over content. He found a methodological way out of the nationalist predicament by developing a radical new pedagogy of drawing, which stimulated a rethinking of education policy in Chile and Peru as well as Argentina.

Malharro grew up in Azul, a frontier town in the province of Buenos Aires, 'in the profound solitudes' of the pampas, which he recalled as 'a temple of art' where light, colour, scent and motion combined to create the conditions for an intense apprehension of life.[33] Like so many others at that time he moved to the capital city, aged fourteen, to study drawing in printing workshops and at the Sociedad de Estímulo de Bellas Artes (Society for the Promotion of Fine Arts).

This society was Buenos Aires' privately funded equivalent of an official academy, where Malharro first felt the constraints of the copying method and began to question the assumption that the starting point for Argentine art should be the masterpieces of the European tradition. In Paris, working as an illustrator (1895–1901), he was intrigued by, but critical of, the impressionists, coming to see their method as one more manifestation of the positivist materialism that was beginning to dominate the age.[34] On returning to Argentina in 1903, he started the work in Argentine public education through which, as he emphasised, he came to understand the true potential of teaching drawing from nature. He gave hugely popular courses in drawing to trainee schoolteachers from all over Argentina, reviving a subject in decline by replacing 'the antiquated [practice of copying] from prints' with the radical method of 'direct copying from nature'.[35] At a time when high rates of immigration had prompted major public debates about how to make state education more 'Argentine' in content,[36] Malharro campaigned successfully against attempts to remove drawing from the curriculum and replace it with lessons on national history or culture. He argued, specifically invoking his independence-era predecessors such as Father Castañeda,[37] that learning to draw was a way of synthesising the full range of human capacities—intellectual, practical, aesthetic and moral. Through their drawing practice, students would be able to overcome what Malharro saw as false and destructive divisions between the arts and sciences and between pure and applied knowledge. Education had to be 'one, integral and indivisible' otherwise, in his view, it was not education.[38] Teaching children to draw by the 'natural method' of close observation of their immediate environment would lead them, through a profound understanding of the particular, to appreciate more generalisable principles of beauty and morality. He wanted each school to be a museum or theatre of wonders, which could be opened up for the general public to enjoy on Sundays. Malharro also called for a national repository of images, 'in order to interest Argentine children . . . in the spectacle of our own way of life [and] to help them to get to know [. . .] the multiple regions which constitute the patria'.[39] Yet he insisted that Argentine education should be the product of local conditions in form and practice as much as in content.

So it was that Malharro's experiences of teaching drawing to Argentine schoolteachers and children showed him a way to overcome the limitations of what he called 'patrioterismo' (chauvinism or jingoism).[40] Art had no 'flags or pennants', he argued, yet neither could there be 'any universal ideal of beauty in an absolute sense'. Art 'had to be national' in that it was bound to reflect a specific cultural environment: 'the conception of feeling and of action is not the same in our land as it is in Europe, just as it is not the same in Europe as in Japan or China'. Yet those nations conventionally associated with great art were those whose artists were deemed to have transcended their national context, painting 'without *patrioterismo*, without any ideal other than Art'. Those cultural gatekeepers who lauded 'Italian' art or 'French' art were trying to have it both ways, enthroning 'absolutes that had no more value than the sly artifice' behind them. But given the established recognition of Italian and French art as both national *and* universal, any artist born in Argentina was obliged to forget—which meant first having to learn—'all the best from the European schools of art'. For an artist from anywhere deemed to be peripheral, winning national, let alone universal, recognition entailed challenging global hierarchies of knowledge that excluded all but the most culturally confident societies from the possibility of transcending local specifics.

The way forward, argued Malharro, was for artists in the Americas to take American nature, not European art, as their point of departure. What he advocated was the creative interpretation of encounters between human beings and their surroundings, a dynamic process he saw as the opposite of naturalism or copying. It was not just a question of American content to fill European forms, but rather of a new method, a new vantage point, a new way of looking at the world. Artists—or citizens—had 'to have their roots in the country, adapting themselves to its conditions, to its natural, historical and social principles',[41] but from that starting point they could then engage confidently with the rest of the world, applying 'a relative [that is, not absolute] criterion of adoption and an American criterion of adaptation'.[42] Malharro was steeped in all the international theories of education ('from Rousseau, Pestalozzi and Froebel, to Spencer, Ravaisson, Guillaume, Tood, Rouma and others'), but his method, he insisted, had been developed in Argentina, which had drawn upon all the experiences of the past 'to transform completely these teachings, moving ahead of several countries in Europe, where they are still discussing where to begin'.[43] Malharro's studio, in Belgrano, a leafy northern neighbourhood of Buenos Aires, became an informal intellectual centre, frequented by scientists and theatre people as well as artists, all interested in debating how to create an art—and an education policy—that was both of universal significance and true to its social context.

Malharro's experiments in Buenos Aires were admired in Chile, where similar ideas were aired about the importance of drawing in building a curriculum suited to local conditions. A lecture given at the University of Chile in 1906 entitled 'The teaching of drawing' was a landmark of change.[44] The author, Juan

Francisco González, had taught drawing at the Liceo de Hombres in Valparaíso for eleven years from 1884, and later served as professor of sketching and drawing at the Escuela de Bellas Artes in Santiago, from 1908 to 1920. In an updated version of the claims of Manuel de Salas, he argued that drawing was necessary to a complete education. He laid especial emphasis on the importance of good teaching, opening with a quotation from the minister of public instruction, Antonio Huneeus, to the effect that teaching well was as difficult as 'constructing cities, building railways or conquering provinces', and urging the need to professionalise the role of the drawing teacher.[45] His intervention came in the context of a wider social critique of an overly theoretical—for which read humanistic—emphasis in the curriculum, which had allegedly weakened Chile's capacity to compete with its neighbours in industrial production. Only an education based on the practice of drawing could teach students to see the whole, allowing them to develop the capacity for synthesis necessary to complement the analytical methods of science.[46] Only cultivation of the eye, through close observation, could stimulate the critical faculties of the intelligence. González did not depart from the conventional view that students should be shown examples of the artworks 'of the great centres of Europe' in order to instil 'good taste in a people like ours, lacking in contact with the arts'.[47] But he also suggested that through closer contact with nature, Latin Americans would be able to make progress towards the kind of integrated artistic and industrial education he envisaged as the hallmark of the future. It was Japan that had come closest to this ideal, he argued, because 'from very remote times, through very active education, they have come to possess, atavistically, the skill, the good taste and the naturalness that today are scarcely beginning in European art. Japanese art is all action and character, absolutely national in kind, and without any sign of European tendencies, to such an extent that its creators know by heart the [. . .] movement of the living, in all its power'.[48] González often urged his students 'to see the big picture', taking inspiration from the Japanese. But it was in Buenos Aires that he had witnessed the most promising innovations in the teaching of drawing as a visual language for seeing the world as a whole. He was thinking of the work of Martín Malharro.

Gerardo Seguel (1902–1950), writing in 1929, offered an even more expansive conception of the significance of drawing to the elaboration of an American point of view. Seguel has mostly been discussed as a Spanish Civil War poet and a scholar of literature written in Chile during the viceroyalty, but he also spent many years as a drawing teacher and a militant in a teachers' union. He was a communist, but he saw art as a vehicle for the more spiritual approach to life that he hoped would accompany political revolution, a view shared by other Latin American Marxists of the era, notably José Carlos Mariátegui and his comrades in Peru. For Seguel, it was therefore 'a fundamental social duty' to teach children to draw in order to equip them for an age in which the 'logical methods' that had dominated the nineteenth century were being replaced by 'the intuition of those spirits well aligned with the precepts of life'.[49] Seguel drew selectively and critically on a transnational field of theories of 'new education', in which subjects were replaced by thematic, participatory learning, to develop a distinctive philosophy of education based on drawing. His main inspiration, however, was the drawings done by young children he had taught at an Escuela Industrial, or by his students at the Escuela Normal José Abelardo Nunez, eleven black-and-white reproductions of which illustrated his book. His distinctive contribution was to draw attention to the importance of point of view, in relation to differences in time, space and place, in each instance illustrating his point with examples from the teaching of drawing. Teachers had long followed Pestalozzi's principle of moving from the simple to the complex, without recognising that what is psychologically simple for an adult, such as a straight, geometrical line, might well not be for a child. Young children were expected to start learning to copy the external world at a stage when they wanted to express spontaneously their internal world of the imagination. Perspective was conveyed as a mathematical formula, when 'each artist'—and he saw everyone as a potential artist—'acquires an individual form' of expressing space, 'because not everyone sees the world through the same eyes'. Instead of being taught the history of art as a tale of ancient Greek, early modern Italian and modern French genius, children should learn that the artistic production of different societies—Egyptian, Greek, Chinese, American—'took different paths' but that none was superior to any other. In 'our America', a contemporary art would be the product of 'all the past contributions' of 'the Incaic and the Chilean' which in turn were 'nourished by Tiahuanaco which preceded them', together with 'the characteristic influences' of the local environment and the 'rhythm of the spiritual tensions of the cultural world that surrounds us'. In the same year, work began on introducing indigenous artistic techniques into the mainstream curriculum.[50]

In Peru, Elena Izcué (1889–1970) led the way in a radical transformation of visual practices to create a 'Peruvian art' based on pre-Columbian cultures, which had ramifications both in Peru and in the imaginaries of the industrialised world. Icons and symbols of Peru's ancient and medieval societies are now so ubiquitous, 'from pieces of crockery to items of clothing to printed logos', that it is easy to forget that this was not always so.[51] Two art historians from Peru, Natalia Majluf and Luis Eduardo Wuffenden, have shown how central Izcué and her sister Victoria were to the history of this imaginary. The conditions of possibility for their work included new developments in educational theory, especially the theory of object lessons, which were championed by the US inspectors appointed to oversee Lima's schools in the early twentieth century. There were also new archaeological discoveries: Hiram Bingham's excavation of the magnificence of Machu Picchu caused an international sensation, but in many ways the most significant of the new sites were those that revealed the sheer variety of pre-Columbian societies that had previously been regarded as 'an undifferentiated continuity'.[52] Both transnational and local dynamics interacted here: Romantic nationalism throughout Europe and the Americas, which was a constrained echo of the Romantic internationalism of the early nineteenth century, prompted a 'search for vernacular sources for modern design', medieval rather than classical this time around.[53] There was an international vogue for primitivism, folklore and the democratisation of art in the objects of everyday life. Izcué both drew upon this wider context and challenged some of its assumptions.

Izcué was able to attend the first drawing classes in Lima to be taught from life, held in the open air by Teófilo Castillo (1857–1922), who, unusually at that time, welcomed women students.[54] Castillo was a friend of Malharro and shared his rejection of academic training in favour of cultivating the expression of emotion stimulated by nature. Izcué continued to experiment with drawing from life while teaching in the state primary schools of Lima, which she did from 1910 until she went to study at the newly founded Escuela Nacional de Bellas Artes in 1919. She developed a practice of giving object lessons using pre-Columbian artefacts, combining the idea that studying drawing brought out inventiveness in children with her own insight that the beauty and variety of Incaic designs offered an 'inexhaustible' source of inspiration.[55] She found that young children naturally responded to the 'instinctive sense of beauty' in ancient Peruvian art, spontaneously acquiring its qualities of drama, colour and harmony.[56] Izcué explicitly saw her way of teaching drawing using pre-Columbian materials as a stimulus to patriotism as well as a framework for a child's intellectual life. The books are adorned with sequences of pre-Columbian-style animals, birds, fish and insects, marching across the top of the page and into the classroom. It was an alternative nationalist aesthetic, different from both that of José Sabogal, who drew upon popular art of the colonial period, and that of Manuel Piqueras Cotolí, who combined Spanish and indigenous elements, enacting *mestizaje*

(racial mixing) on canvas. Izcué's approach was also different in that she continued to pursue the decorative arts. Supported by Rafael Larco Herrera, from 1923
she worked at his private archaeological museum, running workshops on decorative arts, the products of which—household goods of all kinds—began to
feature in fashionable shops in central Lima.[57]

The 'Inca room' curated by the Izcués at the reopened Museo Nacional was
heralded at the time as 'the starting point of the reconstruction of our artistic
past'.[58] Like the national library, the museum had been ransacked in 1881, but
no Ricardo Palma was appointed to restore its collections and they did not
begin to revive until the 1920s. The revalorisation of what became known as
'Peruvian art', displacing the term 'antiquities', was marked by two essays written by two brothers. In 1908 José García Calderón sent from Paris a disparaging
account of pre-Columbian aesthetics, in the mould of racial pessimism; in 1924,
his brother Ventura García Calderón wrote a preface to Elena Izcué's textbook
El Arte Peruano en la Escuela, optimistically claiming Inca culture as a living
tradition, 'interrupted, but not dead'.[59] Her textbook was intended to make up
for the lack of artefacts within easy reach, given the scarcity of museums and
the difficulty of reaching them, even in Lima. It was published in two volumes,
the first for primary schools, the second for artisans and more advanced school
students. As Majluf and Wuffenden have pointed out, Izcué's decision to present her materials purely as models to be used in teaching drawing, with no
explanation of cultural context or differentiation between the various societies,
eras or modes of production, tended to fuse a multiplicity of styles into 'a common spiritual heritage'.[60] Her claims that infants were likely to be receptive to
archaic art because of its 'simplicity' also tended to sustain a reductionist view.
But her work to promote the artisanal production of everyday items based on
pre-Columbian designs and decorations, which she resumed on returning to
Peru in 1939 after a successful career as a fashion designer in Paris and New
York, laid the foundation for a successful export industry. Her educational endeavour also had lasting effects. Her work as a teacher of drawing helped to
change the way that the pre-Columbian past was seen, both in Peru and internationally: as subtle, complex and civilised, rather than crude and barbarous.

Conclusion

Debates in Spanish America about how to teach drawing went far beyond
matters of artistic practice to address the epistemological questions raised by
independence and the foundation of new political communities. How was the

specificity of local conditions to be related to universalist aspirations? What should be the foundation of education for citizenship? During the wars of independence and the early republican period, debates about drawing reveal the potential—mainly unrealised at this time—for seeing the world anew by making connections between different fields of knowledge. Half a century or so later, in revived form, they began to open up a space for criticism of dominant modes of understanding and representation, both symbolic and political. To reject the copying of European masterpieces in favour of the creative imitation of American nature meant to question a series of claims underpinning the model of scientific progress: that nature was there to be exploited by humankind; that sciences and humanities were unrelated; that reason could be isolated from ethics and aesthetics; that nationalism and universalism were opposed. Instead, it was suggested that mimesis could be a route to emancipation and that education could be holistic in approach rather than restricted to instilling any particular set of skills or attributes. Similar arguments were made in mid-twentieth-century Europe by members of the Frankfurt School in their critique of the Enlightenment. Adorno, who saw mimesis—understood as a creative response to nature rather than the passive production of a replica—as a repressed presence in Western history, suggested that it made possible an ethical relationship to the world that could counter the violence of instrumental rationality.[61] In Spanish America, throughout the twentieth century drawing continued to be a significant means of cultural expression and exchange for people marginalised by the written word—for example, in Chile the famous linocuts of working men and women by Pedro Lobos (1919–1968). Gerardo Seguel, fleeing Chile in 1930, spent several months in Rio de Janeiro, where he contributed to the lively debates there about the place of drawing in an educational reform designed to develop a whole new conception of life's possibilities.[62] The discussion continued in Brazil, and it is probably no coincidence that drawing played a fundamental role in the methods for consciousness-raising advocated by the great Brazilian educator Paulo Freire and in the award-winning literacy campaigns inspired by his work in Cuba, Nicaragua and other developing countries.

5

Touchstones of Knowledge

MOST OF THE TERMS used to talk about knowledge in Latin America are hard to translate, especially into English. One example that might be familiar to readers of literature is *pensador*, a nineteenth-century coinage widely used well into the twentieth century. The literal equivalent 'thinker' is too vague, failing to capture the direction of intellectual work towards political ends that was characteristic of *pensadores*, who carved out their role in societies where thought and action were usually conceived as complementary rather than mutually exclusive.[1] Yet 'philosopher' is too specific, because *pensadores* were polymaths who ranged freely over politics, literature, art, language, ethnography and natural science as well as philosophical matters, in a refusal to be constrained by the conventions of any single area of knowledge. 'Intellectual' is not quite right, either, implying as it does more of a differentiated social role than was typically associated with the *pensadores*, most of whom built up their income and their reputation from a variety of occupations (some intellectual, others not). A university professor would not typically have been referred to as a *pensador*, because the term also implies someone with a visionary capacity to see the big picture, floating free from the moorings of a body of scholarship to rethink the world anew. To characterise Borges as 'basically a *pensador*' was to acclaim his sheer inventiveness in working out philosophical problems through literature, rather than in terms of academic *filosofía*, even though he was steeped in knowledge of philosophies from many areas of the world.[2]

In short, *pensador* is a term that can be only glossed in English, and the same is true of many other markers of how knowledge was conceived and practised in the countries of Latin America. In time, it struck me that the difficulty could be turned into an advantage by analysing these untranslateable terms as touchstones of knowledge, barometers in themselves of the epistemic atmosphere of the societies in which their usage rose and fell. Such terms testify to the varying social status of different kinds of knowledge, to the range of people who had access to knowledge, and to the qualities associated with those individuals who were recognised as producers of knowledge. They are eloquent sources for tracing changes in the values, biases and preconceptions of the order of knowledge in any particular society, especially assumptions that go unspoken. Analysis of these touchstones makes it possible to look beyond the specific currents of nineteenth-century Latin American intellectual history, so often presented as a sequence of isms—liberalism, positivism, idealism, Marxism—to identify the underlying features of the landscapes of knowledge. For example, although political terminology changed rapidly after independence, epistemological terms remained saturated with the tensions of continuity and change well into the nineteenth century. Touchstones of knowledge therefore offer an alternative set of clues for understanding the oft-noted gulf between discourses and events in the decades after independence (perhaps a more reliable guide than the conventional political oppositions of liberal and conservative, secular and ecclesiastical). They also shed light on the extent to which the rules and conventions that converted subjects into disciplines were established in institutions and gatherings where intellectuals from Latin America had little say or sway. This chapter focuses on the verb *ilustrar*: to enlighten, instruct, explain, illustrate; and its related noun *la ilustración* and adjective *ilustrado/a*. During the wars of independence nearly all public figures, including those who supported Spanish rule, argued that it was crucial 'to enlighten the people', but what did they mean by that?

From *la Ilustración* to *el Pensamiento*

The closest to a singular term for knowledge at the time of independence was *la ilustración* (enlightenment), sometimes *la Ilustración*, which was the standard antonym of ignorance. That small slippage from lower to upper case *I* takes us to the heart of the history of knowledge during the transition from colonies to independent states. *La Ilustración* was the most common Spanish word for what is now referred to in English as 'the Enlightenment', a term which is so taken for granted in anglophone countries that its history as an ideologically charged European invention of the early twentieth century is familiar only to intellectual historians.[3] Although the Enlightenment (and its equivalent terms in other European languages) was retrospectively ring-fenced as the achievement of certain 'core' European countries,[4] a wealth of recent research has shown that they were far from the only places where comparable changes in epistemology occurred during the eighteenth century.[5] Enlightenment signified a set of methods for acquiring new knowledge of the natural world and of human societies, through discovery, exploration and experimentation. Such approaches were evident at universities in Spanish America—notably at the Universities of Santo Domingo, of Mexico and of San Marcos in Lima—certainly from the mid-1700s, and probably earlier—antedating the Bourbon Reforms of 1759 onwards, which used to be credited with introducing scientific methods into Spanish America.[6] The Spanish monarchy's wish to improve the economic efficiency of its American lands did lead to the creation of certain modern scientific institutions, such as the Seminario de Minería in New Spain (1792), where research into how to revive a declining industry led to the discovery of a new element.[7] Yet many of the late-colonial scientific bodies were instigated by American-based enlightened thinkers, such as the Escuela Naútica and the Academia de Geometría y Dibujo, founded in Buenos Aires in 1799 by Manuel Belgrano, or the first astronomical observatory in the Americas, opened in Bogotá in 1803 on the initiative of the medically trained botanist and mathematician José Celestino Mutis. The royal authorities' desire to extract more from their American territories led them to permit new institutions of knowledge that were advocated by Americans precisely in the hope of reducing their dependence on training in Spain. Beyond the sciences, even though many texts of Enlightenment political philosophy were banned by the Inquisition, the American Sociedades Económicas de los Amigos del País openly debated the new subjects of political economy and public administration.[8] Challenges to scholasticism were invariably persecuted but nonetheless they kept being made, often by clergymen. By the beginning of the nineteenth century, there was a well-established strand of thought which intellectual historian José Carlos Chiaramonte has analysed as 'the enlightened critique of reality' (la crítica ilustrada de la realidad).[9] He preferred to characterise it thus rather than as 'the enlightenment', in order to acknowledge other influential ways of thinking and knowing in the Americas at the time: the baroque and the neoclassical; the theological debates between reformist and orthodox currents within the Catholic Church; the natural law theories exploring the possibility of moral precepts applicable to all times and places.

At this stage there was little or no explicit concept of 'American' knowledge (in the later, nationalist, sense of its being authentic rather than imported). Scientists and scholars in the Americas saw themselves as participants in a transatlantic field of new discoveries: they may have envied the superior resources available to their European counterparts but rarely expressed any sense of intellectual inferiority. The nature of interactions between European and American investigators can be seen in the histories of the four great voyages of exploration sponsored by the Spanish king Carlos III, who invested more than any other European imperial power in compiling a scientific inventory of overseas territories. Long journeys were undertaken to Peru and Chile (1778–88); to New Granada (1783–1803); to Mexico, Cuba, Guatemala, Santo Domingo and Puerto Rico (1787–1803); and—most famously—to the Pacific, led by Alessandro Malaspina (1789–94). These expeditions, which made invaluable (and still underappreciated) contributions to the emerging fields of geography, botany, zoology, medicine, astronomy and oceanography, created transnational communities of scientists, intellectuals and artists in the Americas, especially in Bogotá and Lima. The Europeans brought the latest tools and techniques, but their view of the Americas as a testing ground for theories formulated in Europe often led them to wildly inaccurate conclusions about local conditions. They depended heavily on their American colleagues, who had devoted years to investigating their surroundings and who then spent a good deal of time patiently correcting and enlightening their visitors. Accounts of their meetings reveal a mix of mutual respect and reciprocal mockery.[10] If Europeans betrayed a conviction of their own superiority, it was also evident that Americans required them to prove it in the exacting environment of the Americas.

Inevitably, the wars of independence caused great disruption to the creation of knowledge. The Muses fled in horror, sighed Mariano Moreno, as temples of learning were converted into barracks.[11] A whole generation of scientists and scholars was lost to the Americas: some departed for Europe; many of those who stayed to fight for independence either died in battle or were executed by royalists.[12] At the same time as knowledge creation became harder in the Americas, the wars of independence brought to power those who argued for Enlightenment subjects of study: political economy, drawing, mathematics, modern languages and philosophy that was distinct from theology. The *ilustración* that during the late colonial period had been produced in the Americas as well as in Europe was from the early republican period onwards primarily identified by the new rulers as something that had to be imported. This was partly because the period of the independence wars coincided with a period of impressive success for science, technology and medicine as practised in Europe and the United States: there was a dazzling succession of inventions, from the electric lightbulb in 1809 to the internal combustion engine in 1826, with the stethoscope, the bicycle, the steamship, the steam locomotive, the lathe and Portland cement in between. The new countries of Latin America emerged in the 1820s with an acute sense that northern Europe and the United States had forged ahead in technology and healthcare (vaccination being the prime example). At a time when the main requirement of knowledge was that it should be *útil* (useful), it seemed that the only way—or at least by far the quickest way—to benefit from the advances of the early nineteenth century was to import them. Thus, although at the start of the wars of independence *la ilustración* was *not* deemed to be external to the Americas, by the end of them it *was* perceived to be so.

The independence-era identification of knowledge as *ilustración* embedded a bias towards forms of knowledge that over the course of the nineteenth century came to be defined and jealously guarded by its practitioners in Europe and the United States. It therefore had profound and lasting consequences for the status of the various kinds of knowledge produced in Latin America. Amid the repeated references to *la ilustración* in early constitutions, the acknowledgements of alternative possibilities are striking in their rarity. In some countries, isolated occurrences of the term *costumbres* registered an uneasy recognition of the presence of ways of being and, by implication, ways of knowing other than those represented by *ilustración*. The preamble to the Uruguayan Constitution of 1830 stated the wish to identify the form of government for the country that was 'most consistent with its customs [and . . .] adaptable to its current circumstances and situation; according to our knowledge (*nuestro saber*) and the dictates of our conscience'.[13]

In Guatemala (1825), where indigenous peoples were in the majority, trial by jury was proposed 'as soon as the progress of *la ilustración* and of popular customs permit'.[14] The Bolivian text of 1826 stipulated that 'no kind of work, industry or commerce can be prohibited, so long as it is not opposed to the public customs, the security or the healthiness (*la salubridad*) of Bolivians'.[15] In Ecuador (1830), on the other hand, the new ways were championed more forcefully: 'Everyone can freely exercise any commerce or industry that is not opposed to good customs.'[16] The expressed desire of the new rulers was that the *costumbres* (hitherto unchanging) of the common people would be converted, through a dynamic process of *ilustración*, into *buenas costumbres*, which referred to a combination of hospitable manners, personal and domestic hygiene, and a decorous—for which read modern European-style—appearance. Typical was the attempt by Buenos Aires Director Juan Manuel de Pueyrredón to replace the local popular songs accompanied by a guitar with orchestral music in classical style, through the Society for the Promotion of Good Taste in Theatre.[17] In particular, the *usos y costumbres* of the *pueblos originarios* were not conceptualised in mainstream discourse as *saberes y conocimientos* until the late twentieth century. They were confined to a static ontological category— an unchanging way of being—rather than a potentially transformative epistemological one.

All of the above, taken together, constitutes the context for understanding the calls made from both sides of the independence struggles for the enlightenment of the people.[18] Of course, the term carried a range of connotations, one of which concerned *derechos* (rights). When the pro-independence Chilean priest Camilo Henríquez wrote in 1812 that 'in order to make the people happy it is necessary to enlighten them' (*para hacer a los pueblos felices es preciso ilustrarlos*), he was trying to drum up support for the provisional government.[19] To Henríquez, who had spent time in a Lima jail awaiting trial by the Inquisition for reading Rousseau and Montesquieu, enlightening the people meant making them aware of their natural rights to liberty and self-government. If left in 'ignorance' of such rights, they would be condemned to servitude. The *ilustración del pueblo* proposed by Henríquez thus entailed awareness of collective, not individual, political rights. Like most other intellectuals at the time, he envisaged a knowledge elite. Here he introduced another notion key to nineteenth-century conceptions of knowledge in Latin America: the idea of natural talent, which arose from his commitment to what was God-given. It was the talented—*los buenos ingenios* (the good, sharp minds)—who should study public law and political theory, but the fate of the republic would ultimately depend upon popular understanding of their right to freedom, which was, he maintained, perfectly compatible with the Catholic faith. Indeed, in a deft alignment of his readings of Rousseau with his interpretations of the Bible, he argued that the people owed their eternal rights 'to the supreme Author of nature' (*al soberano Autor de la naturaleza*).

Such associations of *ilustración popular* with knowledge of political rights were soon marginalised by an emphasis on the corresponding duties of republican life. In this respect, the intense preoccupation of all parties with the moral state of the populations becomes sharply apparent: in nearly all the sources of the era, references to 'morality' are frequent and insistent. While there was a lasting concern to disseminate *ilustración* in the sense of certain skills and methods associated with economic progress, the overwhelming priority of the new governments was to fulfil the programme articulated by Andrés Bello for Chile—namely, to ensure that everyone had sufficient 'educación' to bring them to 'true knowledge of their duties and their rights'.[20] The term *educación* referred to a complete preparation for life as a social being. It involved the cultivation of morality and what were called *buenas costumbres* (good habits) in children, rather than the acquisition of certain skills or information, which was called either *instrucción* (formal instruction) or *enseñanza* (training), let alone political awareness. In the first constitutions of Chile (1818), Argentina (1819) and Peru (1823), a commitment was made to *educación*—that is, what was deemed necessary to create a well-behaved population—rather than to *ilustración popular*, with its promise of a participatory political culture. Varying emphases with lasting consequences in the different societies could be detected in these early documents: in Argentina, the focus was on a uniform programme of *educación pública*; in Chile, on *educación* for economic and social development; in Peru, where *educación pública* was a whole chapter of the section 'On the means of conserving the government', it was *instrucción* that was specified as necessary for all and it was the government that had to become *ilustrado* in order to ensure the conservation 'of public and private rights' and the rule of law.[21]

The pressing need to promote *la ilustración popular* to counter the ills attributed to ignorance was asserted by all the new governments, but there were sharp divides about what it entailed. A few potentially radical projects emerged, defining popular enlightenment as an emancipatory process of intellectual, ethical, aesthetic and physical development for all children (see chapter 10). There were arguments made for educational policies designed to foster connections between *ciencias*, *letras* and *artes* (meaning the industrial arts). What prevailed everywhere by the 1830s, however, although there was no need for it to have been so, was an impoverished version of *ilustración* as basic literacy and numeracy alongside virtuous behaviour. The literacy primers of the era were all steeped in morality. As was brought out in some savage critiques from the mid-nineteenth century, projects to form a critically aware citizenry ceded to the perceived urgency of ensuring a docile population willing to respect property rights. The idea of rights to be exercised was displaced by a concern to instil the duty of good behaviour. Moreover, although the new governments opted to import expertise from Europe as a temporary measure to kick-start the local production of modern knowledge, the result was that European approaches—and individual European carriers of knowledge— acquired greater status than their local counterparts. The problem was compounded by the fact that, in many of the new countries, recurrent civil wars meant that the disruption to the knowledge field begun in 1808 persisted for half a century or more. Looking back from the mid-1840s, Esteban Echeverría dedicated his manifesto for a new Argentina to a long list of martyred men who should have spent their lives in 'science and reflection' rather than being sacrificed in battle.[22] By mid-century, the concept of *ilustración* was increasingly subject to sharp criticism in the Americas for being elitist and European.

Even so, the very word *ilustración* continued to carry the radical promise of knowledge as transformative *process*, inherently characterised as something to be locally created and publicly circulated. Changes in the terminology for intellectuals are revealing in this respect. One such category that has been widely discussed in the historiography is the *letrado* (lettered one), meaning a graduate in law and, by extension, a generally learned individual. Freighted with the weight of colonial legalism, the dual meaning of the term arose from the royal preference for appointing lawyers to administrative posts. In his influential study *La ciudad letrada* (*The Lettered City*; 1984), Angel Rama argued that the continued usage of the term *letrado* during the nineteenth century testified to a persistent association of civilisation with cities and learning. While appreciating Rama's insights, I suggest that the emphasis given to the lettered city, since his intellectual tour de force, has been misleading in several respects, especially in relation to the half century after independence, a period which he discussed only briefly as a prelude to the 1870s.[23] The continuing presence of the term *letrado* is not surprising, given that the majority of university students in Spanish America took law degrees until well into the twentieth century, in response to the demand for lawyers to draft and test out new laws. But the conditions that supported *letrado*'s connotations of general learning did not endure. One significant change in this respect was the ending of the pre-independence university requirement for students to follow the *Studium generale*, which had given anyone with a law degree a good grounding in all fields of knowledge. It was not in the universities that polymaths were formed, but in periodicals and newspapers, printing works and bookshops, libraries and politico-cultural societies. In the gap between the colonial *letrado* and the figure of the modern *intelectual*, which began to feature in the late nineteenth century,[24] the use of a variety of terms to refer to bearers of generalist knowledge points to two significant features of the landscapes of knowledge: (1) recurrent initiatives to extend the circulation of knowledge, and (2) autodidacticism.

More prevalent than *letrado*, especially from the 1830s onwards, was the term *publicista*, which is defined by the Spanish Royal Academy as someone 'who writes for the public', usually with a political end in mind.[25] Some of the most powerful individuals of the nineteenth-century knowledge environment were known as *publicistas*. The term located them at the intersection of culture and politics, at the gates of the polis. As noted in chapter 2, during the wars of independence publication was seen as a route to liberation. Even the most militarily engaged of independence leaders were publishing on all subjects— constitutionalism, pedagogy, meteorology, natural history—as if the *patria* would perish were the ink to run dry. In the aftermath of independence, when institutions were weak and borders insecure, the new political communities took form primarily as fragile collages of text and image, pieced together from the newspapers and periodicals, pamphlets and flyers that flew off the few printing presses available.[26] Print was invested with quasi-magical properties as the medium through which the public good could transcend private interests. Freedom of the press was furiously defended, not least because it was often blatantly traduced. It was precisely *not* the *letrados* who were the alchemists of the new nations, but, rather, all those involved in the new practice of publication in print.

The idea of the lettered city obscures a transformation that happened during the wars of independence: the *purpose* of writing changed along with the new means of dissemination, printing. To aspire to sovereignty was not only to conjure with constitutions, laws and borders; it was to conceive of a people to be mobilised and a citizenry to be instructed. It is still overlooked that one of the commonest words in Latin American sources, deep into the nineteenth century, was *público*, which was used primarily as an adjective at first, especially in *la opinión pública*, but rapidly became a generic term in its own right: *lo público*.[27] The learned no longer wrote solely for their peers in the lettered city, but instead for a wider public interested in anything that might bear on the future of a new political order. The point was not so much that the topics changed—after all, compendious periodicals covering everything modern under the sun had been published in several of the late viceregal capitals.[28] It was more that those who wrote for publication changed their tone, style and approach to address—or try to shape or thwart—the demands of the emerging nation-states. The emphasis shifted from acquisition of knowledge to its communication. The language of these new publications crackled with the electricity of events, replacing the steady hum of science with a sparkling effervescence geared to evoking the possibility of socio-political transformation.[29] The opportunities both to read and to write for these publications created other routes to recognition for learning apart from the qualifications offered by institutions of higher education. The shift from the inscribed letter of the law to the printed page was more significant than Rama's account implied.

By the mid-nineteenth century, being characterised as *ilustrado* did not necessarily imply either higher education or any particular employment: an individual who was broadly well informed and able to converse about modern science and culture could be deemed 'as *ilustrado* as anyone, although not a man of letters'.[30] The idea of *la ilustración* sustained an alternative way for a minority of those excluded from the lettered city to carve out a role as consumers and sometimes even as creators of public knowledge. Claims to cultural authority were based less on formal qualifications than on participation in public life and certain personal and intellectual qualities. A few exceptional women, denied the chance to become *letrada* because they were not allowed to take university degrees, nonetheless won social recognition for being *ilustrada*.[31] More broadly, certain middling sorts, the kind of people who aspired to become *gente decente* (decent people), began to use the informal acquisition of knowledge as a route to social betterment. A range of publications were targeted at such people, indicating the importance of autodidacticism in mid-nineteenth-century Spanish America (see chapter 3). The biographies of autodidacts are invaluable sources of information about the opportunities any particular society offers to acquire cultural capital. It was the autodidacts who produced some of the most scathing critiques of the debasement of *ilustración* to good conduct and good taste, European-style, attempting to revive a more radical and participatory model of enlightenment.

The problem of knowing what and how to know was addressed head-on by Andrés Bello in his speech at the opening ceremony of the University of Chile in 1843, one of the earliest indictments of the uncritical adoption of ideas from elsewhere. The last thing Chileans needed was to accept 'the synthetic results of the European Enlightenment (*la Ilustración europea*)' without examining the bases upon which they were obtained or collecting and analysing evidence for themselves, which was 'the only way to acquire true [kinds of] knowledge [*verdaderos conocimientos*]'.[32] It is still insufficiently recognised that, after independence, intellectuals in the Americas continued to pursue their own routes to *ilustración*, criticising, revising and—perhaps most importantly—sometimes ignoring European theories, especially but by no means only those about the Americas. Bello's speech was a clarion call to return to first principles, to question all received wisdom, to become self-grounding in all things. As new countries, the societies of the Americas had to study numerous examples, especially from history, as the only reliable guides to creating the knowledge they required. In the increasingly visible gap between European categories and American experience, the terms *pensar*, *el pensamiento* and *el pensador* (think, thinking and thinker) came to the fore to stake out claims to agency in knowledge creation. A year earlier, inaugurating the Sociedad Literaria, José Victorino Lastarria had captured the zeitgeist: 'Now our Chile is beginning to think (*empieza a pensar*) about what it is and about what it will be.'[33] In most Spanish American countries around the mid-century, there were arguments made for a return to the founding ideals of emancipation as the route to genuine enlightenment and for a revival of an American conception of *ilustración*, distinct from and critical of the European version. Related themes were a critique of the press for failing to ensure impartial debate and informed opinion; an argument that ignorance was not confined to the masses but only too manifest among the supposedly educated ruling elites, who knew nothing about their own countries; and a renewed emphasis on *practical* enlightenment as a crucial element in the formation of an active citizenry.

A characteristic example is the weekly review *La Ilustración Argentina: Museo de Familias* published in Buenos Aires in 1853–54, soon after the defeat of Rosas.[34] This periodical was one of the first of many published in Latin America during the second half of the nineteenth century to feature *ilustración* in the title, echoing the independence era, but now asserting a distinctively national provenance. One of the contributing editors was the educationalist Juana Manso (1819–1875), who was deeply committed to 'la ilustración de las masas'—how much bloodshed might have been spared, she wrote, had it been implemented immediately after the Revolución de Mayo, as Moreno had envisaged. Manso's starting point was identified in her famous article on the rights of women to an intellectual life in the public sphere: 'The woman who is *free, learned* (*ilustrada*), *emancipated* from the antiquated concerns that used to condemn her to intellectual inactivity, that destined her to the perpetual status of *victim*, is a dangerous enemy', because those 'pigheaded ones' who were used to treating women as property would be obliged to recognise her as an equal.[35] The possibility of acquiring knowledge was not, however, necessarily accompanied by recognition of the right to create it: Manso wrote that she 'preferred to translate because my [own] ideas might not have authority'.[36] Yet by making herself *ilustrada*, through her own efforts Manso challenged the assumption that enlightened knowledge was the exclusive preserve of the social elites who sought to emulate a European way of life.

La Ilustración Argentina played on the dual sense of illustration as enlightenment and as visual imagery, which defined the later wave of *revistas ilustradas*
(illustrated magazines) designed for popular consumption. The publisher of
Manso's periodical was a recent Spanish migrant called Benito Hortelano
(1819–1871), a refugee from the post-1848 repression in Madrid, who recalled
that he had specially ordered fine engravings from Europe in order to show
'the Americans that Spaniards were not as backward as they thought'.[37] The
high-quality illustrations, mostly sketches of Buenos Aires by French artists,
symbolised the magazine's overall project of importing technology from Europe in order to disseminate knowledge of the Americas. The very first article
in *La Ilustración Argentina* was an extract from what was later published as *El
Tempe argentino* (1858), by the Uruguayan autodidact, naturalist and educator
Marcos Sastre (see chapter 2). It carried no attribution but was so famous that
most readers would probably have recognised it. In general, the editors sought
to counter the extensive coverage of Europe (mainly Britain and France) in
the liberal press, such as *El Nacional*,[38] by publishing local writers, including
the Uruguayan Alejandro Magariños Cervantes (1825–1893), one of the first
to develop Americanist themes. There were articles about the Argentine
Church in which religion was declared to be 'the most solid foundation of any
human society', in a clear rejection of the 'ultra-liberalism' of the 1820s and its
attempts to discredit Catholicism as an element of Spanish despotism.[39] The
project of *ilustración* was failing not because of the ignorance of the masses, it
was claimed, but because the educated classes were equally if not more ignorant in a different way—namely, in not knowing their own country.[40]

Above all, *La Ilustración Argentina* derided what had passed for *ilustración
popular* to date. The magazine gleefully mocked the manuals of good conduct,
the entertainment columns which were supposed to sugar the pill of improving articles and the political catechisms which purported to teach the people
their rights while neutralising the capacity to exercise them. In place of the
'many and varied [. . .] rules that have to be observed at table' according to the
etiquette manuals, the readers of *La Ilustración Argentina* were given instructions on how to prepare Argentine dishes.[41] True enlightenment for Argentine
families required that they should know their own culinary traditions. The
patronising assumption that instruction had to be leavened with amusement
was satirised in an article which copied out a list of improbable tricks—making
a tortilla in a sombrero, making the answer to a question appear from a random
egg—from a book by a travelling magician, a certain Mr Alexander, apparently
of German birth, who had acquired a certain notoriety when he visited Buenos

Aires.[42] And the inherent absurdity of the question-and-answer format of the catechism, which had been widely adapted for civic education, was brought out in a subversive, 'truly democratic' version:

> Are governments infallible?
> No.
> Do they often err?
> Yes.
> And on a grand scale, isn't it true?
> Yes.
> Is this odd?
> No.

Rehearsing Rousseau's arguments against despotic power, the text went on to affirm that citizens were entitled to withdraw their obedience from an abusive government and indeed that in so doing they would not only be 'exercising their rights' but also 'be giving a shining example, worthy of being immortalised in history'.[43]

Corresponding criticisms of the elites for being educated but not wise rumble around in the depths of the *Diccionario para el pueblo* (Dictionary for the people), published by Juan Espinosa (1804–1871) in Lima in 1855.[44] Espinosa pointedly laid claim to legitimacy not as an intellectual (although he was head of the Colegio San Carlos in Puno and the author of several published works on history and politics) but, as advertised on the frontispiece, as a 'former soldier of the army of Andes'. He was indeed a veteran not only of the 1817 Andean campaign, but also of the struggle to liberate Peru and Upper Peru from 1820 to 1825. Like Manso, he sought to revive the founding ideal of *ilustración popular* in order to highlight the travesty that it had become. As 'a good soldier', he averred, he would not have embarked upon 'such a bold enterprise' had there been more learned people in Lima willing to undertake it, but—he observed scathingly—nobody was prepared to devote any time 'to the instruction of the *common herd* (el *Vulgo*)'. He mocked their excuses: 'they had so much to do!', 'they were so tired of politics!', 'they saw our situation as so contemptible!'.[45] In the context of mid-1850s Peru, where corruption was rife, Espinosa claimed the purity of his republican commitment, rather than any specialist knowledge, as the basis of legitimation for his attempt to stimulate readers to think and develop their own views. He wrote most of the entries himself, indicating with an asterisk those few contributed by others, all of whom remained anonymous. None of the authors, he emphasised, were *científicos* (formally trained scientists). In time, he hoped, dictionaries would be written 'treating each subject scientifically, and not crudely like us'; such a marriage between good republican intentions and evidence-based knowledge would, he argued, create the perfect work of enlightenment. By implication, those whose republicanism was in any doubt could not create enlightened knowledge. Meanwhile, Espinosa pleaded indulgence from his readers on the grounds that the great Spanish author Cervantes 'was not learned [*literato*]' and was not even addressed as '*Don* Miguel, such a plebeian was he'.[46] By disrupting the conventional association of learning and elite social status, Carmen McEvoy has suggested, Espinosa posited a more popular version of republicanism as the field in which the new kinds of knowledge required in Peru could be cultivated.[47]

The dictionary—a quintessentially Enlightenment genre—was superior to the catechism, he argued, because if you learnt by catechism, when someone asked you a different question, 'you often [didn't] know how to respond', whereas a dictionary, which presented information alphabetically and concisely, enabled you to find things out for yourself—that is, to become an autodidact.[48] Like Manso, he challenged the tenets of a model of learning in which knowledge was passed uncritically from teacher to pupil: his dictionary was designed not to teach but 'to give ideas on things that are of most interest to the people'; all its ideas were 'subject to controversy': 'I don't impose them, I only set them out' to be accepted or rejected as the reader chose. At some points in the text doubts were raised about the very possibility of definite knowledge promised by enlightenment: all knowledge was provisional and subject to change; ideas, like fashions, sometimes seemed extravagant at first but then appeared in time to be the most rational.[49] It was no longer clear in Peru where learning was located, but certainly not in the once great universities. The title of 'doctor' was no longer 'a great thing'; university degrees had lost status partly because of the increasing opportunities to be 'deputies, advisers, ministers, presidents' or at least 'heads of a department, a province or a district', which did not mean, he noted, that ignorance could not be found 'in the chairs of philosophy, in the ministries and even in the presidency'.[50] And if ignorance was bad, then error was worse. In the entry on 'Error', he attacked the Colegio de San Carlos in Lima for teaching erroneous ideas—for example, denying popular sovereignty as a principle of republicanism and insisting that sovereignty came only from God.[51] Espinosa's stated aim was to foster a critical public opinion to hold the elites to account and to counteract corruption and *caudillismo*. This was in tension with his assertion of the importance of moral education (seen as mainly the responsibility of the family) and his plans for state school training in the practical skills to create a skilled and industrious artisanal sector of model citizens. In her survey of the intellectual context of Espinosa's work, Carmen McEvoy identified him as a moderate reformer, related to a mid-century strand of Catholic republicanism that sought to make the people more like the educated minority, rather than arguing, as others soon began to do, that the culture of the people was the only reliable source of republican legitimacy.[52] Espinosa's republican dictionary was designed to inspire a Peruvian version of *ilustración*, committed to independent critical thought, fostering a spirit of invention rather than mere imitation of Europe and preserving the moral consciousness of Catholicism while abandoning the formal constraint of the catechism. A transitional text, it was saturated in the tensions of *ilustración* as a process that promised emancipation but only on condition of following a prescribed route towards it.

Conclusion

Analysing the touchstone term *ilustración* opens a window onto the main areas of dispute within the knowledge environment: What was socially recognised as knowledge and who was entitled to it? When more nineteenth-century Spanish American publications, especially the press, become available in digitised, searchable form, it will be easier to trace more extensively the relative usages of the various terms relating to knowledge. Even so, it already seems fair to conclude that the potentially radical conception of popular enlightenment as the exercise of political rights persisted as a counter-current to the conservative version of civic duty. The idea sown during the independence period was revived around the mid-century. From the 1870s onwards, a flurry of periodicals carrying the word *ilustración* in their titles bore witness to new possibilities for making this particular kind of knowledge available to a wider audience. There were periodicals directed at artisans, workers and immigrants,[53] many of which explicitly played on the dual sense of *ilustración* as visual imagery and as exposition, making bold use of new printing techniques.[54] Some of them had continental ambitions, aiming to create transnational communities for exchanging modern ideas and approaches.[55] The political implications of becoming *ilustrado* varied—a few of these publications were official—but overall the term *ilustración* continued to carry a promise of greater participation in the republic through the acquisition of knowledge deemed to be modern. Knowledge, ideally, was public, communicable and accountable, as is indirectly confirmed by one term of abuse that came to the fore in the late nineteenth century: *académico*. There was widespread contempt for knowledge that was locked away to muster in exclusive institutions, dry knowledge detached from life, sustained by only its own pedantry and sophistry. By this time, the main target was no longer scholasticism but all approaches to knowledge that relied solely on a reasoning reason that looked only to itself.

The touchstone term *ilustración* can also help to gauge changes in the relationship between knowledge from Europe and knowledge from the Americas. By the mid-century, the well-established tradition of Americans criticising European errors and misapprehensions about American conditions was developing into a more fundamental critique of what they saw as a European conception of knowledge that separated out intellectuality from morality and spirituality. When Bello referred to 'the European Enlightenment', he was actually marking it out as a model *not* to be followed: his point was precisely that Americans had to develop their own ways of knowing. Espinosa argued, in his *Diccionario para el pueblo*, that it was possible to be too *ilustrado*: after all, 'enlightened Europe' had been just as ignorant of the Chinese invention of printing of images as had 'innocent America'.[56] For all Europe's accumulation of knowledge, it had no monopoly on creativity or open-mindedness to new discoveries. The Rousseauvian echo of the negative consequences of (too much) organised learning fits with Espinosa's claim that the natural spontaneity of the Americas meant that it was bound to surpass Europe in due course.

The crux of the matter lay in conceptions of the relationship between enlightened thinking and Catholic faith, an epistemological question that cannot be reduced to institutional power struggles between church and state. If conservatives, both clerical and nonclerical, continued to make the argument that true *ilustración* could be founded only on the word of God, it was also the case that many committed Catholics advocated modern methods for the study of the natural and human worlds. Even radical liberals who battled to exclude the Catholic Church from the public sphere tended to see the Enlightenment goal of thinking for yourself in religious terms. For the Chilean Francisco Bilbao (1823–1865), who was twice forced into exile for blasphemy and for criticism of the clergy, the sovereignty (of an individual and, by extension, of a nation) was intrinsically bound up with both the ability to think well *and* the capacity to apprehend 'the light [and] the word of the Eternal'. What Bilbao in 1855 called right thinking, based on an understanding of liberty, equality and fraternity, required full freedoms to be exercised throughout the knowledge environment: freedom 'of thought, belief, worship, speech, teaching, the press, the tribune, the university chair, art'.[57] Any restriction on freedom of thought constituted an interference in each person's sovereign right to 'communion with the mind of God', 'separating us radically from the land of the spirit', which would lead to a hellish existence.[58] This bias towards the view that both reason and spirit were required for the full realisation of sovereignty persisted throughout the nineteenth century and into the 1900s. The *Arielista* movement, for example, set a supposedly 'Latin American' consciousness of spirituality and beauty against materialist and utilitarian outlooks associated with the United States.

Another clue to the increasingly widespread sense in Spanish America of the inadequacies of European-style enlightenment lies in the adjective *culto*, one of the most prevalent terms in the sources throughout the nineteenth century. It captured the great hope—and the lingering doubt—expressed about any Spanish American nation: *¿Puede ser culto?* Could it (we, they) be, or at least become, well, what exactly does it mean?—educated? cultured? cultivated? learned? *civilised*? As a noun *el culto* has usually meant 'worship', in both the general sense of veneration and the specific one of a set of rites and convictions. No adjectival usage escaped these fundamentally religious connotations. As an adjective applied to an individual, it denoted someone of good *educación*, which meant having strong morals and refined manners in addition to being well informed. If a biography—or an obituary—concluded that its subject was *además, el tipo perfecto de los hombres cultos* (besides, the perfect example of a cultured man),[59] it explicitly signalled qualities over and above talent, learning and nobility of character: it emphasised that he was a man of faith *and therefore* a man of broad—catholic—learning, sympathetic understanding and open-minded toleration. Later, during the twentieth century, characterising someone as *culto* began to carry negative connotations of being affected or pretentious, but in the nineteenth-century sources it was normally a term of approbation.

When *culto* was applied to peoples or nations, the implication was often that a religious sensibility was constitutive of both collective self-consciousness and recognition by others. There were many references to 'all the *pueblos cultos*' to evoke the kind of countries with which Spanish American policymakers identified, usually France, Britain and Germany. But to become *un pueblo civilizado y culto* it was not enough to establish stable government, the rule of law and cultural institutions: religiosity was constitutive of the capacity to move beyond barbarism and create a moral society.[60] The term *culto* captured the higher state of human perfectibility—combining ethics, aesthetics, intellectuality and spirituality—envisaged for the republics of Spanish America. During the early twentieth century, many arguments of various hues turned on the shared assumption that no intellectual process pursued in isolation, for its own sake, could result in true *ilustración*.

PART II

Knowledge for Nation-Making

6

Languages

UNIVERSAL, NATIONAL AND REGIONAL

Soy un huérfano del idioma
(I am an orphan of the language)

—CÉSAR VALLEJO

AMONG THE LESS NOTICED WAYS of commemorating the recent bicentenaries of independence was a series of new national dictionaries. The differences in title of these apparently similar publications, all of which were published by local branches of the Spanish Royal Academy (RAE), pointed to notable variations in scope and emphasis. The Peruvian lexicographers presented their work—*DiPerú, Diccionario de Peruanismos* (Dictionary of Peruvianisms, 2016)—as a celebration of nine thousand new words and locutions 'created by Peruvians to reflect the culture and reality of our country'.[1] In contrast, the Chilean version—*Diccionario del uso del español de Chile* (Dictionary of the use of the Spanish of Chile, 2010)—was emphatically declared *not* to be a dictionary of *chilenismos*, because 'with globalization [. . .], it becomes more difficult by the day to think in terms of a lexicon that is exclusive to any one territory'. Instead, it was billed as an aid to understanding the current vocabulary used in Chile that did not (yet) belong to 'the general pan-hispanic vocabulary of the Spanish language'.[2] It nonetheless contained about the same number of entries as the Peruvian compilation. The far more compact Argentine *Diccionario del habla de los argentinos* (Dictionary of the spoken language of the Argentines, 2003) expanded steadily to reach 1,439 entries in its third edition of 2017, prompting concerns that greater expressivity had come at the

121

cost of good taste.[3] These are subtle indications of significant differences in histories of language and nation-making.

A century earlier, it looked as if the question of language had been officially settled. Local branches of the Royal Academy were opened in most Spanish American countries from the 1880s to the 1920s, all committed to defending 'the purity and splendour of the Spanish language'.[4] Angel Rama has pointed out the contrast with Brazil, where a special committee was established to oversee and regulate a future Brazilian language in preference to conserving Portuguese.[5] After campaigns waged by various Spanish American intellectuals, the RAE granted recognition to certain American variations of Spanish as a quid pro quo for a degree of acquiescence to Spain's role as arbiter of the rules. During the same period, there was a veritable industry of compilations of words and phrases distinctive to particular countries (*-ismos*). Most of these works were didactic and normative, intended 'to purify' what was still usually referred to as 'Castilian' from the 'vices' of local variation. Linguistic nationalism assumed the form of campaigns against those foreign borrowings deemed to be undesirable, especially from US English: 'why say *sport* when we have *deporte*, a word as ancient as it is pure?' (*tan antiguo como castizo*).[6] Whole tracts were written to join battle against the use of *lunch* instead of *almuerzo*, *pic-nic* for *jira* or—a recurrent bugbear—*etiqueta* for *rótulo* (label).[7] By the time of the independence commemorations, correctness in Spanish usage was both pillar and ornament of the edifice of virtuous and decorous patriotism constructed by those in power. National newspapers saw it as their mission to educate readers in how to avoid 'solecisms, barbarisms, words and phrases that disfigure the language', not least because there were no clear linguistic principles behind what operated as an exclusive social code. The Argentine national daily *La Prensa* advised its readers in 1919: 'you must write *inficionar* not *infeccionar*', because the Spanish Royal Academy decreed that it was so; '*Leibniz* and not *Leibnitz*', because that was how the philosopher himself spelt it; '*mexicano* and not *mejicano*', for which they could give no reason but insisted upon nonetheless.[8] There were vigorous and substantial debates, especially among educators, about whether the most effective route to writing and speaking well lay in grammar or in spelling, in teaching children to read by the syllabic or the analytic method, in learning 'pure' Castillian or its idiomatic local variations. Yet they were all based on the shared assumptions that Spanish was the national language and that correct usage correlated to high social status, even—or perhaps especially—in those countries where indigenous languages had long been the first languages of high proportions of the population. Only one country built a national identity around an indigenous language: Paraguay, where most people, including politicians and intellectuals, spoke both Guaraní and Spanish.[9] Even so, Guaraní was not made an official language until the bilingual constitution of 1992. Other countries granted official recognition to indigenous languages in the late twentieth or early twenty-first centuries,[10] and some governments took steps to preserve or promote them, but Paraguay remains unique in its cross-class experience of bilingualism.

Yet the unity confected around (certain versions of) Spanish at the centenary celebrations thinly veiled a long history of deep and persistent unease about language. The sense of orphanhood conveyed by Peruvian poet César Vallejo at the time of the centenary arose because his native tongue gave him neither an inheritance acceptable to him nor universal reach for his writing. As a Marxist champion of social justice, how could he write in the language of colonialism and oligarchic rule? Without the words to be truthful to the particularities, how could he speak to the general human condition? Vanguard writers everywhere sought to express the intractability of language, but Vallejo conveyed the predicament of being trapped between marginal status abroad and oppressor status at home—a double silencing. Hence the literal breakdown of syntax, spelling and semantics enacted on the printed page of his collection *Trilce* (1922): '999 calorías / Rumbbb . . . Trrrapprrr rrach . . . chaz'.[11] For authentic modernist alienation, the Left Bank of the Seine could not begin to compare with the university town of Trujillo on the north coast of Peru. A generation later, José María Arguedas (1911–1969), the first Peruvian novelist to write bilingually in Quechua and Spanish, wove together autobiography and politics of language in declaring himself an orphan of his Spanish-speaking father and stepmother, having learnt Quechua from indigenous servants who took care of him. Vallejo's and Arguedas's preoccupations with language were closely related but have rarely been seen as so, perhaps because the history of language in Spanish American countries is a striking example of the restricted view that can result from disciplinary divides. The history of Spanish has been studied by scholars of literature; the history of Quechua, Aymara, Mapudungan and a host of other native languages by historians, anthropologists or sociolinguists.[12]

Most of the existing historiography on the Spanish of the Americas has focused on the region's most distinguished scholars of language, notably Andrés Bello (1781–1865), a Venezuelan based in Chile, and the Colombians Rufino José Cuervo (1844–1911) and Miguel Antonio Caro (1843–1898).[13] They all wrote justly celebrated works on Spanish, geared towards preserving its integrity and informed by their deep knowledge of classical Latin and Greek, logic and philology. In the early twentieth century, the German-born Rodolfo Lenz (1863–1938), who introduced modern scientific linguistics into Chile, explicitly rejected the established view that grammar should be taught to aid 'the art of speaking and writing correctly' and reduced its place in the school curriculum to the mínimum necessary to aid practical language learning.[14] Lenz also became interested in what he referred to as 'Chilean popular dialect' and compiled a remarkable, if controversial, dictionary of words derived from indigenous languages.[15] These influential scholars shaped the contours of debate about language, but as was the case in other areas of study, there were many other, lesser-known individuals working on language. This chapter focuses on them, particularly those who were interested in the languages and idioms of the various ethnic groups that made up the national populations. By bringing a range of language debates into a single frame, it becomes easier to see how misleading is the still common assumption among comparative historians of nationalism that the question of language was unproblematic in Spanish American nation-making.

Spanish and Its Discontents

The first point is that what constituted 'Spanish' itself was a matter of contention from the outset of the new republics. After the wars of independence, periodicals featured opinion pieces lamenting that accurate Spanish was rare, especially in writing, and urging the importance of teaching the rules of Castilian grammar, both to prevent Spanish American republics losing their *lingua franca* in a Babel of dialects and to ensure precise drafting of new constitutions and laws. It was no easy matter to foster the correct use of Spanish, however, not least because many of the peninsular Spaniards who had taught the language returned to their native land.

In the early years of the republics, there were a few visionary intellectuals— liberated from the dictates of the Royal Academy, along with other imperial authorities—who sought to establish new ground rules for how to write, spell and pronounce the language they spoke. The most famous example was Bolívar's tutor Simón Rodríguez, who drew upon his extensive experience of listening to spoken popular language as he travelled throughout the Americas to argue for a simplified version of written Spanish that would challenge the linguistic monopoly of the well educated as well as the cultural imperialism of the RAE. He envisaged a republican form of language that would extend citizenship and combine universal communication with the particularities of American ways of thinking.[16] Others were thinking along similar lines, but such initiatives were overtaken by moral concerns about the need to promote decency and good conduct. One notorious example was the battle to moderate intemperate language in the press, especially those newspapers financed by pay-to-publish contributions (*remitidos*), which were often used to conduct personal vendettas over matters too costly to pursue through the courts. The controversies (*polémicas*) waged within or between periodicals were often at least as much about the appropriate or inappropriate use of language as they were about the specific matter in dispute. Thus, not only grammatical accuracy but also tone and expression, or—to introduce that ubiquitous term of nineteenth-century public writing—*style*, became a marker of not only social but also political and even moral status. Boundless admiration was expressed for anyone who could write well; conversely, there was irredeemable contempt for ignorance of the language. Although such concerns were undoubtedly imbued with elitist norms of good taste, there were deeper reasons for unease. The quality of public debate was at stake.

For anybody involved in knowledge creation, there was an equally urgent matter: how to establish the legitimacy of Spanish as a language for the exchange of knowledge. By the time of independence, French, English and German accounted for most scientific (understood in the widest sense of formal knowledge) publication and communication. Until well into the eighteenth century, the use of Latin for scholarly exchange in Europe had made it possible for scholars at institutions of higher education in the Iberian Americas to participate on more or less equal terms in international debates to which they made major contributions, notably in theology and jurisprudence. The Universities of San Marcos (Lima), Mexico, Santo Domingo, Córdoba and Chuquisaca (now Sucre, Bolivia), to mention only the most distinguished, were prominent sites of knowledge generation, especially in the seventeenth century.[17] Missionaries were among the most remarkable linguistic scholars ever known, with their vast endeavours of recording and analysing—mostly in Latin—indigenous languages. Yet the scientific revolution, which endorsed information obtained through specific experimental methods as more legitimate and prestigious than any other kind of information, was encoded in the vernaculars of the most powerful centres of knowledge production: Britain, France and Germany. Thereafter the scholarly output of other European countries—notably, for the argument here, Spain, Portugal and Italy—became increasingly marginalised. These languages lacked terms for many of the new findings and were forced to borrow them from French, German or, increasingly, English (which itself eventually displaced French and German to become the dominant medium of scholarly dissemination by the mid-twentieth century). After Spanish American independence, there were repeated calls in most of the countries for state provision in modern European language tuition, which did feature in some of the secondary colleges. In most places it remained the preserve of private tutors, usually foreign visitors, until the late nineteenth century; the children of the wealthy learnt French, but even among individuals who dedicated their lives to learning, familiarity with English or German was rare.

Anxiety about the relative decline of Spanish as a scholarly language was a factor in some of the post-independence debates about correct usage. The fear was that if Castilian developed into a series of dialects in the newly separate countries of the Americas there would be no hope of securing its acceptance as a language of international communication. This was a significant concern for both Bello and Sarmiento, whose famous language polemic of 1842–43 has usually been observed through the lens of Europeanism versus Americanism. There was indeed a marked difference between the two intellectuals along those lines: Sarmiento called for Americans to stop deferring to the RAE in matters of grammar, while Bello maintained that it was in Americans' own interests to abide by those rules. Yet their dispute was also about the social role of language. Bello's purism was grammatical rather than lexicographical: a common grammar would prevent Spanish in the Americas from degenerating into 'a multitude of irregular, undisciplined, and barbaric dialects [, . . . reproducing] in America what happened in Europe during the dark period of the corruption of Latin'.[18] Sarmiento rejected as scholastic any emphasis on grammar as an ordering principle, arguing that Spanish Americans had to be free to express their experiences of life in their own terms, unconstrained by residual elements of colonial power. Their disagreements arose partly from their different locations in the knowledge order: the university-educated Bello coolly insisted that adherence to the rules of grammar would aid communication; the self-taught Sarmiento bellowed that it would thwart creativity. These notable controversies have distracted attention from the fact that Bello and Sarmiento shared several assumptions about the role of language in independent Spanish America. Both were committed to the use of Spanish as a shared medium of correspondence, commerce and public life in the Americas. While Bello sought to ensure consistency through grammar, Sarmiento preferred to standardise spelling.[19] Neither wished to see variations in the Spanish of individual countries develop into distinctive vernaculars—at this time, the term *idioma/lengua nacional* referred to the Spanish spoken throughout the Americas rather than to the variations distinctive to individual countries. Both Bello and Sarmiento took it for granted that any knowledge created in the Americas would be created and communicated in Spanish. Both of them located the Spanish of the Americas in the context of modern European languages rather than in that of the indigenous languages from which it had been borrowing for centuries.

The obstacles to participation in international exchanges of ideas using the Spanish language became increasingly intractable as French and English steadily expanded their reach. The RAE did not provide much help to those working in the Americas, particularly anyone concerned with public education. Marcos Sastre, as inspector-general of schools in Buenos Aires during the 1850s, criticised their publications on both general and specific grounds: the RAE dictionary lacked etymologies and synonyms, as well as being 'very deficient' in vocabulary from the Americas. The official orthography was designed for individuals well versed in Latin, he observed, adding that even for them it was 'an incomplete aid', because it had been produced without what he saw as the prerequisites of an orthology (guide to pronunciation) and a prosody (study of patterns of stress and intonation). In order to bring the rules of correct Spanish 'within the reach of the whole people', Sastre produced his own orthography, which was adopted in state schools in Chile as well as Argentina.[20] Following Sarmiento, he recommended spelling over grammar as the best route to widespread use of correct Spanish, which in turn would improve primary education, the inadequacy of which he held to be the main cause of 'the scientific and industrial inferiority of all the Spanish-speaking countries'.[21] Sastre based his orthography on the RAE's three determinants of spelling—etymology, pronunciation and usage (by eminent writers). Yet he laid particular emphasis on a fourth law of his own invention: 'foreign proper names and, in general, any exotic word' required to follow new scientific discoveries should at first keep their original spelling 'so that their meaning is known', until 'the intelligent people' had decided whether or not the new term was necessary. If so, it could be 'Castillianized' on the principle of analogy with previous importations, such as 'Pequin from Pe-king', 'Confucio from Kong-fou-tseu', 'toaleta from toilette', 'Zar from Czar' or 'sicologia from psycologia'.[22] Other terms, in contrast, had not been Castillianized: 'Havre, Civita-Vecchia, Ukrania, Azof, Rousseau, Saint-Pierre, Washington, Francklin [*sic*], kilógramo, polka, zinc' and so on down a long list of examples mostly from English, but also from Quechua, French, Portuguese and Latin.[23] Sastre devoted pages to identifying which proper names, place names, scientific terms and words for fashion trends had or had not been Castillianized. The apparent randomness of his selections reveals the extent of the problem: there were so many borrowings, so many sites of potential misunderstanding, so many absences.

In mid-nineteenth-century Spain relatively little translation was done (unlike in Italy, where a practice of translating anything and everything published abroad was established soon after unification in 1861, partly as a means of establishing a uniform version of Italian). The few translations of foreign-language scholarship available in Spanish America were done either there, usually at the instigation of individuals, or in Paris, where from the 1850s onwards the publishing house Rosa y Bouret began to commission translations into Spanish specifically for the Spanish American market. More common was the practice of translating short extracts or summary accounts for serialisation in periodicals, which made it possible to follow debates conducted overseas but did little to help anyone to participate in them. How was it possible to discuss certain theories or evidence in a language that lacked the terms for them? 'When science has to wait for the word, where there is no word there is no science', noted the compiler of the first etymological dictionary in Spanish.[24] His words were cited in a heartfelt passage by Emilio H. Roque, an Argentine scholar-statesman based in Córdoba, who proposed to address the problem by compiling a *Diccionario metódico de la lengua castellana*. This work never came to fruition, as far as I know, but Roque's account of his plans for it is revealing about the scale of endeavour he thought necessary to revive the scholarly status of Spanish.

In a long letter of 1888 seeking advice and approval from 'the leading linguistic authority in our country', Vicente Fidel López, Roque made the case for his methodical dictionary, namely that while standard dictionaries 'teach us to understand the idea that the words represent, methodical ones supply us with the words that represent the idea'.[25] Thus he was trying to counter the problem that if words did not exist for an idea, the idea was more likely to be lost in transmission or, even if communicated, quickly forgotten. His work was intended to be 'useful for its practical application in the daily struggles against forgetting or ignorance of the language', and it would particularly help 'studious people to learn the common terms, and those of all branches of human knowledge'. He acknowledged the existence of similar works in French and

Italian,[26] but claimed that his would be the first in Spanish. His plan was vast in conception: the first of five volumes would be a standard dictionary, including all the definitions, although not the etymologies, from the RAE dictionary, plus 'many biographical and geographical names and more than one thousand nouns' of American usage. The following volumes were to cover natural history; sciences, arts and industries; geography and biographies; and, last, common words, selected terms, synonyms and verbs. Each of the volumes was divided into chapters and then into further sections, in the relentless classifying spirit of the age, but two points stand out: first, the collocation of subjects based on modern scientific method, such as physics, chemistry and astronomy, with the ancient, spiritually guided processes of alchemy and astrology; and, second, the organisation of material initially by subject and then by linguistic category—nouns, adjectives and verbs—thereby drawing attention to the dependence of knowledge on linguistic form. Roque's plan was apparently designed to relativise the production of knowledge and to compile a vocabulary to make it possible for knowledge created in the Americas to be given its due.

Researching Indigenous Languages, Rethinking History

The prominent controversies over the grammar, spelling and lexicon of Spanish as used in the Americas have overshadowed the fact that there was a notable body of research on indigenous languages carried out during the nineteenth century by Spanish American intellectuals, despite claims made at the time, and later, that little or nothing was done until European and US archaeologists and ethnographers arrived. Before archaeology and anthropology, fundamental questions about the indigenous peoples and their histories were explored mainly through the study of their languages. The context of these investigations was the social Darwinist conviction, shared by most but not all of these intellectuals, that the indigenous peoples were on an inexorable path of decline and were unlikely to survive beyond the next few generations. Work in indigenous languages was a major element in the 'studies of the Americas', for which a market was created from the 1870s onwards (see chapter 3) and involved transnational exchanges throughout the continent, sometimes mediated by Europeans. In Mexico, for example, Joaquín García Icazbalceta compiled extensive 'Notes for a catalogue of writers in indigenous languages of America' and printed sixty copies of the manuscript himself.[27] The publishing house Trübner of London sent one of them to Bartolomé Mitre (1821–1906) in Buenos Aires, who spent the last thirty years of his life collecting information and publications on languages throughout the whole Americas, from Tierra del Fuego to Greenland. Three years after his death, the museum established to house Mitre's archive published a catalogue of these materials, intended to make known all the existing work on native American languages, dating back to the earliest missionaries, and to assess its scientific value case by case.[28] Through their interest in language, nineteenth-century intellectuals began to rediscover the scholarship of the colonial period. This catalogue was introduced by Luis María Torres, himself a distinguished archaeologist and director of the Museo de La Plata, who drew attention to the research of 'a nucleus of South Americans'—mainly Chileans and Brazilians, plus more than ten from the River Plate. The pioneer of them all was Pedro de Angelis, a Neopolitan *publicista* who arrived in Buenos Aires in 1827 and became an inveterate collector of documents on the history of the River Plate;[29] other leading figures included the polymath Vicente Fidel López and the founding director of Argentina's national archives, Manuel Ricardo Trelles, both of whom were assiduous collectors of materials in and on indigenous languages.[30] None of these connoisseurs of language were formally trained in the German scientific approach to sociolinguistics that Rodolfo Lenz introduced into Chile during the 1890s, but as Torres pointed out, as a result they were not imprisoned by European models that did not fit the Americas, so they had the potential to 'break the intellectual mould and make an original contribution in the only way possible for most modern countries like ours.'[31]

Indeed, it was through critiques of classical philology that certain scholars in Latin America, working against the grain, raised questions about the relative status of languages, proposed new ways of thinking about both the past and the present of their societies, and formulated arguments to challenge the emerging Eurocentrism of knowledge. In Argentina, Samuel Lafone Quevedo (1835–1920) pursued what we would now call an interdisciplinary approach to language, combining study of existing works of philology and history with archival research and fieldwork. An Anglo-Argentine, son of the owner of a copper mine in the northern province of Catamarca, Lafone Quevedo did a master's degree at the University of Cambridge, one of the leading centres of classical philology. On his return to Catamarca in 1859, he began to combine running the family business with studying the local languages in light of 'the principles of Bopp and Grimm', but 'applying them in my own way' (*haciendo mis aplicaciones*).[32] Franz Bopp and Jakob Grimm were the famous comparative linguists who systematically elaborated William Jones's insight of 1786 that there were possible connections between Sanksrit, Greek and Latin. Lafone Quevedo spent many years travelling in the interior provinces, gathering oral testimony from informants, listening to local speech, collecting artefacts, taking notes and making drawings.[33] He aimed to publish something 'on every single one of the Argentine languages', at least partly in order to refute the claims of Europeans that Americans did nothing to make known the languages of their lands.[34]

Lafone Quevedo's method was to scrutinise all the material he could find on any particular language, evaluating it in light of recent scientific practice. For example, his account of the Vilela language of the Argentine Chaco was explicitly based upon 'the works [of] Hervas, Adelung and Pelleschi'. He referred here to two early nineteenth-century philologists, a Spaniard and a German, both of whom aimed to compare all known languages, as well as an Italian engineer, who had collected a remarkable vocabulary of Vilela during the eight months he spent in the Chaco region.[35] He gleaned further information from eighteenth-century Jesuit works on ethnography (Martin Dobrizhoffer) and natural history (José Jolis), plus political histories—for example, one by Spanish explorer Félix de Azara (1746–1821), or Gregorio Funes's history of the River Plate, the first to be written by a native.[36] The Jesuit studies of the interior were the only ones available at a time before the archives in Spain had been investigated or all the papers in local family collections identified. When locals heard about Lafone Quevedo's interest, especially if he was collecting for one of the national exhibitions, they came to tell him of 'curious traditions' and to bring him all kinds of fragments of antiquity they found lying around (*antiguallas sueltas*), among which he detected great treasures.[37] From the outset, he sought to understand languages in their historical context, working on the assumption of a mutual relationship between social and linguistic change. In so doing, he subverted the principles of philology, which approached a language as a source for deducing information about a society.

For Lafone Quevedo, evidence from the Americas provided a fundamental challenge to many of the generalisations made in Europe. In a series of publications, he first identified affinities between the languages of the various indigenous groups of the northern River Plate, then made a case for analogous grammatical forms between those languages and Andean Quechua and Aymara (a hypothesis which would be broadly accepted by experts today), gradually building towards a theory that all the native languages of the Americas constituted a single family (which current scholars reject). He also saw corresponding lexical and grammatical forms, particularly pronouns and prefixes, in South American and Pacific languages, which led him to suggest that Polynesians arrived in the Americas before Europeans, an idea for which recent DNA analysis has provided some corroboration.[38] What is most significant about Lafone Quevedo's work is his demonstration that 'many of the philological rules of the Old World have no application here', because they were 'the products of the classrooms, more or less artificial, impositions from above; while in America we have a product of nature'.[39] Indeed, after many years working on indigenous languages he came to doubt the very validity of philology, arguing that its concern with written language rendered it artificial, because it was in 'the mouths of peoples [*razas*] free from the influence of the classroom', as they were in the Americas, that the real clues to language development lay.[40] Just as in botany, 'a truly scientific classification' would arise from studying wild rather than cultivated specimens. Anticipating twentieth-century European developments in the study of languages, Lafone Quevedo emphasised that he saw his field of endeavour as 'linguistics and not philology'.[41] It followed that he rejected the claim that language was an indicator of racial differentiation, with all its social Darwinist connotations of languages and peoples moving from primitive to civilised states, a view which was increasingly dominant in late nineteenth-century Europe, although it did not go unchallenged. Throughout his work Lafone Quevedo used terms such as 'hybridisation', 'mixings' (*las mezclas*), which he explained sociologically rather than philologically as the outcome of 'political and geographical changes, migrations, etc'.[42] And he hinted, without fully developing the suggestion, that the same processes probably occurred in Europe.[43]

In Chile, Daniel Barros Grez (1834–1904) was also conducting linguistic research that led him to challenge social Darwinist claims. Now remembered mainly for his founding contributions to Chilean theatre, Barros Grez was a polymath, unusual in his aptitude for both science and literature. After training as an engineer, one of the first to qualify at the University of Chile in 1850, he combined a distinguished career in water engineering works—notably a prize-winning irrigation device and a commission from the Ecuadorian government to introduce drinking water to Guayaquil—with writing successful collections of original fables (prescribed as a set text for primary schools), dramatic comedies and novels, which made him one of the most popular authors of his time.[44] He was born and spent much of his life in Colchagua and Talca, two provinces of Chile's central valley, where he gathered thousands of popular sayings and expressions. Yet Barros Grez's interest in language took him far beyond literary *costumbrismo*: his commitment to scientific methods of experimentation and theoretically informed analysis led him to explore recent findings in comparative philology. What he found prompted him to embark on research for a hugely ambitious *Diccionario enciclopédico etimológico*, parts of which were published in periodicals in 1884–85. Barros Grez's revisionist thinking on the appropriate methods for studying language in Chile is evident in his review of the *Diccionario filológico-comparado de la lengua castellana* (12 vols, 1880–1916), compiled by Matías Calandrelli (1845–1919), the first five volumes of which had come out in Buenos Aires by the end of 1882.[45] Calandrelli himself, now little known, was an intriguing figure, an Italian-born specialist in classical philology and Sanskrit who emigrated to Argentina in 1871, responding to Sarmiento's call for people to come and contribute to building a national education system. Most of his teaching career in Argentina was spent as professor of classical philology at UBA, a position created in 1874 by the incoming rector, Vicente Fidel López, who was himself greatly interested in languages. Calandrelli's monumental dictionary is now regarded by specialists as a work of synthesis, but among his contemporaries he was esteemed for applying a broad comparative perspective to the Spanish language, relating it not only to ancient Greek, Latin and Sanskrit, as had been done before, but also to Semitic languages, Basque and 'American languages'.[46] Yet Barros Grez proposed to go much further than Calandrelli in relation to indigenous languages, presenting 'the five principal languages of [...] Mexican, Guaraní, Aymara, Quechua and Araucano' as comparators in their own right. In examples from his own etymological dictionary, words from these and other languages of the Americas were given equal status to the analogous terms from other ancient languages.[47] He rejected conventional philological classifications of languages as 'monosyllabic' or 'polysyllabic', maintaining that *all* languages probably started out in prehistory as monosyllabic and then were compelled by 'social necessities and the progressive development of the human spirit' to form more complex words until they had effectively evolved into a different language.[48] What was presented as a merely technical point had major ideological implications: Barros Grez was arguing that no language was innately 'primitive' or 'advanced'; instead, it was a question of where the language sat on a continuum of historical change.

In a further challenge to philological method, Barros Grez sought to compel rethinking about what was meant by *writing*. In a passage arguing that it was not possible to know if the proto-Indo-European language postulated by comparative linguists had assumed written form, he suggested that if so it could have been only an elementary kind of writing. By comparison, he continued, the *quipus* (knotted and coloured threads) of the Andean peoples, which he placed alongside Egyptian hieroglyphs, the cuneiform of Chaldea in ancient Mesopotamia and the knotted ropes of ancient China, would have looked 'relatively modern'.[49] What is pertinent here is not his (long super-seded) argument about Indo-European, but rather his ascribing equal validity to graphic and material forms of recording information that classical philology would have placed in a hierarchy of gradually increasing levels of abstraction, culminating in alphabetic script. In later work, Barros Grez insisted that the markings on ancient ruins in southern Chile were by no means 'capriciously drawn', as had hitherto been claimed by those who wished to categorise them as the random daubing of inferior peoples, but, to the contrary, 'intentionally drawn and with the most admirable logic [in] conception'.[50] With 'thorough study' it was possible to understand even the perforations in the stones as 'visible expressions of ideas [. . .] signs comparable with the pictographs'; he coined the term 'geroplasts' for these 'figures which I am sure symbolize some idea'.[51] He named one monument in the valley of Rapiantu 'the Olympic stone' because it represented the gods of the Cauquen people, on a 'voyage through the Earth, Heavens and Hell of this *Divine Comedy*, imagined and sculptured on the rocks by the Dantes and Michael Angels [*sic*] of barbarism'.[52] He repeatedly drew comparisons with examples of pagan inscription from ancient Egypt, China, India or Greece.[53] The Cauquen images were 'hiero-glyphs', he insisted, contesting José Toribio Medina's reference to them as pictographs, because 'each one of them is the figurative expression of an object or of an idea' and together they constituted 'the written [. . .] narration' of a battle, 'consigned to stone for all time', just as the Egyptians had inscribed their history on the walls of temples and on obelisks.[54] Even if his philological analy-sis was wrong, he concluded, the very existence of these markings proved that 'before the expeditions undertaken by the Incas of Peru to civilise the Chil-eans, in the Andes there existed tribes who used hieroglyphic writing to per-petuate the memory of their great deeds'.[55] Comparative philology could lead to radical history.

Work on etymology in the Americas was based on conceptions of the rela-tionship between past and present that were different from approaches often taken in Europe. While many European scholars of language pursued etymol-ogy as proof of linguistic origins, it was more common for linguists in the Americas to argue that the very idea of an origin was fanciful. Eduardo de la Barra, member of the RAE, cited Saint Augustine to the effect that etymology was 'as arbitrary as dreams' and that etymological disputes were no more than enjoyable word games, with no possibility of proving one version over another.[56] For Barros Grez, as for many linguists in Spanish America, etymology was primarily a method for experiencing a sense of connection with the past:

> The history of each word [shows the reader] how today we use the same words, more or less modified, that sounded on the lips of the most ancient of peoples. It is as if we were talking to those peoples, across the centuries. Now scarcely a record of those nations survives; yet we possess and we use their very words. [...] Because of that, our souls commune with theirs.[57]

As an inveterate collector—of butterflies, buttons and hairy spiders as well as words and phrases—Barros Grez saw 'the whole background of an item' (where, when and by whom it was created, plus the story of its subsequent travels) as what Walter Benjamin called 'a magic encyclopedia' of the past.[58]

The Quechua drama *Ollantay* could be seen in that light. The history of its discovery and translation, which involves scholars from Peru, Switzerland and England, is a vivid illustration of how much was at stake in the study of language in the Americas during the nineteenth century. First published in Quechua in 1857 and in Spanish in 1868, *Ollantay* became an international phenomenon, generating translations into many languages—including Latin—and an array of spin-off plays, poems, novels and settings to music. The play consists of three acts, in verse form, set in sixteenth-century Cuzco. It recounts the tale of Ollanta, a warrior of humble birth, who had been elevated to the nobility, in recognition of his loyalty and valour, by the Inca Pachacútec. Ollanta went too far, however, when he fell in love with the emperor's daughter, Cusi Coyllur, and sought her hand in marriage. Pachacútec banished him and imprisoned Cusi Coyllur, who gave birth to a daughter by Ollanta. The outcast warrior established a centre of resistance, known as Ollantaytambo, lying to the north of Cuzco in what is now called the Sacred Valley of the Incas. A force led by the loyal warrior Rumañahui vanquished the rebels, who were captured and sentenced to death by the new Inca, Tupac Yupanqui. At the last moment they were reprieved and the drama ended happily, with Ollanta restored to high status, Cusi Coyllur released from prison and the two of them united in wedlock. Most of the existing historiography discusses the text in terms of the politicised struggles of the early twentieth century to claim the Inca past, which was deftly reinvented as the cradle of national civilisation, instead of a shameful period of barbarism to be swept aside in the grand march of progress. The failure of an opera based on *Ollantay* in 1900 and its success only twenty years later when revived at the newly

opened 'symbol of cosmopolitan modernity', the Teatro El Forero, are book-
ends to the rapidly changing attitudes towards Peruvian antiquity among elite
limeño society.[59] *Ollantay*'s history of multiple manuscripts and disputed origins is also a register of transnational debates about language which, especially in the era of social Darwinism, served as proxy debates about who was
civilised and who was not.

The main controversy was over the dating of the play. Was it a pre-Hispanic
text, an authentic piece of Inca literature, or was it a confection of the colonial
era? In the absence of any contextual evidence, the arguments were conducted
in terms of linguistic analysis, but a good understanding of Quechua was rare
among Spanish-speaking Peruvians, so the credibility of anyone's conclusions
relied on their reputation for knowing the language well. Peruvian scholars
discreetly wielded this weapon in their disputes with European scholars who
intervened in the debates, especially the Swiss explorer Johann Jakob von
Tschudi (1818–1889), who was often credited with discovering the play. The
true story is more complicated. A natural scientist and physician by training,
Tschudi spent five years travelling round Peru (1838–42), initially in search of
flora and fauna, but he soon started also to collect material on Peru's ancient
past and on the Quechua language. The first publication of *Ollantay* came in
the form of extracts in the first major post-independence study of Peruvian
antiquities, of which Tschudi was credited as joint author. In fact, most of the
material in *Antigüedades peruanas* (1851) came from research conducted by the
other author named on the cover (albeit in smaller print), Mariano Eduardo
de Rivero y Ustáriz (1798–1857), the director of the Museo Nacional de Lima.
Rivero had spent much of the 1830s making arduous journeys to 'abandoned
places, through thick, impenetrable forest' to unearth evidence of Peru's ancient past.[60] The dangers of research were succeeded by the difficulties of finding a publisher for a massive tome that required extensive illustration of ruins
and artefacts. Even the well-connected Rivero could not persuade the Peruvian Congress to sanction a sufficiently large subsidy, although many politicians became keener to see his work published as Claudio Gay's monumental
Historia física y política de Chile continued to roll off the Parisian presses (1844–
54).[61] Increasingly anxious that his work would be superseded before it had
even appeared—the US historian William H. Prescott's *History of the Conquest
of Peru, with a Preliminary View of the Civilization of the Incas* was published in
1847 and translated into Spanish three years later—Rivero eventually decided
to publish his own material jointly with Tschudi, whose scholarly reputation
(in other fields) enabled him to arrange for publication in Vienna. In return

Rivero included material by the Swiss on Peruvian skulls (with which he almost certainly disagreed) and on the Quechua language, a substantial element of which was a discussion of *Ollantay*. Acknowledging the care that Tschudi took in overseeing publication of the text, he observed that the Swiss scholar had at his disposal 'the copious works and manuscripts of the Imperial Library of Vienna, materials which we lack in Peru'.[62] It is a small irony of history that publication was further delayed because the price of paper had shot up in Vienna after the 1848 revolutions.[63]

Tschudi went on to publish a text of the whole play as an appendix to his study of Quechua (1853), which was followed by a separate bilingual edition, in Quechua and German translation, in 1857.[64] Although he was the first researcher to publish a complete text, Tschudi was certainly not the play's discoverer, because *Ollantay* had been discussed two decades earlier in the Cuzco periodical *Museo Erudito*. This publication, one of a succession launched by liberal journalist José Palacios to spread 'las luces' (enlightenment), was aimed at a general audience. By republishing complete articles from the late-colonial learned journal *Mercurio Peruano* (1790–95), it explicitly revived their stated purpose of correcting European errors about Peru, especially in relation to antiquities.[65] In 1837 *Museo Erudito* published the first discussion in print of the drama *Ollantay*, based on a manuscript handed down from a local priest, Antonio Valdez (d. 1816), who was thought to be the author, both in Cuzco at the time and by some mid-twentieth-century historians. No reference was made to the *Museo Erudito* material either in *Antigüedades peruanas* or in Tschudi's 1857 book.[66] The articles, almost certainly written by Palacios, identified various discrepancies between the play and the versions of the legend circulating as a local oral tradition. His main concern was to evaluate the credibility of the play, which he saw—as most scholars do today—as a late-colonial literary rendition of an oral tradition, rather than a primary source for Inca history. Like other Cuzco specialists in Quechua at the time, he worked on the basis of a genealogical method, finding clues to ancient modes of writing from talking to the shepherds who used quipus (knot-records) to count their flock.[67]

For Tschudi, however, the play was a piece of ancient Inca literature. His view came to be shared by the British geographer Clements Markham (1830–1916), who spent nearly a year travelling in Peru (1852–53) and then returned for two years (1859–61) on a mission to collect samples of cinchona bark so that quinine could be introduced into India. Markham built his early scholarly reputation on work in Peru, publishing an account of *Ollantay* in 1856, as part of the memoir of his first journey, then a full translation into English in 1871.[68] As Sara Castro-Klarén has argued, the play served to enhance his interpretation of Cuzco as a living ruin.[69] Given the nineteenth-century vogue in Europe for all things indigenous, European scholars may have been predisposed to find ancient authenticity in *Ollantay*. What is more noteworthy is that the same view was taken, contrary to the opinions of the Cuzco experts, by José Sebastian Barranca (1830–1909), the Peruvian translator of the first Spanish version, published in Lima in 1868. Barranca was an able linguist, botanist and minerologist from a modest background in the valley of Camaná, south of Arequipa. After attending a secondary school in Lima, where he learnt Latin and ancient Greek, Barranca spent many years in the southern provinces, where he taught, practised medicine, studied indigenous languages and translated Christian doctrine into Quechua. By 1870 he was back in the capital city and holding down four jobs: chair of natural history at San Marcos, teacher of Greek at the Colegio de Guadalupe, and director of the botanical garden and of the Museo Nacional. He was well connected both in Peru and internationally, having had reports on Peruvian plants and minerals published in European journals.

Acknowledging at the beginning of his edition of *Ollantay* that the consensus in Peru was that while the subject was pre-Columbian the oral tradition had been written down in Hispanicised form, Barranca nonetheless argued that the play was actually a fine example of 'indigenous literature', which patriotism compelled him to recover.[70] All that Valdez had done, he claimed, was to put an ancient text in order and add a few embellishments 'in the time of Tupac-Amaru, protector of letters'.[71] Barranca was writing during the early stages of a 'Quechuist boom', which reached a peak under the government of Manuel Pardo (1872–76), who promoted Quechua as an instrument of national identity. What was increasingly referred to as 'the national language' was introduced into the syllabus of Lima's elite secondary school, the Colegio de Guadalupe, and the government commissioned a Quechua grammar, in what seems to have been a serious if short-lived initiative to teach 'the language of the Inca empire' to the Spanish-speaking elites.[72] In this context, Barranca's introduction to his translation of *Ollantay* deftly adduced the authority of 'the foreign experts' who had visited Peru 'motivated only by a love of science' in support of his own arguments, while at the same time subtly criticising and correcting them.[73] Manuscripts of the play were not so rare, he said—by implication, not nearly as rare as the foreigners had claimed. Indeed, one of his eleven reasons for concluding that the text was ancient was that he had found significant discrepancies between manuscripts, which he judged to go beyond what could be accounted for by mistakes in copying. Barranca judged that Tschudi's version was based on 'one of the most correct' manuscripts, but emphasised that he himself had 'corrected' (by implication, from his superior understanding of Quechua) many passages that were unintelligible. He had more substantial criticisms of Markham's text, not least the Englishman's rendering of *quipu* as 'a heap of wool'.[74] As Barros Grez did later in Chile, Barranca had a broader conception than Markham about what was meant by 'writing'. Whereas Markham dismissed the word *Quellca*, meaning 'to write', as 'of doubtful antiquity', Barranca countered: 'Qqullcca, paper; and Qquellccani, to write. If the ancients knew of paper and had the verb to write, it is because they knew of writing'.[75] Thus what Markham translated as 'All that has ever happened / Is present to me, as on a quipu', Barranca rendered as *como si estuviera escrito* (as if it were written).[76] His knowledge of contemporary spoken Quechua was important to his case for the antiquity of the piece, because he could recognise words in the text that were no longer in use.[77] His seventeen pages of notes made extensive comparative reference not only to the classical languages and myths but also to ancient Hebrew and Sanskrit, in a survey of world literature designed to support his conclusion that some passages in *Ollantay* 'could not have been done better' by Sophocles or Euripides.[78]

The case for *Ollantay* as a great work of literature and, by analogy, for Inca society as a great civilisation to which modern Peru should lay claim, was revived in a later Spanish translation by José Fernández Nodal,[79] who was a strong advocate of 'Incaism' as a basis for national identity. Fernández Nodal, a lawyer from Ayacucho, was a scholar of both Quechua and—far more unusually at that time—Aymara.[80] His published work on Quechua was more learned than that of the state-supported Anchorena and he campaigned for Quechua to be a language of instruction.[81] In a bid to convince the Peruvian elites that *Ollantay* was one of 'the literary glories of Peru', he deployed his expertise in Quechua poetry and song to translate the play into verse (Barranca's version was in prose).[82] With a similar aim, but directed this time at an international audience, the Peruvian poet Gabino Pacheco Zegarra (1846–1903) published in Paris a translation into French (1878), with a critical study and a vocabulary of Quechua. Pacheco Zegarra had learnt Quechua as a child, in his hometown of Ayaviri, near Puno, and was probably the greatest nineteenth-century authority on the language.[83] He spent many years in Paris and Madrid, and was one of a handful of scholars from Latin America to attend the first Congress of Americanists, held at Nancy, in north-eastern France, in 1875. Indeed, Pacheco Zegarra's paper on Quechua was the only contribution by a Latin American scholar to be published in the proceedings.

These congresses, which were the first formal occasions for researchers on the Americas to meet, are revealing about how difficult it was for scholars from the region to be heard in Europe. The congresses were initiated by French members of the Société Américaine (an 1850s product of French imperial interest in the region) to promote 'ethnographic, linguistic and historical research on both Americas, especially the pre-Columbian epoch'. The first ten meetings were all held in Europe, but in 1895 the organisers ventured to Mexico City. As the congress became established as an annual event, it was occasionally held in a Latin American country, once a decade or so. The proceedings were published in French until 1892, when the meeting was held in Madrid as part of the commemorations of Columbus's landing—Pachecho Zegarra's paper was included because although he gave it in Spanish he 'was obliging enough to produce a version in French' for publication.[84] The only other work by a Latin American to be discussed was Vicente Fidel López's *Les races aryennes du Pérou*, which had been published in Paris in 1871. The response to it at Nancy was dismissive on the grounds of its lack of scientific rigour.[85] Yet many of the hypotheses presented to the first few congresses by so-called experts from Europe were later described as 'more or less fantastical' in their claims about the ancient civilisations of the Americas.[86] For example, Philippe-Édouard Foucaux (1811–1894) of the Collège de France, an expert in Tibetan, spoke uncritically about a comparison between Otomí and Chinese, deriving from the alleged presence of Buddhists in Mexico in the fifth century.[87] Despite calls to exclude 'these eighteenth-century imaginings', in the early congresses there were repeated claims—more often than not based on supposed correspondences between native American languages and others—that the Americas were the site of Atlantis, or the biblical flood, or about the presence of Phoenicians, Hebrews, Finns and Etruscans.[88] José María Torres Caicedo, a Colombian-born intellectual and diplomat, long based in Paris, drew attention to the unspoken assumption that 'the great civilisations of the Americas' must have derived from importation of other civilisations, rather than being 'born of the natural development of the human spirit in the Americas'. In other words, in debates about language above all, what was deemed to be 'scientific' was a matter of dispute in Europe as much as it was in the Americas.

Conclusion

Just as in the eighteenth century there were natural scientists in the Americas who refuted European claims about the degeneracy of American nature (de Pauw, Buffon), so in the nineteenth century there were linguists in the Americas who emphasised the rich expressiveness of American languages to counter social Darwinist claims that they were 'primitive' or 'barbaric'. In the process, these linguists not only drew upon the methods of the emerging field of comparative philology but also presented a range of challenges to its mainstream positions: rejecting linguistic purism; arguing that the societies of the Americas, past and present, had to be understood in their own terms; and paving the way for the scientific study of popular language. Comparative philological methods were applied to demonstrate that American variations in Spanish were by no means all errors arising from a state of barbarism. Although many of the numerous compilations of Chileanisms, Argentinisms and so on that appeared in the late nineteenth century were normative in outlook, there were dissenting works that deployed comparative philology to raise the status of popular idiom. In each of the nations of Spanish America, language debates took different forms, responding to their distinctive histories, demographies and politics, but most of these countries had 'a language debate', with specific historical outcomes in terms of the values attached to language in relation to national identities. In snapshot form, the bicentennial dictionaries mentioned at the beginning of this chapter suggest that in Argentina, language became the marker of a distinctive national style; in Chile, of an internationalist outlook; in Peru, of an ideal of plurality within unity. In all cases, the questions about language were more fundamental than the famous dispute over Spanish rules versus American inventions. Debates about language turned on claims that American societies were both comparable to and different from European ones, so that new ways had to be found to communicate their realities.

7

Land and Territory

MAKING NATURAL NATIONS

AS THESE NATIONS were being fought for, the beauties of their lands were being sung: in new national anthems, in reams of patriotic verse and in popular ballads. Images of providential nature—biblical in inspiration, classical in form, scientific in orientation—appeared everywhere long before European travellers introduced the Romantic sublime. Once lithography had arrived in the 1820s it became possible to illustrate printed matter with beautiful scenic engravings, but even before then publications featured tiny smudged sketches of a typical flower, a characteristic bird, a native tree. Look at the Peruvian shield of 1825, which depicted a vicuña, a cinchona tree (from which quinine is extracted) and a cornucopia of coins, symbolising the country's wealth in fauna, flora and minerals. Such evocations of distinctive natural phenomena constituted a rare element of continuity between the creole patriotism of the late eighteenth century and the post-independence debates about the future. The idea of the Americas as a gigantic scientific laboratory (analysed in chapter 2) was reinforced by the extraordinary voyages of exploration undertaken by Humboldt (1799–1804) and Darwin (1832–35). Both utility and utopianism were enfolded into investigations of the biblical and secular paradise of American nature. From the outset, the land was imbued with purpose and virtue. Bello's famous *Ode to Tropical Agriculture* (1826) summoned its audience to live out the freedom won by independence through working the soil, exhorting them not to let the prodigious bounty of tropical fruits lure them into sterile idleness. Nature was the source not so much of aesthetic inspiration or philosophical consolation, as it was for the European Romantics, but rather of a more robust, collective commitment to liberty, purity and a glorious future. The Argentine anthem mapped out the battlegrounds where liberty had been won; the Chilean one, in successive versions, celebrated the clarity of the sky and the purity of the air, the tranquillity of the sea and the majesty of the mountains; the Peruvian one symbolised the dawn of God-given freedom, with the sun rising magnificently over the Andes.

The nations of Spanish America may not have been founded on a territorial vision,[1] but they quickly acquired one. True, the very first constitutions made little or no mention of territory, but they were drafted before any certainty about the physical extent of the new political communities was possible, because wars were still being fought. As soon as it became at all plausible to make claims about territorial reach, that was done. Peru's Constitution of 1823 gave *territorio* pride of place in the first section and specified that its limits were to be fixed by Congress as soon as 'the total independence of Upper and Lower Peru' was secured.[2] The Argentine Constitution of 1826 specified the thirteen existing areas entitled to political representation and likewise charged Congress 'to demarcate the territory of the State and fix the limits of the provinces, without prejudicing the permanence of those enumerated'.[3] In the 1853 version, *territorio* was mentioned twenty times and *suelo* (ground, land) almost as frequently, even though its intellectual author, Juan Bautista Alberdi (1810–1884), famously rejected simple Romantic nationalism: 'The *patria* is not the soil.'[4] Article 1 of Chile's Constitution of 1833 set out a bold and precise vision of the republic's extent: 'The territory of Chile extends from the Atacama Desert to Cape Horn, and from the Cordillera of the Andes to the Pacific Ocean, including the Archipelago of Chiloé, all the adjacent islands, and those of Juan Fernández.'[5]

Soon after independence, the new governments laid ambitious plans to map their territories, establish their borders, survey the mineral wealth, navigate the rivers and coasts, and chart the skies. Although Spanish engineers had carried out extensive mapping of some parts of South America during the late colonial period—for example, Felipe Bauzá (1764–1834) on Alessandro Malaspina's voyage to the Pacific of 1789–94—little of this work was available to the new governments.[6] They were largely starting from scratch, which gave the study of geography and natural history a political charge from the outset. The economic and strategic motivations for acquiring such knowledge are readily apparent and have been well researched by historians. Governments hoping to foster new industries needed to know where their mineral resources lay. Most borders, both external and internal, were disputed and much of the charting of the territories of these would-be nation-states was carried out by *Comisiones de límites* (border commissions), whose main purpose was to establish an agreed demarcation. In Argentina, the state topographical office had its origins in a commission established to serve the 1825 military campaign led by Rosas to force indigenous people out of southern Buenos Aires province;[7] more than fifty years later, the Oficina Topográfica Militar was organised to coordinate map-making for all-out war against them (see below). In Chile, too, scientific expeditions to the southern regions yielded information that was later used to support first agricultural colonisation, then military occupation and war against the indigenous peoples. Expeditions to navigate the Amazon claimed many lives, especially among the native inhabitants. Not only was science deployed in the service of war, but wars were seen as opportunities to pursue science. Many of the border commissions included men with an interest in science, who jotted down observations on the movements of the stars, the patterns of the weather, and the characteristics of flora and fauna as they went about their strategic calculations. Science and war acquired an uneasy but unmistakable connection—particularly during the second half of the nineteenth century, as states acquired greater capacity to enforce territorial nationalism. These points are all well known and follow the findings of the large body of historiography that has analysed the various ways in which science was abused to justify imperial practices, in this case internal colonialism.[8] I fully recognise the importance of these arguments, but my focus here is different. I suggest that knowledge of the land also played a part in developing a sense of nationhood among a wide variety of people, beyond statesmen and intellectuals. This was especially so during the half century after independence, before public schooling began to expand.

This chapter presents evidence to show that there were high levels of *popular* interest in the natural environment, which is what made it such a significant factor in nation-building. This evidence has been derived mainly from reading published sources against the grain, following small or buried leads to build up a picture, albeit fragmentary, of a popular reservoir of curiosity and detailed knowledge about observed natural phenomena. There were so many people in Latin America who contributed to knowledge of the land in addition to the famous scientists recruited from Europe, who have received the most attention. There has already been a shift in the historiography of science in Latin America away from these scientists as heroic individuals (white and male) towards the networks in which they participated.[9] Even so, the generation of knowledge about the land involved a lot of other people, most of whom have escaped attention. Many a government official posted to a provincial capital with few amenities occupied his time collecting information about the local environment, in all likelihood assisted by the women and children of the household.[10] Sailors ploughing up and down the Pacific coast regaled the taverns of Valparaíso and Callao with tales of the conditions and creatures they had seen. Peru was said to be 'a veritable "botanical garden"', because so much expertise in cultivating plants for medicinal use was handed down from generation to generation, often through women.[11] The scientists on their journeys of exploration, lugging around cabinets full of curiosities, were as popular a draw as travelling showmen. In effect they functioned as mobile research centres, magnets for the specimens and information collected by a wide range of amateur observers of nature, many of whom had highly specialised knowledge of their environment.[12] Some of them were no doubt motivated by the payments offered, but it is clear from the expedition reports that this was by no means always the case. For example, the leader of the scientific commission sent by the Spanish government from 1862 to 1866, as part of a wider initiative to reassert influence in the Americas, recorded how impressed his men had been by the expertise and dedication to inquiry of the people they met on their long journey through Argentina, Chile, Peru and Ecuador.[13] Accounts of explorations and discoveries by both locals and foreigners were published in local newspapers as well as in the capital cities. Popular almanacs and teach-yourself manuals all contained information about the natural world. Astronomy and meteorology featured regularly in most periodicals from the independence era onwards, with readings sent in to Santiago from ever more far-flung sites around the country. Towards the end of the century, it became possible to make a career out of the public communication of science, as was done by, for example, Eduardo Holmberg and Pedro Scalabrini in Argentina.

The cumulative significance of knowledge of the land in nation-making has been obscured by the fact that different aspects of it have been studied by historians with different interests (natural science, cartography, art, literature and so on). If we bring all these areas together, it becomes easier to see some neglected aspects of the process: the range of locations in which it took place, beyond the capital cities; the contribution of what would now be called citizen science; the recurrence of intersections between state and society in the elastic category of the semi-official policy or institution; and the variety of people who were involved apart from the well-known transnational experts or liberal public intellectuals.

The theme of the land also provides a powerful lens through which to view the transnational processes of nation-making that were profoundly shaped by the simultaneous rise to prominence of European science and technology.

One intriguing example is the great vogue for dahlias in Chile during the 1830s, when society women vied with each other to create the finest displays, even managing to induce the august scholar Don Andrés Bello to scour his library for tips on how to grow them.[14] Dahlias have a transnational history characteristic of the ages of empire and revolution: native to Mexico (where they were declared the national flower in 1963), they were first taken to Europe in 1777 by a French botanist on a mission to steal the cochineal insect in order to break New Spain's monopoly on the production of carmine dye. Humboldt later sent dahlia seeds to England. The excitement about growing them in Chile went beyond an elite fad, a mere echo of the European craze for black tulips, to become symbolic of deeper conflicts about whether to import exotic specimens of cultivation or to start with native species. As historians of modern imperialism have shown, there were close connections between the extension of European power and the conversion of natural history into the disciplines of the natural sciences.[15] By the mid-nineteenth century, botanical gardens, crucibles of advances in medical and agricultural knowledge, were deemed a prerequisite for being counted among the civilised nations.[16] Europeans, divided over almost everything else, were impressively united over their claims to a monopoly of legitimate knowledge. Yet American nature brought out the limitations of European claims to universal knowledge. Works on American nature written by scientists based in the Americas, both immigrants and natives, very often started from a position of correcting a claim by a scientist based in Europe. A scientific version of Romanticism, opposed to absolute universalism and emphasising the starting point of the particular observer, questioned the Enlightenment view of a naturally perfect order.[17]

Knowledge from the Americas, Knowledge from Europe

A New Methodology

It was not only that the scientists who came to the Americas from Europe depended upon local expertise, but that such knowledge had to be integrated into the methods of those scientists in order to make possible their endeavour of connecting American nature to European science. For example, Claudio Gay was trained in France at a time of burgeoning confidence in human capacity to classify and thereby explain nature. He arrived in Chile in 1830 to find that the majority of the plants, insects and reptiles he saw, even in the urban areas of Santiago and Valparaíso, did not fit the taxonomies he had learnt. Historians of science Mario Berrios and Zenobio Saldivia have argued that Gay developed a methodological solution to this dilemma through a series of footnotes to his own descriptions of plants. These addenda recorded information about their habitat, or life cycle, 'according to the peasants', providing a source complementary to the explanatory framework of European science and enabling Gay to connect those categories, which had acquired the status of being scientific, with the specifics of local conditions.[18] In order 'to publish a work of full utility to Americans and especially Chileans', Gay dealt with the vexed question of botanical names by referring to a plant in Latin where possible, then in Spanish if a Spanish name already existed, then by what it was called in Chile (which in some cases varied from province to province). The example he gave was the Berberis, which was *el agracejo* in Spanish, but usually known in Chile as *michay*, derived from an indigenous term. If, however, 'the names were entirely the country's own, and in common usage, [...] in that case we conserved them scrupulously and did not even permit ourselves to translate the scientific name they had been given'.[19] Thus did 'universal' science and local specificity coexist in uneasy tension.

Later, in a precursor of citizen science, the Italian naturalist Antonio Raimondi (1826–1890), who explored much of Peru in the forty years he spent there, called upon Peruvians to conduct their own research on local environmental conditions:

> if you like geography, you can do a detailed description of your birthplace and its surroundings [....] Each one of you, oh young Peruvians, from all corners of the Republic, can make your small contribution to science. And just as in Nature small causes can produce great effects, so joining together all these partial works will in a short time give us an exact knowledge of the whole country.[20]

Such invitations to contribute to the national scientific endeavour were repeated in scientific publications in all three countries.[21] Many people responded, as was evident in the leading periodicals and newspapers, which published reports on journeys of exploration, botanical drawings, geological finds and—a particular favourite—meteorological observations, assiduously collected by amateurs following instructions in one of the dedicated teach-yourself guides.[22] If Raimondi in Peru, or Gay in Chile, did a great deal to 'create a geographical awareness' of the national territory, it was 'the work of the explorers, the sailors, the miners, the rubber tappers, the farm labourers and the workers' of Peru and of Chile who 'engraved the block of granite raised by' the immigrant scientists.[23]

Spanish American Research: The First Atlas of Peru

The study of geography in Peru owed a great deal to one family, the Paz Soldáns, and above all, to two brothers, Mateo (1812–1857) and Mariano (1821–1886), who between them published the first Geography of Peru (1862), the first atlas (1865) and the first geographical dictionary (1877).[24] They were both sons of an immigrant from Panama, who occupied a post in the colonial bureaucracy in Arequipa until 1825.[25] They were men of modest fortune, able to travel to Europe in pursuit of their scholarly interests, but who spent most of their lives in a succession of public roles in Peru. Both men have been characterised as autodidacts, because they had no formal scientific training, but it is unlikely that their intellectual achievements would have been possible without certain educational opportunities they enjoyed from growing up in Arequipa. Peru's third city, high up in the southern Andes, had a long history of learning and was also a transit hub where new ideas, both scientific and political, circulated freely. By the 1830s Mateo Paz Soldán, who became known as 'the astronomer of Arequipa', had acquired a reputation as a man of vast learning, both humanistic and scientific, and clearly had remarkable intellectual gifts. In Arequipa, unusually in Peru at that time, he was able to learn mathematics to an advanced level,[26] and also drawing, taught by José Recabarren at the Universidad de Arequipa (founded in 1765), both of which skills contributed to the only major work of his to appear during his lifetime: a treatise on astronomy, which was acclaimed by natural scientists in Europe, including Humboldt.[27]

Mariano's talent, as he described it himself, was for compiling information, which he did on a remarkable scale. Of special interest here is his discussion of the methodological problems involved in collection and organisation. His starting point was to conduct an extensive review of all the existing work on Peru that he could find, both in Peru and in Europe, in order to differentiate between works that were credible and those which were not. In Paris, looking through all the material there, he concluded that if these foreigners' reputations were to be judged by their accounts of his country, often written on the strength of only a fortnight's stay, they would be condemned as 'audacious charlatans'.[28] His dictionary of 1877 included an appendix of over twenty pages listing all the printed works available on the geography of Peru, including colonial scholarship, indicating which ones he had used himself.[29] His main sources were studies recently published by local officials or clerics who had collected data about the regions where they served,[30] as he had done himself during his first post as a judge in Cajamarca,[31] plus accounts of recent voyages of exploration into the Amazon. Mariano Paz Soldán was eloquent about the methodological problems posed by the sources available to a researcher of Peru's geography. Like other cartographers in Latin America at that time, he expressed concern about the lack of common measurements (*leguas*, *varas* and *metros* were all used, although there was not always agreement about how to define them). He opted to rely upon calculations made by engineers for railways, irrigation works and the mail service, supplemented by a set of measurements ordered by President Ramon Castilla, in 1845, of distances between department and provincial capitals. It was hard to gauge the accuracy of any figures; the best he could do, in the absence of resources to take his own measurements, was to deduce estimates by cross-checking a variety of sources.

A difficulty that he saw as particular to Peru was the place names, many of which were from Quechua, Aymara or other indigenous languages. The authors of grammars and dictionaries of these languages, which had non-alphabetic forms of writing, had all used different roman letters to capture the sounds; Paz Soldán acknowledged that he really needed to acquire expertise in etymology in order to produce accurate maps. Small places were particularly difficult to identify, not least because of the indiscriminate use of at least eleven terms to refer to them: 'Pueblo, Caserio, Pago, Aldea, Parcialidad, Barrio, Estancia, Asiento, Ayllo [. . .], Villorio and Rancheria'.[32] There was great variation in different areas of the country and even over small distances. For political reasons, or just from sheer lack of information, official documents often classified places inappropriately; to call somewhere a Caserio, for example, would create the expectation of a moderately sized place, when it might actually be 'a squalid little hamlet of barely more than seven shacks with 15 or 20 inhabitants'.[33] Further confusion was created by the lengthy history of boundary disputes: both viceregal and republican governments drew borders for provinces or districts 'according to the needs of the moment',[34] without troubling to fix them precisely, so that they were always open to challenge by individuals with something to gain. In another work, Paz Soldán quoted the story of the 'Indian' who refused to be nominated Corregidor in the 'Bolivian' section of an area disputed by Peru and Bolivia. The pretext he gave was 'that he was a Peruvian citizen', but 'the real motive' was that his property lay on the 'Peruvian' land so had he accepted the post he would have been considered a Bolivian and required to pay Bolivian tribute.[35] While large landowners were particularly well placed to ensure 'the silence of Congress' in these legal entanglements, many other people had an interest in keeping things vague. The result for any unfortunate geographer was that the same place—its name differently spelt—might be claimed for various districts or provinces in different official documents. Over more than three decades, Paz Soldán laboured to make sense of over thirty thousand place names. What he had done, he claimed, was to collect and arrange in alphabetical order 'the information dispersed in thousands of books and authentic documents that can be judged credible', to produce 'the least incorrect' compilation available.[36] In effect, he acted as an informal office of statistics, before the state was able to establish one.[37]

Mariano Paz Soldán's historical work was harshly criticised by twentieth-century historians, notably José de la Riva Agüero, in 1911, for his lack of modern methods, exclusive focus on elite political history and dry prose.[38] Jorge Basadre characterised him as the product of a certain tradition in Peruvian thought of taking a 'procedural approach to ideas' (*tramitación administrativa de las ideas*), 'which came from the antiquity of the State in the country, from the importance of bureaucratic practices and curial, legal and clerical formulations' (*los formulismos curialescos, forenses y oficinescos*).[39] Yet Basadre saw this 'bureaucratic' thinker as the 'creator of modern Peruvian geographical research, [the] first author of the general map of the Republic that subsequent generations have continued to improve upon'.[40] Raimondi, whose map of Peru was adopted as the country's official one in 1900, was working later and therefore enjoyed the advantage of being able to use the surveying work of railway engineers, as well as more advanced hydrography.[41] Even so, his map of Peru drew upon Paz Soldán's work.[42]

Two Reviews of Raimondi

What was at stake in knowing the Americas, particularly those areas where there were known ancient civilisations, was inadvertently displayed in two very different critical responses to Antonio Raimondi's studies of the natural history and geography of Peru. The first was by an established French scholar, Ernest Desjardins, and published in the *Bulletin de la Société de géographie* in Paris in 1863; the second, published in Lima in 1878, was by a young Peruvian medical doctor, Pablo Patrón (1855–1910).

For Patrón to criticise Raimondi's work was audacious, given that he was only twenty-three and had yet to establish his own reputation in any area of scientific study (he later became well known for studies of indigenous history, medicine and languages, particularly the claim—which has enjoyed a long if non-scientific afterlife—that Quechua was related to ancient Sumerian). He was one of many individuals of that period who built on a professional training in one field to teach himself a wide range of other subjects. Patrón's arguments were careful, moderate in tone and mainly concerned to draw attention to sources that had been overlooked.[43] Raimondi publicly acknowledged that some of his points were valid.[44] The exchange between the scientist of grand repute and the young autodidact was a model of respectful scholarly debate.

The tone of a review of Raimondi by the eminent French geographer and historian Ernest Desjardins could hardly have been more different. The work in question was Raimondi's study of the north-eastern Amazonian region of Loreto, based on a visit of nearly two years, which was included as an appendix to Mariano Paz Soldán's edition of his brother Mateo's *Geography of Peru*, published in both French and Spanish in 1861. All the data carefully compiled by Mateo was ignored by the learned fellows of the Parisian Geographical Society, but they did appoint Desjardins to write a review of Raimondi's account of Loreto, jointly with a two-volume history of ancient Peru by the Spaniard Sebastian Lorente. The reviews of both works were so hostile that they prompted a point-by-point rebuttal by Manuel Rouaud y Paz Soldán,[45] nephew, assistant and translator to Mateo and Mariano. Desjardins might have been motivated partly by professional rivalry, because he had recently departed from his usual work on ancient Italy to publish a study of pre-conquest Peru, which was based—like most others at that time—on the chronicles of Garcilaso de la Vega (1539–1616) rather than on original research.[46] But the sheer brazenness of Desjardins's misrepresentation of Raimondi's work left a clue that far more was in jeopardy. The Frenchman accused the Italian of being an 'official geographer' who had doctored his findings in order to support Peru's territorial claims against Ecuador, even to the extent of falsifying Quechua place names.[47] He added, for good measure, that Raimondi was committed to propagating the myth that there was fabulous gold and silver wealth in Loreto. Even more dramatically, Desjardins attacked Raimondi for proposing a colonisation scheme 'exclusively for the profit of the white race'.[48] Such an approach to colonisation went against all the scientific evidence, maintained Desjardins, who was committed to the view that 'whites' did not adapt well to the tropics, as the French were indeed finding as work continued on the Suez Canal.[49] As Rouaud y Paz Soldán was easily able to show, none of the positions attributed to Raimondi could be found in his text; indeed, on colonisation his arguments were diametrically opposed to those attributed to him.[50]

Evidently it was Desjardins who was politically motivated. In 1859, as the Peruvian government sought to take advantage of civil war in Ecuador to extend its territory, conservative politician Gabriel García Moreno of Quito—who later became renowned for promoting science and education in Ecuador—requested a French protectorate to help him defeat his pro-Peruvian rivals in Guayaquil. The late 1850s and early 1860s were a period of French overseas expansion in both Asia and Latin America: what did not come to pass in Ecuador transpired in Mexico during 1862–67, when France occupied the country and installed the emperor Maximilian. As Rouaud y Paz Soldán pointed out, it was Desjardins, not Raimondi, who devoted half of his review to supporting the territorial claims of Ecuador, while claiming to take no view on the matter. But the review reveals more than a political motive: it goes to the heart of the mid-nineteenth-century battle over claims to legitimate knowledge. Given that the French imperial project relied on the nation's self-image as the fount of modern knowledge, any pretensions to scientific discoveries by other Europeans, especially migrants to the Americas—note that Desjardins ignored completely the work of Peruvians—had to be sharply rebuffed. Raimondi had seen less of scientific value in 1843–44 than Charles Marie de La Condamine, the first European scientist to navigate the Amazon,[51] a century earlier, asserted Desjardins. Neither Raimondi nor 'the famous expedition made in 1859 by the Sociedad de Patriotas de Amazonas' had made any significant advance on the work done by Bohemia-born Jesuit missionary Samuel Fritz, who in 1707 drew the first accurate map of the Amazon River, establishing its source as the Marañón—along the banks of which lay the famous missions.[52] In fact, the 1859 expedition had charted two large rivers, the Cristalino and the Nieva, never previously mapped. By denying the achievements of recent explorations of Peru, Desjardins, who was closely connected to Napoleon III's entourage,[53] was raising the imperial flag not to claim the actual territory of the Amazon basin, but instead to assert the exclusive right to explore it, to discover it, to *know* it.

Knowledgeable Entrepreneurs

One leading example of an entrepreneur who championed the importance of applied science was Eduardo Olivera (1827–1910), known as the first Argentine agronomist.[54] He played a leading role in founding the Sociedad Rural (1866)

and the Escuela Práctica de Agricultura y Ganadería at Santa Catalina (1872).
From an elite family, originally with close connections to the colonial administration, he is usually presented as someone who sought to model Argentina
on Europe, but that claim needs qualifying in various ways. Eduardo was the
son of a migrant from Ecuador, Domingo Olivera (1796/8–1866), who had
moved his family to the River Plate after the Quito declaration of independence in 1809—the first in the Americas. Domingo Olivera's estate at Los Remedios, on the outskirts of Buenos Aires, became a testing ground for new
techniques, notably for improving the quality of livestock. He became famous
for breeding the Argentine Rambouillet sheep, a synthesis of the best breeds
from Spain, Austria, France and Germany, a hardy beast which produced both
wool and meat of high quality. During a hard drought he undertook an arduous journey to move his cattle and horses more than two hundred kilometres
to find water,[55] at which point he was obliged to leave his son Eduardo, then
only fourteen, temporarily in charge of Los Remedios. A few years later, Eduardo went to study agronomy at the renowned Institut Grignon in France, and
he later travelled round northern Europe, observing patterns of landholding
and techniques for increasing yields. Much has been made of Eduardo's time
in Europe as the supposed source for his commitment to developing the Argentine countryside through scientific understanding of how best to work the
land, with modern equipment, but it seems likely that he was at least as influ-
enced by observing the difficulties overcome by his father. Much of his time
in Europe was spent analysing the market conditions there, with an eye for
gaps Argentina could exploit. [56] His own testimony was that he acquired his
interest in working the land through growing up on his father's estate, 'isolated
from the world of horrors surrounding us, [cultivating] the sensitivity that
develops through daily contact with nature'. His determination to become a
trained agronomist was reinforced on a visit to Montevideo in 1853, when he
saw at first hand the effects of 'the war of desolation and extermination' that
had just ended. Scientific method, he concluded, was the best way 'to transform the cruel and ferocious habits of our herdsmen (*pastores*) into the gentle,
civilised ways of the farmer'.[57] Back in Argentina, from 1857 to 1863 and then
permanently from 1866, Olivera constantly sought to stimulate scientific debate and, as founding editor of the *Anales* of the Sociedad Rural Argentina
(SRA), encouraged all readers 'interested in the public good' to contribute
information about the harvests, the rainfall, the condition of the lands, the
sales of livestock and so on.[58] In trying to promote technical training at all he
was going against the grain of an elite consensus that privileged the professions

of law and medicine. His plan for a rural credit bank, intended to help create smallholdings, received no support from the powerful ranchers who could buy land very cheaply.

Olivera's commitment to agrarian development was imbued with the sense of entitlement to claim territory for modernising Argentina from the native inhabitants that characterised the policy of all nineteenth-century governments but which was pursued most relentlessly in the War of the Desert (1878–84). As that war was beginning, Olivera published four volumes on his study of European agriculture, summarising a chapter on 'Education among Us' as follows:

> It is to be hoped that the almost complete disappearance of the ravaging Indian from our fields, which we are currently witnessing as the happy outcome of the change in our frontier, will give us greater security to work [the land] and to establish permanently the agricultural man (*hombre de campo*) that we so sorely need.[59]

The racist outlook was widely shared among his contemporaries; the distinctiveness of Olivera's 'civilising mission' lay in its focus on the countryside. He revived the arguments of independence-era champions of practical enlightenment, such as Belgrano, Rivadavia and contributors to *La Abeja*, all of whom had argued for the importance of agriculture at a time when conventional wisdom gave primacy to trade. He also criticised the 'concentration of all the intellectual energies of the ruling classes' on *urban* culture, instead celebrating the rural way of life as 'the source of all feeling of liberty' and a vast arena for the human desire to improve their lot through hard work.[60] Olivera developed a kind of conservative utopianism, in which cultivating the land was the bedrock of social stability and virtuous civic conduct. He admired England as the model of a well-ordered, aristocratic rural society, more than as a source of advanced agricultural techniques. Unlike José Hernández, the main alternative source of a ruralist ideology at this time, Olivera did not question rural social structures.[61] What concerned him was the gap emerging in Argentina between the urban-oriented ruling elites and those actually engaged in making the economy work. He noted that there were agricultural societies, fairs and exhibitions going on throughout the interior, and he wanted to establish an institute near Córdoba to experiment with new possible activities such as growing sugar-cane.[62] Olivera certainly sought to introduce into Argentina various institutions and practices that he saw working in Europe: agricultural exhibitions; a society to bring together landowners, agronomists and scientists in pursuit of agricultural modernisation; technical training for agricultural workers; immigrant colonies to introduce new activities; and banks tailored to the agricultural cycle to provide credit. Yet he argued against many of his contemporaries in advocating investment in the development of native stock as best adapted to Argentine conditions, rather than importing costly foreign breeds. He championed homegrown expertise by sponsoring the posthumous publication of Daniel Pérez Mendoza's *Manual del pastor* (1863), an extensive compendium of detailed knowledge of sheep raising in Uruguay and northern Argentina.[63] The scientific orientation that Olivera and others instilled at the SRA proved crucial to Argentina's economic development during the late 1870s, creating the conditions of possibility for the livestock grandees to spot the opportunities created by the invention of the refrigerator ship (see chapter 9).

Geographical Societies and Institutes

The range of ideological possibilities arising from visions of nationhood based on the land became evident when the study of geography was institutionalised during the late nineteenth century. Political leaders were driven by the strategic imperatives of territorial nationalism: demarcating international borders, securing access to natural resources and extending state control over disputed territory. Yet even the official versions of patriotic geography contained elements of alternative ways of thinking and knowing, not least because they entailed contesting the claims of European scientists about the environment of the Americas. The geographical societies established in Peru (1888), Chile (1911) and Argentina (1922), which were joint initiatives by governments and groups of civilians, each created opportunities for new perspectives and positions to be brought into debates about the role of the land in nationhood. [64]

A unifying impulse was most evident in Peru, where the Sociedad Geográfica de Lima (SGL) was founded in 1888, specifically to support the national regeneration effort after defeat and territorial loss (to Chile) in the War of the Pacific (1879–83). It was a semi-official body, the outcome of close connections between the government of Andrés Cáceres and the leading newspaper *El Comercio*, which had long served as a forum for scientific discussion. The distinguished surgeon Luis Carranza, joint owner of *El Comercio*, had persuaded the government to found a geographical society by pressing home the argument that Peru's ignorance of neighbouring countries, especially Chile, had 'contributed not a little to the disastrous war'.[65] The first meeting took place in the Senate; later, rooms were found on the unused top floor of the national library (although the society had to find funds for repair and redecoration).[66] The list of founding members was a roll-call of the leading intellectual lights of Lima, and the SGL went on to become the main learned society for a wide range of knowledge practitioners throughout the country.[67] Its administrative location under the aegis of the Ministry of Foreign Relations reflected the first of its twin aims, namely to 'correct grave errors propagated abroad by superficial observers, not only in European public opinion but also in scientific centres'—especially myths that threatened plans for modernisation through foreign investment and immigration, such as the claim that Europeans were unable to adapt to Peru's climate or that the inhabitants were unfit for work.[68] By this time, the need to counter misinformation about Peru had become a political and economic imperative as well as an intellectual one.

The society's second stated aim was to ensure that public policy was based on accurate and comprehensive information. Even so, the SGL started out with no funding and Luis Carranza, as its first president, had to work hard to persuade public opinion that geography was important to 'the practical life of the country'.[69] From the outset, the society made sure to assist in resolving Peru's various border disputes, dispatching its leading members to survey territory and to serve on commissions. It also publicised its willingness to establish national offices of hydrography and meteorology, if given the resources. From 1891 onwards, the relative stability provided by a modest monthly government grant, plus membership dues and donations, enabled the society to maintain its own library of geographical works, a map collection, a cartographic office and, from 1891, to publish a regular bulletin of its activities, which received a prize at the Paris World Fair of 1900, and has continued to the present day.[70] Led by distinguished figures, such as the engineer José Balta (president, 1913–18), the society's achievements were impressive. It mapped Peru's coordinates, demarcated political boundaries both external and internal, lobbied for a common time throughout the country, financed expeditions, founded an observatory, and oversaw the publication of two final volumes of Raimondi's materials. The SGL established geography as the Lima establishment's preferred framework for scientific knowledge of Peru. It represented a civilian bid to control geographical consciousness, which was successful until the 1930s, when the military asserted its own claim and the SGL's unrivalled prominence in geographical research came to an end.

In Argentina, in contrast, the study of geography was driven by military imperatives from the 1870s until the 1920s, at which point civilian geographers and engineers, led by women, established an alternative approach. In order to understand the history of geographical research in Argentina, it is crucial to be aware that the first dedicated institutions, the Instituto Geográfico Argentino (IGA; 1879–1934) and the Sociedad Geográfica Argentina (1881–97), were both products of the so-called Conquest of the Desert. This term refers to a series of military expeditions in the 1870s and 1880s sent by governments in Buenos Aires to defeat and—many historians argue—to exterminate the indigenous peoples of the southern territories. As has been well documented, various pseudoscientific arguments, blending social Darwinism, positivism and racial pessimism, were deployed by influential politicians and intellectuals to justify these wars on the grounds that indigenous peoples were obstacles to economic exploitation, to the consolidation of national borders and indeed to any prospect of a 'civilised' Argentina. [71] Since 2005, an organisation of Argentine social anthropologists has published evidence of the human rights abuses that occurred at the Museo de La Plata, where captured indigenous people were taken to be studied as examples of a species on the verge of extinction, and has supported the claims of indigenous peoples for the removal and restitution to their communities of the human remains on display in the museum. [72] Most of the members of the IGA had either taken part in or supported the wars against the indigenous peoples, not least the main founder, Estanislao Zeballos (1854–1923), who only the year before had hastily written the justification commissioned by General Julio Roca to help him persuade the Argentine Congress to finance another military attack on the *pueblos originarios*. [73] The same was true of the Sociedad Geográfica Argentina, which was founded by Ramón Lista (1856–97), a military man who spent two decades exploring the southern coastal areas, including Tierra del Fuego, where he was responsible for a massacre of Ona (or Selk'nam) people. [74] When Lista died in 1897, the society closed and its members joined the IGA, which continued in existence until 1934, when its functions were subsumed into the state bureaucracy. The IGA received state funding, which enabled it to maintain a permanent administration; to finance a series of scientific expeditions to explore the vastly expanded Argentine territory, especially Patagonia; and to sponsor the publication of notable scientific works, such as Florentino Ameghino's internationally recognised research on mammalian fossils. The deep past of life on earth uncovered by the palaeontologists helped to avert the public's gaze from the recent atrocities of Argentine state-building. Thus did the IGA's work contribute to the reimagining of sites of war as frontiers of knowledge. By the 1920s, however, the IGA had been eclipsed by two new institutions of geographical research, one military and one civilian. The Argentine military established its own dedicated organisation, the Instituto Geográfico Militar (IGM), in 1919. A product of the professionalisation of the Argentine military that took place during the early twentieth century, the IGM was a more ambitious version of previous topographical departments in the Ministry of War, where the maps had been prepared to service the Conquista del Desierto. In 1941 the IGM was charged with mapping the whole country.

Another way of approaching geographical work, in reaction against an agenda of exploitation and conquest, developed at the *escuelas normales* (teacher-training colleges) founded during Sarmiento's presidency (1868–74).[75] It ultimately resulted in the creation in 1922 of the first civil association dedicated to geography: GÆA, the Sociedad Argentina de Estudios Geográficos.[76] It was symbolically significant that the foundation of GÆA took place in UBA's botany lecture theatre, which was located in the Manzana de las Luces, the historic centre of Argentina's knowledge order. The new geographical society was concerned more with national identity than with territorial nationalism: its purposes were education and research with a view to creating a shared collective experience based on the Argentine environment. There was only one trained geographer among the founders, who included people with a wide range of expertise related to study of the environment—five engineers, two geologists, two natural scientists, a surveyor, an anthropologist and a translator.[77] They chose the name—referring to 'the earth' or 'the land' as a whole—and set the remit as 'geographical studies' rather than 'geography' in order both to invite comparative exchange between different areas of knowledge and, it is reasonable to deduce (although it was not stated), to signal a move away from the militaristic territorial nationalism of their predecessors. The membership was almost entirely civilian. The society's first president, Elina González Acha de Correa Morales (1861–1942), who served for twenty years until her death, was one of the first graduates of the Escuela Normal de Buenos Aires.[78] She had spent many years teaching geography in schools and to trainee teachers, writing textbooks on the subject for children—for which she won awards in the United States—and conducting her own research into insects, birds and plants.[79] One of her particular interests was the question that has preoccupied many geographers of the Americas, namely how to develop a nomenclature and taxonomy that was fit for purpose.[80] González Acha was part of the Buenos Aires elite circle of scientists and apparently became the first woman member of the IGA in the early twentieth century.[81] Yet, as happened with women educators in other fields, her practice of teaching seems to have led her to question, on intellectual grounds, the IGA's relatively narrow conception of geography (as territorial exploration) and to argue for a less instrumental, more socially conscious methodology, informed by debates between various fields of knowledge.

In Chile, there was a long tradition of teaching geography in public educational institutions, dating back to before independence. The enlightenment intellectual Manuel de Salas (1754–1841) introduced it in 1809 to the school he founded in Santiago. Salas's curriculum at the Real Academia de San Luis, which was the first school in Chile not controlled by the church, was designed to provide the advanced technical education he advocated in order to make nature productive and society prosperous. Geography was continued in the syllabus of the main educational institution of the new republic, the Instituto Nacional (of which the Academia de San Luis formed the nucleus); it was also taught for periods of time in various secondary colleges during the 1820s and 1830s. Scientists from Europe, commissioned by the government to bring their expertise to Chile, played an important part in keeping the subject alive at this time, most famously Claudio Gay, who arrived in 1830 to study the country's natural history, and Pedro Amado Pissis, invited in 1848 to lead the preparation of a map of Chile. One of Gay's legacies was to cement the close connection with history that has characterised the evolution of geography in Chile. A Sociedad Chilena de Historia y Geografía was founded in 1839, a forerunner of the cluster of knowledge institutions created under the government of Manuel Bulnes during the 1840s. It was not active for long, perhaps mainly because in 1843 geography was one of the new subjects introduced when the Universidad de San Felipe was reorganised and reformed to establish the Universidad de Chile. By 1853 it was possible to study for a degree in geographical engineering, which by the late nineteenth century had formed in a cohort of specialists, particularly in physical geography, able to supply the state's increasing demand for geographical knowledge for economic and infrastructural development. Towards the end of the century, schoolteachers were trained to teach geography at the Instituto Pedagógico, led by German immigrant Hans Steffen.

As was the case with natural history, the state's commitment to teaching geography laid the basis for a range of public lectures, exhibitions and publications on the subject. It is striking how many Chilean intellectuals felt compelled to turn their hand to writing a geography textbook in the second half of the nineteenth century, from José V. Lastarria, who was known mainly for his studies of positivist philosophy, in 1846, to Diego Barros Arana, whose reputation derived from his historical research and literary criticism, in 1888. Debates about Chile's future were channelled through discussions of the strengths and weaknesses of these geographical textbooks.[82] The history of geographical investigation was also deployed as evidence for the argument that knowledge was relative to different times and places, which was the necessary starting point for thinking about what was best suited to Chile. If Ptolemy was the first geographer, it was argued by leading astronomer José I. Vergara (1837–1889), the central sites of discovery in the field had moved around over the centuries—from ancient Alexandria to Arabia, to Toledo in the thirteenth century and later to London, Paris and Washington—in what might now be referred to as shifting centres and peripheries.[83] For all the importance that has rightly been attached to the role of historians in creating Chile's national identity, it is worth bearing in mind that for many of them it was through the relationship between geography and history that Chile's past, present and future could be seen in microcosm.

Territorial acquisition lay behind the allocation of state resources to geographical research in Chile, just as it did in Argentina. The reach of the Chilean state was extended first to the south by the military occupation of Araucanía from 1860 to 1883 and then to the north by lands gained at the expense of Peru and Bolivia in the War of the Pacific. From the 1840s onwards, the demand for land to grow wheat to supply first the northern mining areas, then—after the gold rush—California and Australia had resulted in indigenous peoples being defrauded of their lands. The resistance of some of the Mapuche peoples was met by the Chilean state with fortification in 1862 and then full-scale war during 1867–69. The military strategists who planned these invasions doubtless found information in the accounts of the region written by Gay and Domeyko after their visits in the 1840s, but their main sources were the hydrographical studies conducted during the 1850s by Chilean naval officers, especially Francisco Vidal Gormaz (1837–1907) and Francisco Hudson Cárdenas (1826–59).[84] During the 1870s, after a peace accord, it was mainly state railway engineers, building the Ferrocarril del Sur, who charted the territory and whose maps were used by the military during their repression of a general Mapuche uprising from 1881 to 1883. After the War of the Pacific, the central government financed the exploration and mapping of the Atacama Desert, led by mining engineer Francisco J. San Roman.[85]

In the early twentieth century Chilean intellectuals deployed arguments about geography to express increasing frustration with their nineteenth-century forebears' reliance upon imported knowledge. An article by Alberto Edwards, published in the first edition of the *Revista Chilena de Historia y*

Geografía in 1911, was symptomatic of an increasing tendency to criticise Chile's previous reliance on the work of foreigners which, it began to be argued, was not as scientifically advanced as had been assumed. Edwards pointed out that Claudio Gay's atlas of 1854 had not been based on any trigonometry, but he directed the real force of his scorn at the map drawn in 1872 by Pedro José Amado Pissis (1812–1889), who had presented it to the Chilean government as the result of a complete survey applying the technique of geodesic triangulation. Edwards condemned Pissis's map, which had been taken as the basis for all subsequent ones, as 'deplorably' inaccurate.[86] Pissis's claims to scientific accuracy had been 'extraordinarily detrimental to our progress in geography', wrote Edwards, because in fact 'a map made with a compass and a pedometer', drawing upon the hydrography carried out in the 1860s by the Chilean Navy with the advice of the British Admiralty and 'the known astronomical positions', 'would not have been very inferior' and would have had 'the advantage of not having deceived the geographers, the government and the public'.[87] The new map of Chile ordered by the government to mark the centenary of independence drew mainly upon the maps of the Andes produced by Chilean members of the border commission of 1906–12, charged to determine the boundary with Argentina.[88] This map, drawn by Luis Risopatrón, a geographical engineer trained at the Universidad de Chile, was, Edwards claimed, the most advanced map in the Americas, given that even the United States lacked a complete map of its whole territory based on modern surveying techniques. Even so, Risopatrón himself continued to revise and improve it.[89]

The revival of the Sociedad Chilena de Historia y Geografía in 1911 was indicative both of widespread public interest in geography and of mounting criticism of the state's emphasis on studying physical geography for the purposes of economic development. The instigator, Enrique Matta Vial (1868–1922), whose scholarly reputation derived from his compilations of historical documents on Chilean independence, took the opportunity afforded by a government commission to curate an exhibition about the first national government to launch the *Revista Chilena de Historia y Geografía* in May 1911. The first editorial of this publication, which has been published with only brief interruptions to the present day, declared a wish to be open to all views and invited contributions from anyone interested in subjects related to geography or history: 'ethnology, ethnography, folklore, linguistics, numismatics, geology, meteorology, seismology'.[90] The success of the journal encouraged Matta Vial to revive the society, the inaugural meeting of which brought together over seventy people in the main room of the Biblioteca Nacional.[91] The society was divided into sections to work on geography, history, archaeology, genealogy and folklore. The geography section oversaw the publication of Luis Risopatrón's landmark *Diccionario jeográfico de Chile* (1924). Both the journal and the society provided a forum for wide-ranging investigations into Chile's nature and culture, within a framework of promoting a national identity compatible with the integration into international circuits of knowledge exchange.

Conclusion

The interaction between humans and the land was fundamental to the distinctively American version of love of country that evolved in the region, mainly but not exclusively among creoles, during the nineteenth century. In a characteristic account published in Peru in 1879, shortly before the War of the Pacific, it was declared that in the Americas, *patria* (homeland) meant far more than place of birth: it was the site of fields of battle upon which your ancestors fought for liberty and the rights of man, converting monarchical rule into republican government, '[redeeming] virgin land with blood'; it was also the land your forebears had 'wrested (*arrancaron*) from barbarism or from nature' to work productively. Later, the racism that glossed over the history of conquest and seizure by Europeans and their descendants as a necessary step towards 'civilisation' was challenged. What endured was the idea that the identity of an American human being was no abstract construct confined to a particular bounded territory, but a lived experience 'drawn from his head, his heart and his arm', at once specific to a certain place and generalisable to all the other lands of the Americas that had similarly been forged through the epic struggles to build a 'temple of Liberty'.[92] Of course the emphases and the values varied in different countries and at different times: it could be claimed that in Argentina the land has been primarily associated with liberty and, if not equality, perhaps a certain democratic levelling; in Chile, with decency and clean living; in Peru, with health and well-being. Specifics aside, however, the broader point holds. The land was seen not—or not only—as a resource to be exploited, or as a source of aesthetic inspiration, but, above all, as the site of a historical commitment to a certain kind of society based on political freedom and social justice. This is why it is hard to understand the history of national identities in Latin America in terms of the conventional distinction between patriotism (as benign loyalty to the land of one's birth) and nationalism (as promotion of the interests of a particular nation-state). The predominant forms of nationalist discourse in Latin America, at least until the mid-twentieth century, hovered between *patria* and *estado-nación*. It was through working the land for which all Americans had fought—and many had died—that the nations of the future would be made. The Cartesian divide between nature and culture had little significance in this context, a point of view that anticipated the recent position of radical geographers that 'it is impossible on the ground and in the streets to see where nature ends and culture begins'.[93]

The land became, literally, the *terrain* of nation-making in nineteenth-century Latin America. It was where the foundations for nationhood were laid, in the period before any degree of consensus could be engineered, even among the privileged, about national history. In the alternative domain of natural history, the boundaries between formal and informal knowledge, or between transnational and local approaches, were particularly porous. The classifications and methods that were recognised as 'scientific' because they were developed in Europe did not necessarily aid understanding of the very different conditions in the Americas; at worst, they fostered ignorance. Trained scientists remained reliant upon the specialist knowledge of a variety of informants, many of them indigenous people. Study of the land, sea and sky of the national territory therefore brought a wider range of people into the processes of nation-making than did any other area of knowledge production. Examples can be found even among those Latin American countries where there was great natural diversity: Nancy Appelbaum's study of mid-nineteenth-century Colombia showed how geographical knowledge of regional specificities of habitat (as well as of population) stimulated an awareness of the potential for unity in diversity that undermined the elite's dreams of homogeneity.[94] The point may be applicable to other nations in other regions of the world: an awareness of the environment they share gives the inhabitants of a country a sense of something lasting in common, even when they are divided by history, language, belief or way of life. The seasons they weather, the birds they watch, the plants they grow—all contribute to a set of everyday experiences that are not limited by class, race, religion or gender (even if they are bound to be variously affected by all those factors). It is therefore easier for nation builders to stimulate identification with the nation through appeals to the shared natural environment than through virtually any other means.

8

Not the 'Dismal Science' but the 'Lifeless' One

CRITIQUES OF CLASSICAL POLITICAL ECONOMY IN LATIN AMERICA

IN THE 1950S a whole new approach to political economy—development economics—was pioneered at the United Nations–founded Economic Commission for Latin America in Santiago de Chile. Led by the Argentine Raúl Prebisch (1901–1986), economists from across the region built on his argument that the terms of trade for primary products were bound to decline as technological advance accelerated, thereby exacerbating structural inequalities between the 'centre' and the 'periphery'.[1] This work blew the idea of comparative advantage out of the water, directly refuting the long-standing claim of classical political economists that agricultural produce was bound to increase in value as populations rose. Out of this new theory, known as structuralism, came a raft of policies to promote industrialisation and reduce reliance on imports in the developing world. As is well known, import-substitution industrialisation ran into various difficulties, and Prebisch himself modified his analysis in the 1960s. Nonetheless, despite the resurgence of geopolitically fuelled neo-liberalism in response to debt crises in the 1980s, the commission's fundamental ideas remained influential on the dependency school, the world system theorists and the policy-making of the New Left that achieved power in the late twentieth century.

Yet Prebisch's ideas did not come out of nowhere. This chapter questions the still widely held assumption that classical political economy (CPE) was hegemonic in Latin America from independence until the Second World War.[2] The conventional story goes like this: Smith and Ricardo were widely cited; John Stuart Mill's *Principles of Political Economy* (1848) became 'a bible'; the idea of comparative advantage was naturalised. So (the causation is assumed rather than traced) laissez-faire governments sat back, parroted the theory and allowed the proceeds of primary product exports to accumulate in the hands of a minority, with little concern for the rest of the economy. If industrialisation took place—and economic historians have found more and more of it, earlier and earlier—it was despite, not because, of any deliberate policy, let alone a theory.[3] This bold outline is easy on the eye but casually drawn, incomplete and deeply misleading about the relationship between political economy and economic policy. If the classical theories really did go unchallenged, how do we explain economic nationalism, which caught international attention as a clause in Mexico's revolutionary new constitution of 1917, but was also evident in Brazil's manipulation of coffee prices in 1906 and in the founding of a state-owned oil company in Argentina (1922)? How do we account for the proliferation of societies and schools for the promotion of industry—some civil, some state—throughout Latin America during the late nineteenth century? What about the emerging interest in 'scientific'—or technocratic—government, which paved the way for major reforms in Chile and Peru during the 1920s, when new state economic institutions were created (including a central bank in Chile) and major programmes of public works undertaken? Moreover, even during the period of supposedly unchallenged free trade, from 1880 to 1914, tariffs in Latin America were among the highest in the world.[4] Although it would be easy to rattle off a long list of endorsements of free trade by Latin American public figures of this era, broader historical developments imply that economic thought was far more diverse than the image of unchallenged laissez-faire implies.

The subject of political economy was a product of the Age of Revolution and a self-consciously modern intellectual endeavour from the outset. It was widely believed to hold the secrets to success: '[Most revolutions fail] under the weight of disunity, ambition, vested interests and cowardice. A lack of [. . .] political economy plays a great part in these unfortunate outcomes', noted *El Monitor Araucano* of Santiago, in 1813.[5] It is hardly surprising, then, that some of the earliest chairs of political economy in the world were founded in Latin America,[6] where part of the case for independence had been to introduce the modern knowledge supposedly denied by Iberian rule. Political economy was usually taught as part of a law degree and it was also included in the curricula of colleges that prepared students for university, so most people who had gone beyond elementary education would have taken it. From the late eighteenth century onwards it featured often in general-interest periodicals and newspapers; from the 1850s onwards it was further popularised through teach-yourself manuals, reference works and encyclopedias.[7] During the late nineteenth century a gradual process of professionalisation began, with the production of a small number of research theses, the founding of specialist journals and the convening of academic conferences.[8] Yet even though political economy was widely promoted in Latin America as a standard-bearer of modernity, many of those who studied and taught the subject were sceptical about several elements of the classical approach. Their criticisms have been overlooked because of the blindspots caused by the fact that the history of the discipline of political economy was written mainly during the late nineteenth century in Britain or the United States.[9] In the newly independent countries of Latin America, however, the classic texts were interpreted and evaluated differently, for both theoretical and empirical reasons. In what follows, my examples are drawn mainly from Argentina, Chile and Peru, but preliminary further research suggests that the arguments below could also apply to other countries of the region.

CPE and Its Critics in Latin America

Adam Smith's *Wealth of Nations* (1776) was undeniably a gift to independence leaders seeking international recognition, especially in London, for their case against mercantilism. As Smith's work increased in prestige, so it became more persuasive for Latin Americans to cite him in support of freedom to trade, with whichever country offered the best terms, rather than free trade, which—they rightly suspected—would work to the advantage of the more industrialised economies.[10] In that respect, their borrowing of Smith's arguments was closer to his own purposes—namely, to establish that a country's wealth should be measured by its productive capacity rather than by its bullion reserves—than most later appropriations of his ideas by advocates of laissez-faire. Everyone was *librecambista* at first, out of hope for a prosperous modern future, one free of antiquated colonial restrictions.[11] But when new governments began to grapple with the challenges of adjusting to severed trade routes and of building economic institutions from scratch, CPE had less to offer. Its theories had been developed in societies in which the rule of law, territorial borders and fiscal legitimacy were all relatively secure; the main threat was deemed to be from populations outgrowing productive capacity. In the underpopulated lands of Latin America, the spectre of a Malthusian crisis did not loom large.

The hidden hand of the market, which Smith's successors emphasised far more than he had done, patently could not perform its transformative magic in societies where, as Argentine Esteban Echeverría pointed out in 1837, 'nothing is stable, everything is unforeseen' and neither property rights nor contract law could reliably be enforced.[12] To many nation builders in Latin America, it looked as if the causation had to be reversed: law, institutions and education would create an efficient market, not the other way around.[13]

Intellectuals in Latin America were among the first people anywhere to argue that CPE, far from being universal, was very much of its age—and of its place. Starting in the first courses taught in the 1820s, efforts were made to determine the extent to which CPE was applicable to local circumstances. It is often observed that the textbook for the first course at UBA was James Mill's *Principles of Political Economy* (1821), which blended David Ricardo's theory of comparative advantage, published in 1817, with utilitarian principles. It is less often noted that Rivadavia's decree specified the need to adapt CPE to 'the practicalities of new countries' and stipulated that the second year of classes should be spent discussing how to apply the theory to the economy of the River Plate.[14] Rivadavia also established a statistical register (1822–27), arguing that it was essential to the successful application of economic theory.[15] In 1837 Esteban Echeverría called for 'a truly Argentine economic science'; at the inauguration of the University of Chile in 1843, Andrés Bello declared that in studying 'the special features of Chilean society from an economic point of view', the university intended to be 'entirely Chilean: if it borrows from Europe the deductions of science, it does so to apply them to Chile'.[16] In Peru, Juan Espinosa noted in his widely consulted dictionary (1855) that political economy was 'a science of experiments' which, like medicine, required 'many modifications depending on the state of the societies' in which it was practised.[17] The drive towards applied knowledge was strengthened because political economy was written in Latin America by individuals who were involved in making and implementing policy: as had happened in the Kingdom of Naples in the eighteenth century, economic ideas were tested for practical efficacy as well as theoretical rigour.[18]

Many of the early courses in political economy given in Latin America were based on the work of Jean-Baptiste Say.[19] In the Anglo-American tradition, Say was assimilated as the great clarifier of Smith, credited with distilling a coherent system from Smith's exuberant mix of ideas but not with adding many of his own. In Latin America, however, Say was read as a republican working out how to adapt enlightenment principles derived from small-state models to a large, modern country,[20] which was precisely how republicans in Spanish America (and, in different ways, policymakers in imperial Brazil) saw their own project. Say's appeal lay above all in his famous law—supply creates demand—which refuted the physiocrats' view of consumption as the engine of an economy and opened up the attractive possibility of achieving prosperity by boosting production. Many other aspects of his work resonated in Latin America: his clear definition of the public good and exhortation to pursue it before private self-interest; his rejection of hierarchical social ranks; his emphasis on virtuous manners; and his efforts to popularise political economy, notably in the famous catechism, which was widely distributed throughout the region.[21] Similarly, by the mid-century John Stuart Mill's *Principles of Political Economy* (1848) was attractive to many Latin Americans not for its echo of his father's work but for its critique of reductive utilitarianism and a renewed emphasis on the wider social context of economic decision-making.[22]

In any case, it was by no means only the classical political economists who were read in Latin America. Everyone writing about political economy anywhere made ritual reference to Smith as the founder of the subject and Say as its great populariser. But a wide range of other readings fertilised thinking in Latin America. The Neapolitan school (Genovesi, who from 1755 occupied the first chair of political economy in the world, Filangieri and Galiani) became known through the same late-colonial routes as Smith and his French disciples: Manuel Belgrano, translator of Say,[23] was as well versed in Italian and Spanish political economy as he was in the French and British work. When UBA's chair of political economy was revived after the fall of Rosas, the first course was taught by an Italian, Clemente Pinoli, who replaced the study of James Mill with his own 'eclectic' syllabus, based almost entirely on Italian economists, particularly work on 'social economy' by Antonio Scialoja (1817–1877).[24] Spanish works of political economy, notably Manuel Colmeiro's survey of general principles, featured regularly on booksellers' lists throughout the nineteenth century;[25] and the famous Spanish debate of 1841 on free trade versus protectionism was covered in the Spanish American press. Latin Americans read successive generations of French critics of CPE: Argentines debated Saint-Simon and the early socialists in the 1830s; Chileans discussed the *solidarisme* of Charles Gide and Paul Leroy-Beaulieu in the 1890s. Peruvians encountered the French schools of economic thought directly through the teaching of Saint-Simonian Paul Pradier-Fodéré, appointed in 1875 as the first professor of political economy at the Universidad de San Marcos, whose work on social economy had been translated into Spanish by Manuel Fuentes.[26] They also happily deployed John Stuart Mill's observation that high tariffs might be beneficial in 'a new country' hoping 'to naturalise a foreign industry' (for him, the only circumstances in which they were justified) to co-opt the liberal *par excellence* for their own cause. Comparative reference was made to protectionist thinkers elsewhere, especially the United States, from Alexander Hamilton's infant industry arguments to the more fully developed models of Henry Carey and the German-American Friedrich List (1789–1846). As is usually the case in the generation of ideas, however, the main stimulus to thought came from their own circumstances.

A text that was typical in its range of references was the ambitious study of landownership published in 1865 by the twenty-eight-year-old Nicolás Avellaneda, future president of Argentina, then professor of political economy at UBA. This work made reference to classical economists and their critics, both French (Sismondi) and US American (Carey); to the eighteenth-century Spaniard Gaspar de Jovellanos; to the Frenchman Courcelle-Seneuil, whose initial commitment to low tariffs was substantially modified during his years teaching at the University of Chile in the 1850s; and to the Argentine J. B. Alberdi, who had gone a lot further down the road of rejecting CPE's relevance to his own country.[27] Avellaneda's prescient analysis of the risks for an emerging economy of over-reliance on foreign loans may have been launched by quotations from Smith and Say, but—given the complexities of landholding in Argentina—it moved into areas that they did not even touch upon.

Thus, there was from the outset a widespread sense that CPE did not fit the circumstances of the new countries of Latin America. There was also a major philosophical objection, expressed by both conservatives and liberals. For its critics in Latin America political economy was not so much the "dismal science", to cite Thomas Carlyle's famous protest against its pessimism, as the "lifeless science". CPE's analytical separation of the economic from the intellectual and the moral was seen by many Latin American thinkers as a 'mutilation' of human nature. Alberdi expressed a common view in calling for a more philosophical approach to economics, to take 'law, morality [and] religion' into account, because 'neither the individual nor society are maintained by material needs alone' and 'economic production is not the whole purpose of society'.[28] Similar arguments against *homo economicus* reappear over and over again, in a wide variety of sources, well into the twentieth century. By the mid-nineteenth century, the self-regulating market was hardly mentioned in discussions of economic policy in Latin America.[29] There was widespread rejection of a commodified idea of virtue and, indeed, of the very concept of an 'economy' that could be isolated from other elements of society. In certain contexts, such unorthodox thinking began to be translated into policy-making.

Currents of Economic Nationalism

A steady stream of historical research over the last few decades has shown that there were strong pockets of protectionism in various Latin American countries: Peru in the 1830s and 1840s and the 1870s; Mexico, among conservatives, in the 1850s; and the better-known Argentine López-Pellegrini School in the 1870s.[30] In both Chile and Argentina, economic historians have identified persistent strains of protectionist thought throughout the nineteenth century.[31] What I want to highlight here is that from the 1870s onwards there was a gradual shift away from the kind of protectionism compatible with a liberal framework (a limited role for the state in the exceptional circumstances of new countries building infant industries) and towards a version that questioned the fundamental principles of liberalism by presenting the state as an engine of development. Analysing these debates in terms of 'free trade versus protectionism' tends to limit the discussion to the question of tariffs on imports and exports, which were undeniably important, but more significant still is that even though debates often started with tariffs, they rarely ended with them. Thinking about the implications of laissez-faire led to wider doubts about the supposedly beneficial role of foreign powers in the economy, including criticism of the repatriation of profits and concerns about control of resources. One often overlooked contribution of economic thinkers working in Latin America during the late nineteenth century is their argument that desirable state support for local industries went far beyond tariffs to encompass a range of measures designed to 'establish the rule of the social interest over the private interest', as Vicente Fidel López put it.[32] The real debate, as it developed in the 1890s and 1900s, was between proponents of a free market and advocates of *fomento* (fostering), a term which increasingly came to the fore as a marker of the role of the state in stimulating economic activity.

Argentina has often been characterised as the epitome of free trade, yet a close look at ideas and policies there shows that the picture was far more mixed. A bold official commitment to free trade was made during the presidency of Bartolomé Mitre (1862–68), who famously declared that the Paraguayan War (1865–70) was a victory not only for Argentina but for free trade. There was an element of truth to his claim, in that merchants in Buenos Aires and Entre Ríos had made a fortune importing supplies for the allied troops of Argentina, Brazil and Uruguay. But the reaction against free trade for the whole country was immediate, in the López-Pellegrini School of the 1870s, which has been identified as an early manifestation of economic nationalism. One major factor behind this rapid emergence of a counter-current to the embrace of CPE was the historical experience of the confederation (1854–61), when President Urquiza tried to organise a nation without Buenos Aires.[33] Archives in Entre Ríos contain documents recording Urquiza's investments in a huge range of enterprises: banks; all kinds of transportation; agricultural industry; and societies to promote local industry, agriculture and commerce.[34] One relatively well documented example was an attempt by visionary local businessman Baltazar Aguirre (1809–1881) to modernise sugar production in Tucumán, replacing mules with steam-powered machinery from Britain.[35] The enterprise failed (mainly owing to drought), like Urquiza's overall project, but the confederation's economic experience must have weighed heavily on Vicente Fidel López, who had fought for Urquiza against Rosas in 1852. Observing events from Montevideo, where he taught political economy and later became director of the London and River Plate Bank, he had ample opportunity to contemplate the inadequacies of CPE, especially for the economies of the interior provinces.

Back in Argentina in 1871, López was also concerned to refute the arguments of Malthus and Ricardo,[36] which ran directly contrary to Argentina's policy of attracting immigrants, who in the 1860s had begun to arrive in large numbers. He interpreted Argentina's 1873 balance-of-payments crisis as the result of exporting primary products with no value added and henceforth became the leader of a campaign for moderate economic nationalism. Even though arguments for a full embrace of protectionism were famously defeated in congressional debates of 1875–76, the period of national organisation (1862–80) saw a degree of state support for industry (for example, wine, flour and textiles) in the form of credits, guarantees, tax exemptions, infrastructure-building and the spread of technical education—a set of policies close to what Adam Smith himself had advocated. It may not have been enough to create the conditions for real success (Argentina was still heavily dependent on imported textiles in 1913),[37] but it does not fit the picture of unquestioning acceptance of the doctrine of comparative advantage. It was scarcely surprising that free trade was official orthodoxy during the 1880s, given the high rates of growth achieved through the expansion of exports and the resulting hold of the agro-exporters over the state. But in the 1890s the debate was rejoined once again, after the uprisings led by the Unión Cívica Radical, founded by Leandro Alem, who had taken López's course in political economy at UBA.

Even though exporting primary products to Europe did bring high rates of growth to Argentina, the argument was soon made that in the longer term such policies went against what was beginning to be identified as the national interest. In 1870, Emilio de Alvear, a fully paid-up member of the Argentine oligarchy and a legal representative of British firms, set out the risks of Argentina's reliance on two primary products and one buyer.[38] He called for reform of the 'exaggeratedly liberal' laws on trade and industry, arguing that 'with wool and hides' Argentina would never be a great nation, especially as the price was set by the consumer so that the country did not even retain the value of its two main exports. Free trade was good for Britain but it meant 'degrading servitude' for Argentina, which needed its own industry as a matter of basic security: if there were to be a prolonged war or a blockade, 'we would have no bread to eat, because even flour is imported'. Moreover, it was absurd to transport clothes and household items all the way from Europe when there were plenty of European workers in Argentina who could make them. Writing from the United States, where he read Henry Carey's letters to Lincoln arguing for protectionism for US industry, Alvear advocated flexible tariffs for Argentina (with exemptions for provincial industries) and lower internal transportation costs. The main argument he adduced from Carey was that a healthy external balance of trade required an expansion of internal trade, so free trade was for the internal not the external market. Protectionism was *natural*, he argued, manoeuvring to dislodge the association between the free market and nature. Far from being limited to tariffs, his version of protectionism encompassed technical education as well as infrastructure.

Anticipating opposition to his proposed reforms, Alvear deployed various examples intended to pique or flatter patriotic pride. In its current precarious state, Argentina was outdone by Paraguay, which, despite 'worse conditions of government, climate and topography, has been self-sufficient during five years of unremitting war'. Even France, at its relatively advanced stage of industrialisation, was debating ending the free-trade treaty with England after ten years. And Britain itself was not always in favour of free trade: it had applied tariffs to silverware and even to its literary works; moreover, if the cotton mills were threatened by a revival of production in the US South, London might 'react against its own system'. Alvear drew attention to different stages of the history of the United States, England and France to bolster his case, choosing the examples he knew would resonate with his critics. It was pointless trying to outdo the United States in liberalism, he argued; instead Argentina urgently needed to develop the one thing he saw in the United States that was missing in his own country, namely a consistent commitment, independent of changes in government, to the national interest. If the United States, with a larger population (thirty million) and better infrastructure, needed protection for its industry, labour and interior market, how much more did Argentina, which lacked any of those advantages? Liberty was not 'an absolute good', especially in trade, where 'liberty without equality is deceptive, because it tends to disarm and leave some peoples at the mercy of the will and rapacity of others'. It was not the case, as free-traders argued, that Argentina could import goods more cheaply than it could make them at home; rather, the lack of industry in Argentina had created an incentive for industrialists in Europe to manufacture poor-quality goods for the Argentine market. If Alvear did not explicitly formulate the concepts of centre and periphery found in structuralist economics, the basis was certainly there. Even clearer precursors of dependency theory have been identified in Peru, where the early experience of a commodity boom and bust (guano) prompted Juan Copello and Luis Petriconi to explore the disastrous consequences for overall development of relying on a single primary product. Notably, their study was published in 1876, before the war with Chile (1879–83) compounded the damage. Twentieth-century Peruvian economic historians plausibly saw Copello and Petriconi's work as 'the lodestone of dependency interpretations of the republican era'.[39]

Even the more cautious political economists increasingly combined ritual obeisance to liberalism with policy prescriptions that stretched any conventional definition of it to the limits. José Antonio Terry, three times minister of the Treasury in Partido Autonomista Nacional governments, described a liberal framework as fundamental to the international connections 'that the solidarity of modern civilisation requires', but nonetheless he came to advocate moderate state intervention in the economy, including the use of taxation to address social inequality. As professor of public finance at UBA (from 1899 until his death in 1910), he opposed *dejar hacer, dejar pasar* with the argument that a government should be an engine of progress, an organ of public opinion and a protector of all legitimate rights. Terry argued that after the Constitution the most important law was the fiscal budget, 'because its provisions show us the state of moral and intellectual culture of the people, their material advances or retreats, and their economic or financial situation. It is the most important manifestation of sovereignty'. In a highly esteemed analysis of the Argentine economic crisis of 1892,[40] he discussed the advantages of 'socialismo del estado', testing out ideas from thinkers of the French Third Republic, such as Léon Gambetta. He analysed the difficulties that followed from Argentina's dependence on foreign investment, especially in infrastructure, arguing that Argentina needed to generate more of its own capital and make itself 'as independent as possible [. . .] from foreign influence' if it wanted to avoid 'a poverty unworthy of modern societies'.[41] His methodology, like that of many critics of CPE, was comparative and historical—again, placing him closer to Adam Smith than to those who claimed to be Smith's heirs. In practical policy, at the Treasury in 1892 Terry had not supported the attempts of his predecessor, López, to curb the power of British banks.[42] Yet his theoretical positions later led him, as a senator, to resist a proposal in 1901 to transfer Argentina's public debt to several European syndicates. The most objectionable aspect of the proposed deal was the requirement to remit a proportion of customs revenues to the Banco de la Nación to pay off the debt, which nationalists compared with what was being demanded of the Dominican Republic by the United States. Terry argued in a lecture at UBA that the proposal contravened sovereignty because it opened up the possibility of foreign intervention if the terms were not met. Student protests ignited public opinion against the proposal, which the executive eventually withdrew. Even in Argentina, where it was most markedly the case that 'the main lines of political economy were drawn from London',[43] those lines did not go unchallenged.

Chile was the only one of my three case studies where CPE was systematically taught at university level. It was introduced by the Frenchman Gustave Courcelle-Seneuil (1801–1892) from 1856 to 1862, then continued for the next half century by his disciples, some of whom were more dogmatic than he was, notably Miguel Cruchaga and Zorobabel Rodríguez. Courcelle-Seneuil himself modified his approach substantially during his time in Chile, adopting a comparative framework to write a highly regarded analysis comparing Chile's circumstances to those of Britain, the United States and France. By the end of the century, there had been a marked shift away from CPE to advocacy of *fomento*. One marker of change came in 1886, when one of Courcelle-Seneuil's students, Marcial Martínez (1832–1918), published a series of letters to his former teacher in which he argued that the fall in value of the Chilean currency since 1878 and the corresponding increase in import prices created an opportunity for industrial development if protectionist measures were carefully applied.[44] The situation was made urgent, declared the Sociedad de Fomento Fabril (Society for the Promotion of Manufacturing) in 1884, by the rapid increase of wheat production in California, which was likely to render Chilean wheat farming, on its relatively limited extent of land, uncompetitive within a few years. In any case, they added, there was no case for continuing to allow the rich and varied produce of Chile 'to leave our land to be processed elsewhere and immediately sent back to our country to be sold at prices that take from us far more than was gained from the sale of the primary product'.[45] Chile had already seen the benefits of strategic protectionism in the mid-1870s, when the government banned the importation of vines from France, preventing phylloxera (the disease that ravaged French vineyards) and thereby giving the Chilean wine industry a unique competitive edge because it was the only place where certain grape varieties survived. [46]

There was even a popular novel in favour of protectionism, *Luis Ríos, o una conversación al proteccionismo* (1884), by Manuel Aristides Zañartu (1840–1892), perhaps intended as a riposte to Harriet Martineau's fictional homilies on laissez-faire, the *Illustrations of Political Economy* (1832).[47] One of the central characters in *Luis Ríos* was 'The Economist', a champion of free trade who appeared in a most unflattering light: 'cowardly, gluttonous, lazy, petulant, without knowledge or wit', as noted in an irascible review by Zorobabel Rodríguez, a staunch opponent of any state intervention in the economy.[48] Rodríguez, who didn't even trouble to get the name of the author right, attacked the medium rather than the message, citing a chunk of Spencer to support his own contention that the state could not be trusted, but couching his objections in terms of poor style and bad taste. Zañartu, who was briefly minister of the Treasury under Balmaceda, planned to found a national bank that offered low-interest loans to help promote agriculture and industry, thereby anticipating the creation of the Banco Central in 1925, but revolution broke out. Even without the institution, it has been argued that his plan provided a basis for financial planning and stability in Chile for more than three decades.[49] By the time of the centenary, Francisco Encina's famous diagnosis of Chile's ills—in *Nuestra inferioridad económica* (1912)—as foreign dominance of internal trade, primary resources (nitrates and copper), banking, insurance and merchant shipping was widely shared, even if his attribution of the causes to a weakness of national character was not.

In all three countries, efforts were made to promote industrialisation during the late nineteenth century: societies of industrialists were founded in Argentina (1875), Chile (1875) and Peru (1896). They organised lectures, edited periodicals and held a series of major exhibitions of industrial products.[50] The Unión Industrial Argentino, created in 1887 from a merger of two earlier organisations, became a quite powerful interest group, on occasion able to win policy concessions from governments.[51] In Chile, the government created the

Sociedad de Fomento Fabril (1883) specifically to boost manufacturing industrialisation; most of the industrialists themselves, already meeting in their own associations, initially kept their distance from the new group. With government funding, however, the Sociedad de Fomento Fabril gradually increased its membership and influence: it collected the information behind Chile's early twentieth-century social legislation, successfully argued for the protectionist measures of 1897 and 1916, established a *museo industrial*, and by 1921 was running thirteen *escuelas industriales*.[52] One element in Chile's relative success in industrialising compared with Argentina and Peru may have been its early establishment of a national office of statistics, in 1843, initially concerned with censuses but soon extending its remit to produce an annual statistical review.[53] In 1930 its role in economic development was recognised when it was moved to the new Ministerio de Economía, Fomento y Turismo. In Argentina, Alejandro Bunge, the first national director of statistics (1915–24) and professor of political economy at UBA, introduced systematic collection of statistics on the Argentine economy, arguing that the available information was 'ten or twenty years out of date.'[54] Bunge's insistence on full and accurate data was absorbed by his student and teaching assistant Raúl Prebisch.[55] In Peru, Pedro Emilio Dancuart (1847–1911) and José Manuel Rodríguez (1857–1936) spent many years compiling a remarkable twenty-four-volume collection of data from the Peruvian Treasury, covering 1821 to 1895.[56] In 1895 the government of Nicolás Piérola founded a Ministerio de Fomento y Obras Públicas, hoping to emulate the success of the Mexican equivalent (1877), and began to gather information to support policy-making. Rodríguez, who seems to have been mainly self-taught in economics, published a series of innovative studies exploring the ramifications of the guano boom and bust, criticising direct foreign investment, analysing capital flight, and condemning the parasitic behaviour of Peru's economic elites.[57] Liberal in outlook at first, he advocated selective protectionism in practice and increasingly favoured state interventionism to promote development, during the 1920s drawing inspiration from European fascism. Economic historian Carlos Contreras Carranza, who has uncovered the little that is known about Rodríguez's life, described him as 'one of the first Peruvian economists.'[58] Perhaps most importantly, he founded the periodical in which most debate about Peruvian economics took place for three decades, *El Economista Peruano* (1909–40). His own articles consistently emphasised the close relationship between economic policy and quality of life in moral as well as material terms, a concern which also came to the fore in other countries.

In early twentieth-century Chile, it became 'fashionable' to teach 'social economy',[59] which studied the working and living conditions of the labour force and their voluntary associations. The change was reflected in the renaming of the chair of political economy at the University of Chile to the chair of political and social economy in 1901. For Armando Quezada, the first occupant of the renamed post, the lack of a social dimension was 'a serious deficiency' of CPE.[60] Quezada used a metaphor of nature to illustrate his sense of 'a new spirit' in economic thinking: the 'compacted ice' of the 'great mountain' that was CPE had begun to thaw in the warmth of 'currents of ardent life'. In some places, the melting ice exposed 'arid rocks', but in others it revealed 'verdant oases'.[61] With the rise of 'the social question' and the teaching of social economy, solidarity was proposed as the route to prosperity. Here the Chileans were drawing on late nineteenth-century French ideas, but their interest in them can be understood only in light of the long tradition of doubts about CPE. The extent to which a humanistic outlook grounded in nature and informed by classical references began to displace economic individualism is captured in the following quotation from Quezada: 'our country, endowed with a beautiful and bounteous Nature, populated by a people [una raza] not yet abundant but intelligent and vigorous, could be the Arcadia dreamed of by the poets', if everyone could forget 'political or class distinctions' and work together in solidarity.[62] Such courses in political and social economy, taught to law students at the University of Chile and the Catholic University, were part of the intellectual formation of individuals like Pablo Ramírez (1886–1949), an early technocrat who led comprehensive economic and administrative reforms under President Carlos Ibáñez in the late 1920s.[63]

But there were also more politically radical positions adopted by proponents of social economy. A leading example is Malaquías Concha Ortiz (1859–1921), whose analysis of unequal trading relations between Latin America and Europe, presented at the fourth Latin American Scientific Congress of 1908, was no less trenchant than that of the dependency school of the 1960s.[64] When competition occurred between nations at different levels of industrialisation, he averred, 'the most dominant crush the most backward [...] deprive them of any industrial future and condemn them to [...] economic servitude'[65]—in other words, what the dependency theorists called the development of underdevelopment. Competition was a means of attack for powerful nations, protectionism the only means of defence, in a 'Darwinian struggle for existence in the economic domain',[66] he argued, reflecting the fears evoked in Latin

America by Darwin's emphasis on the possibility of extinction. The risk Concha identified was the closing of markets for agricultural produce, rather than the fall in relative prices that later preoccupied Prebisch. Most significantly for the argument here, he saw the European triumph as an intellectual one: Latin American policymakers had been conned into 'an absurd, unthinking cosmopolitanism, calculated in the interest of the nations where it was created'.[67] Concha called for Latin America to regain the initiative by urgently producing new ideas and organisations in 'industry, commerce, navigation and credit' to serve their own interests. [68] Social economy was a substantial field in Latin America during the early twentieth century, culminating in the Congreso Internacional de Economía Social held in Buenos Aires in 1924. There was a revival of interest in the twenty-first century in relation to co-operative movements and community development policies.

In sum, during the late nineteenth century a variety of new approaches to political economy were developed in Latin America, based on the ideas of *fomento* and social economy. These critiques of CPE came from individuals working from disparate perspectives, from high statesmen to university professionals to workers' leaders. Yet they shared a common theoretical concern, which was to retain a conception of the public good. Their diverse assaults on CPE stimulated a wide range of economic analysis that has only recently come to the attention of historians. There were studies of currency, taxation, banking, infrastructure, communications and public land use. One particular concern was how to ensure that foreign-owned banks worked in the national interest. There were several attempts to create national banks to finance industrialisation, stymied by the reluctance of locals with capital or of financiers in Europe—who were well aware of the threat to their own positions—to support them. Some of the policy prescriptions in this body of work are striking in the light of recent findings by economic historians about what might explain the surprisingly rapid industrialisation that occurred in some Latin American countries from 1870 onwards. In 2008 Williamson and Gómez Galvarriato identified protectionist tariffs as one of two key factors in enabling industrialists in certain places to take advantage of market conditions (the other being real exchange rate policies that kept exports competitive).[69] By the late nineteenth century, many political economists throughout Latin America were advocating such policies, even if their views did not always prevail. There were also extensive discussions about technological change, which was notoriously underappreciated in the classic theories of comparative advantage. Proposals to introduce technical education were supported by exhaustive studies illustrating its beneficial effects in more industrialised countries (see chapter 10). Arguments against excessive foreign involvement in the economies of Latin America ultimately resulted in the set of policies that became known as economic nationalism after the famous article 27 of the new Mexican Constitution of 1917.

Conclusion

All the elements of development economics were in place, albeit not systematically so, in the work of political economists in Latin America during 1870–1930. They had developed critiques of the theory of comparative advantage, arguing that it worked more to the benefit of industrialised countries. Although they did not use the term 'informal empire' (a mid-twentieth-century coinage to characterise Britain's role in Africa), they were analysing the situation of unequal advantage it denotes, including the notion of local collaborative elites. Concerns had been expressed about over-dependence upon export markets; about repatriation of profits by foreign investors; and about relinquishing control of banking, infrastructure and natural resources to foreigners. Doubts about the applicability of CPE to the new countries of Latin America surfaced early on, but continued to be expressed within the framework of liberal economics for the half century or so after independence. Towards the end of the nineteenth century, however, a decisive shift took place in how the role of the state was conceived, with increasing advocacy of an active role for the state as a promoter of industrialisation, and attention to the interconnectedness of economic, political and social developments. Present-day economists, notably Amartya Sen, have focused on the detrimental effects of thinking in terms of a separation between economics and ethics; similar points have been widely and consistently made in Latin America since the 1830s.

As in other areas of intellectual endeavour in nineteenth-century Latin America, a comparative and historicising methodology was seen as the best way to bridge the gap between the realities of circumstances in the Americas and the theories developed in Europe yet projected as universal. The distinction between theoretical and applied knowledge was, and still is, one of the divisions most ruthlessly policed by gatekeepers of knowledge. Originality was confined to the free-floating zone of theory, which immediately rendered derivative any work applying principles to different contexts, even though that was exactly the method followed by Adam Smith in the works that founded the subject. So often it is said that a Latin American economist was not innovative because they did not produce a new theory; even Prebisch—who was nominated for, albeit not awarded, a Nobel Prize in 1977—has been branded more of a policymaker than a theorist.[70] Yet as Latin American economists have repeatedly pointed out, the economic history of Latin America shows all too clearly the dangers of applying inappropriate theories that are actually only the applied knowledge of other societies that happen to be wealthier.

9

Infrastructure

ENGINEERING SOVEREIGNTY

THERE IS A WIDESPREAD VIEW that economic nationalism was born with the Mexican Revolution and that before then Latin American countries both needed and welcomed foreign innovation and expertise, especially for technically demanding infrastructure projects. The legendary escapades of certain larger-than-life individuals, plus the undoubted importance of foreign financing and foreign-made equipment, have distracted attention from the fact that many of the continent's first railways were built by Spanish American engineers under contract to the respective states, contrary to the common belief that British or US American companies always led the way.[1] When local experts were not the protagonists, projects generated huge public controversy. They were contested, often over many years, in debates that went back and forth between the two houses of Congress, the executive, the official bodies responsible for public works, the professional organisations of engineers and sometimes the courts. Everyone made their bids for public support, generating a volley of reports, prospectuses and manifestos; there were public exhibitions, award ceremonies and gala openings, all of which were featured in the press. Rival newspapers, which from the 1870s onwards took advantage of the new transportation routes to develop more extensive distribution networks, took opposing sides in what they all had an interest in framing as 'national' debates.

In light of the visibility and intensity of public concern about the relationship between science and sovereignty in late nineteenth-century Latin America, this chapter highlights three themes. First, these disputes were framed in terms of questions about the status and legitimacy of knowledge. Representatives of European or US companies claimed that they offered the only sure route to scientific progress; engineers working in Latin America countered that the outsiders knew nothing of American conditions. Even though political, economic and diplomatic factors all conditioned decisions about such potentially lucrative projects, it is hard to understand the outcomes without due regard to the history of emerging hierarchies of knowledge. Next, there has been an overlooked history of resistance in Latin American countries to handing over infrastructure projects to private companies, especially if they were foreign-owned. This point relates to disputed conceptions of the role of the state and provides further evidence for the argument—now gaining in traction—that free-market liberals did not have it all their own way in nineteenth-century Latin America (see chapter 8). Finally—and this is the crux of the matter—scientific expertise developed in the region was crucial to the success of major infrastructural projects, some of which turned into expensive disasters for lack of it, or, rather, for lack of appreciation of its importance. Science from the Americas was required to complement science from Europe, despite European claims to universalism.

These themes are illustrated by analysis of four encounters between foreign and local engineers. The first two cases concern the modernisation of the ports of Callao and Buenos Aires. In Callao, there was vociferous protest when the company Templeman and Bergmann was granted the concession in 1869, in preference to several alternative bids. Although Templeman and Bergmann had been founded in Lima in 1821 by a German-Jewish immigrant, the firm had developed close connections in Paris which undermined its national credentials, particularly when it sold the concession on to a French bank in 1874. The controversy was fuelled further over the next three decades as it became increasingly obvious that Templeman and Bergmann's engineering was inadequate and had to be rectified by local experts. A similar trajectory characterised the history of port works at Buenos Aires, where Argentine-trained engineer Luis Huergo was outmanoeuvred by a nexus of pro-British interests, only to be vindicated by the complete failure of their construction to meet the needs of Argentina's late nineteenth-century export boom. These two episodes are early examples of the problems caused by direct foreign investment, but they also demonstrate a decline in the prestige of knowledge from Europe and a corresponding rise in the importance attached to homegrown expertise. The increasing conviction that knowledge from the Americas was both useful and legitimate was a necessary condition for making economic nationalism seem not only desirable but also possible.

The third example is the invention of the *frigorífico* (refrigerator ship), which has been variously attributed to a Frenchman, an Argentine and a

Uruguayan. The development of the technology to keep meat cold and in perfect condition for the duration of a trans-oceanic voyage was crucial to the
growth of the economies of Argentina, Uruguay and also Australia during the
late nineteenth century, not to mention the benefits for European populations
in terms of improved diet. It is unsurprising, therefore, that the credit for the
invention of the refrigerator ship has been the subject of bitter disputes, both
at the time and subsequently. These claims and counter-claims are particularly
revealing about hierarchies of knowledge and what it took to achieve recognition for intellectual innovation. There are so many elements in the process of
invention: imagining the theoretical possibility, conducting the technical experiments, seeing the social implications, testing the technique in real-world
conditions. The enduring myth of Romantic genius rolls them all up together
as the product of a single heroic individual, but it rarely happens like that in
practice.

My fourth example is the transandine railway (*el trasandino*), a remarkable
feat of engineering over the mountains from Santa Rosa de los Andes, east of
Valparaíso in central Chile, to the balmy wine-growing slopes of Mendoza in
Argentina. It was begun in 1874 under the leadership of two Chilean brothers
of Argentine and British parentage, but their business had been taken over by
a London-based company by the time the railway opened in 1910. The history
of the *trasandino* allows for a comparison of the shifting and varying relation-
ships between local and foreign knowledge in the two countries. In concert,
these four case studies vividly convey that it was not, as has often been claimed,
a lack of local knowledge that allowed foreign expertise to prevail in late
nineteenth-century Spanish America. Rather, it was a murky convergence of
factors that artificially elevated the status of foreign knowledge at a critical
period of technological development.

The Port Works at Callao

The development of modern facilities at Peru's main port of Callao, just west of
Lima, is a prime example of a Latin American government opting for a costly
prestige project with foreign partners instead of a local design appropriate to the
conditions. Work to build a new *muelle* (wharf) at Callao started as a Peruvian
state project in 1865, but was interrupted by war with Spain in 1866 and then
suspended again the following year, apparently because of uncertainty about
which way it should be extended out into the bay. Even so, three government-
commissioned inspectors, all engineers, reported in March 1869 that the

construction was solid, within budget and well managed by Ingeniero del Estado (State Engineer) Alejandro Prentice, a Scotsman who had worked in Lima for nearly twenty years and was well regarded for having introduced gaslight to the city.[2] Early in 1868, however, the government received an outline proposal to build more ambitious facilities in the form of a *muelle-dársena* (wharf and enclosed dock). It was submitted by José G. Rivadeneira, with backing from Buenaventura Sánchez, a businessman from the rival port of Valparaíso.[3] Just a few months later, Templeman and Bergmann proposed an almost identical design.[4] Although the Peruvian government expressed interest in Rivadeneira's plan and requested further details from him, he soon withdrew, for reasons that remain unclear. Templeman and Bergmann then cited the reports favourable to the Rivadeneira and Sánchez scheme as evidence for the general desirability of a *muelle-dársena*. The Peruvian Congress granted the firm the concession, by a slim majority, in August 1869, despite strong public resistance, orchestrated by the Callao Chamber of Commerce and its allies in the local press. Templeman and Bergmann appointed Mario Alleón, one of the few local experts who had supported its bid, as chief engineer for the purposes of the inauguration ceremony, but a few weeks later it contracted the work out to the English company Thomas Brassey & Co. The *muelle-dársena* opened in 1877, by which time Templeman and Bergmann had sold the concession to the French bank Société Générale.[5]

Once the docks were operational, the main focus of the controversy—and the aspect of the affair that has attracted most attention in the historiography—was the generous terms of the concession. Templeman and Bergmann was initially granted a monopoly of forty years, with even longer periods later being advocated before Congress reduced it, after lengthy and bitter debate, to twenty-five years in 1887.[6] The French company—which quickly realised it had been sold a pup—exploited its monopoly ever more ruthlessly in an attempt to recoup the losses it had made on the project.[7] By then, the fact that Société Générale was being run by associates of Auguste Dreyfus, the protagonist of the notoriously disadvantageous guano contract of 1869, cast the dispute in terms of the Peruvian national interest against an exploitative foreign enterprise. This had not been the case at the outset, however, when the point at issue was not the terms of the concession but the need for any such project. The fundamental choice in the late 1860s was between completing the *muelle* already in place and scrapping that work to embark on a *muelle-dársena*. Although there were differences of opinion about technical possibilities, the decision turned on different assumptions about which kind of knowledge was most legitimate.

The most damning commentary on the whole affair was made in a report by Mariano Paz Soldán, author of the first Peruvian atlas (see chapter 7), in his capacity as a former director of public works.[8] Paz Soldán refused to go quietly when his office was abruptly closed down by the government in November 1868, while arguments about the future of the port were in full swing. He was not himself a trained engineer, although his map-making work must have given him an understanding of the principles of surveying, but he justified his authority on the basis of ten years' experience at the Office of Public Works, spent reviewing and discussing a wide range of projects with engineers of all kinds. By the time he published his views, in 1870, the concession had already been granted, but he nonetheless evaluated Templeman and Bergmann's plans as if he were doing so in an official capacity. His report was a measured evaluation based on three criteria: necessity, technical competence and value for money. In later years, as the scale of the disaster began to unfold, it was repeatedly invoked as a model summary of the case against the *muelle-dársena*.

The crux of Paz Soldán's argument was that Callao did not need a *dársena* (enclosed dock), because the Peruvian harbour was 'naturally favoured' with calm waters, unlike ports such as Southampton, where enclosed facilities had made a big difference in protecting ships from tempestuous seas.[9] What Callao needed was precisely what was already being built, namely a new wharf. Even with only the existing short, rickety platform it had been possible to manage loads of great weight, observed Paz Soldán, so a new, longer and more solidly constructed *muelle* would serve all of Callao's present and future needs, making the proposed *dársena* 'a pure luxury'.[10] What was also required, in his judgement, was a *malecón* (embankment) to protect against flooding, but he insisted that given the benign conditions it did not need to be an expensive one and could easily be developed as an extension of the current *muelle*, in collaboration with local waterfront dwellers. His recommendation was to finish the new *muelle* already started by Prentice and adapt it to allow for a *malecón*. He maintained that no engineer who knew anything about the conditions of Callao would have advocated building a *muelle-dársena* and concluded that the engineer responsible must have known full well that the idea was not worth pursuing, because the drawings were anonymous. No engineering plan without a signature to guarantee 'precision and thorough study' would be admissible 'in any office or by any government'.[11] The proposed *dársena* was too small to accommodate current traffic, let alone provide for any expansion. Furthermore, the architect of the plan displayed his ignorance of Peru's customs administration, because the proposal would, if anything, exacerbate the problem of smuggling.[12] Paz Soldán's report went on to compare in detail the high costs of operating the *dársena*, claiming that on the basis of the charges envisaged by Templeman and Bergmann Callao would become more expensive a port than Liverpool.[13] It would be cheaper to unload at the port of Pisco, 127 miles down the coast, and transport goods by rail to Lima, than to dock at Callao.[14] In sum, the whole scheme of the *muelle-dársena* was inappropriate for Callao. The project was inherently expensive and would become even more so precisely because the conditions there were not right. All informed scientific opinion was against it.[15] If it went ahead, he accurately predicted, Peruvians would 'eternally rue the day'.[16]

Paz Soldán included a set of documents to show that the customs authority, the municipality of Callao and the *Fiscal* (Public Prosecutor) shared his doubts about the scheme. There is indeed plenty of evidence of local opposition. The Callao Chamber of Commerce campaigned vigorously against it, publishing a succession of critical reports and compiling a large dossier of documents to support their case that the whole venture was undertaken in disregard of 'the demonstrations of science' as well as in contravention of 'the spirit of the Constitution and the law'.[17] Yet a series of government-appointed commissions all came out in favour of the *muelle-dársena*, albeit without scrutinising the technical aspects of the proposal. The Commissioners of Public Works claimed that between the five of them they had little capacity to 'come to a scientific judgement' on the matter and had to rely on other reports. They duly chose to rely on those reports that supported the proposal. Even two professional engineers asked to comment on Templeman and Bergmann's plans confined themselves to enthusing that the *muelle-dársena* would be 'a colossal work, which would be [. . .] the first of its kind in South America'.[18] It seems that they were all, as Paz Soldán claimed, 'fascinated by the dazzling idea of seeing a *muelle-dársena* and *malecón* built at Callao'.[19]

In lobbying for the work, Templeman and Bergmann insisted that their scheme was the only one that constituted true modernisation, exhorting members of the Peruvian Congress to show that they were 'moved by that spirit of progress that tends to elevate modern peoples to the most advanced civilisation'.[20] The company made much of its connections in Europe, while adroitly playing the nationalist card by promising to use Peruvian materials. They accused their critics of deliberately suppressing 'the knowledge' (*el conocimiento*) that would make it possible to calculate the true costs of continuing with only a *muelle* and invoked the authority of the renowned Madrid reference work the *Diccionario de comercio y navegación* as 'proof' of their case.[21]

The sheer modernity of the *muelle-dársena* was impressed upon readers' minds by reiteration of the English word *docks*, in itself an inscription of the impossibility of comparison with the mere *muelle*, which simply did not belong in the same category.[22] The fact that no one with any serious expertise in port engineering had been consulted, as the newly established State Engineering and Architecture Corps concluded in 1874,[23] could not compete with Templeman and Bergmann's claims that its proposal was 'in harmony with the most advanced and liberal economic principles'; that it was the only one supported by accurate documentary evidence; and that anyone who opposed it was condemning Peru 'to the primitive age, when the forces of the intelligence could not transform matter'.[24] After Peru's defeat in the War of the Pacific, the *muelle-dársena* was duly paraded in upmarket illustrated magazines as 'one of those magnificent constructions that say much for the level of civilisation and advancement attained by Peru, in spite of its recent misfortunes'.[25]

Argentina's 'First Engineer' and the Port of Buenos Aires

Buenos Aires is a famous and significant port, but it is not a natural one.[26] Shallowness, silting, sand banks drifting in wayward winds and tides—all make for major engineering challenges. As late as the 1980s, when the Argentine government defied the United States by selling grain to the Soviet Union, not the least of the problems involved in this act of Cold War brinkmanship was that the huge Soviet grain tankers could not dock at Buenos Aires. Even today, there is a constant need for dredging. It is hardly surprising, then, that the port's nineteenth-century development was fraught with difficulties. By 1870 all there was to show for repeated attempts to build a modern wharf was a heap of discarded plans. These frustrations were partly caused by political factors—a series of costly wars, both internal and external, and the uncertain constitutional status of the city of Buenos Aires in relation to the rest of the country—but there was also a lack of consensus about the best technical solution, making it harder to secure finance for a project fraught with risk.

In the late nineteenth century, the building of a new port caused the first public controversy in Argentina that could meaningfully be described as national. It was played out in the two recently founded newspapers aspiring to national coverage, *La Nación* and *La Prensa*, which took opposing sides. The protagonists were Luis Huergo (1837–1913), known as 'the first Argentine engineer' because he was the first to graduate, in 1870, from the engineering degree newly established at the University of Buenos Aires, and Eduardo Madero

(1823–1894), a wealthy businessman and international trader. Engineer Huergo was already a public figure, elected to Congress while still a student. He was a founder and first president of the Argentine Scientific Society (1872). Unusually for an Argentine at that time, he had been educated in the United States, at a Jesuit college in Maryland, where he learnt English. Back in Buenos Aires, he trained first as a surveyor, then from 1865 as an engineer. In contrast, Madero, who had inherited a role in his family's business, had no technical training. After spending several years in Montevideo, however, he returned to Argentina preoccupied, some said obsessed, with ensuring that Buenos Aires had the modern facilities that would enable it to trump Montevideo's natural advantages. By 1870 he had already presented two plans for the development of Buenos Aires, both drawn up in collaboration with British engineers, neither of which had attracted sufficient political support.

There was a long-established practice, dating back to the 1820s, of inviting foreign—mostly British—engineers to tender for the modernisation of Buenos Aires port. In 1870, the very year in which the first cohort of university-trained engineers achieved their degrees, President Domingo Sarmiento commissioned yet another foreign expert to find a solution: Juan F. Bateman, whose plan—drawn up after spending less than a month in Buenos Aires—involved cutting a long canal in order to build the docks close to the heart of the city. It attracted 'a deluge of criticism' from locals, who argued that Bateman had completely underestimated the problems and the costs involved in such extensive dredging.[27] A government-appointed commission made up mainly of other 'foreign engineers' concluded that it would cost at least seven times what Bateman had estimated.[28]

It was in this context that Luis Huergo successfully argued for the development of the existing facilities at the alternative site of Riachuelo, just south of the city centre, in the area now known as Boca. As a reformist politician, recently elected as senator for the province of Buenos Aires, he wanted to avoid the huge costs he anticipated from pursuing any version of Bateman's scheme.[29] He sought a realistic proposal not a prestige project. Huergo's own design was supported by both politicians and engineers. It received state funding in 1876, and by 1883 works had progressed so well that one of the new transatlantic steamers, *L'Italia*, was able to dock at Buenos Aires for the first time. This event was hailed in the press, both in Italy and Argentina, as a vindication of the plan devised by 'a creole engineer, without authority in the scientific world and in opposition to the powerful opinions of an expert of European fame like Mr Bateman'.[30]

In light of this success, in 1882 Huergo submitted detailed plans to extend the docks northwards. The next thing he knew, apparently from reading it in his daily newspaper, was that the government had decided instead to back a third plan championed by Eduardo Madero, drawn up by the British company of Hawkshaw, Son and Hayter, with the promise of finance from Barings. The well-connected Madero had returned from a visit to London; sought an urgent meeting with President Roca, which he obtained through the good offices of his uncle, the vice-president; and persuaded Roca to support a plan supposedly designed by the great engineer Sir John Hawkshaw. In fact, Sir John had handed the project over to his son, who in turn passed it on to someone else. In general, the company specialised in railways rather than port works. Their plans were very sketchy and had been drawn up without even the briefest of visits to Buenos Aires; they ignored Riachuelo and all the existing facilities; and, indeed, they were very similar, with the same problems, to the Bateman project rejected in 1871. Yet Madero's proposal was forced through Congress by President Roca.

The legislature did, however, stipulate that the final version of the plans had to be endorsed by the Department of Engineers. The government first tried to circumvent this requirement by establishing a commission of experts, two out of the five of whom were English and US engineers. This commission reported that the drawings Madero had supplied were too sketchy to evaluate. What happened then, it later emerged, was that the president simply sent for the head of the Department of Engineers and ordered him to ensure that a set of suitable drawings was made, along the lines indicated by Hawkshaw, Son and Hayter.[31] When these supposedly 'definitive' plans were presented in 1884, they were approved by decree and Roca summoned three former presidents, no less—Mitre, Avellaneda and Sarmiento—to join him in ceremonially signing the contract with Madero.[32]

This public display of official preference for British over Argentine expertise unleashed a storm of criticism. The Argentine Assembly of Engineers of 1886 came to two unequivocal conclusions. One was that Hawkshaw, Son and Hayter's plan would not result in a good port for Buenos Aires (on the contrary, the high costs of its construction and operation would 'impose a burden incompatible with the general interests of trade'). The other was that Huergo's far more detailed design not only met 'the technical, general and commercial demands of a port for Buenos Aires' but also would cost only a third of Madero's plan.[33] Nevertheless, the government pressed on with the Madero-negotiated contract. Huergo and the head of the Department of Engineers both resigned and were publicly supported both by their colleagues and, more remarkably, by the thousands of people who turned out to cheer the awarding of a medal to Huergo in Boca del Riachuelo.[34] Work on what became known as Puerto Madero began in 1887 and was completed a decade later. It ran way over budget: even the supportive *La Nación*, which had always championed the project, estimated in 1919, conservatively, that it had cost at least twice the amount originally specified; French engineers simply dubbed it 'the most expensive port in the world'.[35] It was already congested by 1902 and ceased functioning altogether in 1925. In 1909 the government decided to build a new port, along the lines of what Huergo had envisaged back in 1882.

There are two key points to this story. The response of the English engineers to any of the specific criticisms set out by locally based engineers was to claim that their proposals were 'as advised by modern science and practice'.[36] Yet the experienced and distinguished Luis Huergo had actually done more than most individuals anywhere to modernise engineering. He carried out many other inventive projects, including sanitation and irrigation works throughout Argentina and in Paraguay, always undertaking extensive research into human health and nutrition to inform his engineering.[37] Despite all of these pioneering scientific endeavours, Huergo was denied the mantle of modern expertise.

The second point—which is perhaps even more telling—is that President Roca could not have secured the detailed drawings he needed to force this project through Congress had it not been for the fact that an engineering degree had been started at UBA in 1865, creating a cohort of trained, capable staff at the government Department of Engineering. Roca was reliant upon home-grown expertise to rectify the technical defects in the work of the foreign company he wished to impose.

The Invention of the *Frigorífico* (Refrigerator Ship)

In the historiography written by Spanish American historians, there are three main figures in this tale of an invention: the French scientist Charles Tellier (1828–1913), who carried out the necessary experiments; the Uruguayan landowner and entrepreneur Francisco Lecocq (1790–1882), who may have given him the basic idea; and the Uruguayan statesman Federico Nin Reyes (1819–1890), who saw the implications for international trade and funded the necessary trial runs. The point here is not to adjudicate between these and other competing claims, but rather to explore the basis upon which they were made and the resulting implications for understanding the politics of knowledge at that time.

Tellier's own account of the invention of the *frigorífico*, which was published long after the event, was a conventional reworking of the Romantic myth of the lone heroic genius battling against lack of support and recognition. Tellier protested, perhaps too much, about two points above all. First, he claimed that there was often confusion between the two methods of conserving meat: freezing with ice, which he noted was very ancient, and freezing with dry cold, which he insisted he had been able to do since 1867.[38] This was true, but misleading in that it conveniently omitted to mention the modern methods of freezing meat pioneered in Australia during the 1860s, which had been well covered in the European press. Second, he was equally keen to establish that the voyage of the steamship *Frigorifique* from France to Argentina in 1876, fitted with refrigerating equipment, was the first time that 'any meat or perishable goods conserved by cold' had been successfully carried 'between nations'.[39] His own experiments of 1867 were unknown in South America, he claimed, citing as 'proof' one fact from a report by Pierre Bergès, a renowned professor of palaentology at UBA, to the Congrès International du froid in 1908, referring briefly to a prize offered in Argentina in 1868. This was false: Tellier's work *was* known in South America, because after he had met Lecocq and Nin Reyes in Paris in 1867, Lecocq had paid for a test model of Tellier's machine, jointly hosted a banquet at which the meat was proven to be of high quality, then returned to Buenos Aires to try to raise funds to commercialise the invention.

Tellier did mention the two Uruguayans who visited him in Paris in 1866 and acknowledged their 'great influence on the direction' of his work, but he referred to them only *anonymously*, as 'two friends from the River Plate'.[40] He gave them credit for inspiring him with 'the desire, more ardent than ever' to find a way of transporting meat in cold conditions, but did not recognise any intellectual input from them.[41] While it is impossible to reconstruct exactly what transpired during these conversations, there is plausible evidence that Lecocq's contribution was, at the very least, of consequence to Tellier's subsequent success in developing the game-changing technique of dry refrigeration. Indeed, it is likely that Lecocq had the original idea of using dry cold rather than wet cold, which apparently occurred to him from observing how Uruguayan farmers hung carcasses on trees to preserve them for weeks in the cold, dry mountain air. Lecocq was sufficiently knowledgeable about modern science to be aware of the potential significance of his finding. He had some formal scientific training and on his estate in Uruguay he had, for some years, imported new plants and breeds of livestock into Uruguay and conducted a series of experiments in wine production, fruit-tree growing and silkworm cultivation, work which became well known internationally. In 1919 a move was made at the Exposición Agricola e Industrial Sud Americana (South American Agricultural and Industrial Exhibition) to recognise Lecocq's contribution to the refrigeration industry. His main champion, historian Ramón Carcano, argued that during 1865–68 Lecocq, aware of research in Europe, the United States and Australia into various ways of conserving meat with ice, travelled to Europe three times with the aim of trying to promote the alternative idea of dry cold.[42] Carcano presented evidence of patents Tellier secured in both Paris and London in 1866 for the use of dry cold for preservation, a year or so before Tellier's invention. But despite trying to mobilise contacts in London, Lecocq was unable to attract sufficient interest to exploit his intellectual property. In Paris the following year, he found Tellier at an impasse because his own machine for freezing meat in ice had proved costly and reduced the quality of the meat. The conclusion drawn by champions of Lecocq is that he gave Tellier the idea of using a current of cold air, which Tellier then implemented by designing a new mechanical process. There is even a contract signed by Lecocq and Tellier, article 5 of which recognised that 'Sr Lecocq is the owner of the idea'.[43]

Claims that Federico Nin Reyes had a scientific input into the invention are less convincing,[44] but what is well documented is that as a former finance minister of Uruguay he had an acute appreciation of the socio-economic implications of a successful refrigeration process. Tellier himself acknowledged that it was Nin Reyes's vision of Europe well fed and South America prosperous that spurred him on through a series of failures. Once Tellier had developed a fully functioning system, it was Nin Reyes who found a sponsor to test it on the successful voyage of the *Frigorifique*, carried out in a blaze of publicity. Tellier's failure to give full recognition to his Uruguayan colleagues or, indeed, his Argentine financial backers is particularly poignant, given that Tellier, himself challenged in the French courts by Ferdinand Carré, the inventor of a more economical system of dry refrigeration, ended up impoverished and reliant on financial aid from the governments of Argentina and Uruguay.

Given the enduring focus on the role of individuals in scientific invention, it is worth adding that both the Argentine state and the civil association of landowners, the SRA, played crucial enabling roles in the development of the frozen-meat industry. Thanks to the interest in new technologies stimulated by

its founders (see chapter 7), the SRA was quick to spot the opportunity to replace the declining salted-meat industry with a more lucrative export. In 1868
they offered a prize for the invention of a way of keeping meat cold without
impairing its quality. It went unawarded, but the SRA continued to promote
the possibility and made a major contribution to funding the test voyage of
1876. The following year, the SRA successfully lobbied the Argentine Congress
to keep exports of frozen meat tariff-free, a measure that enabled the nascent
frozen-meat industry to flourish, initially with mutton, later—again at the instigation of the SRA—with beef. One of Argentina's most successful export
industries was certainly not the outcome of laissez-faire, but of an intricate set
of transactions, over several decades, by governments, learned societies, civil
associations, and individuals who were scientists, entrepreneurs or a combination of the two. Nor was it wholly the result of European science, but rather of
a transnational process of collaboration, exchange of ideas, mobilisation of
contacts and pulling of strings in both the River Plate and northern Europe.
The same is true of perhaps the most ambitious of all infrastructure projects
undertaken in South America at this time: the transandine railway.

The Transandine Railway

A railway across the Andes between Argentina and Chile was first seriously
mooted in 1872 and finally completed in 1910, just in time for the independence
centennials of both nations. Some of the intervening delays were caused by
economic or political crises either in South America (the War of the Pacific,
1879–83; Chile's civil war of 1890–91; the flare-up of a border dispute around
the turn of the century) or in London, where the finance had to be raised (a
recession in the late 1870s; the banking panic after the Barings crisis of 1890).
Moreover, the whole undertaking posed huge technical challenges—the
Andes were far higher than the European Alps, where railways opened in 1903
and 1910. There were uncertainties among even the most experienced railway
engineers about the best route to take and the safest means of construction,
particularly of the tunnels. The persistence of problems was less remarkable
than the fact that they were all eventually overcome. For the first time, historian Pablo Lacoste has pointed out, a world-leading engineering project was
driven by countries that were not world powers.[45] In the midst of the various
political, financial and diplomatic factors that affected the history of the *trasandino*, one constant theme is the shift in public opinion from privileging foreign
expertise to recognising and advocating the importance of precise knowledge

of local conditions, both geological and political. It is also a revealing example of changes in conceptions of the role of the state and the related need for national control over infrastructure projects.

The story began in 1872, when two Chilean-born entrepreneurs, Juan and Mateo Clark, petitioned the Congresses of both Chile and Argentina for the concession to build a railway across the Andes. The Clark brothers of Valparaíso, born in 1840 and 1843 to an Argentine mother and a Scottish father, had made their reputations as bold and commercially astute engineers by raising capital to build a telegraph line between Argentina and central Chile, opened in 1872. The responses in the two countries to their projected railway could not have been more contrasting. In Argentina, the proposal was embraced as the means of realising the nation's true destiny as a conduit of people and goods between Europe and the Pacific. The Clarks played skilfully on the self-fashioning of Sarmiento's Argentina as a beacon of civilised prosperity, marshalling endorsements from influential foreign "friends of Argentina" such as William Wheelwright and Admiral Robert FitzRoy, who in an address to the London Royal Geographical Society had mentioned the transcontinental railway as potentially the shortest—and therefore the least costly—route from Europe to Australia. President Sarmiento himself was sceptical, noting that most of the world's trade circulated in the northern hemisphere and arguing that for any commercial benefits to be secured there would first have to be 'a direct war' against the Ranquel Indians.[46] But as he acknowledged in a letter to Manuel Montt, 'the mood of the public [...] recognised no limits, and the project had irresistible support in the legislative chambers'.[47] There was little scrutiny of the Clarks' plans, and their tender for what was customarily referred to in Argentina as 'the inter-oceanic railway' was quickly accepted. Moreover, the Clarks' route through the 3,800-metre-high Uspallata Pass was approved in preference to the alternative way through the Planchon Pass, which was favoured by two earlier surveys conducted by an Italian and a British engineer.[48] The Clarks succeeded in establishing their proposal as the most prestigious, posing greater challenges but also offering greater rewards than the alternatives, because it took the railway close to the main centres of population. In the Argentine Congress, the Clarks were well served by their boldness, which chimed with the optimism of the times. Argentina must take a risk, Vicente Fidel López urged the Chamber of Deputies, in 1873, to extend 'our personality and civilisation [...] by means of railways', just as in earlier times Argentina had sent 'weapons and freedom' to help liberate its neighbours from Spanish rule.[49]

In Chile, however, there was more immediate resistance to the Clarks' plans. When the Chilean Congress finally granted them the concession in 1874, it was not on the terms they had requested. At the same time, another concession was awarded to Chilean engineer Francisco J. San Román to build a trans-Andean railway to the north, across the Atacama Desert. The Clarks argued that the terms of their Chilean contract made it impossible for them to raise the necessary funds in London, because they could not guarantee financiers sufficient returns on a highly risky undertaking. A sympathetic fellow engineer wryly observed that each time the Clarks petitioned Congress for better terms, they ended up worse off.[50] When work began on the Chilean side, in 1889, it was partly funded by the Clarks themselves. In 1903 Congress finally agreed to terms almost identical to those they had refused back in 1874,[51] enabling the railway to be completed, although by that time the Clarks had lost control of the concession and were reduced to the role of advisers.

A review of the debates in the Chilean Congress in the 1870s shows that one concern expressed by opponents of the bid was reluctance to accept a role for the state as guarantor. At this time laissez-faire economics tended to set the parameters of debate. State capital should not subsidise private profit, it was maintained.[52] At a session in the Chamber of Deputies at the end of 1875, it was forcefully argued that the government had been too generous in relation to the trans-Andean railway schemes, thereby triggering unsolicited bids for support from other private companies, which should be firmly refused.[53] By 1897, when the terms of the Clarks' contract were discussed yet again, there was far less reluctance to see state involvement in such a project (see chapter 8). Indeed, some congressmen argued that the government should buy the line and finish it themselves, because even though 'governments are not in general good builders', even the 'least careful' of them could hardly do any worse than this particular private enterprise.[54] The Chilean engineer Luis Risopatrón (1869–1930), later the author of a classic *Diccionario jeográfico de Chile* (1924), went further in arguing that an international railway should always be under state control, never 'in private hands, much less in the hands of foreigners'.[55] The minister of the interior, forced onto the defensive about whether the railway would ever cover its costs, appealed first to a *local* authority: Enrique Budge Prats (1834–1924), 'former engineer of the State railways' and 'someone whose opinion could not be doubted', who had argued that, in time, the *trasandino* would become profitable. Only after dwelling on Budge's unassailable position as an expert on the subject did the minister mention the supporting view of Chapman, 'a great authority in construction works of this kind, not only in America but also in Europe'.[56] National experts were by then the primary source of legitimacy, and great concern was voiced about the lurking presence of the expansionist New York–based multinational company Grace Brothers among the Clarks' funders. The Clarks' remaining defenders in Congress had to insist that they were not 'vulgar crooks' but 'unfortunate industrialists who deserve our protection'.[57] In the court of public opinion, the Clarks had become denationalised.

Conclusion

The oft-reiterated claims that Latin American countries 'needed' foreign technical expertise in order to develop should be subjected to close scrutiny, because in the major projects surveyed here it was not that local expertise was lacking but that it was undervalued by those in power. Local engineers and their champions did their best to make their voices heard. Peruvian artist Federico Torrico, who knew many engineers from their shared days as drawing students, wrote a compelling case in 1868 for revising a contract with Henry Meiggs to give locally trained experts more control over building the Arequipa railway. He also advocated making the State Engineering Corps fully functional to ensure that their views could not be ignored.[58] In the late 1870s, Argentine state engineers succeeded in delaying approval of an amendment to the Clarks' contract so that the government was compelled to take the initiative in extending one of the state railways instead of waiting for the Clarks to start work on it. The presence of foreign companies was always contested. Throughout Latin America, specialists who knew the territory pointed out the faults of designs by engineers from abroad with little or no understanding of conditions on the ground. Yet it proved hard for local experts to prevail. The European or US companies traded on their capacity to reassure financiers, but in at least some cases a high level of foreign investment was required only because the designs were so exorbitantly expensive in the first place. The question of funding was often a smokescreen, or at most a partial explanation for dismissing pragmatic designs by locals in favour of grand schemes by foreigners.

What swayed opinion at key moments was that the European companies aggressively promoted their claim to be at the vanguard of modern science, insisting that only by supporting their plans could a nation's legislators demonstrate their disinterested commitment to progress, modernity and civilisation.[59] Any opposition was attributed to narrow self-interest or even baser

motives—for example, local traders contesting the Société Générale's claims
to a monopoly of Callao were accused of being the beneficiaries of smuggling.[60] Many congressmen were the products of an elite education, with its
ritual study tour of Europe, so they simply assumed that expertise from abroad
was superior. The status of the heroic technological pioneer was deemed to be
the preserve of foreigners: William Wheelwright or Henry Meiggs were portrayed as ruthlessly subduing the wildernesses of Latin America through sheer
force of character, while local engineers were discredited or ignored. The tendency to privilege foreign knowledge created huge gaps in expectations: foreigners were permitted—indeed expected—to present plans of a general nature, in accordance with their role of offering *a vision*; locals were required to
provide specific, detailed information, *a blueprint*. The results of accepting
sketchy outlines by engineers who did not know the local conditions in detail
included some disastrously inappropriate and expensive projects. It is hearten-
ing to note that Luis Huergo, whose skills were so casually dismissed by the
Roca government in its pursuit of links with London-based capital, spent his
last years campaigning for Argentina to establish state control over oil deposits, [61] which eventually happened in 1922 with the founding of Yacimientos
Petrolíferos Fiscales, the first wholly state-run oil company in the world.

10

Education for Citizenship

BEYOND MORALITY AND PATRIOTISM

EVERYONE WAS TALKING about popular education during the wars of independence.[1] It was one of the few priorities upon which royalists, reformers and revolutionaries could agree. Social order was the main rationale, but political legitimacy was also a widespread concern, as was, for a radical minority, public accountability: 'People: enlighten yourselves, enlighten yourselves, [then] you will recognise the farces and the comedies for yourself without the need for moral guides.'[2] In urban areas, the new periodical press, whether official gazette or self-proclaimed people's tribune, was passed around in markets and drinking dens, read aloud at bullfights and from the pulpit, discussed in general stores and at impromptu gatherings on street corners. If most people could not read, many of them would have known someone who could. The salience of the new printed matter as a public source of information and mobilisation made more people conscious of the power of literacy. It was not only that the elites were concerned to educate the people into becoming virtuous solders and citizens, but also that there were popular demands for knowledge to be shared. Expectations ran high: education was seen as the route to promoting political rights, industrial prosperity and social integration.

The independence era produced bold proposals for popular education policies that were radical in inclusivity (whom to teach), in approach (what to teach) or in method (how to teach). The rhetoric of inclusion sometimes sounded ringingly modern. In Lima, Fernando López Aldana (1774–1841), a migrant from Bogotá, in 1812 advocated education for all Americans—'the poor artisan, the unhappy Indian, the sad black, the *pardo*, the ignoramus [. . .] all have the right to hear and be instructed.'[3] In Buenos Aires, Mariano Moreno argued that schooling was the natural complement of the press in creating the capacity for informed public debate. In Santiago, the founders of the Instituto Nacional envisaged it as open to all on the basis of merit. Even if historians have shown that the actual plans were far less socially radical, entailing a hierarchical system of differential access to education,[4] the idea that education was a universal right was nonetheless in the air at the birth of the independent states. In Peru, the Constitution of 1823 stated: 'Instruction is a common necessity, and the Republic owes it equally to all its individuals.'[5] And the commitment to inclusion was not wholly nominal. In Buenos Aires in the early 1820s, primary school attendance was declared compulsory and one of the earliest schools for girls in the world opened, over a decade earlier than in Massachusetts. With respect to the curriculum, there were ambitious visions of integrating practical and political enlightenment in elementary education programmes in order to foster the industrial arts alongside humanistic learning. New methods were explored, notably teaching children to draw as a fundamental technique for opening both eyes and minds, integrating theory with practice, and arts with sciences (see chapter 4). Herein lie the seeds of a tradition of innovative thinking about education, which ultimately yielded famous fruits in the twentieth century with the radical pedagogy of Paulo Freire (1921–1997), the great Brazilian advocate of education as a means of consciousness-raising; the widely emulated literacy campaigns in Cuba during the early 1960s and Nicaragua during the early 1980s; and in contributions to the current body of theory known as social pedagogy.[6] This chapter will focus on the revival of this radicalism from the 1870s to the 1920s, a time when the partial successes of state policy brought a far wider range of people into debates about education hitherto dominated by intellectuals and policymakers.

In practice the independence-era dreams of a complete education to equip the population for life in a modern industrial republic gave way to a curriculum geared towards instilling basic literacy and the rudiments of civic patriotism through rote learning. The Lancasterian method, by which the most able pupils instructed the others in what they themselves had just learned from a teacher, was widely adopted, not least because it enabled many children to be taught by one trained teacher.[7] Nearly all governments declared it a priority to extend elementary education, but few of them did so consistently until the 1870s at the earliest. While the explanations for these histories of failure lie mainly in the absence of political stability or secure state revenues, historians of education have also identified a cultural preference among those in power to ensure that public education did nothing to challenge the social status quo. *Buen gusto* and *buena conducta* were prioritised over political rights or

industrial skills. The religious orders continued to provide most of the schooling available, at least in the rural areas, until the late nineteenth century. Even
the liberal Argentine education minister Vicente Fidel López, who was deeply
committed to providing state schooling, contemplated inviting the religious
orders to open schools in 1852 because they were the only people willing to
teach in the interior.[8]

These decades were not without innovation: there were notable instances
of experimental pedagogy, particularly in relation to the teaching of literacy,
the continual public discussion of educational policy and a dedicated periodical literature from early on. And there were individuals who continued to
argue for an ambitious vision of what schooling might achieve beyond civilising the supposedly barbarous masses. The most famous of them was Simón
Rodríguez (1769–1854), known outside the Americas mainly for the short
period of his early life as Bolívar's tutor, but who dedicated many years to testing out his educational theories in schools he founded in a succession of the
independent republics. He advocated schooling that was mixed by both race
and gender, secular, and dedicated to encouraging children to think and act
for themselves. His ideas were found to be still relevant in the second decade
of the twenty-first century.[9] Rodríguez's work has been widely discussed elsewhere,[10] so I won't dwell upon it here, where the most relevant point is that
he was far from alone in thinking deeply about the potential of education to
further the dream of emancipation. His career as a schoolmaster, which was
repeatedly interrupted by clashes with clergy, municipal officials and parents
in a succession of South American countries, also bears witness to the limits
of radicalism in education during the three decades after independence.

The mid-nineteenth century marked the beginning of what became known
as the *estado docente* (teaching state), which is in several respects a story of
achievement. I draw a few key points from the extensive historiography on
the expansion of state primary education in nineteenth-century Latin America,[11] in order to sketch out the context for my discussion of the criticisms
that came to the fore during the centenary years. Of my three case studies,
Chile was the first to establish a comprehensive school-building programme,
in the Ley General de Instrucción Primaria of 1860, which, on the basis of
census information collected by the Central Statistics Office, established in
1843, mandated the extension of free 'primary instruction' to create a school
for every two thousand inhabitants. The target was technically met by 1915,[12]
although the distribution of schools did not fully map on to the spread of
population, but there were sufficient school places to introduce compulsory

primary education in 1920. Famously, it was in Argentina, under the presidencies of Domingo F. Sarmiento (1868–74) and Nicolás Avellaneda (1874–80), that the most rapid programme of school-building anywhere in Latin America was carried out. Elementary schooling was declared free, compulsory and secular in 1884. By the early twentieth century, around 70 per cent of Argentine children were receiving at least some primary education and literacy rates in the society overall were relatively high, in comparison both to elsewhere in Latin America and to some parts of Europe.[13] In Peru, provision was far patchier, especially of state schools, with virtually no coverage in the highland areas of majority indigenous population, until José Pardo's government transferred responsibility from the municipalities to the central state in 1905; after which expansion into rural areas began, although it remained slow until the 1940s. Despite the undoubted problems, all three countries had certain achievements in public education to feature in official celebrations of the independence centenaries. The Argentine government highlighted its network of *escuelas normales* (teacher-training colleges) and its early promotion of education for women; Chile could point to its Servicio Médico Escolar (School Medical Service) and its introduction of secondary education for women in the 1890s; in Peru, the focus was on the provision of adult education for workers in Lima.[14]

For all these achievements, the *estado docente* had severe limitations, which are eloquently conveyed by Gabriela Mistral's dismissal of it as 'a kind of trust for the manufacture of unanimous minds'.[15] Dedicated to the teaching of morality and patriotism, it was a project endorsed by the combined authorities of civilian governments and the national militaries as they began to professionalise. In the justly admired teacher-training schools, swathes of the syllabus were devoted to *ciencia moral y urbanidad*,[16] so that the trainees could pass such precepts on to their pupils. The role of the military in this process of socialisation is worthy of note, especially in Chile, where between 1900, when military service was made obligatory, and 1920, when state primary education became compulsory, many young Chilean men were drilled in basic literacy and nationalism in barracks organised as 'schools of the people' by Prussian advisers.[17] In Argentina, military mores were conveyed directly into the state schools, in the form of a *Cartilla militar*, written by a military officer to prepare young people to defend their country, which in 1905 the government ordered to be distributed free to all pupils.[18] In all three countries, the virtues of obedience, work, charity, honour, hygiene, punctuality and—above all—patriotism were propounded in the educational press and in new teaching materials.[19]

The *estado docente* was a two-tier system of primary education for the common people and secondary education for the privileged.

There was no shortage of critics of state education who remained untroubled by the regressive effects of teaching basic literacy and good citizenship to the poor and liberal humanities to the well-connected in preparation for university. These elite-oriented critics championed a variety of ways to make the *estado docente* more efficient: extra resources, a broader curriculum, the use of home-produced rather than imported textbooks, and more teaching of national history. All of these policies, which were often sharply contested, made a difference to elementary education, but when major change occurred it came from outside these elite circles of statesmen-intellectuals in the cities. By the 1880s, one of the consequences of the expansion of public schooling was that a more socially diverse range of people acquired a stake in education policy. Once again, everyone was talking about education and the radicalism of the independence era was revived. In this chapter, I will focus on challenges to the model of education as morality and patriotism arising from social sectors to whom its limitations were all too apparent: women, artisans, industrial workers, immigrants and indigenous leaders. Even though many of the ideas aired during these years did not begin to be implemented until later in the twentieth century, they were crucial in keeping alive the vision of popular education as a means of furthering social inclusion, equality and justice.

Three strands of critical analysis developed, directed at pedagogic method, curriculum content and social purpose. Each of these lines of argument was present in all three countries, but for the sake of clarity I will illustrate each one with evidence from the country in which it was most prominent. The first critique countered the idea that children were receptacles to be filled—what Paulo Freire later called the 'banking' model of education—and advocated instead various models of participatory learning designed to foster individual agency and, as positions radicalised, collective solidarity. This case was first made by teachers thinking about how best to motivate small children— particularly in Argentina, where women did most of the teaching in primary schools; it also featured there in debates about adult education in workers' mutual aid societies, unions and political parties. The second critique challenged the academicism and humanism of a primary school system that reinforced social prejudices against any kind of work apart from the liberal professions, seeking instead to revive the independence-era interest in practical enlightenment. In Chile, led by leaders of organised labour and later by teachers, a two-decade campaign for vocational, technical and manual skills to be taught in primary schools alongside the traditional academic subjects achieved some success in legislation of 1920. The third and most radical critique sought to change the very purpose of education, transforming it from a means of reproducing social divides into a vehicle of social reform and even revolution. Such an approach was pioneered by indigenous educators and certain *indigenistas* in Peru.

Against Automatism: Participatory Learning

There was a flourishing market for teach-yourself manuals in Spanish America during the mid-to-late nineteenth century, mainly among the various middling sorts who were often well connected but not necessarily well off (see chapter 3). People from such backgrounds, especially women, often had a few years of formal instruction, enough to equip them to continue learning by their own means. Given those experiences it is unsurprising that they took a particular interest in how to stimulate people to learn. One leading example was Juana Manso (1819–1875), who was one of the first people in the Americas to elaborate an informed critique of rote learning. Born in Buenos Aires, Manso was able to attend one of Argentina's early schools for girls (run by the Sociedad de Beneficencia, created as part of a programme of secularisation in 1823), which antedated those in the United States (Massachusetts, 1837); but there was nothing for women beyond primary level until the 1850s, making them all in effect autodidacts.[20] Exiled in Montevideo during the Rosas years, Manso opened her own girls' school in order to earn her living. On finding that teaching required more than a knack for improvisation, she set herself to study modern pedagogic theory, which was possible in the relatively liberal cultural conditions of recently independent Uruguay, where she could discover Pestalozzi (1746–1827), advocate of 'learning by head, hand and heart', and Fröbel (1782–1852), inventor of the kindergarten. Manso was one of the earliest Argentine educators to be well versed in the international literature on education, having taught herself languages so that she could read it, and to have visited schools in a variety of countries, including Cuba and the United States. Back in Argentina during the 1850s she battled on all fronts for improvements in popular education, urging the importance of spacious, airy buildings, statistical data to inform policy-making, training for teachers and rigorous inspection procedures. She was an early champion of the controversial policy of laicising the state schools, leaving the child's religious instruction to the family and the church.

Many of the reforms enacted during the 1870s by Presidents Sarmiento and Avellaneda originated in Manso's work. Yet in several respects her model of a republican education was far more ambitious than state policy. In her view the purpose of education was to equip children for active participation in civil society, for which they would require a curriculum with 'all the seeds of the scientific ideas that preparation for modern life requires'.[21] Manso inveighed against the poor quality of textbooks—'woolly readings [*lecturas fofas*] will leave individuals woolly-minded [*fofos*] for their whole lives'—taking particular exception to Sastre's *Anagnosia* (1849), long the prescribed text for learning to read, which 'made idiots of children', she argued, reducing them to 'automatons'.[22] A child's mind was not 'a kind of basin or bag', to be filled up with 'church prayers, grammatical definitions, geographical descriptions', but fertile ground for cultivating 'the appetite for investigation, and the love of knowledge' necessary 'to resolve practical questions of life'.[23] Countering Sastre's metaphors of manufactured containers with images of living nature, she argued that children were endowed with 'natural perception', and 'a lesson in natural history is preferable to one in catechism'.[24] She thought, as Pestalozzi had done, about what kinds of teaching methods were likely to stimulate the creativity of small children. A school would ideally be a 'small museum of curiosities',[25] synchronising its efforts to stimulate self-motivated learning with a network of other cultural institutions, such as *academias libres* (private colleges offering specialised training, usually in a practical skill), libraries and theatres. Manso herself founded various popular libraries and she also wrote plays intended for popular, rather than elite, audiences.[26] But what really made the difference was that her commitment to stimulating children to find things out for themselves was shared by many other primary school teachers during the early twentieth century, four-fifths of whom were women.[27] In the 1930s and 1940s, Rosario Vera Peñaloza (1873–1950), famous for her work creating kindergartens, also ran a government-supported programme of museums attached to primary schools.[28]

Arguments against any passive mode of learning that focused on the mind in isolation resonated far beyond the state primary schools. It was a widely shared view that *educación* implied far more than formal instruction in schools, its meaning being closer to a complete preparation for participation in society—political, economic, cultural and moral. Civil educational and cultural associations, some entirely private, others partly supported by the state, came to play an important part in the development of Argentine education, especially among immigrants and workers, during the late nineteenth century.

An extensive network of popular libraries was created, which is still internationally admired today: in 2015 the Colombian government commissioned Argentine advice on how to establish popular libraries to help promote reconciliation in former conflict zones. The original enabling legislation was passed during Sarmiento's presidency, in the Popular Libraries Act of 1872. The idea was that these libraries would be autonomous civil associations, created by groups of local people, who could apply to the state for recognition and grants to contribute to their activities. Apart from collections of books and periodicals (and later other media), many of them organised programmes of cultural and social events. The majority of the libraries were created during the 1920s and 1930s, but some of the most active ones dated back far earlier.[29] The oldest example, which became a model for many others, was instigated in Buenos Aires by a Catalan immigrant printer, Bartolomé Victory y Suárez (1833–1897), attached to the mutual aid association the Sociedad Tipográfica Bonaerense.[30] The scale and scope of these local popular libraries and cultural centres varied at different places and times, but cumulatively they significantly extended opportunities to participate in the creation as well as the consumption of knowledge, especially for women.[31] Thus was the relationship between formal and informal education embedded.

Beyond the Humanities to Industrial Skills

In Chile a workers' education movement was started soon after the 1860 act, at least partly to compensate for what labour leaders saw as the inadequacies of state provision. Mutual aid societies spread rapidly throughout Chile over the next three decades,[32] and many of them tried to sustain adult education programmes. The main gap they sought to fill was the teaching of practical skills. Although the State took over many of these night schools in 1889, some of them retained their early commitment to offering workers the opportunity for technical education. A key figure was Fermín Vivaceta (1829–1890), one of Chile's earliest home-trained architects, who designed some of the major buildings of Santiago, notably the central market and the main building of the University of Chile. My interest here is in his experience of benefiting from educational opportunity and the work he subsequently did to create such opportunities for others. Vivaceta was born into a poor family and was still a young boy when his father died. His mother 'made every effort to give her son an education'—how many stories of social mobility hinge on a mother's tenacity—and she managed to secure him an apprenticeship. From that position, he was able to take advantage of the evening classes in drawing at the Instituto Nacional, introduced in 1846 to foster industrial skills among Chile's artisans and taught by José Zegers. Later on, in 1850, he joined the new architecture classes given by Frenchmen Claude Brunet de Gaines and Lucien Ambroise Hénault. He also benefited from a government decree of 1854, declaring that no degree was required to practise as an architect or mining engineer, so he was able to work as an architect although not formally qualified.[33] Vivaceta made haste to pass on his skills: picture him, still a student himself, spending his Sundays and holidays showing Santiago's painters and decorators how to supplement their broad-brush skills with fine ornamental work. [34]

In 1862, Vivaceta was one of the founders of a mutual society for artisans, the Sociedad Unión de Artesanos, which continued for fifty-four years and became one of the most important workers' organisations in Chile. [35] It was at his instigation that the society began to offer workers technical education alongside mutual aid. The society developed its own adult education programme, the Escuela Nocturna 'La Unión', later renamed after Benjamin Franklin, the archetypal example of social mobility, and later still after Vivaceta himself. Many of Chile's most distinguished public figures spent time teaching workers for free at La Unión, in what became something of a rite of passage for a political career. A delegation of government ministers, including the president, José Joaquín Pérez, attended the inauguration of the Escuela Nocturna, which was given the blessing of the *estado docente* as a model of workers' education.[36] Vivaceta himself became well connected and was invited in 1858 to serve on the board of the Sociedad de Instrucción Primaria, a private educational society formed in 1856 by liberal intellectuals, and later to select and judge the entries at the first Exposición Nacional de Artes e Industrias, staged in 1872. Even so, in continuing to make drawing a prominent element in its curriculum the school posed a permanent challenge to the absence of technical education in the state curriculum. La Unión's night school offered workers the chance to develop their practical skills, unlike other institutions of adult education, such as those founded by the Sociedad de Instrucción Primaria, where rote learning was rejected in favour of encouraging pupils to think, but the syllabus otherwise followed the academic and moralistic orientation of the state schools. By the early twentieth century, several thousand workers had studied at La Unión (over one hundred a year),[37] some of whom went on to campaign for popular education that was 'useful for the life of the arts and industries'.[38]

The efficacy of teaching practical skills was fully demonstrated by the work of the Servicio Médico Escolar, begun in Santiago in 1898, then extended to other areas of Chile and run for over thirty years by Eloísa Díaz (1866–1950). Díaz was the first woman in Chile to qualify as a medical doctor (at the University of Chile, in 1887, after the Amunátegui decree of 1877 had made women eligible for university degrees).[39] In her roles as doctor to an Escuela Normal and head of the medical service, Díaz carried out pioneering research on the conditions for successful learning, especially for teenage girls, insisting on the need for good ventilation, cleanliness, fresh air and the absence of hunger.[40] It was at her instigation that the Chilean state started to provide school breakfasts, to turn schools into centres for the vaccinations that were just becoming available against contagious diseases such as smallpox and typhoid, and to replace rudimentary toilet facilities with modern lavatories. The Servicio Médico Escolar also taught basic hygiene and preventative healthcare. There were undoubtedly many other school inspectors and medical personnel who helped to raise awareness of the possibilities for schools to be centres of practical education for daily life, although less is yet known about them.

Teachers themselves were enthusiastic advocates of applied learning. One of the concluding resolutions of the first Congreso Pedagógico in 1889 was to include manual work in the curricula of primary schools.[41] The next such Congreso Jeneral de Enseñanza Pública, convened by the rector of the University of Chile in 1902, became known for launching a campaign to make primary education compulsory, in light of persistently high rates of illiteracy (an estimated 60 per cent in 1907) and low rates of attendance.[42] A long debate also took place about the desirable balance between intellectual and practical education, with opponents of change registering anxiety that any shift towards the practical would result in materialism and a loss of morality among the population. That discussion ended in stalemate, but the next national education congress in 1912 resolved that manual skills should be introduced into all schools in order to enhance the status of industrial jobs. Teachers and educationalists also argued strongly for extending access to secondary education in order to promote national economic development.[43] The 1920 law to make four years of 'primary education' compulsory for all children also stipulated the teaching of practical skills in all primary schools—woodwork for boys and needlework for girls. Moreover, scientific subjects were to be taught 'in accordance with the economic necessities' of the locality, so that techniques learned in school could be applied outside. At the same time, the emphasis on national history and civic education was retained. The fact that an element of practical training had been introduced into the general curriculum meant that there seemed to be less need for specialist institutions. In 1920 nearly 5% of school-aged students were learning industrial skills, up from 1 per cent in 1900.[44] Clearly, the proportion was still low and it was to remain so. Advocates of dedicated technical and vocational training had to keep on making their case throughout the twentieth century and were still doing so during the disputes of the 2010s. Even so, Chile has done more than many other countries, in Latin America or elsewhere, to make technical education available.

Education for Social Transformation

It has been argued that autodidacts by definition shared the *iluminista* view that education was the route to a better life and were thereby complicit in the elite project of education for patriotic citizenship. Analogous claims have been made about the education programmes for workers run by anarchists and socialists: while they refused to teach patriotism, religious doctrine or morality, they nonetheless conceived of education as a means of individual, rather than collective, liberation. While there is some force to these arguments, I do not think they tell the whole story. Evidence from the writings of anarchist and socialist leaders implies that what might have started as a fundamentally individualist conception of education gradually mutated into a commitment to various kinds of social purpose. In this respect, labour leaders appear to have been radicalised by their constituencies, rather than the other way around. One such case was the Argentine anarchist Julio Barcos (1883–1960), whose activism as president of the Liga Nacional de Maestros from 1911 onwards took him away from anarchist libertarianism and advocacy of US models and towards a commitment to an Escuela Social geared to active learning for full participation in the community. He relentlessly attacked state schools for instilling passivity and obedience into children.[45]

After leading the first national teachers' strike in 1918, Barcos went into exile, where his observations of schooling in other parts of Latin America, especially Central America, increased his advocacy of the Escuela Social, which he repeatedly (albeit unsuccessfully) urged upon the Argentine minister of instruction. His ideas had more resonance in post-revolutionary Mexico.[46]

A well-known Chilean example of radicalisation from militancy is Luis Emilio Recabarren (1876–1924), the leader of the Partido Obrero Socialista (Socialist Workers' Party) founded in 1912, which ten years later became the Chilean Communist Party. Over nearly two decades of writing, mostly published in the workers' newspapers and periodicals produced by the socialists,

Recabarren's ideas about education transformed. In 1910, Chile's centenary year, when the government was making much of its commitment to education for all, Recabarren attacked the premise that improvements in literacy rates signified social progress. Knowing how to read and write did the poor no good, he argued, if they had no use for those skills in their everyday lives; indeed a little literacy was likely to prove a dangerous thing, in that individuals could be duped into signing documents they did not fully understand.[47] In this piece, he was thinking within a liberal framework that promoted education as a way to improve the lot of the poor, even though he was critical of the government's standard of judgement about what constituted 'progress'. Five years later, having lived among the nitrate workers of Iquique, he cast revolutionary politics as a struggle between two forces: 'the force of the past which holds us back' and 'the force of the present which opens the door to a marvellous future'.[48] The state school curriculum, with its 'out of date ideals, antiquated formulae, hypocrisies, immoral teaching', all of which enslaved and corrupted children, was now an enemy of the people against which revolutionary struggle had to be waged.[49] In order to do so, the Partido Obrero Socialista committed its scarce resources to a network of publications, lectures, adult education centres, reading groups and socialist theatre, in the belief that there would be no socialism without a new culture and that, as war laid bare how 'barbarous' Europe had become, the future of the modern world lay in the Americas.[50] By 1924, Recabarren had brought together a printing works, a library and a lecture theatre, which he identified as 'powerful tools for building [. . .] the future life of the revolutionary proletariat' that would transform the Chilean nation.[51] From seeing (informal) education as a vehicle for bringing civilisation to the working class, he came to regard it not only as a necessary component of workers' emancipation but also as the means by which a working-class version of civilisation, based on solidarity and a participatory culture, could be brought to Chile.

Extensive evidence of workers adapting educational theories to suit their own needs can be found in the Peruvian labour press. The first anarchist periodicals in Peru were founded by intellectuals, notably Manuel González Prada,[52] but the anarcho-syndicalist organisations created in the 1900s did not welcome the involvement of students or intellectuals,[53] so their publications were increasingly written, produced, circulated and funded by workers themselves, notably *La Protesta* (1911–26) and *El Obrero Textil* (1919–25).[54] After 1920, when the government destroyed the printworks where these journals were produced, labour organisations clubbed together to fund an *imprenta proletaria* to keep them going.[55] These periodicals contain accounts of and publicity for an extensive network of informal cultural resources created by and for workers: libraries and reading groups; centres for concerts, plays and the popular *veladas literario-artísticas*; evenings of recitation, music, song, short stories and comic sketches, often ending in a dance.[56] Most of this informal cultural life took place in or near Lima, but workers' cultural centres could also be found in cities such as Trujillo and Arequipa, a transit point for anarchist currents from Argentina.[57] Many activists used pseudonyms, because government repression was severe, particularly after the mass demonstration against the consecration of Peru to the Sacred Heart of Jesus on 23 May 1923. It is therefore hard to identify them all with certainty. Even so, historians of the Peruvian labour movement have collected plenty of evidence that anarchist workers played a prominent role in advocating the importance of art, culture and education to any process of social liberation.[58]

In their journals, workers deployed anarchist arguments against state provision of education. In 1915 the leader of the bakers' union, Delfín Lévano, one of the main architects of the successful campaign for an eight-hour day, deplored the fact that anyone 'who could read and write to an average level' could open a school, so long as they could find someone in the government to protect them. Such impoverished instruction, geared to teaching a child 'to scribble his name' or 'to count the daily pay of a worker or the tip given to a sergeant', 'perverts a child's sentiments, confuses his intelligence and impairs his reasoning.'[59] In any case, even good instruction would not guarantee a true education, he argued, in a speech of 1921 to peasant workers: instruction was the absorption of knowledge, while education entailed making the most of that knowledge 'in order to live better' and to direct all one's efforts towards goals that were 'useful and beautiful, just and noble'.[60] A school could be a prison in which children were locked away 'to mutilate their intelligence, crush their will, restrict their independence and atrophy their brain', or it could be 'a temple dedicated to truth' where 'fraternity and liberty' could reign. It was up to the workers to claim 'the rational life' to which they were entitled.[61] The anarchist press also contested the political merits of initiatives by Marxist intellectuals to educate the workers, debating whether the Universidades Populares or the Bibliotecas Obreras were devices for co-opting workers to the bourgeoisie or a resource for destroying bourgeois society.[62] The anarchist workers of Lima did not need to listen to José Carlos Mariátegui to know that culture was an arena of struggle between capitalists and workers, or that art could be either liberating and life-enhancing or 'second-rate and commercialised'.[63] 'As workers of muscle that we are,' Delfín Lévano said in defence of the Centro Musical Obrero (Workers' Musical Centre), 'we want to serve, in the same way as the painter, the actor and the progressive pedagogue, the poet, journalist and revolutionary orator, the great cause of spiritual dignity and social emancipation'.[64] Indeed, when Mariátegui returned from Europe in 1923 and set out to politicise the Universidades Populares, 'defending the Russian Revolution, preaching internationalism and the united front, eventually overcoming the protests of the anarchists',[65] it is likely that the influence was not all one-way and he took on board some of their arguments. When Mariátegui made his famous arguments that culture was a crucial element in revolution,[66] he drew upon years of observing the cultural and educational practices of Peruvian workers' organisations.

Indigenous Educators

One of the most transformative visions of popular education at this time was elaborated in Peru by José Antonio Encinas (1888–1958). Encinas was born and raised in Puno, a city and province high up in the south Peruvian Andes, with a majority of indigenous people who, as became evident in an official survey of 1901, had no access to any schooling, either state or Catholic.[67] In his writings and those of other Puno-based *indigenistas*, we are given glimpses of the experimental pedagogy of certain indigenous educators in the region, which evidently informed and inspired his own practice. After training as a teacher in the first cohort of the Escuela Normal de Varones, opened in 1905 in Lima—without its own library! he recalled in amazement—he returned to Puno to run an experimental 'new school', the Centro Escolar 881 (1907–11).[68] In his account of this school, written fifteen years after its closure, Encinas observed that he had opened it at a time when the indigenous peoples were represented in the public sphere as victims of oppression (a decade before the separatist rebellion of 1915–16, led by Rumi Maqui in nearby Azángaro, shattered stereotypes of stolid passivity[69]) and excluded from what was deemed to be culture in Peru. The nation's Lima-based writers were oriented towards Europe, he claimed, its students wrote dissertations on Dante or Shakespeare, its poets sang the glories of Napoleon—no one was interested in indigenous art or music, no one studied their social, economic or legal affairs. The 1870s vogue for Quechua had passed; the 1920s literary and artistic embrace of *indigenista* themes had not yet begun. The municipality of Puno banned indigenous people from playing their music in the city, deeming it to be more

important that they learn how to dance the waltz, observed Encinas causti-
cally, than that their usurped lands be restored. In such circumstances, it was
incumbent upon the new school to create 'a true spirit of social equality' and
to become a microcosm of social harmony. Encinas's school taught, in Quechua, all the usual subjects—reading, writing, arithmetic, history, geography
and natural sciences—plus daily 'manual work', which included geometry and
drawing, as well as the artisanal skills of carpentry, shoemaking, pottery, iron-
work and printing.[70]

Encinas encouraged his pupils to think for themselves, mocking the
question-and-answer format of the pedagogic catechism in a passage that demanded: 'What is an automaton?' (Answer: 'a pupil who repeats what he does
not know').[71] He also discarded the conventional textbooks, arguing that too
much book learning ('la escuela libresca') depleted students' mental energy
and thereby weakened their capacity for observation and experiment.[72] He
criticised the internationally fashionable object lessons, on the grounds that
such an approach 'mechanised teaching', overcomplicating simple objects with
explanations fit for only casuistical medieval theologians. At his school, he
declared, they 'archived that famous book by Sheldon' and took the students
out to look at nature.[73] In history lessons, 'we set aside that whole catalogue
of names and the dates on which they were martyred', approaching the subject
instead as a means of 'awakening and fortifying the children's critical sense,
principally from a social point of view'.[74] Geography was taught in the context
of history; no one was required to memorise lists of the world's rivers or the
mineral products of distant lands. He encouraged the students to put on plays
and concerts for local residents and he founded a periodical at the school, *El
Educador de los Niños*, to increase awareness of his model. There was no religious instruction and morality was taught more to foster sociability than to
instil individual good conduct. Teachers in Peru had no need to resort to the
Bible to explain the origin of the world and humankind, Encinas argued,
because they could call upon the legend of Wirakocha, the Peruvian god that
'not only creates, but also organises, encourages and impels life'. Wirakocha
created humankind not as individuals, like the Christian God, but instead as
peoples (*naciones*): where Jehovah sowed division, Wirakocha brought unity,
thus providing the appropriate spirit for a modern, enlightened republic.[75]

Encinas's memoir identified two predecessors. One was the Escuela de Per-
fección, which was run by indigenous teacher Telésforo Catacora (1880?–
1906) in collaboration with the Sociedad Fraternal de Artesanos of Puno. Even
though it followed the official agenda in teaching citizenship and hygiene

together with basic literacy, it was closed down by the local authorities after less than a year (1903–4). Later, it came to be seen as a precursor of the popular universities of the 1920s. A young Encinas (aged fourteen or fifteen) worked there as a secretary, and Telésforo Catacora later trained alongside him at the Escuela Normal. When Catacora tragically died after the first year of teacher training, Encinas became friends with Francisco Chuquihuanca Ayllu, who was equally committed to transforming Peruvian education to favour the interests of the indigenous peoples.[76] The second early indigenous school was initiated by Aymara leader Manuel Camacho Alka, who began teaching literacy in his house in Utalwilaya, Platerías, in 1902, the success of which caused intense local hostility resulting in its closure in 1908.[77] Camacho Alka then took a strategic decision to invite US Seventh-Day Adventists, with whom he had made contact during a visit to the United States, to establish a mission in the region, because in his experience 'gringos were good at getting along with the authorities in Peru'.[78]

Encinas became increasingly critical of all aspects of state elementary education, arguing that a lack of effective planning or a clearly defined purpose had undermined the isolated attempts that had been made to improve it—that is, Manuel Pardo's efforts of 1876 to create a network of popular libraries and José Pardo's decision of 1905 to transfer control over schools from the municipalities to the central state—so that neither initiative achieved anything like what had been done in Argentina.[79] When the government opted in 1909 to contract US teachers, they had done so without due diligence, not even taking the obvious step of approaching universities, which would have been at least an indicator of competence and seriousness. As a result, the US Americans who came knew little about Peru or did not speak Spanish.[80] In any case, Encinas deemed official education policy to be inappropriate to Peru in almost every respect: it was urban-based, when three-quarters of the population was rural; it rewarded book learning when most people sought practical skills; it was individualist rather than collective in orientation; it failed to reconcile tensions between nationalism and Christian universalism; and it stubbornly adhered to mind-numbing rote learning.[81] Everybody in the educational system had the spirit of innovation crushed out of them: the whole approach was geared to 'quash [*concluir con*] the child's personality'; teachers were undervalued, inspectors were entangled in bureaucracy.[82] The situation was particularly bad for the indigenous peoples, declared Encinas, whose ways of life were entirely disregarded in state education policies. It was not surprising that indigenous people had resisted various state initiatives—'mobile schools, propaganda campaigns, boarding schools, workshop schools'—that all had the same purpose, namely to compel them to abandon their own culture and community for a few years of nationalist indoctrination only to return them to unskilled manual labour or use them as cannon fodder.[83]

In the context of an ongoing debate in early twentieth-century Peru about whether the state's priority should be to create active citizens or skilled industrial workers, Encinas questioned the very premises of that discussion.[84] He drew upon the ideas of the international New School movement, but went far beyond them to elaborate a comprehensive new policy that he called 'social education'. Encinas started from the argument that a school had to serve the surrounding community in its day-to-day activities. Rather than designing a curriculum and a timetable on solely 'pedagogic' grounds, as if the school were an enclave, he argued that 'it should be organised socially, creating in the village different groups to improve agriculture, care of livestock, architecture, public and private hygiene, sport, dance, music, cooperative societies for production and consumption, and mutual aid societies to protect infants, the elderly and the sick'.[85] Peru could not afford to postpone the social benefits of schooling to some future, unspecified date. Any educationalist who focused only on pedagogy understood nothing about how children learn, he argued. He argued that through 'direct contact with the needs of society and with the phenomena of nature', a small child would soon acquire the capacities of observation, reasoning and judgement,[86] which would gradually eliminate superstition from its spirit. It was crucial to this delicate process that teaching methods were never didactic or authoritarian, but instead designed to create an atmosphere of trust in which students had the confidence to ask questions, express doubts and develop at their own pace. Although he did not begin by focusing on 'indigenous education', he came to the view that the practices that had worked well with students of indigenous background were a good way forward for the primary schooling of all children. In Encinas's view, the qualities that helped such a mode of learning were particularly strong among indigenous people: 'The man of the Andean high plateau is distinguished by sobriety in speech, exactitude in imagery, precision and acuity in observation, persistence in effort, loyalty to a principle and by a permanent desire for renovation.'[87] 'The Indian', he insisted, was 'dynamic' in his approach to life, not static as often portrayed, engaged in 'permanent action' the whole time: it was 'absurd' to accuse him of 'mental passivity'. Directly refuting the stereotype of the fatalistic Indian 'sitting on a rock, playing mournful songs (yaravíes)', Encinas emphasised that the indigenous people had 'created an empire and today were still as brave, auda-cious and energetic as before'.[88]

Encinas's own pedagogy came to be founded more and more on the ethics and teaching practices of the *ayllu* (self-governing and self-sustaining Andean indigenous community). He began to champion indigenous social organisa-tion as the basis for the transformation of Peru. Like Gamaliel Churata and also Mariátegui, he argued that a change in the economic situation of the in-digenous peoples was necessary before education was likely to benefit them. Their lands had to be returned to them in a policy of 'Escuela con tierra propia', as proposed in post-revolutionary Mexico and Russia.[89] But Encinas rejected the Soviet view of education as geared towards material production, instead presenting the indigenous self-governing community of the *ayllu* as the ideal model for a complete education that would integrate individual and social development, theoretical and practical learning, intellectual and ethical ex-pression. The *ayllu*, which was organised around common land ownership, shared labour and reciprocal exchange, was based on 'a profound social ethic', which was 'stronger, more humane and more noble than the Christian ethic'.[90] Rather than inculcating patriotism or industriousness, for Encinas the purpose of education was to create new men and women, energised by the natural world, to be the agents of a socially just future. Increasingly, he saw the 'incor-poration of the aboriginal element [. . .] into national life' as Peru's greatest priority.[91] Unlike many activists at the time, including those who identified as *indigenistas*, he argued, in his doctoral thesis, that Peruvian law should adapt to the Indian rather than the other way around.[92] Instead of advocating sepa-rate schools for indigenous people, as did the influential Asociación Pro-Indígena,[93] Encinas championed indigenous ways of transmitting knowledge as a model for the education of all Peruvians.

It took decades for the Peruvian state to improve educational provision for the Andean indigenous population. During the 1920s, the supposedly *indigeni-sta* government of Augusto Leguía (1919–30) promoted a policy of teaching indigenous children in Spanish, even by Quechua- or Aymara-speaking teach-ers.[94] The estimated rate of illiteracy in 1940 of 87.5 per cent was even slightly higher than the 86.9 per cent of 1902. When APRA (Alianza Popular Revolu-cionaria Americana) came to power in 1945, the anthropologist and activist Luis Valcárcel became minister of education, publicly acknowledged the shameful history of failure and began a serious programme to make education available to the indigenous populations, but it was abruptly curtailed after the coup of 1948. Reform was not seriously attempted again until the military government took power in 1968. Even so, Encinas's work, based on his knowledge of the ideas and techniques of indigenous educators, had introduced into Lima's public awareness the idea, which proved ultimately impossible to dismiss, that attempts to Hispanicise the indigenous peoples through state schooling were bound to fail.

Conclusion

This chapter has highlighted a series of struggles about the purposes and methods of primary education, starting from the very foundation of the new states in the 1820s. It is a story of short-lived achievements, of many reverses, in all three of the countries that provide my case studies. The overall shape of events can be summarised briefly: the demand for the sharing of knowledge arose in the time of the wars of independence, as shown by the enthusiasm for the creation of libraries in the new states. Such ambitions were frustrated by the period of war and conflict. When oligarchic governments were in a position to pursue consistent education policies, they opted for a curriculum focused not on the extension of learning and skills but on the instilling of rudimentary academic knowledge in the pursuit of state-approved morality and patriotism. From the late nineteenth century onwards, however, the extension of public schooling brought many new actors into the frame of debate—notably teachers, many of whom were women, and unionised workers—who began to campaign against rote learning, the dominance of the liberal professions, the lack of technical training and the poverty of ambition about what popular education could be. A tradition of autodidacticism stimulated a range of new ideas about the conditions for successful learning and about the social purposes of education.

Although, for most workers, denial of opportunity continued to be the hallmark of the educational system during the early twentieth century, there is, all the same, clear evidence that the efforts of the workers' education movement did have lasting successes in extending the skills and knowledge of working people. They provided night schools, libraries, speakers, pamphlets, newspapers, magazines and even popular universities, all operating on the slenderest of means but nonetheless often conveying news and ideas of remarkably cosmopolitan reach. Workers could learn about the struggles of their counterparts not only in the Americas and Europe but throughout the world. They saw images of the Haymarket Affair in Chicago and of Kemal Ataturk; they heard lectures on the New Zealand welfare state and the Indian strike movement of the 1920s. It is worth emphasising how transnational these networks of labour publications were: through the policy of *canje* (exchange), the popular libraries in workers' cultural centres had copies of publications from neighbouring countries and sometimes further afield. In the library of the Casa del Pueblo (run by Lima's Centro Socialista), for example, a reader could find 'workers' periodicals from all over the world'.[95] The new ideas propounded by the workers' education movement created opportunities for organised labour to contest conceptions of citizenship geared to the maintenance of class hegemony and to develop more participatory alternatives. It took several more decades after the 1920s—beyond the Second World War—for states to develop inclusive popular education policies. Yet during the early twentieth century, looking beyond the formal state system and the prominent intellectuals uncovers a collective endeavour of popular nation-making through educational practice.

Conclusion

MY SURVEY of landscapes of knowledge in Spanish America over the hundred years or so after independence has led me to three conclusions about the history of knowledge in general:

First, the recognition of knowledge matters as much as the production or distribution in analysing outcomes of past and present struggles to extend access to knowledge. How is it that certain ways of knowing are deemed worthy of being received as knowledge? Who decides what actually counts as knowledge, even before it is subject to validation?

Second, a nation-state can be revealingly interpreted as a community of shared knowledge, which provides a more flexible and more grounded analytical framework than Anderson's idea of an imagined community.

Third, the knowledge order of a society will affect its capacity to achieve integration, constitutional legitimacy and political participation.

Recognition of Knowledge

Thinking about how knowledge was recognised makes it possible to bring into the same analytical framework three fields of enquiry that are often treated separately:

1. Global hierarchies that privileged knowledge made by imperial powers, first in Europe, later in the United States of America;
2. The dynamics of any particular society, including state-building at all levels (central, provincial, municipal) and contending with legacies of colonialism; and
3. Epistemological communities of varying scope and reach. The evidence from Spanish America shows that all three of these elements need to be considered in order to understand what happened.

Take, for example, the claims by independence leaders that ending Spanish rule would open the doors to modern knowledge. In making such claims, the Liberators of Spanish America chose to situate themselves and their potentially sovereign states within international circuits of recognition, both diplomatic and cultural. There were sound anti-colonial reasons for this decision, related but not reducible to the more obvious strategic motivations of manoeuvring to secure support from European powers. The concept of sovereign statehood entailed the enlightened philosophy and experimental science that would usher these countries into the modern age, freeing them from scholasticism, superstition and ignorance. There was to be no looking back: 150 years before Frantz Fanon wrote about the decolonisation of the mind, Spanish Americans proclaimed that life after colonialism would require new ways of thinking, a new epistemology.

The claim to be founding a new order of knowledge resonated because it contained a significant element of truth: there was an influx of the ideas later identified as 'the European Enlightenment'. Like most foundational statements, however, it contained a measure of falsehood. Methods very similar to those that came to be associated with Enlightenment thinkers in France, Germany and Britain had been practised in Spanish American universities, such as San Marcos in Lima, since the late seventeenth century. In other words, the leaders of independence were continuing a long-standing debate in the region about the extent to which 'enlightened critique of reality' should be privileged over divinely revealed knowledge. In most of their texts, the Liberators pursued the long-established practice of criticising ideas from Europe in light of evidence from the Americas, but their strategic positioning embedded from the outset the idea that 'modern' knowledge came from *outside* the region rather than from within it. This idea seemed to be confirmed by the fact that the wars of independence overlapped with a remarkable period of successful invention in Europe and the United States.

Everybody has always borrowed ideas and techniques from elsewhere, as Voltaire deftly conceded when he defined originality as judicious imitation. Over the course of the nineteenth century, however, various forces combined to create hierarchies of knowledge in which some acts of imitation were celebrated as of wide general applicability while others were dismissed as only of relevance in the specific locale of their production. The travelling show that was 'European' knowledge had an impressive range of props at its disposal: the invention of the romanticised figure of the scientist; the creation of disciplines, with their international congresses and supposedly open journals; the validation ceremonies conducted by men in frock-coats buttressed by classical plaster casts and cut-glass chandeliers in the learned academies of the imperial capitals. As a wealth of work has shown, concepts, classification systems and modes of thinking produced in the particular contexts of European countries were gradually projected, through imperial power, as of universal validity. By the time new republican governments began to design policy in the 1820s, there was a dominant view among policymakers that the knowledge required to make a modern polity would have to be imported. Even though many Spanish Americans, throughout the nineteenth century, drew attention to the inadequacies of European philosophy and science in the contexts of the Americas—after all, the logic of empiricism is that theory is deduced from specific, observable evidence—'European' ways of knowing became the standard by which other kinds of knowledge were evaluated and normally found wanting. Given the precarity of their position, the upper classes had their own reasons for privileging a certain kind of knowledge to which they could control access. Before the requirement to be national came the requirement to be decent, to demonstrate good taste and good behaviour, all of which came cloaked, literally, in European garb. In the specific historical conjuncture of the first quarter of the nineteenth century, what started out as a move against formal colonialism ended up opening the door to informal empire.

The consequences were profound, lasting and damaging. Most tragically of all, the kinds of knowledge produced in indigenous communities went unrecognised as knowledge that was applicable to anybody else, dismissed as tradition or superstition irrelevant to the making of a modern polity, thereby laying the epistemological groundwork for policies of violence and exclusion. There were always critics of this point of view—for example, at the University of Cuzco—but they were isolated and had little impact on mainstream thinking until the 1920s, when indigenous peoples' organisations began to operate at the national level. During the century after independence, the republic of knowledge was in principle open to all, and in practice a perhaps surprising number of *individuals* from outside the upper classes succeeded in establishing a place for themselves, but the price of admission was acceptance of the imperative to become modern, which came to mean being integrated into a nation-state. Any group of people that preferred to continue as a distinctive community was denied the status of knowledge producers.

The prestige attached to knowledge from Europe by those in power during the early republican period meant that the knowledge created in colonial institutions of learning, by creole, indigenous and mixed-race intellectuals, was also largely ignored. Intellectual historians have only recently begun to highlight the contributions of scholars in the universities of Spanish America to intellectual debates that took place across the common cultural field of Europe and the Iberian Americas during the seventeenth and eighteenth centuries. The field became separated out over the course of the nineteenth century, partly because of the European claims to universal knowledge, partly because of an *Americanista* response. From the mid-century onwards, Spanish Americans began to create canons of their own knowledge, especially in history and literature. In this new context, it became something of an anti-colonial act for Spanish American intellectuals to visit the archives in Spain to copy documents from the colonial period that were unavailable in the Americas (whether they did so to reject the colonial past or to recuperate it as part of American history). From the 1870s onwards, as nation-states increased in capacity, there was an increasing emphasis in public debates on 'national' or homegrown knowledge. The history of school textbooks, the contents and authorship of which were often fiercely contested, exhibits the transition from the mid-nineteenth-century preference for translating French or English versions to the late nineteenth-century insistence on commissioning nationals to write them from first principles. What didn't change much was the requirement to learn European ideas and theories first, making them what was necessary to know, while reducing knowledge of and from the Americas to a supplementary role. And nationalism created all the pressures of the burden of representation: knowledge practitioners were increasingly denied universal reach, instead expected—both abroad and at home—to be authentic expressions of their local culture. As the Peruvian poet César Vallejo put it in the 1930s: 'Why do I always have to be "Peruvian" when I write?' Although Vallejo had been living in Paris for over fifteen years, he still felt condemned to be national, denied the possibility that anything he said or thought could be deemed of interest beyond its relevance to the country where he happened to have been born; that is, he felt—and he was—denied the possibility of being fully human.

Latin America was generating knowledge throughout the nineteenth century, but it was not always recognised, either at home or abroad. My findings contribute to an expanding historiography that challenges perceptions of Latin America as peripheral to grand narratives of political and economic modernisation led by the North Atlantic countries.[1] This book has highlighted the importance of conceptions of knowledge in sustaining the analytical frameworks that condemn some parts of the world to playing eternal catch-up. My case studies of infrastructure projects have demonstrated how expensive the privileging of foreign expertise could be. In other fields of knowledge, American realities brought out the inadequacy of scientific terminology and classification schemes. In important ways European science depended on science from elsewhere, not the other way around. Strategies of appropriation are usually identified in the reception of ideas *from* Europe, but it was the Europeans—not to mention the US Americans—who were past masters of the art. Imperial powers scooped up other peoples' knowledge alongside more material booty, appropriating or discarding in ruthlessly instrumental fashion what they deemed useful. The secret of their success lay in their capacity to dissemble, casting a 'civilising' net to disguise the loot and plunder of histories and cultures. The freedom to imitate without being dismissed as derivative is a privilege indeed.

The lack of recognition of knowledge from Latin America is a loss for everyone in the post-imperial nations as well as in the region itself. There's a long history in Latin America, dating back to the early colonial period, of probing the limits of knowledge from Europe: correcting European errors, criticising European misunderstandings and challenging European abstractions in light of conditions in the Americas. After independence, debates took an epistemological turn, resulting in the creation of work on themes that are strikingly current today. To give three examples: critiques of instrumental rationality that sought to retain what might be called a democratic, rather than an imperial, role for reason; questioning of binary divides that laid the foundations for later work on hybridity; and scepticism about absolute universals that sought to avoid full relativism. It became almost a convention to preface any report on knowledge with a history of whichever area of knowledge was under discussion; an argument for a common meridian, for example, started with a history of geography, moving from Ptolemy in Alexandria to the Arabs after their conquest of Iberia, with the thirteenth-century meridian at Toledo, then to northern European countries and, later still, to Russia and the United States—the effect being to highlight how centres and peripheries of knowledge generation shifted across time and space, an early example of 'provincialising Europe'.[2] Critiques of the Enlightenment and of modern science were produced elsewhere, including of course in Europe itself, but they featured strongly in Spanish America because of the region's distinctive history of the early end of colonial rule combined with early experiences of informal empire.

Attention to the processes by which knowledge is recognised is the most effective way of countering diffusionism and Eurocentrism. It rejects diffusionism but avoids the pitfall of 'local' determinism. Indeed, I suggest that the term 'local', which retains connotations of being limited, should be abandoned. The global versus the local is another of the problematic binary divides that reinforce the status quo. Some of the knowledge produced within the framework of the supposedly 'universal' categories of the enlightenment project was specific to its own conditions of production; some of the knowledge produced from Andean *ayllus* had universal implications. No knowledge is innately 'universal' or 'local': how it is categorised depends, again, on processes of recognition. It is also valuable to keep within the frame questions about spatiality while reinstating the significance of change over time—the historical. Likewise, it keeps within the frame questions about materiality of knowledge while making it possible not to lose sight of the importance of content. A great deal has been learned from all the work on geographies of knowledge, but I suggest that both the spatial and material turns are due for a corrective. Not everything is about movement or connection: many of the stories of intellectual life in nineteenth-century Latin America—including some of the most creative moments—were about stasis and isolation.

Above all, human agency matters, which the politics of recognition highlights, avoiding the residual determinism of perspectives in which coloniality or imperialism is central to the analysis. In this book, I have tried to keep colonial and neocolonial effects in sight without assuming that they were always central. Sometimes they were, but instead of prejudging them to be so I've worked on the basis that there was always the potential (albeit not always realised) for an element of agency that escapes the colonial or neocolonial imprint. This element is not reducible to occidentalist options of collaboration, rejection or resistance. It arises out of having lived in a different place from the dominant culture, with a different environment and a different set of everyday practices: in sum, a different *starting point*, to apply Stuart Hall's idea of a non-essentialist identity. Like any other dominant power, coloniality itself will be seen in clearer relief if it too is decentred, as will other significant elements of the historical scenario. For example, it will become more visible that in the 1920s the Peruvian Marxist José Carlos Mariátegui published not only a far-reaching critique of coloniality but also a political programme for a revolution to overcome both internal and external colonialism. Mariátegui was unusual in his intellectual gifts but he was far from alone in his thinking, much of which drew upon his discussions with indigenous activists rather than his knowledge of Gramsci. There is a long and varied history of *reflection upon* coloniality from Latin America, as well as an equally compelling history of debates about many other aspects of human experience. Yet most of this work has been ignored, except among specialists, because the idea of coloniality itself loomed so large that it became hard to see what else was there.

Last, the politics of recognition retains the idea that the sphere of knowledge has its own dynamics and is not merely subsidiary to wider economic, political and social processes, while acknowledging that it will be affected by them just as it affects them in turn. Through its primary purpose in the modern era—publication, or the making of knowledge public—it intersects with both the state and the market. There are various features of the republic of knowledge that are worth emphasising for comparative purposes. It is constantly striving for autonomy and self-determination. It has its own vocabulary, its own conventions, practices, rituals of belonging and sociability. Its ideals of enquiry, root metaphors and repertoires of reference are all clues about its workings. Like its political counterpart, it can be quite wild at times. Personal charismatic authority was often a notable feature; 'caudillo intellectuals' wielded arbitrary power and, like their military counterparts, knew how to make institutions work to their advantage. The republic of knowledge is democratic in principle, but in practice it may be dominated by gatekeepers, whose power is sometimes reinforced, sometimes undermined, by a series of mediators, brokers and other varieties of go-between. In the republic of knowledge, ideas matter. It was from the republic of knowledge that people who were marginalised in the political republic were able to engage in a continuing struggle to give meaning and substance to the founding ideal of enlightenment for all.

Nations as Knowledge Communities

I suggest that modern nations are best thought of as communities of shared knowledge, rather than as imagined communities. This idea makes it possible to understand them in new ways, bringing together features that are often analysed separately: how nations are experienced and performed as well as how they are imagined; how they are created by transnational as well as local dynamics; how they are constituted by a political framework (usually but not necessarily a state) as well as a cultural one. Knowledge, however imperfect or fragmentary, is more substantial and evidence-based than imagination. Focusing on it helps us to account for the variety of agents who contribute to creating and sustaining national consciousness, without losing sight of hierarchies of power. It helps to explain why some elite blueprints for a nation worked while others failed to resonate. It makes it possible to historicise coloniality and nationalism: through the lens of knowledge we can trace when, where and how the national took form, coalesced, dissolved and assumed a new shape again, giving due attention to the processes of destruction that make a nation as well as those of creation. It reminds us to keep in mind the sheer variety of networks and exchanges that contribute daily to making and remaking a nation, some of which are geared to the society within state borders, others to the world beyond them. In relation to the inhabitants of any particular nation, an analysis of their access to knowledge, which also involves thinking about what kinds of knowledge are denied to them, is a powerful way of capturing the peculiar mix of the everyday and the remarkable that constitutes a national identity. Above all, it frees us from deterministic accounts of race, culture or language to explore the historical choices made about how to interpret them, while still keeping us anchored in lived experience. Thinking about nations as knowledge communities helps us to explain why it is that a strong sense of national identity can exist even in countries—like those of Spanish America— where there are few factors to both unify and differentiate. The field of knowledge brings together history and geography, time and space, encouraging historians of modern nations to think beyond the assumptions of the one-nation, one-culture model, with its emphasis on homogeneous, empty time. There's a history of ideas of plurality of time, of space, of nations. In Peru at its centenary, after a century of separation between the knowledge of indigenous communities and the knowledge of Lima, it was possible to detect the beginnings of the twenty-first-century model of multiple nations within one state, the stirrings of a recognition that the knowledge of indigenous peoples could be a source of inspiration and enrichment for modern Peru. The history of independent Spanish America could be encapsulated as the history of struggles to compel those in power to acknowledge that homogeneity was not a realistic—or desirable—option.

The history of knowledge provides a way of looking at state-building and nation-making together. These two processes, which in Spanish America evolved in relation to each other, over comparable periods of history, have usually been analysed separately. The classic accounts of state-building (Tilly, Skocpol, Mann) rarely looked at questions of identity, belonging or sociability; historical analyses of national identities have tended to assume the integrity of socio-cultural processes. One important category neglected by both parties is that of the semi-official organisation, the many collaborations between the state and members of civil society that featured in the formation of

nationhood in Spanish America. Telling examples are the geographical societies discussed in chapter 7: founded in Peru after defeat in the War of the Pacific, when history seemed anything but glorious, or in Chile in the midst of a
national preoccupation with decline after a brief but intense civil war dis-
rupted a historical narrative of institutional stability. A focus on the history of
knowledge reveals the extent to which the land and nature were significant
elements of national consciousness in Spanish America: natural history was
at least as important as history in this respect, particularly in the decades before state primary education became widespread. The emphasis on the land
signified more than a territorial nationalism; instead, it was a manifestation of
the spirit of the country, to be known by its people in interaction with their
natural environment.

The history of knowledge highlights another, often overlooked aspect of
nation formation, namely the variety of other places to which people looked
for ideas and experiences that were relevant and useful. Evidence from Spanish
America has alerted me to two key aspects of transnationalism which, despite
recent work, are still not as widely appreciated as they deserve to be. First,
there was a far greater diversity of presences from beyond the region than has
usually been appreciated in the historiography, which still tends to focus on
connections with (if not imports from) the commercial powers of Britain,
France and the United States. These were undeniably important, but so too in
terms of ideas were connections and exchanges with many other places, not
least other European countries, especially Germany, Italy and (often overlooked) Spain. The general point is that the history of knowledge takes us
beyond the history of empire. For some countries on the Pacific Ocean, the
allure of anywhere in Europe was at least partially eclipsed by the lustre of
Asian civilisations, which was given material reality by trading routes on which
the ports of Callao, Valparaíso and Acapulco were key staging posts. Such
places were transnational before they were national.[3] There were other com-
pulsions to look westwards: for example, South American philologists identified analogous lexical and grammatical forms in the languages of the Andeans
and the Polynesians and began to speculate about ancient connections to
Oceania. Transnational imaginings—often stirred by snippets of information
culled from the publications slung onto the docks from ocean-plying merchant vessels—increasingly ranged all over the globe. News from Egypt and
Russia and Japan appeared not only in broadsheet newspapers but also in the
labour press. Transnational encounters, both experienced and imagined, were
a feature of many people's lives, beyond the socially privileged and the

migrants who have been the subjects of most historiography. Workers, indigenous travellers, soldiers, were all affected.

The second point concerns what I call *localised transnationalism*—that is,
the multitude of exchanges and connections, and comparisons, that took place
between the countries of Latin America and affected most social groups. Such
transfers of knowledge from other parts of the region played a crucial role in
nation-making, because they were more likely to be assimilated into a local
outlook than to be received as explicitly foreign imports. My accumulated evidence on transnationalism illustrates the sheer diversity of worlds of reference
both in Latin America and in the wider world, thereby making an empirical
contribution to the endeavour of refuting claims that the region's intellectual
life was derivative of Europe's.

Knowledge Matters

When young Spanish American radicals reassessed the future in the wake of
the First World War, it was the universities, rather than any political body, on
which they focused their attention. For activists in the University Reform
Movement, universities were targeted both as anachronistic bastions of colonial ways of thinking and as potential crucibles of the ideal republic of equality
and social justice envisaged by the founding fathers. The reformists' demands
typify the significance of knowledge in the constitution of a political community. They focused on teaching methods, curriculum content, co-
government, and entrance requirements and fees—in other words, respectively, on questions of authority, the right balance between homegrown and
imported knowledge, student participation in decision-making and the creation of knowledge, and accessibility to people of any social background. For
a short time in the 1920s, universities in Spanish America were among the most
radical in the world, not only in political terms (which was more common,
with Japanese universities the sites of socialism; Chinese universities those of
revolutionary nationalism) but also in terms of knowledge equity. Although a
top-down power structure was restored in many universities, other aspects of
the reform persisted, at least in certain faculties or courses, and universities
were central to a long list of radical political events—not least the revolutions
in Cuba (1959) and Nicaragua (1979).

Looking at the twentieth century in Latin America, then, it is not hard to see
how the history of knowledge affected politics and policy-making. The same
is true, if less immediately obvious, for the nineteenth century. Questions such

as how a society decides whose knowledge to value, or what kind of knowledge came to be regarded as 'natural', or who were the gatekeepers to high-status knowledge, are not of second-order significance. It is sometimes possible to trace shockingly direct connections between the production of knowledge and the actions of governments: Argentine historians have shown that thinking of the Argentine 'desert' as a deserted—that is, uninhabited—space, together with the social Darwinian idea that the people there were in any case destined for extinction, made it possible for President Roca to legitimise a war of extermination against the indigenous peoples in a relatively liberal climate of public opinion. More often, answers to questions about the knowledge order reveal the conditions in which it became possible to think about some options and not others; free trade, for example, was deemed the only realistic policy in certain countries for most of the nineteenth century, despite the robust arguments against it, because it acquired the status of naturalised knowledge. In this book, I have explored ways of collecting evidence to identify how the history of knowledge shapes what Koselleck called the horizons of expectation and the spaces of experience, which in turn form the environment in which actions and decisions are taken. Assumptions, biases and preconceptions about what can or should be known set the limits to what is possible in a society. Their effects may be oblique or tangential, but they are cumulative and over time their consequences are major.

In Western societies we tend to miss much of this, or see it only in fragments, because of the persistent biases not only of Eurocentrism in general but of European Romanticism in particular. Romanticism was, of course, a diverse current of thought, with very different emphases in its various European sites, but Romantics did share certain ideas about the creation of knowledge and it is those notions that have continued to exercise a powerful hold over the imaginations of Western intellectuals. Postmodernists have taken Enlightenment thinkers apart, for logocentrism, grand narratives, instrumental rationality and so on, but the Romantics—ostensibly critics of modernity— have remained largely untouched. In addition to the privileging of the metropole, the capital city and the university as sites of knowledge production, Romanticism embeds another bias towards the figure of the individual creative genius (literary or scientific). This bias means that prominent generators of knowledge are discussed at the expense of the many other individuals who created the conditions for that knowledge to be produced, circulated and recognised. It means that creativity is emphasised over the transfer of skills; creative writers over other kinds of intellectuals; dedication to the pursuit of knowledge over part-time work in the field (with inherent class biases). Because intellectual production is classified as either literature or science, historians of culture study writers and historians of science study scientists. Key figures fall outside these remits, such as collectors of artefacts and documents, compilers of dictionaries or encyclopedias, librarians and bibliographers, editors of journals, translators and publishers. Many of these individuals had huge influence as gatekeepers. Focusing on the ideas and practices of those who passed on fundamental skills, rather than the famous writers or scientists, uncovers evidence to challenge the claim that only the highly educated had access to knowledge. I chose drawing teachers, but the pedagogy of music or mathematics would probably have been equally revealing. There were far more people committed to a life of learning than had an institutional base for scholarship or research. Autodidacticism was a significant phenomenon among a variety of people below the upper classes, as indicated by the range and sales figures of self-help manuals directed at them. This is not to say that the work of celebrated intellectuals does not matter. Of course it does, but it matters at least partly because it was recognised, either at the time or by later generations, as articulating concerns shared by a wider range of people. The creation of knowledge is a collective endeavour and it is only by analysing it as such that we can begin to understand its significance to questions of societal cohesion, institutional stability and democratic practice.

Throughout history, including the current age, when things go wrong it is blamed on ignorance. If ignorance can be an explanation, then it must follow that we have to ask questions about the role of knowledge. What is referred to as ignorance is likely to be the privileging of one or more kinds of knowledge over other kinds: for example, knowledge of a specific place over knowledge of global processes; knowledge derived from emotional experiences over knowledge validated as factual; knowledge offered by experts over knowledge of the common people. More knowledge in itself is no panacea: there are many examples down the ages of thinking that there is an excess of knowledge, meaning too much of a certain kind, including, in a commercially oriented nation such as Peru, too many 'men of letters' instead of 'men of enterprise'.[4] The factors that shape the knowledge order are mainly qualitative, although resources, especially state capacities to provide, usually make a notable difference to outcomes. There is no ideal type (all that I have said about the importance of specific social context precludes that). Even so, it is possible to identify certain principles and practices that make it more likely that knowledge can be created and distributed freely and fairly, and that practitioners of knowledge will be able to work in creative tension with the wider society. It's a vision, like the dreams of various people in Spanish America during the wars of independence, rather than a blueprint.

To pursue that vision for a moment, a 'good' republic of knowledge would be a place where it was widely acknowledged, both by those in government and across the whole society, that it is a never-ending process to sustain a public realm in which genuine communication of ideas and information can take place. Such a space is always elsewhere, in a perpetual state of becoming. Its existence depends upon a constant struggle to create it, a sustained resistance to the manoeuvres of those who seek to control knowledge in their own interests, a repeated exposure of hierarchies in order to make the landscape of knowledge open to being shaped by everyone in the society. In other words, a well-functioning knowledge order would keep open the possibility for epistemic challenges to be heard. Many knowledge institutions, not least the academic disciplines, put up major barriers to any questioning of prevalent methods or assumptions. Removal of these barriers requires knowledge practitioners to stay alert to their own values, biases, and prejudices in order to keep at bay the would-be caudillo gatekeepers, with their authoritarian tendencies. Given the persistence of global hierarchies that privilege certain kinds of knowledge, an openness to ideas from elsewhere has to be balanced by the core values and principles that make it possible to encounter other ways of thinking with integrity, creating an environment in which both the hybrid and the homegrown can flourish. Innovation in knowledge production can be stimulated by keeping open channels to connect different fields of endeavour in order to avoid the limitations of thinking in silos. Both specialisms and established routes to move between and across them are desirable, as is alertness to the epistemological implications of capacities that are fundamental to a variety of fields: drawing, mathematics, languages. Above all, it is crucial to maximise opportunities for people from all walks of life to become not only consumers or distributors of knowledge but also creators in their own right.

For the closing scene, let me take you back to Mendoza, where this book began, to see how this nascent republic of knowledge fared over the hundred years after independence. The city's history continued to illustrate in sharp relief the contours of the history of knowledge in many other places in Spanish America. The story is partly one of tragedy: in 1861 much of Mendoza was destroyed by an earthquake, in which perhaps half of the population perished. During the city's reconstruction, the centre was relocated and refashioned on the principles of European urban planning, in a lengthy process overseen by

French surveyor Julio Balloffet. The huge public squares and wide avenues were intended to help protect against earthquake damage, but they were also a clear statement of the local elites' preference for Parisian design. From the mid-1860s to the mid-1880s European ways of knowing had high social prestige in Mendoza, as was the case in Buenos Aires, which was gradually converting itself into the capital of a territorially expanding nation. In the 1860s and 1870s the reconstruction of Mendoza city along European lines became closely bound up with the federal government's military campaigns against the indigenous peoples. Balloffet built fortresses as well as neoclassical theatres; both he and another key figure in the work of reconstruction, the Mendoza-born topographer and cartographer Colonel Manuel Olascoaga, carried out the surveying for the maps that made the Conquest of the Desert possible. In 1885 a railway opened to Buenos Aires, bringing trainloads of immigrants to work the stolen lands. The provincial elites oversaw a transition in the region's economy from grain and livestock production to viticulture, with rapid success. As has happened so many times in histories of territorial expansion, science facilitated war and colonisation. Mendoza experienced some of the cruellest consequences of the founding bias towards knowledge that came to be associated with Europe.

Yet the history of knowledge in Mendoza, as elsewhere in Spanish America, is not only about suppression or separation. It is possible to see there the effects of that *other* founding commitment, namely to make knowledge accessible to everyone. Even though in many cases the ruling classes were able to manipulate this source of legitimacy to their own advantage, by ensuring that the kind of knowledge disseminated was geared towards instilling patriotic obedience and 'modern' modes of conduct, they found it impossible to maintain full control. The creation and communication of knowledge in and for the Americas created its own dynamics, which in turn created spaces for many kinds of people to contest elite visions of what and how to know. Such sites were usually small in scope and often ephemeral, but what is remarkable is the persistence with which they were recreated and the ingenuity with which their potential was realised as far as possible even in adverse situations. By the early twentieth century, Mendoza's cultural life had been transformed by the presence of immigrants, Italian and Spanish, Arab and Jewish. Around the centenaries of independence, an expanding middle class, increasingly powerful in local government, and a rising labour movement created new cultural institutions, clubs, societies and associations, in which the public exchange of ideas and information was usually a central activity. In 1911 a new Museum of Natural

Sciences and Anthropology opened, which, in its exhibits of archaeological fragments from the late Inca period, presented an (as yet tentative and patchwork) alternative to the official version of the region's history that invariably started with San Martín.[5] Every popular organisation seemed to publish its own periodical, of which there were nearly two hundred registered in the four decades from 1890 to 1930.[6] The province of Mendoza's Constitution of 1916, which remains in place, was world-leading in its provisions for social rights and cultural liberties.[7] The city's first institutional university opened later, in 1939 (the Universidad Nacional de Cuyo), but a Popular University functioned for most of 1921 before the authorities closed it down.

This is not to say that by the 1920s Mendoza had fully become the oasis of 'enlightened critique of reality' that it had briefly aspired to be one hundred years earlier. When 'the Gaucho' José Néstor Lencinas was elected as governor for the Radical Party (1918–20), in office he responded to popular challenges much as the national Radical president Hipólito Yrigoyen opted to do, namely with top-down reform and repression of protest. In Mendoza the decisive event was a strike of teachers, which emerged in the wake of protests against the 'Tragic Week' of January 1919, when hundreds of workers in Buenos Aires were killed by government forces, who particularly targeted Jewish people. From March 1919 to January 1920 the primary school teachers of Mendoza, 84 per cent of whom were women, 'took the school onto the street', in a campaign to be paid a decent wage. Teachers were paid very little, precisely because they were women who were assumed to be happy to act as 'second mothers' to schoolchildren while being kept by their husbands' salaries. Astutely, the women teachers continued to offer classes throughout the strike, holding them wherever they could: in union buildings, their own living quarters or the homes of their pupils. They turned this difficult situation to advantage by developing a new approach to popular education in response to the direct needs of working families. Their work was supported actively by students, intellectuals and organised labourers.[8] A repressive reaction by the authorities meant that teachers' conditions did not improve very much as a result of the strike. But the process of mobilisation around what and how the children of workers should be taught had lasting effects. Once again, it was the process of communicating knowledge that became a forum in which wider social issues were debated, contested and taken forward in a creative response. Nowadays, Mendoza brands itself not only as the 'land of good wine' but also as the 'land of museums'. Behind that apparently minor manifestation of civic pride lies a remarkable history in which knowledge played a founding part.

ACKNOWLEDGEMENTS

This project would not have been possible without the generous backing of the Leverhulme Trust, which awarded me a three-year Major Research Fellowship, giving me the time to orient myself in a new field, to read a large volume of primary material, to visit Latin America for archival work and, above all, to think. I also appreciate the dependable support of the UCL History Department, both in allowing me to take the time away from normal duties to pursue this work and in funding some additional research trips to look at materials held in the Iberoamerikanisches Institut in Berlin and the International Institute for Social History in Amsterdam.

I would like to thank the anonymous readers commissioned by Princeton University Press for their helpful suggestions for improvements to the first draft. I'm also very grateful to the following friends and colleagues who gave their time to read chapters and to offer constructive criticism, tactfully mixed with enthusiasm: Maurice Biriotti, Matthew Brown, Camila Gatica Mizala, Axel Körner, Catherine Merridale and Caroline Zealey. For invaluable research assistance, my warm appreciation goes to Ignacio Solminihac and Ed Shawcross. My overall thinking about the nineteenth century has benefited greatly from participating in the working group on 'Reimagining Democracy in Latin America and the Caribbean, 1770–1870', organised at Oxford University by Joanna Innes and Eduardo Posada-Carbó. As is the case with any supposedly 'single-authored' book, many colleagues and students have helped me to identify sources, work out ideas and clarify my expression of them during the course of discussion in seminars, workshops and conferences. I thank them all.

A special thanks goes to my editor, Ben Tate, for his consistent faith in the project and his good-humoured accommodation of the reality that writing always takes longer than one hopes. All the staff I've encountered at Princeton University Press have been a pleasure to deal with. The copy editor, Ben Wilson, made many careful changes that cumulatively had a strongly beneficial effect on how the text reads.

It's customary, but it also happens to be true, to say that this book would have taken far longer without the loyal backing and day-to-day involvement of my husband, John North. He has been ever willing, over six long years, to discuss ideas, read drafts, restore my motivation and—not least—help me to see when it was time to stop. This book is, above all, for him.

NOTES

Introduction

1. Peter Schmidtmeyer, *Travels into Chile, over the Andes, in the Years 1820 and 1821*, Longman, London, 1824, 180.

2. Ricardo Cicerchia, 'Journey, Rediscovery and Narrative: British Travel Accounts of Argentina (1800–1850)', *ISA Research Papers*, no. 50, London, 1998, 15: https://sas-space.sas.ac.uk /3412/; Schmidtmeyer, *Travels*, 171–73.

3. Alexander Caldcleugh, *Travels in South America during the Years 1819–20–21*, John Murray, London, 1825, 286; Samuel Haigh, *Sketches of Buenos Ayres, Chile and Peru*, Effingham Wilson, London, 1831, 79, 86; Schmidtmeyer, *Travels*, 177.

4. On churches, see 'El Plano Espinosa de la ciudad de Mendoza en 1822', reproduced in Jorge Ricardo Ponte, *Mendoza, aquella ciudad de barro*, CONICET, Mendoza, 2008, 125–26; on schools, Juan P. Ramos, *Historia de la instrucción primaria en la República Argentina, 1810–1910*, vol. 1, Jacobo Peuser, Buenos Aires, 1910, 330–32. Mendoza had more schools, including schools for girls, than any other province at that time, even Buenos Aires.

5. None of this is visible today, because the earthquake of 1861 destroyed most of the city, which was then rebuilt with the explicit intention of consigning the Spanish legacy to the past. The old colonial centre was duly relocated, but urban historians have deduced the former shape of Mendoza: see the CONICET video 'Reconstrucción: Los años de San Martín en Mendoza', at http://www.mendoza.edu.ar/reconstruccion-los-anos-de-san-martin-en-mendoza-2/. On the library, notable for its acquisition of more than two hundred published volumes of the *Encyclopédie* in its revised form of *L'Encyclopédie méthodique ou par ordre de matières* (1782–1832), see Arturo Andrés Roig, *Los orígenes de la Biblioteca Pública 'Gral. San Martín'*, Edición de la Biblioteca Pública 'Gral. San Martín', Mendoza, 1966.

6. John Lynch, *San Martín: Argentine Soldier, American Hero*, Yale University Press, New Haven and London, 2009, 76.

7. Caldcleugh, *Travels*, 288.

8. Respectively: *El Verdadero Amigo del País* (1822–24); *Registro Ministerial* (1822); and *El Amigo del Orden* (1822). Antonio Zinny, 'Efemeridografía de Mendoza', *La Revista de Buenos Aires*, vol. 23, year 8, no. 89, Sept. 1870, 476. Zinny recorded a further twelve titles, published 1820–28. See also Jorge Enrique Oviedo, *El periodismo en Mendoza*, Academia Nacional del Periodismo, Buenos Aires, 2010.

9. Arturo Andrés Roig, *Breve historia intelectual de Mendoza*, Ediciones del Terruño, Mendoza, 1966, 28–29.

10. Arturo Roig, Pablo Lacoste and María Cristina Satlari, eds., *Mendoza, cultura y economía*, Caviar Bleu, Buenos Aires, 2004, 526–34, esp. 529; 'El 25 de mayo de 1810 en Mendoza: Historia de la revolución que no fue', *Pirámide Informativa* (Mendoza), 25 May 2014: https://piramideinformativa.com/2014/05/el-25-de-mayo-de-1810-en-mendoza-historia-de -la-revolucion-que-no-fue/; and Carlos Campana, 'Cómo llega la revolución a Mendoza', *Los Andes* (Mendoza), 21 May 2017: https://www.losandes.com.ar/article/bicentenario -490610.

11. Schmidtmeyer, *Travels*, 183–84.

12. The engineer was José Antonio Álvarez Condarco (1780–1855), who had worked at an explosives factory in Córdoba; the munitions expert was Friar Luis Beltrán, a Mendocino brought up in Chile, who was by turns 'mathematician, physicist, carpenter, blacksmith and gunner'. Lynch, *San Martín*, 76.

13. Beatriz Bragoni and Orlando Gabriel Morales, 'Libertad civil y patriotismo en el Río de la Plata revolucionario: La experiencia de los esclavos negros en la provincia de Cuyo, 1812–1820', *Historia y Sociedad (Medellín)*, no. 30 (Jan.–June 2016), 131–67. Bragoni's main sources were local court records.

14. James Thomson, *Letters on the Moral and Religious State of South America*, James Nesbitt, London, 1827, 33, 273–75.

15. Carmen Gutiérrez de Arrojo, 'La música en Mendoza', in Roig, Lacoste and Satlari, eds., *Mendoza, cultura y economía*, 397–433, 410–11.

16. Anthony Grafton, 'A Sketch Map of a Lost Continent: The Republic of Letters', *Republics of Letters*, 1:1, Dec. 2008: https://arcade.stanford.edu/rofl/sketch-map-lost-continent -republic-letters#_ftn11. This article is a good introduction to a large literature. For an in-depth study of how the Republic of Letters worked in practice, see Anne Goldgar, *Impolite Learning: Conduct and Community in the Republic of Letters, 1680–1750*, Yale University Press, New Haven and London, 1995. See also the digital project 'Cultures of Knowledge: Networking in the Republic of Letters, 1550–1750', led by Howard Hotson at Oxford University: http://www.culturesofknowledge.org. Landmark studies of the relationship between cultural and political conceptions of a republic include Roger Chartier, *Les origines culturelles de la Révolution française*, Seuil, Paris, 1990; Robert Darnton, *The Literary Underground of the Old Regime*, Harvard University Press, Cambridge MA, 1985; Daniel Roche, *Les républicains des lettres: Gens de culture et Lumières au XVIIIe siècle*, Fayard, Paris, 1988.

17. Isabel Montoya Ramírez del Villar, *Imprentas volantes en la emancipación*, Biblioteca Nacional, Lima, 1972. An *imprenta volante* carried by liberating troops in northern Argentina was on display in the Museo del Cabildo, Buenos Aires, in 2016.

18. José de San Martín, decree to found the Biblioteca Nacional, 28 Aug. 1821, in *Colección documental de la independencia del Perú, Tomo XIII, Obra de Gobierno y Epistolario de San Martín*, ed. José A. de la Puente Candamo, 2 vols., Comisión Nacional del Sesquicentenario de la Independencia del Perú, Lima, 1975, vol. 1, 294–95, esp. 294. Many other examples can be found among the primary sources in José Luis Romero and Luis Alberto Romero, eds., *Pensamiento político de la emancipación*, Biblioteca Ayacucho, Caracas, 2 vols., 1977, such as: José Amor de la Patria, 'Catecismo político cristiano', Santiago, 1811, vol. 1, 212–19, esp. 219; Antonio José de Irisarri, 'Reflexiones sobre la política de los gobiernos de América', *Semanario Republicano de Chile*, February 1813, vol. 1, 236–40, esp. 236; and Francisco Antonio Zea, 'Manifiesto a los pueblos de Colombia', 1820, vol. 2, 129–36, esp. 135.

19. 'El Gobierno a los Pueblos', *El Monitor Araucano*, no. 34, 24 June 1813, facs. edn. of nos. 1–50 in *Colección de Historiadores y de Documentos relativos a la Independencia de Chile*, vol. 26, Imprenta Universitaria, Santiago, 1914, 230–31, esp. 231.

20. Constitutions of Venezuela (1811), Colombia (1821), Peru (1823), Central America (1824), Uruguay (1830), in Nelson Chávez Herrera, ed., *Primeras constituciones: Latinoamérica y el Caribe*, Biblioteca Ayacucho, Caracas, 2011, pp. 223, 287, 315, 111, 448, respectively. It was also the case in Chile's 1833 Constitution (capítulo 4, art. 6), *Constitución de la República de Chile jurada y promulgada el 25 de mayo de 1833*, Imprenta de la Opinión, Santiago, 1833, 5. Similar provisions were made in Brazil through a naturalisation act: 'Lei de Octubro de 1832 sobre naturalisação dos estrangeiros', http://www2.camara.leg.br/legin/fed/lei_sn/1824-1899/lei-37324-23-outubro-1832-563838-publicacaooriginal-87885-pl.html.

21. Colombia until 1840 (1821, sección 1, art. 15, clause 3); Peru also until 1840 (1823, capítulo 4, art. 17, clause 3); Bolivia until 1836 (1826, capítulo 3, art. 14, clause 3)—in *Primeras constituciones*, 286; 315; 342.

22. 'Decreto constitucional para la libertad de la América mexicana, sancionado en Apatzingán (22 de octubre de 1814)', capítulo 8, art. 117, required Congress 'cuidar con singular esmero de la ilustración de los pueblos' (to take especial care over the enlightenment of the peoples), *Primeras constituciones*, 70; Constitution of Uruguay (1830, sección 4, capítulo 1, art. 17, clause 3) required the legislature (Asamblea General) to pursue 'fomento de la ilustración' (promotion of enlightenment), 450. For what was meant by *ilustración*, see ch. 5.

23. On the meat shortage, see *Representación de los hacendados de Buenos-Ayres al Exmo. Supremo Director. Para el restablecimiento de los saladeros, exportación libre de todos los frutos del país, arreglo del abasto de carnes, y otros puntos de economía política*, Buenos Aires, 1817; and Antonio Millán, *Acusación sostenida contra los saladeros, y advertencies a su defensor D. Pedro Trapani*, Imprenta de la Independencia, Buenos Aires, c. 1820.

24. http://www.presidencia.gob.ec/wp-content/uploads/downloads/2012/10/2011-04-11-Creacion-del-Ministerio-Coordinador-de-Conocimiento-y-Talento-Humano.pdf, accessed May 2017. Chile followed suit in 2018, creating the Ministerio de Ciencia, Tecnología, Conocimiento e Innovación.

25. For reports: http://bibliotecanacional.gov.co/es-co/Bibliotecas-en-Red/bibliotecas-publicas-moviles/actualidad and https://www.radionacional.co/noticia/bibliotecas-publicas-posconflicto. For a study: Orlanda Jaramillo, 'Bibliotecas públicas en Colombia: Territorio de paz', *El profesional de la información*, 25:5 (2016), 815–21.

26. The main instances are summarised in Haig A. Bosmajian, *Burning Books*, McFarland & Co., Jefferson NC, 2006, 172–74. One of the most notorious was the reduction to ashes of nearly fifteen thousand copies of Nobel laureate Gabriel García Márquez's reportage of a famous film director's secret return to Chile: *La aventura de Miguel Littín clandestino en Chile*, Ediciones El País, Madrid, 2nd edn., 1986. General Pinochet's own clandestine activities included collecting a private library of about fifty thousand books: see Juan Cristóbal Peña, *La secreta vida literaria de Augusto Pinochet*, Random House Mondadori, Santiago, 2013. On censorship in Argentina, see Andrew Graham-Yooll, *The Press in Argentina, 1973–1978, with additional material for 1979–1981*, Writers and Scholars Educational Trust, London, 1984.

27. Venezuela (1811, sección 3, capítulo 9, art. 218); Colombia (1821, título 8, art. 180, which specified 'for the knowledge of the nation' rather than 'for the knowledge of all'), in *Primeras constituciones*, 255, 309.

28. The corresponding clause in section 9 of the US Constitution stipulates that 'a regular Statement and Account of the Receipts and Expenditures of all public Money shall be published from time to time'. *The Constitution of the United States, and the Declaration of Independence*, US Government Printing Office, Washington DC, 2007, 8.

29. Constitution of El Salvador (1824, capítulo 12, art. 82), *Primeras constituciones*, 107.

30. José Martí, 'Nuestra América', in *Obras escogidas*, Centro de Estudios Martianos / Editora Política, Havana, 1980, 520.

31. The first multidisciplinary congress was instigated by the Sociedad Científica Argentina and held in Buenos Aires in 1898. For proceedings see *Primera reunión del Congreso Científico Latino Americano, Buenos Aires, 10 al 20 de abril de 1898*, Companía Sud-Americana de Billetes de Banco, Buenos Aires, 1898, which listed about five hundred participants, mainly from Argentina, Chile, Peru and Uruguay, although most countries sent representatives. Further gatherings followed in Montevideo (1901), Rio de Janeiro (1905), Santiago (1908–9) and, again, Buenos Aires (1910). The Chilean organising committee decided to invite the United States, as a result of which the fourth Latin American scientific congress was also designated the first Pan American one: *Trabajos del Cuarto Congreso Científico (Primero Pan-Americano)*, Imprenta Barcelona, Santiago, 20 vols., 1909. While two thousand people attended the Santiago event, by the time of the Third Pan American Scientific Congress, held in Lima in 1924, participation had sharply declined to about three hundred. The United States aggressively promoted its commercial and financial practices at the Pan American Conferences of 1919 and 1920, respectively. There is now a growing body of work on the US deployment of knowledge as a tool of empire, at first in administration and management, later in most fields of knowledge. In order of publication, the key studies are Emily Rosenberg and Norman Rosenberg, 'From Colonialism to Professionalism: The Public-Private Dynamic in United States Foreign Financial Advising, 1898–1929', *Journal of American History*, 74:1 (June 1987), 59–82; Paul Drake, *The Money Doctor in the Andes: The Kemmerer Missions, 1923–33*, Duke University Press, Durham NC, 1989; Paul Drake, ed., *Money Doctors, Foreign Debts, and Economic Reforms in Latin America: From the 1890s to the Present*, SR Books, Wilmington DE, 1994; Marcos Cueto, ed., *Missionaries of Science: The Rockefeller Foundation and Latin America*, Indiana University Press, Bloomington, 1994; Gilbert M. Joseph, Catherine C. LeGrand and Ricardo D. Salvatore, eds., *Close Encounters of Empire: Writing the Cultural History of US–Latin American Relations*, Duke University Press, Durham NC, 1998; David Sheinin, ed., *Beyond the Ideal: Pan Americanism in Inter-American Affairs*, Greenwood Press, London, 2000; Ricardo D. Salvatore, 'The Making of a Hemispheric Intellectual-Statesman: Leo S. Rowe in Argentina, 1909–1919', *Journal of Transnational American Studies*, 2:1 (Mar. 2010), online; Mark D. Petersen, 'Argentine and Chilean Approaches to Modern Pan-Americanism, 1888–1930', DPhil diss., University of Oxford, 2014; and Ricardo D. Salvatore, *Disciplinary Conquest: US Scholars in South America, 1900–1945*, Duke University Press, Durham NC, 2016.

32. One of the most telling critiques is Claudio Lomnitz, 'Nationalism as a Practical System: Benedict Anderson's Theory of Nationalism From the Vantage Point of Spanish America', in Miguel Angel Centeno and Fernando López Alves, eds., *The Other Mirror: Grand Theory through the Lens of Latin America*, Princeton University Press, Princeton NJ, 2000, 329–49.

Chapter One: Public Libraries, Modern Nations

1. Jorge Luis Borges, *Siete Noches*, Fondo de Cultura Económica, México DF, 1980, 146. See also his short story 'La Biblioteca de Babel', *Ficciones*, Alianza Editorial, Madrid, 1971, 89–100.

2. José de San Martín, 'Palabras pronunciadas por San Martín el día de la inauguración de la Biblioteca, el 17 de septiembre de 1822', cited in Antonio Gutiérrez Escudero, 'José de San Martín: rasgos de su personalidad', *Araucaria: Revista Iberoamericana de filosofía, política y humanidades*, 18, 2007, 319–37, 323.

3. Diego Barros Arana, *Historia jeneral de Chile*, vol. 11 (1890), Editorial Universitaria, Santiago, 1999, 56.

4. Simón Bolívar, 'Discurso pronunciado [. . .] ante el Congreso de Angostura' (1819), in Vicente Lecuña, ed., *Proclamos y discursos del Libertador, 1811–1830*, Biblioteca de Autores y Temas Mirandinos, Los Teques, Venezuela, 1983, 202–35, 228.

5. Francisco de Paula Santander, 'El decreto del año doce de la Independencia', 12 Mar. 1822, reproduced in Guillermo Hernández de Alba and Juan Carrasquilla Botero, *Historia de la Biblioteca Nacional de Colombia*, Imprenta Patriótica del Instituto Caro y Cuervo, Bogotá, 1977, 81–82. Santander stated the purpose of the reorganised library to be the 'truly Republican' concerns of '[advancing] general enlightenment and [promoting] the sciences and the arts' (81). The library opened as the Biblioteca Nacional on 25 Dec. 1823 (84). Santander was later held prisoner there, in 1828, where he famously occupied himself counting the books, arriving at a grand total of 14,847 (88–89).

6. Asociación de Bibliotecas Nacionales de Iberoamérica, *Historia de las Bibliotecas Nacionales de Iberoamérica: Pasado y presente*, UNAM, Mexico City, 1995, 54; Timoteo (Washington Bermúdez), *Baturrillo uruguayo*, Imprenta a Vapor y Encuadernación de El Laurak-Bat, Montevideo, 1885, 10.

7. Francisco Araucho, 'Himno a la apertura de la Biblioteca de Montevideo', 26 May 1816, Biblioteca Virtual Universal, 2006: https://www.biblioteca.org.ar/libros/130771.pdf.

8. Miguel de Cervantes, 'El discurso de las armas y las letras', *Don Quijote* (1605), ch. 38, online at https://cvc.cervantes.es/literatura/clasicos/quijote/edicion/parte1/cap38/default.htm.

9. 'El 154° aniversario de la Biblioteca', *La Nación* (Buenos Aires), 10 Sept. 1964.

10. Nicanor M. Saleño, *Literatura: La Lira Argentina—La Abeja Argentina*, Biblioteca de Mayo / Senado de la Nación, Buenos Aires, 1960.

11. *Historia de las Bibliotecas Nacionales*, 148.

12. Cincuentenario de la Sociedad Geográfica de Lima, 1888–1938, Imprenta Gil, Lima, 1937, 7.

13. For example, see Biblioteca Nacional de Chile, *Sesquicentenario de la Fundación* [. . .] *Homenajes, Historia-crónica-recuerdos, Album de la biblioteca*, Ediciones de la Biblioteca Nacional / Revista Mapocho, Santiago, 1963.

14. Mariano Moreno, 'Fundación de la Biblioteca Pública', in *Doctrina democrática*, Librería La Facultad, Buenos Aires, 1915, 178–180, esp. 180; Francisco Antonio Pérez, Agustín Manuel Eyzaguirre and Juan Egaña, 'El Gobierno a los Pueblos: Proclama de Fundación de la Biblioteca Nacional', *El Monitor Araucano* (Santiago), no. 57, 19 Aug. 1813, facsimile in Guillermo Feliú Cruz, ed., *Colección de Historiadores y de Documentos relativos a la Independencia de Chile*, vol. 27,

Dirección General de Talleres Fiscales, Santiago, 1930, 33; and José de San Martín, decree to found the Biblioteca Nacional, 28 Aug. 1821, in *Colección documental* [. . .] *del Perú*.

15. Moreno, 'La educación', 179.

16. Ricardo Levene, 'El fundador de la Biblioteca Nacional', *Boletín de la Academia Nacional de Historia* (Buenos Aires), vol. 12, 1939, 267–351, 283.

17. For General William Beresford's statement justifying the British commandeering of public property, with the exception of 'the public archives', see 'Condiciones bajo las cuales se convino en la entrega de la Plaza de Buenos Aires á las armas británicas, el día 27 de Junio de 1806', in Juan Coronado, *Invasiones inglesas al Río de la Plata: Documentos inéditos*, Imprenta Republicana, Buenos Aires, 1870, 71–72.

18. Néstor Forero, *La patria saqueda, 1806–1825*, Librería de la Paz, Resistencia, Chaco, Argentina, 63–65.

19. *Gazeta de Buenos Ayres*, 15 Nov. 1810, 388; 10 Jan. 1811, 507–8; 24 Jan. 1811, 224; 7 Feb. 1811, 548; and *Gazeta extraordinaria*, 25 Sept. 1810, 11–12; 2 Oct. 1810, 11–12; 15 Oct. 1810, 11–12; 23 Oct. 1810, 10–12. There were over one hundred donations listed in 1810, with thirty-eight the following year and further intermittent contributions thereafter.

20. *Gazeta Extraordinaria*, 25 Sept. 1810, 12; and *Gazeta Extraordinaria*, 23 Oct. 1810, 11. For estimates of a porter's wages, see Leticia Arroya Abad, Elwyn A. R. Davies, and Jan Luiten van Zanden, 'Prices and Wages in Argentina, Bolivia, Chile, Colombia, Mexico and Peru', database at http://www.iisg.nl/hpw/data.php#southamerica.

21. Paul Groussac, *Historia de la Biblioteca Nacional* (1893), Biblioteca Nacional, Buenos Aires, 1967, xi–xii.

22. Hugo Acevedo, 'Argentina', in Asociación de Bibliotecas Nacionales de Iberoamérica, *Historia de las Bibliotecas Nacionales*, 7–8.

23. Acevedo, 'Argentina', 7.

24. 'Rejistro Estadístico de la Provincia de Buenos Aires, semestre 20 de 1823', cited in Vicente G. Quesada, *Memoria de la Biblioteca Pública Correspondiente a 1871*, Imprenta del Siglo, Buenos Aires, 1872, 5. Groussac argued that counting up the donations listed in the *Gazeta* led to an underestimation and that the total was about four thousand books in response to the first call if you included the whole collections given by individuals: *Historia de la Biblioteca Nacional*, xi.

25. Letter from the Primer Triunvirato to the first librarian, Luis José de Chorroarín, 30 Dec 1810, in Levene, 'El fundador', 102; see also Alejandro E. Parada, *Los orígenes de la Biblioteca Pública de Buenos Aires*, Universidad de Buenos Aires, Buenos Aires, 2009, 158–63, 311.

26. 'Reglamento', 1812, reproduced in Parada, *Los orígenes*, 181–84.

27. Successive biographers of Manuel de Salas referred to a letter he wrote, soon after becoming librarian of the Biblioteca Nacional de Chile in 1818, to Domingo Zapiola, who worked at the Buenos Aires public library, with a long list of precise questions about how it worked. See M. L. Amunátegui, *Don Manuel de Salas*, Imprenta Nacional, Santiago, 3 vols., 1895, vol. 3, 68–72.

28. For further discussion, see Andrés Baeza, 'Enlightenment, Education, and the Republican Project: Chile's Instituto Nacional (1810–1830)', *Paedagogica Historica*, 46:4, Aug. 2010, 479–93.

29. 'El Gobierno a los pueblos', *El Monitor Araucano*, 57, 19 Aug. 1813, in *Colección de Historiadores*, xxvii, 33.

30. The initial donations were recorded in *El Monitor Araucano*: 63, 2 Sept. 1813; 68, 14 Sept. 1813; 71, 21 Sept. 1813; and 75, 30 Sept. 1813. Raúl Silva Castro, *Los primeros años de la Biblioteca Nacional (1813–1824)*, Imprenta Universitaria, Santiago, 1951, 21–25.

31. 'Decreto para que la Biblioteca Nacional se instale en el edificio de la Aduana', 19 July 1823. Online at http://www.memoriachilena.gob.cl/602/w3-article-124342.html.

32. 'Crónica de la Biblioteca Nacional: Celebración del centenario (1813–1913)', *Revista de Bibliografía Chilena y Extranjera*, Sección de Información de la Biblioteca Nacional, Imprenta Universitaria, Santiago, 1:7, July 1913, 131–40, esp. 134.

33. 'Crónica de la Biblioteca Nacional', 135.

34. *Colección documental* [. . .] *del Perú*, 13:1, 295.

35. *Colección documental* [. . .] *del Perú*, 13:1, 294–95.

36. *Colección documental* [. . .] *del Perú*, 13:1, 297.

37. José de San Martín, 'Reglamento de la Biblioteca Nacional', 31 Aug. 1822, *Colección documental* [. . .] *del Perú*, 13:1, 296–99, esp. 297.

38. *Colección documental* [. . .] *del Perú*, 13:1, 295.

39. Mariano Arce, 'Oración', Lima, 8 Oct. 1821, in *Colección documental* [. . .] *del Perú*, vol. 1, 299–303, esp. 299.

40. Pedro M. Guibovich Pérez, *El edificio de letras: Jesuitas, educación y sociedad en el Perú colonial*, Universidad del Pacífico, Lima, 2014. See also Marcela Aspell and Carlos A. Page, eds., *La biblioteca jesuítica de la Universidad Nacional de Córdoba*, Universidad Nacional de Córdoba, Argentina, 2000; Guillermo Fúrlong Cárdiff, *Los Jesuitas y la cultura rioplatense*, Nueva edición corregida y aumentada, Buenos Aires, 1946; and José del Rey Fajardo, *Las bibliotecas jesuíticas en la Venezuela colonial*, Academia Nacional de la Historia, Caracas, 1999. On Chile, there is a brief account of the 'plentiful profane literature' in the library of Colegio de San Miguel: 'Las bibliotecas coloniales de Chile. VI. Bibliotecas de la Compañía de Jesús', in *Revista de Bibliografía Chilena y Extranjera* 1:9, Sept. 1913, 141–44, esp. 142. On Jesuit intellectual life in Spain, see María Dolores García Gómez, *Testigos de la memoria: Los inventarios de las bibliotecas de la Compañía de Jesús en la expulsión de 1767*, Universidad de Alicante, Alicante, 2012.

41. For the circulation of material between Europe and China through Jesuit networks, with a tantalisingly brief mention (454–55) of the route from New Spain (Mexico) to Manila and on to Macau/Canton: Noël Golvers, *Libraries of Western Learning for China: Circulation of Western Books between Europe and China in the Jesuit Mission (ca. 1650–ca. 1750)*, Ferdinand Verbiest Institute, Leuven, vol. 1, 2012.

42. Manuel de Salas, the first librarian of the BNCh, noted that what remained of the Jesuit collections was mainly 'the least estimable' and that all the materials had been badly kept at the Universidad de San Felipe. Amunátegui, *Don Manuel de Salas*, vol. 1, 78.

43. Levene, 'El fundador', 293. His appendix of documents includes two lists of books from the Temporalidades de Córdoba, Jan. 1811, 305–9. On the tactics of the inventory compilers for keeping the books in Córdoba, see Acevedo, 'Argentina', 6. A process of restitution was begun in the 1990s: Aspell and Page, *La biblioteca jesuítica*, 11.

44. Vicente Arlegui, 'Primera historia de la Biblioteca Nacional mandada escribir por Andrés Bello en 1857', in *Ediciones de la Revista Mapocho* (Biblioteca Nacional de Chile, offprint) 4:3, 1965, 24–26, esp. 24.

45. 'Chile', in Asociación de Bibliotecas Nacionales de Ibéroamerica, *Historia*, 136.

46. *La Biblioteca Nacional del Perú: Aportes para su historia* (150th-anniversary BNP publication), Lima, 1971, available at http://www.cervantesvirtual.com/obra-visor/la-biblioteca-nacional -del-peru-aportes-para-su-historia/html/ff3f0240–82b1–11df-acc7–002185ce6064_10.html.

47. John Lynch, *San Martín. Argentine Soldier, American Hero*, Yale University Press, New Haven and London, 2009, 180.

48. 'Catálogo de la biblioteca que poseía San Martín y que regaló a la ciudad de Lima', in *Colección documental* [. . .] *del Perú*, 13:2, 440–53. See also Lynch, *San Martín*, 180.

49. Notably Francisco Xavier de Gamboa, *Comentarios a las ordenanzas de minas*, Mexico, 1761. On Mexican mining expertise, see María de la Paz Ramos Lara and Juan José Saldaña, 'Del Colegio de Minería de México a la Escuela Nacional de Ingenieros', *Quipu: Revista Latinoamericana de Historia de las Ciencias y la Tecnología*, 13:1 (Jan.–Apr. 2000), 105–26.

50. Benedict Anderson, *Imagined Communities: Reflections on the Origins and Spread of Nationalism*, Verso, London, 1983 (revised 1991). Anderson was referring to continuities after a revolutionary change in the political order, which he saw as 'sometimes' of personnel such as 'functionaries and informers' and 'always' of laws, documents and records of all kinds, 1983 edn., 145, and 1991 edn., 160.

51. *El Argos de Buenos Ayres*, 1 Sept. 1821.

52. The BNP began to open in the evenings in 1905, the BNCh in 1910. In Buenos Aires, despite intermittent initiatives, the national library appears not to have opened regularly in the evenings until after Paul Groussac's death in 1929.

53. Paul Groussac, *Historia de la Biblioteca Nacional* (1893), Biblioteca Nacional, Buenos Aires, 1967, xxi.

54. Groussac, *Historia*, xlvi.

55. Arlegui, 'Primera historia', 26; Manuel Atanasio Fuentes, *Estadística general de Lima*, Tipografía Nacional de M. N. Corpancho, Lima, 1858, 246.

56. 'Chile', Historia de las Bibliotecas Nacionales, 148.

57. Benjamín Vicuña Mackenna, cited in Vicente G. Quesada, *Las bibliotecas europeas y algunas de la América Latina*, Imprenta y Librería de Mayo, Buenos Aires, vol. 1, 1877, 129.

58. For Chile, the *Revista de Bibliografía Chilena y Extranjera* of 1913 gives snapshot data on what was consulted at the BNCh, divided by language and subject: 1:7 (July 1913), 69, and 1:8 (Aug. 1913), 139–40. Literature accounted for nearly all the books borrowed (965 of 1,171 in July 1913 and 1,001 of 1,249 in Aug. 1913). In the reading rooms, 'General works', which could not be borrowed, were those most often consulted (1,981 in July; 2,508 in Aug.), followed by 'Literature' (1,347 July; 1,466 Aug.), 'Social sciences' (843 July; 978 Aug.), 'History and geography' (706 July; 922 Aug.), 'Applied sciences' (309 July; 418 Aug.) and 'Pure sciences' (310 July; 352 Aug.). In total 5,729 consultations were recorded in July and 6,973 in Aug. On the situation in the 1930s in Argentina, see *Los 2600 libros más pedidos en la Biblioteca Nacional*, Imprenta de la Biblioteca Nacional, Buenos Aires, 1936.

59. Guillermo Feliú Cruz, 'Andrés Bello y la Biblioteca Nacional', in *Ediciones de la Revista Mapocho* (Biblioteca Nacional de Chile, offprint), 4:3, 1965, 13–23, 19–20.

60. Pablo Buchbinder, *Los Quesada: Letras, ciencia y política en Argentina, 1850–1934*, Edhasa, Buenos Aires, 2012, 89.

61. Decree of 11 Feb. 1870, cited in 'Las Bibliotecas públicas', *Boletín de las bibliotecas populares, Buenos Aires*, 1 (1872), xxxii–xliii, esp. xxxix.

62. Benjamin Franklin Ramiz Galvão, *Bibliothêcas publicas de Europa—Relatorio apresantado āo Ministerio dos Negocios do Imperio*, Rio de Janeiro, 1874.

63. *Borges, Director de la Biblioteca Nacional: Diálogos entre José Edmundo Clemente y Oscar Sbarra Mitre*, Biblioteca Nacional Argentina, Buenos Aires, 1998, 21.

64. 'A próposito de un libro de Vicente Quesada', orig. in three parts, *La Educación Común*, 15 June and 1 July 1877, and *La Tribuna*, 6 Nov. 1877, all together in D. F. Sarmiento, *Páginas selectas de Sarmiento sobre bibliotecas populares*, Comisión Nacional de Homenaje a Sarmiento, Buenos Aires, vol. 4, 1938, 172–88.

65. *Boletín de las bibliotecas populares*, vol. 1 (1872), xl.

66. Oscar Sbarra Mitre, Director of the BNA 1997–2000, in *Borges, Director*, 24.

67. Alberto Manguel, in conversation, event at the British Library, London, 4 Apr. 2017.

68. Feliú Cruz, 'Andrés Bello y la Biblioteca Nacional', 22.

69. 'Correspondencia con la Biblioteca Nacional de Chile, i documentos, desde 1829 hasta 1863, caja 23, vol. 80 [manuscritos]', Biblioteca Nacional de Chile.

70. 'Chile', *Historia de las Bibliotecas Nacionales*, 136.

71. 'Chile', *Historia de las Bibliotecas Nacionales*, 137–39.

72. Horacio Torrent, 'Bellas artes, técnica y arquitectura en Sudamérica: La Biblioteca Nacional en la modernización de Santiago de Chile', *ARQ* (Santiago), no. 29 (Apr. 1995), 25, http://www.edicionesarq.cl/1995/arq-29/. Mauricio Onetto, 'Terremotos recordados, temblores olvidados: Interpretaciones sobre los orígenes de la memoria telúrica en Chile', *Revista de Geografía Norte Grande*, no. 59, 2014, 185–99; Bárbara Silva Avaria and Alfredo Riquelme Segovia, *Una identidad terremoteada: Comunidad y territorio en el Chile de 1960*, Ediciones Universidad Alberto Hurtado, Santiago, 2018. My thanks to Camila Gatica Mizala for drawing my attention to the importance of earthquakes in Chile's national imaginary and for these references.

73. http://www.bibliotecanacional.cl/sitio/Contenido/Noticias/64915:Biblioteca-Nacional-celebra-203-anos-con-libro-y-exposicion-sobre-su-edificio.

74. 'Crónica de la Biblioteca Nacional: Celebración del centenario (1813–1913)', *Revista de Bibliografía Chilena y Extranjera*, 1:7 (July 1913), 131–40, esp. 131.

75. Memoria Chilena, 'Quienes somos': http://www.memoriachilena.gob.cl/602/w3-article-123834.html. For the award of the Stockholm Challenge Award to Memoria Chilena in 2010, see http://www.thisischile.cl/sitio-chileno-recibe-nobel-de-internet-en-categoria-cultura/.

76. Nicolás Díaz Sánchez, 'Biblioteca Nacional del Perú: Historia', at http://www.cervantesvirtual.com/portales/biblioteca_nacional_del_peru/historia/, accessed 3 Apr. 2017.

77. Jorge Basadre (then director), 'La Biblioteca Nacional de Lima, 1943–5', *Fénix* (BNP, Lima), 2–3, 1945.

78. *La Biblioteca Nacional del Perú: Aportes para su historia*. In 1830, and again in 1840, it was proposed to finance library acquisitions through a tax on imported books, the underlying impetus being to transfer resources from those with access to foreign goods to a national institution.

79. Raimundo Lazo, *Vigil, Palma, González Prada. Evocaciones históricas de la Biblioteca Nacional de Lima*, Universidad de La Habana, La Habana, 1943, 7.

80. See Hugo Neira, ed., *Joyas de la Biblioteca Nacional del Perú*, Lima, 2009; and Irma García Gayoso, Dionicia Morales de la Cruz and Silvana Salazar Ayllón, *Incunables peruanos en la Biblioteca Nacional del Perú (1584–1619)*, Biblioteca Nacional del Perú, Lima, 1996.

81. *Diario Oficial de la República de Chile*, Santiago, 22 Aug. 1881; Ignacio Domeyko, *Objetos científicos extraídos del Perú y su destino*, Universidad de Chile, Santiago, 1881.

82. Ricardo Palma, *Memoria que presenta el director de la nueva Biblioteca Nacional en el acto solemne de su inauguración el 28 de julio de 1884*, Imprenta del Universo de Carlos Prince, Lima, 1885; *Memoria que presenta el director de la nueva Biblioteca Nacional en la que compendía 25 años de labor*, Imprenta de San Pedro, Lima, 1908; *Apuntes para la historia de la Biblioteca de Lima*, Empresa Tipográfica Unión, Lima, 1912.

83. Palma, *Memoria*, 1908, 9.

84. Oscar Gonzales, 'La devolución de los libros al Perú por parte de Chile', 2015. http://www.librosperuanos.com/autores/articulo/00000002341/La-devolucion-de-los-libros-al-Peru-por-parte-de-Chile.

85. Bernardo Subercaseaux, *Historia del libro en Chile (alma y cuerpo)*, LOM Ediciones, Santiago, 2nd edn., 2000, 50.

86. Parada, *Los orígenes*, 307. 'Ley de 23 de Sept de 1870 sobre bibliotecas populares', in República Argentina, *Leyes y decretos relativos a la Comisión Protectora de Bibliotecas Populares*, Talleres de la Oficina Meteorológica Argentina, Buenos Aires, 1911, 5–7.

87. Domingo F. Sarmiento, 'El enemigo en campaña', *Ambas Americas*, New York, 1:1, 1867, also in Sarmiento, *Páginas Selectas*, 95–115. Sarmiento denounces, item by item, a list drawn up by the rector of UBA, Juan María Gutiérrez, in response to a request for advice from the Sociedad Auxiliar de la Biblioteca Pública de San Juan. Sarmiento argued that Gutiérrez's recommendations were out of date, irrelevant to the practical needs of the San Juan immigrant economy and designed to deter anyone from reading.

88. An appendix to the *Boletin de las bibliotecas populares*, nos. 2–3, 1872, lists the books sent by the Comisión Protectora to individual libraries. On readers' responses, see Javier Planas, *Libros, lectores y sociabilidades de lectura: una historia de los orígenes de las bibliotecas populares en Argentina*, Ampersand, Buenos Aires, 2017.

89. Arnaldo Ignacio Adolfo Miranda, *Las bibliotecas públicas municipales de la Ciudad de Buenos Aires*, Municipalidad de la Ciudad de Buenos Aires, 1996, 29. Comisión Nacional de Bibliotecas Populares, *Herramientas de gestión social para bibliotecas populares: Las bibliotecas populares y la CONABIP*, CONABIP, Ministerio de Cultura, Buenos Aires, 2017, 24. For an online collection of documents on *bibliotecas populares*, see http://www.conabip.gob.ar/archivo_historico.

90. Miranda, *Las bibliotecas públicas municipales*, 28–29.

91. Walter Benjamin, 'Unpacking My Library', in Hannah Arendt, ed., *Illuminations*, Fontana/Collins, London, 1973, 59–67.

92. Groussac, *Historia de la Biblioteca Nacional*, 374.

93. *Un siglo de periódicos en la Biblioteca Nacional (políticos): Catálogo por fechas, 1800–1899*, Imprenta de la Biblioteca Nacional, Buenos Aires, 1935.

94. Biblioteca Nacional, *Catálogo de la sección americana: América en general*, Imprenta Universitaria, Santiago, 1902.

95. Fuentes, *Estadística general de Lima*, iii–iv.

96. Manuel de Odriozola, *Colección de Documentos literarios del Perú*, Lima, 1863–76; and his *Documentos históricos del Perú*, Lima, 1863–77. For a biography see Alberto Tauro Uriarte, *Manuel de Odriozola: Prócer, erudito, bibliotecario*, Universidad Nacional Mayor de San Marcos, Lima, 1964.

97. Ricardo Palma, *Catálogo de los libros que existen en el Salón América*, Lima, 1891.

98. *Estadística bibliográfica de la literatura chilena* (1862–) and *Anuario de la prensa chilena* (1886–).

99. *Congrès international des bibliothécaires tenu à Paris du 20 au 23 août 1900: Procès-verbaux et mémoires*, H. Welter, Paris, 1901. At this congress, Domingo Figarola-Caneda of Cuba and Fernando Ferrari Pérez of Mexico were vice-presidents (10); and Luis Montt, director of the BNCh, gave a presentation on its history, its current collection of over one hundred thousand volumes, its bibliographical publications and its readership (one hundred people a day, although Montt noted regretfully that many came for 'works of imagination and entertainment'), 221–26, esp. 226.

100. 'Brazil', *Historia de las Bibliotecas Nacionales*, 38–61, 45.

101. Parada, *Los orígenes*, 172.

102. Manuel González Prada, *Nota informativa (acerca de la Biblioteca Nacional)*, Imprenta de La Acción Popular, Lima, 1912, 10–14.

103. Umberto Eco, 'De Bibliotheca' (1981), in Candida Höfer, *Libraries*, Thames & Hudson, London, 2005, 7–14, esp. 8.

104. Groussac, *Historia de la Biblioteca Nacional*, lvii. Groussac stated that he was referring to Auguste Comte's system, as modified by Herbert Spencer in *The Classification of the Sciences*, London, 1864.

105. Groussac, *Historia de la Biblioteca Nacional*, lix.

106. Paul Groussac, *Catálogo metódico de la Biblioteca Nacional seguido de una tabla alfabética de autores*, Buenos Aires, 7 vols., 1893. On the social question, see Eduardo A. Zimmermann, *Los liberales reformistas: La cuestión social en la Argentina, 1890–1916*, Editorial Sudamérica, Buenos Aires, 1995.

107. Before John Dewey worked out his decimal system in 1876, books in US libraries were classified according to size and/or date of acquisition; browsing was not important because there was no public access to the shelves. Dewey's system was adopted after the Second World War in several Latin American libraries—for example, Brazil's national library and Colombia's Biblioteca Luis Ángel Arango.

108. Groussac, *Historia de la Biblioteca Nacional*, 374.

109. On architecture of BNA: http://www.plataformaarquitectura.cl/cl/790683/clasicos -de-arquitectura-biblioteca-nacional-mariano-moreno-testa-bullrich-y-cazzaniga; http:// brutalism.online/brutalist-buildings/17-argentina/459-national-library-of-the-argentine -republic.

Chapter Two: Repertoires of Knowledge

1. The Proyecto Iberoamericano de Historia Conceptual, known as Iberconceptos, has conducted extensive research on the political vocabularies of the región. The key publications are Javier Fernández-Sebastián, ed., *Diccionario político social del mundo iberoamericano: Tomo I, La era de las revoluciones*, Fundación Carolina / Sociedad de Conmemoración Estatal / Centro de Estudios Políticos y Constitucionales, Madrid, 2009; and *Tomo II, Los conceptos fundamentales, 1770–1870*, Madrid, 2014. See also the website http://www.iberconceptos.net.

2. Bernardo Monteagudo, 23 Feb. 1822, *Colección documental* [. . .] *del Perú*, 13:1, 291–92.

3. See ch. 10 on education, esp. 221–22.

4. *El Americano* (Buenos Aires), no. 27, 1 Oct. 1819, 10–15; and no. 28, 8 Oct. 1819, 7–11.

5. Juan Cristóstomo Lafinur, *Curso filosófico dictado en Buenos Aires en 1819*, ed. Delfina Varela Domínguez de Ghioldi, Instituto de Filosofía, Buenos Aires, 1938. This book contains a selection of documents on the controversy.

6. Thomas Aquinas, *De veritate*, question 2, article 3, argument 19.

7. *El Americano*, 1 Oct. 2019.

8. *El Americano*, 1 Oct. 2019.

9. *El Americano*, 8 Oct. 2019.

10. Delfina Varela Domínguez de Ghioldi, 'Prólogo', in Lafinur, *Curso filosófico*, 9–51, esp. 30.

11. Geoffrey Lloyd, *The Ideals of Inquiry: An Ancient History*, Oxford University Press, Oxford, 2014.

12. Alcorta's syllabus was not published at the time, but Juan María Gutiérrez included parts of it verbatim in his *Orígen y desarrollo de la Enseñanza Pública Superior en Buenos Aires* (1868), Ediciones 'La Cultura Argentina', Buenos Aires, 1915, 116–22; and in 1902 Paul Groussac compiled a full version from three fairly consistent manuscripts and printed it in *Anales de la Biblioteca Nacional* (Buenos Aires), vol. 2, 1–177. We therefore have a reliable idea of the syllabus, although of course it is far harder to acertain how much it was modified or embellished in the classroom. An analogous course taught at the Instituto Nacional in Santiago shows many correspondences with Alcorta's but also some intriguing differences, notably an emphasis on spirituality, reflecting the distinct knowledge environments of the two cities/countries. José Miguel Varas and Ventura Marín, *Elementos de Ideolojía*, Instituto Nacional, Santiago, 1830; in revised version as Ventura Marín, *Elementos de filosofía del espiritú humano*, Imprenta de la Independencia, Santiago, 1834.

13. Gutiérrez, *Orígen y desarrollo*, 76; Vicente Fidel López, *Evocaciones históricas: Autobiografía; La Gran Semana de 1810; El Conflicto y la entrevista de Guayaquil*, El Ateneo, Buenos Aires, 1929, 32–34. Alcorta appeared as a character in a novel by his student José Mármol, in which it was claimed that the generation who had been taught by him had become 'his ideas in action, [...] the multiplied reproduction of his patrician virtue, his humanitarian conscience, his philosophical thought'. José Mármol, *Amalia* (1851), Editorial Sopena Argentina, Buenos Aires, 4th edn., 1948, 18.

14. During the French invasion of 1838, Rosas cut funding from 35,000 to 2,900 pesos a year.

15. Paul Groussac, 'Noticia biográfica del Doctor Don Diego Alcorta y examen crítico de su obra', *Anales de la Biblioteca Nacional*, vol. 2, 1902, vii–cxviii; Tulio Halperín Donghi, *Historia de la Universidad de Buenos Aires* (1962), Eudeba, Buenos Aires, 2002, 45.

16. Jean-Luc Chappey, 'Raison et citoyenneté: les fondements culturels d'une distinction sociale et politique sous le Directoire', in Raymonde Monnier, ed., *Citoyens et citoyenneté sous la Revolution française*, Société des études robespierristes, Paris, 2012, 279–90, esp. 287.

17. Varela Domínguez de Ghioldi, 'Prólogo', esp. 19–28, charts the publication of their work in early nineteenth-century Argentina.

18. Jorge R. Zamudio Silva, *Juan Manuel Fernández de Agüero*, Instituto de Filosofía, Universidad de Buenos Aires, Buenos Aires, 1940, esp. 113–14; and Varela Domínguez de Ghioldi, 'Prólogo'.

19. Diego Alcorta, 'Introducción', in *Anales de la Biblioteca Nacional*, vol. 2, cxix.

20. Jorge Cañizares Esguerra, 'How Derivative Was Humboldt?', in his *Nature, Empire, and Nation: Explorations in the History of Science in the Iberian World*, Stanford University Press, Stanford CA, 2006, 112–28; see also Helen Cowie, *Conquering Nature in Spain and its Empire, 1750–1850*, Manchester University Press, Manchester, 2011. Raymond Williams offers a succinct history of the term 'nature', in *Keywords: A Vocabulary of Culture and Society*, Fontana / Croom Helm, London, 1976, 184–89, esp. 188.

21. Famous examples include Juan Pablo Viscardo, 'Carta derijida à los españoles americanos por uno de sus compatriotas' (written 1791), facs. of London edn. of 1801, 1853; Bernardo Monteagudo, *Diálogo entre Atawallpa y Fernando VII en los campos eliseos* (1808), Carlos Castañón Barrientos, La Paz, 1973; and José Servando Teresa de Mier, *Carta de un Americano al Español sobre su número XIX*, W. Lewis, London, 1811.

22. Camilo Henríquez, 'Proclama', 2 Jan. 1811, in José Luis Romero and Luis Alberto Romero, eds., *Pensamiento político de la emancipación*, Biblioteca Ayacucho, Caracas, 2 vols., 1977, vol. 1, 220–24, esp. 221.

23. Diego Alcorta, 'Curso de filosofía', *Anales de la Biblioteca Nacional*, vol. 2, 1–177, esp. 58.

24. Alcorta, 'Curso de filosofía', 155.

25. Rebecca Earle, *The Return of the Native: Indians and Myth-Making in Spanish America, 1810–1930*, Duke University Press, Durham NC, 2007, 10–11.

26. Alcorta, 'Curso de filosofía', 57.

27. Juan C. Lafinur, *Función literaria (Exponense à un examen público los elementos de la segunda parte del curso filosófico)*, Facultad de Filosofía y Letras, Universidad de Buenos Aires, 1820.

28. Alcorta, 'Curso de filosofía', 155.

29. Alcorta, 'Curso de filosofía', 157.

30. Alcorta, 'Curso de filosofía', 155.

31. Alcorta, 'Introducción al Curso de Filosofía', cxix.

32. Fidel López, *Autobiografía*, 34.

33. Marcos Sastre, *El Tempe argentine: Impresiones y cuadros del Paraná etc.*, Buenos Aires, 1858.

34. Alejandro E. Parada, *Los libros en la época del salón literario: El Catálogo de la Librería Argentina de Marcos Sastre (1835)*, Academia Argentina de Letras, Buenos Aires, 2008.

35. Victor Mercante, 'Prólogo', in Marcos Sastre, *El Tempe argentino*, Administración General, Buenos Aires, 1921. All quotations are from this edition.

36. The references were to Aelian, cited in Juan de Guzmán, *Las Geórgicas de Virgil y su décima égloga, traducidas en verso castellano*, Madrid, 1768, 342–46; and to 'Barthélémy', presumably Jean Jacques, an early French Hellenist (1716–1795). Sastre, *El Tempe*, 171–72.

37. Sastre, *El Tempe*, 29.

38. Sastre, *El Tempe*, 16.

39. Sastre, *El Tempe*, 172.

40. Sastre, *El Tempe*, 88–89. Pierre André Latreille (1762–1833) was best known for *Histoire naturelle des fournis, et recueil de mémoires et d'observations sur les abeilles, les araignées, les gaucheurs et autres insectes*, Imprimérie de Crapelet, Paris, 1802. Sastre made no mention of Mandeville's *The Fable of the Bees, or Private Vices, Publick Benefits*, 1714.

41. Sastre, *El Tempe*, 90.

42. Sastre, *El Tempe*, 91.

43. Félix Weinberg, *El salón literario de 1837*, Librería Hachette, Buenos Aires, 1958, includes a list of members.

44. Cited by Mercante, 'Prólogo', 10.

45. Sastre, *El Tempe*, 183.

46. Sastre, *El Tempe*, 102.

47. Sastre, *El Tempe*, 137.

48. Sastre, *El Tempe*, 27.

49. Sastre, *El Tempe*, 175.

50. Sastre, *El Tempe*, 104.

51. Sastre, *El Tempe*, 84.

52. Sastre, *El Tempe*, 87.

53. Manuel L. de Vidaurre, 'Discurso en el Congreso Americano de Panamá', 22 June 1826, in Germán A. de la Reza, ed., *Documentos sobre el Congreso Anfictiónico de Panamá*, Fundación Biblioteca Ayacucho, Caracas, 2012, 184–90, quotations at 184.

54. Vidaurre, 'Discurso', 186–87.

55. Primera reunión del Congreso Científico Latino Americano, 1898, vol. 1, quotations at 72 and 65.

56. Camilo Henríquez, 'La Camila, o, La patriota de Sud-América' (1817), in M. L. Amunátegui, ed., *Camilo Henríquez [. . .] Edición oficial*, Imprenta Nacional, Santiago, 2 vols., 1889, vol. 2, 309–52, esp. 350.

57. Rafael Sagredo Baeza, ed., *Ciencia-Mundo: Orden republicano, arte y nación en América*, Editorial Universitaria, Santiago, 2010, 13.

58. Andrew Laird and Nicola Miller, eds., *Antiquities and Classical Traditions in Latin America*, Wiley, Oxford, 2018.

59. Earle, *Return of the Native*, 34 ff.

60. Elina Miranda Cancela, 'Greece and José Martí', in Laird and Miller, *Antiquities and Classical Traditions*, 157–67, esp. 166.

61. Nicola Miller, 'Classical Motifs in Spanish American Nation-Building: Looking Beyond the Elites', in Laird and Miller, *Antiquities and Classical Traditions*, 144–56.

62. Camilo Henríquez, 'Desventajas del latín para la educación común' (1813), in Raúl Silva Castro, ed., *Escritos políticos de Camilo Henríquez*, Universidad de Chile, Santiago, 1960, 120–22.

63. Escuela Militar de Chile, *Reglamento*, Imprenta Nacional, Santiago, 1862 and *Reglamento*, Imprenta de El Progreso, Santiago, 1883; the Argentine military journal *Ejército argentino: Semanario*, 1883 onwards, regularly featured articles on ancient history.

64. For an example of recitation, see Escuela de Artes y Oficios (Provincia de Buenos Aires), *Programas y horarios de las clases elementales: correspondientes al año 1883*, Escuela de Artes y Oficios, San Martín, Provincia de Buenos Aires, 1883. For a survey of colonial-era rhetoric, see Don Paul Abbott, *Rhetoric in the New World: Rhetorical Theory and Practice in Colonial Spanish America*, University of South Carolina Press, Columbia, 1996.

65. Juan José de Urquiza, who led the forces that defeated the dictator Rosas, said that the first of his obligations was 'to save the *Patria* from demagoguery, after having liberated it from

tyranny': J. J. de Urquiza, 'Viva la Confederación Argentina!', 23 June 1852, in *Manifiesto del Exmo. Sr. Director Provisorio de la Confederación Argentina con otros documentos correlativos*, Imprenta del Estado, Buenos Aires, 1852, 14.

66. Cristiana Bertazoni, '"Apu Ollantay": Inca Theatre as an Example of the Modes of Interaction between the Incas and Western Amazonian Societies', *Boletim do Museu Paraense Emílio Goeldi: Ciências humanas*, 9:1 (Belém, Jan.–Apr. 2014): http://dx.doi.org/10.1590/S1981-8122201400010000.

67. Luis Miguel Glave, *Dama de Sociedad: Trinidad María Enríquez, Cusco 1846–1891*, Red Nacional de Promoción de la Mujer, Lima, 1997, 46; Carlos Ramos Núñez and Martín Baigorria Castillo, *Trinidad María Enríquez: Una abogada en los Andes*, Palestra Editores, Lima, 2005.

68. For example, Sebastián Lorente, *Nociones del estilo*, Lima, 2 vols. (*Prosa* and *Verso*), 1866; *Nuevo Manual Epistolar, ó arte de escribir todo género de cartas según el gusto del día*, Caracas, 1852, and Bogotá, 1857. Diego Barros Arana, *Manual de composición literaria*, A. Raymond, Santiago, 1871; and 'Manual de elocución ó principios de arte de leer y escribir', *Anales de la Instrucción Pública de Colombia*, 2:7, 1881, 42–62.

69. 'Historia de la Universidad Nacional de La Plata', UNLP website: http://www.unlp.edu.ar/historia.

70. Joaquín González, 'Extracto de la memoria enviada al Gobernador de la Provincia de Buenos Aires, Marcelino Ugarte', 12 Feb. 1905, Universidad Nacional de La Plata website: https://unlp.edu.ar/historia/marcelino_ugarte-2791.

71. Guadalupe Appendini, *Historia de la Universidad Nacional Autónoma de México*, Editorial Porrúa, México, 1981, esp. chs. 2, 3 and 4.

Chapter Three: Writing in the Dark: A Market for Knowledge

1. There were earlier examples of hand-printing, the first known of which date from 1776, but this was the first mechanised press in Chile.

2. Victor M. Uribe-Uran, ed., *State and Society in Spanish America during the Age of Revolution*, Scholarly Resources Inc., Wilmington DE, 2001; Luis Miguel Glave, ed., *Del pliego al periódico: Prensa, espacios públicos y construcción nacional Iberoamericana*, Fundación Mapfre Tavera, Madrid, 2003; and Paula Alonso, ed., *Construcciones impresas: Panfletos, diarios y revistas en la formación de los estados nacionales en América Latina, 1820–1920*, Fondo de Cultura Económica, México DF and Buenos Aires, 2004. For a dictionary of where printing first occurred in places throughout Spanish America and Spain, see Antonio Palau y Dulcet, 'Diccionario geográfico-tipográfico', *Manual de Librero Hispano-Americano*, Barcelona, 7 vols., 1923–27, vol. 1, xxi–xxxix. On Brazil, where a modern press was introduced by the Portuguese court in 1808, see Marco Morel and Mariana Monteiro de Barros, *Palavra, imagem e poder: O surgimento da imprenta no Brasil do século XIX*, DP & A Editora, Rio de Janeiro, 2003.

3. There was considerable interim variation: in Peru, for example, 360 newspapers were recorded during 1831–35, which dropped to 52 after the collapse of the Peru-Bolivia Confederation (1836–39), then began to rise again from 1846 onwards. See Carlos Forment, *Democracy in Latin America, 1760–1900*, University of Chicago Press, Chicago and London, 2003, 218.

4. Pablo Lacoste, *El ferrocarril trasandino 1872–1984*, Editorial Universitaria, Santiago, 2000, 126–27.

5. Parada, *Los orígenes de la Biblioteca Pública de Buenos Aires*, 294.

6. Printer-publisher José Alejandro Bernheim, 'the great promoter of the Argentina graphic arts', opened the first foundry for typeface in the 1860s; the following decade his former apprentice Jacobo Peuser founded a paper factory and a binding workshop. Comisión Homenaje, *Don Jacobo Peuser: Rasgos salientes de su vida y de su obra*, Imprenta Peuser, Buenos Aires, 1943, 14–18, quotation at 18.

7. Richard D. Brown, *Knowledge is Power: The Diffusion of Information in Early America, 1700–1865*, Oxford University Press, New York, 1989. See also his *Strength of a People: The Idea of an Informed Citizenry in America, 1650–1870*, University of North Carolina Press, Chapel Hill and London, 1996.

8. Richard E. Easterlin, *Growth Triumphant: The Twenty-First Century in Historical Perspective*, University of Michigan Press, Ann Arbor, 1996, 'Table 5.1. Primary School Enrollment Rate by Country, 1830–1990', 61 and related discussion 60–62.

9. There's now an extensive literature, much of it based on early modern France. For a good general survey and starting point, see Gugliemo Cavallo and Roger Chartier, eds., *A History of Reading in the West*, Polity Press, Oxford, 1999. For a revealing discussion of Argentina, see Alejandro E. Parada, *Cuando los lectores nos susurran: Libros, lecturas, bibliotecas, sociedad y prácticas editoriales en la Argentina*, Instituto de Investigaciones Bibliotecológicas, Universidad de Buenos Aires, Buenos Aires, 2007.

10. Forment, *Democracy*, 218–19.

11. Tomász Hen-Konarksi, 'Cossacks and Gauchos: Myths of Masculinity in the Political Struggles of the River Plate and Ukraine, 1830s through 1840s', PhD thesis, European University Institute, Florence, 2017, ch. 3, 'Luis Pérez and His Gaucho Journalism in Verse', 63–117.

12. Silvia Becerra Riquelme and Zenobio Saldivia Maldonado, *El Mercurio de Valparaiso: su rol de difusión de la ciencia y tecnología en el Chile decimonónico*, Bravo y Allende Editores, Chile, 2010, 29–30 and 39.

13. Carlos Casavalle, *Boletín bibliográfico sud-americano: De la imprenta y librería de Mayo de Carlos Casavalle*, Imprenta y Librería de Mayo, Buenos Aires, 22 issues, 1870.

14. Alejandro E. Parada, *Los libros en la época del salón literario: El Catálogo de la Librería Argentina de Marcos Sastre*, Academia Argentina de Letras, Buenos Aires, 2008.

15. Angel Rama, *La ciudad letrada*, Ediciones del Norte, Hanover NH, 1984. For an example of how the idea has been applied: Carlos Aguirre and Carmen McEvoy, eds., *Intelectuales y poder: Ensayos en torno a la república de las letras en el Perú e Hispanoamérica (ss. xvi–xx)*, Instituto Francés de Estudios Andinos / Instituto Riva Agüero, Lima, 2008. On the salience of visual culture: Serge Gruzinski, *Images at War: Mexico from Columbus to Blade Runner (1492–2019)*, trans. Heather MacLean, Duke University Press, Durham NC, 2001; Magali M. Carrera, *Imagining Identity in New Spain*, University of Texas Press, Austin, 2003; and Daniela Bleichmar, *Visible Empire: Botanical Expeditions and Visual Culture in the Hispanic Enlightenment*, University of Chicago Press, Chicago, 2012. See also the online collection of images: Dana Leibsohn and Barbara E. Mundy, 'Vistas: Visual Culture in Spanish America, 1520–1820', 2018, https://www.fordham.edu/vistas.

16. Alexander von Humboldt, *Personal Narrative of a Journey to the Equinoctial Regions of the New Continent*, trans. and abridged Jason Wilson, Penguin, Harmondsworth UK, 1996, 162.

17. *La Gaceta Mercantil* (Buenos Aires), 19 Nov. 1828.

18. Georgina G. Gluzman, Lía Munilla Lacasa and Sandra M. Szir, 'Género y cultura visual. Adrienne Macaire-Bacle en la historia del arte argentino. Buenos Aires (1828–1838)', *Artelogie*, no. 5, Oct. 2013, http://cral.in2p3.fr/artelogie/spip.php?article245.

19. Rodolfo Trostiné, *Bacle: Ensayo*, Asociación Libreros Anticuarios de la Argentina, Buenos Aires, 1953, 56–58.

20. César H. Bacle, *Estampas de Buenos Aires* (1833), Centro Editor de América Latina, Buenos Aires, facs. edn., 1966.

21. *El Recopilador / Museo Americano*, facs. edn., ed. Hernán Pas, Biblioteca Nacional de Mariano Moreno, Buenos Aires, 2013.

22. *El Tiempo*, 20 July 1829, cited by Trostiné, *Bacle*, 35.

23. Alejo González Garaño, *Bacle Litógrafo del estado, 1828–1838*, Amigos del Arte, Buenos Aires, 1933, 22–25.

24. Nanda Leonardini, *El grabado en el Perú republicano: Diccionario histórico*, Fondo Editorial, Universidad Nacional Mayor de San Marcos, Lima, 2003, 23–24.

25. Ships called at 'Coquimbo, Huasco, Copiapó, Cobija, Iquique, Arica, Islay and Pisco', *El Mercurio de Valparaíso*, 23 June 1841, cited in Becerra and Saldivia, *El Mercurio de Valparaíso*, 25.

26. Pablo Whipple, *La gente decente de Lima y su resistencia al orden republicano*, Instituto de Estudios Peruanos, Lima, 2013, 33.

27. Carreño's text was taken up by Appleton, the New York publishing house that was seeking to extend into Latin American markets, and no doubt benefited from Appleton's distribution networks. Sarmiento noted in disgust that 'this book is adopted in the schools of South America (Appleton)', in *Páginas Selectas*, 114. M. A. Carreño Muñoz, *Manual de urbanidad y buenas maneras para uso de la juventud de ambos sexos*, Appleton, New York, 1854. Most of the work has focused on Carreño's influential manual, but there were many other such texts. See, for example, Beatriz González Stephan, 'Economías fundacionales: diseño del cuerpo ciudadano', in B. González Stephan, ed., *Cultura y tercer mundo 2: Nuevas identidades ciudadanos*, Nueva Sociedad, Caracas, 17–47; Diego Nicolás Pardo Motta, *Manuales de urbanidad: Construcción y destrucción del ciudadano durante el liberalismo radical, 1863–1886*, Ediciones Uniandes, Bogotá, 2016.

28. *El industrial práctico: Colección de recetas utiles de ciencias y artes. Extracto de las obras Secretos raros de artes y oficios, Enciclopedia doméstica, Anales de química industrial, etc., Segunda época*, Imprenta de J. M. Aguilar Ortiz, Mexico, 1873. For the full list of contents, 379–95; for instructions on writing 'at night, without light', by folding and refolding the piece of paper in a logical sequence, 127.

29. Gabriel Moreno, *Almanaque peruano y guía de forasteros*, Lima, 1800, and R. P. Francisco Romero, edition of 1812; *Almanak y kalendario general, diario de quartos de luna, según el meridiano de Buenos-Ayres*, Real Imprenta de Niños Expósitos, Buenos Aires, 1806–7; Bartolomé Muñoz, *Almanak curioso de Buenos-Ayres: Año de 1826*, Buenos Aires, 1826; Mariano Egaña, *Almanak nacional para el estado de Chile*, Santiago, 1824.

30. Carlos Casavalle, description of the *Almanaque popular*, Valparaíso, 1845, in *Boletín bibliográfico sud-americano*, no. 19, 1 Nov. 1870, 76. Another leading example was the *Almanaque rural argentino: Enciclopedia práctica de agricultura*, [...] *etc.*, Igón Hermanos, Buenos Aires, probably published from 1900 (extant copies date 1917 as year 17, 1918 as year 18 and so on; last known copy 1924).

31. Comisión Homenaje, *Don Jacobo Peuser: Rasgos salientes de su vida y de su obra*, Imprenta Peuser, Buenos Aires, 1943, 43.

32. For example, *Almanaque del Rosario para 1876*, Rosario, 1876; *Almanaque de El Comercio*, Lima, 1893.

33. *Almanaque Universal hispano-americano*, ed. José Segundo Florez, Imprenta Española y Americana del Sr Dubuisson, Paris, 1853; *Almanaque sud-americano*, ed. Casimiro Prieto y Valdés, Ramón Espasa é hijo, Buenos Aires, 1877–1902.

34. Carlos Casavalle, in his *Boletín bibliográfico sud-americano*, no. 6, 15 Apr. 1870, 23.

35. *Almanaque comercial y de chistes para 1875*, Lima, 1875.

36. *Anuario bibliográfico de la República Argentina*, 1879, ed. Alberto Navarro Viola, Imprenta del Mercurio, Buenos Aires, 1880, entry 109.

37. J. Armando Guimet, '*Calendario histórico del Perú' (texto escolar): 5 siglos de patria en orden cronológico y alfabético*, Editorial Minerva, Lima, 1939; Pedro J. Ramírez, *Las Efemérides al servicio de la educación: Guía del maestro para las inauguraciones de las clases, arreglada especialmente para las escuelas de Chile*, Editorial Nascimento, Santiago, 1943; Ostende M. Ardiles Morales, *La tribuna del maestro: Efemérides nacionales, biografías de hombres célebres en la historia y la cultura peruana* [...], *En programas completas desarrolladas para la celebración del Calendario cívico escolar*, Editorial H. G. Rozas, Cuzco, 1958.

38. Pedro Rivas, *Efemérides americanas*, Imprenta de 'El Comercio', Rosario, 1879, and Barcelona, 1884.

39. *Anuario bibliográfico de la República Argentina*, 1879, entry 109.

40. *Un riojano universal en Chile: Santos Tornero; Edición facsímil de su obra 'Reminiscencias de un viejo editor'*, Instituto de Estudios Riojanos, Logroño, 2010.

41. Letters from Louis Kuhne to Carlos Casavalle, Leipzig, 4 Jan. and 10 July 1894, Archivo General de la Nación de Argentina (AGN), Colección Carlos Casavalle (hereafter CCC), 2289, 1–2. The collection has been renumbered: the numbers given here are the most recent. There is a collection guide, which in itself is a valuable source for tracing his extensive networks: AGN, Departamento Documentos Escritos, *Colección Carlos Casavalle (1544–1904), Catálogo e índices*, Senado de la Nación, Buenos Aires, 2 vols., 1996. See also Ricardo Piccirilli, *Carlos Casavalle, impresor y bibliófilo: Una época de la bibliografía americana*, Buenos Aires, 1942.

42. Ricardo Palma to Carlos Casavalle, Lima, 7 Mar. 1884, CCC 2293.

43. Carlos Casavalle to Vicente Fidel López, 20 June 1896, CCC 5226; and 17 July 1896, CCC 5227.

44. Carlos Casavalle to Vicente Fidel López, 3 Mar. 1896, CCC 5215.

45. A. Navarro Viola to Carlos Casavalle, 10 Mar. 1882, 1 Oct. 1883 and 19 Jan. 1884, CCC 2292, 12–14.

46. Jorge Faustino to Carlos Casavalle, Buenos Aires, Mar. 1897, CCC 2289.

47. M. R. Trelles to Carlos Casavalle, 22 Apr. 1882, CCC 2296.

48. Ricardo Palma to Carlos Casavalle, Lima, 1 Dec. 1883, CCC 2293.

49. Casavalle, *Boletín bibliográfico sud-americano*. Quotation from matter on the front page of all twenty-two issues.

50. For example, commenting on *Colección de historiadores de Chile, y documentos relativos a la Historia Nacional, Santiago, 1861–4*, Casavalle noted: 'The majority of the documents in this collection are unpublished and extremely interesting', *Boletín bibliográfico*, no. 1 (Jan. 1870), 1.

51. Manuel Torres Campos, *Bibliografía española contemporánea del derecho y de la política, 1800–1880*, Madrid, 8 vols., 1883–98.

52. Graciela Swiderski, 'Estudio preliminar', in *Colección Carlos Casavalle*, 3–14, esp. 5.

53. *Obras completas de D. Estéban Echeverría*, Imprenta y Librería de Mayo, Buenos Aires, 5 vols., 1870–74; Antonio Zinny, *Historia de los Gobernadores de las Provincias Argentinas desde 1810 hasta la fecha*, Imprenta y Librería de Mayo, Buenos Aires, 3 vols., 1879–82. The quality of what we might now call loss-leaders was hailed as a national glory in the Argentine press, but less than half of the editions were sold, according to Bartolomé Mitre, in *La Nación*, 4 Jan. 1871.

54. Vicente G. Quesada, *La vida intelectual en las provincias argentinas (1861)*, Coni Hermanos, Buenos Aires, 1911, 4.

55. It is unlikely that they were all sold, although there was an impressive rise in subscriptions from 159 in January to 641 in July 1861. *Revista del Paraná*, vols. 1 and 7, 1861. See also Alejandro Eujanian, 'Por una historia nacional desde las provincias: El frustrado Proyecto de Vicente Quesada en *La Revista del Paraná*', online at http://historiapolitica.com/datos/biblioteca /pasadoprov_eujanian.pdf, accessed 16 Dec. 2019.

56. Quesada, *La vida intelectual*, 24, 34, 68.

57. Juan B. Alberdi to Vicente Quesada, 23 Apr. 1861, cited in Quesada, *La vida intelectual*, 48.

58. For a decoding of Argentine authors, see Mario Tesler, *Autores y seudónimos porteños*, Ediciones Dunken, Buenos Aires, 2007.

59. This was the style in Casavalle's definitive *Boletín bibliográfico*.

60. *Boletín bibliográfico*, Feb. 1870, 1.

61. Diego Barros Arana, 'Crítica literaria', *El Museo: Periódico científico y literario* (Santiago), 14 (10 Sept. 1853).

62. The articles were published under the pseudonym Víctor Gálvez. *Nueva Revista de Buenos Aires*, vol. 5, Sept. 1882, 177–87, and Oct. 1882, 442–53; vol. 6, Dec. 1882, 36–58, Jan. 1883, 223–42, Feb. 1883, 468–506, and Mar. 1883, 531–46; vol. 7, Apr. 1883, 3–16, May 1883, 237–57, June 1883, 353–405, and July 1883, 657–72; vol. 8, Sept. 1883, 246–60, Oct. 1883, 431–47 (where the title 'Memorias de un viejo' appeared for the first time), and Nov. 1883, 524–49; vol. 9, Jan. 1884, 204–36, Feb. 1884, 345–74, and Mar. 1884, 561–82; vol. 10, Apr. 1884, 151–63; May 1884, 263–68; June 1884, 443–66; vol. 11, Sept. 1884, 161–84, and Nov. 1884, 481–90.

63. *Recuerdos de antaño: Hombres y cosas de la República Argentina*, Chavez Paz, Buenos Aires, 1888. Vicente Gálvez [Quesada], 'Introducción', *Memorias de un viejo: Escenas de costumbres de la República Argentina*, Jacobo Peuser, Buenos Aires, 4th edn., 1889, 10.

64. 'Noticia' (signed 'El Editor'), *Recuerdos de antaño*, i.

65. Antonio Zinny to Carlos Casavalle, Lobos, 24 Apr. 1880, CCC, 2298. Zinny, *Historia de los gobernadores*.

66. Guillermo Feliú Cruz, in 'Homenaje a D. Benjamín Vicuña Mackenna', *Anales de la Universidad de Chile*, 3a serie, Año I, tercero y cuarto trimestres de 1931, 301. Benjamín Vicuña Mackenna, *Catálogo completo de la Biblioteca Americana compuesta de más de 3,000 volúmenes, que posee D. Benjamín Vicuña Mackenna*, Imprenta del Mercurio, Valparaíso, 1861; *Bibliografía completa de las obras de Don B. Vicuña Mackenna: Única nómina completa, revisada i autorisada por el autor*, Imprenta del Centro, Santiago, 1879; *Catálogo de la biblioteca i manuscritos de D. Benjamín Vicuña Mackenna*, Imprenta Cervantes, Santiago, 1886.

67. Abel Pilon i Compañía, *Obras completas de Don B. V. M. Cinco series, 40 volúmenes en cuarto* (a prospectus, with a list of the contents of each volume), Santiago, 1 Oct. 1876. It was addressed 'to the Chilean public in particular and the Spanish-American public in general'.

68. Leading examples were Lucio V. Mansilla, *Una excursión a los indios ranqueles*, 1870; Vicente G. Quesada, *La Patagonia y las tierras australes del continente Americano*, Buenos Aires, 1875; Ramón N. Lista, *Mis exploraciones y descubrimientos en la Patagonia (1877–1880)*, Editorial Marymar, 1975; Estanislao Zeballos, *Descripción amena de la República Argentina, tomo I: Viaje al país de los Araucanos*, Buenos Aires, 1881; Luis Jorge Fontana, *Viaje de exploración en la Patagonia austral* (1886), Ediciones Marymar, Buenos Aires, 1976. See also Florentino Ameghino and Carlos Ameghino, *Reseñas de la Patagonia: Andanzas, penurias y descubrimientos de dos pioneros de la ciencia*, ed. Pablo Chiarelli, Ediciones Continente, Buenos Aires, 2006. Carlos Ameghino made twelve journeys to Patagonia from 1887 to 1903, collecting fossils and other samples for his brother and Francisco P. Moreno. Between the ages of six and eight, General Juan Perón lived in the small settlement of Camarones, province of Chubut, where there now a museum on the site of the family home: see 'Perón en la Patagonia: la casa-museo de su familia [. . .]', *La Nación*, 1 Nov. 2018. He produced his own brief regional study: *Toponomia patagónica de etimología araucana*, Imprenta de la Biblioteca Nacional, Buenos Aires, 1948.

69. For example, M. L. Amunátegui and G. V. Amunátegui, *Juicio crítico de algunos poetas Hispano Americanos*, Imprenta del Ferrocarril, Santiago, 1861; José M. Torres Caicedo, *Ensayos biográficos y de crítica literaria sobre los principales poetas y literatos hispano-americanos*, Paris, 1863, and second series, 1868; Ricardo Palma, *Lira Americana—Colección de poesías de los mejores poetas del Perú, Chile y Bolivia*, Paris, 1865; and Juan M. Gutiérrez, *Poesía Americana*, Buenos Aires, 1867. For an analysis of Gutiérrez's strategy of 'Americanising' through canon formation, see Álvaro Fernández Bravo, 'Un museo literario: Latinoamericanismo, archivo colonial y sujeto colectivo en la crítica de Juan María Gutiérrez (1846–1875)', in Graciela Batticuore, Klaus Gallo and Jorge Myers, eds., *Resonancias románticas: Ensayos sobre historia de la cultura argentina (1820–1890)*, Editorial Universitaria de Buenos Aires, Buenos Aires, 2005, 85–100. The first modern history of the Americas was Diego Barros Arana, *Compendio de historia de América*, Santiago, 4 vols., 1865, which Carlos Casavalle described as 'a complete history of the New World', in his *Boletín Bibliográfico*, Feb. 1870, 58. It did indeed cover most parts of the Americas, including the United States, Brazil, Haiti and Santo Domingo as well as Spanish America.

70. From the back cover of one of this series of 'Argentine Culture', Gutiérrez, *Origen y desarrollo*.

71. 'Editorial y Librería Nascimento (1875–1986)', http://www.memoriachilena.cl/602/w3 -article-3363.html#cronologia. Work is currently underway towards a relaunch, led by Carlos's great-grandson Pablo. Edie Essex Barrett, 'Re-opening Chile's legendary publishing house Editorial Nascimento', 19 Oct. 2018, https://bristolatino.co.uk/reopening-chiles-legendary -publishing-house-editorial-nascimiento/, accessed 7 Apr. 2020.

72. Joaquín Edwards Bello, *Crónicas del tiempo viejo*, Nascimento, Santiago, 1976, 112.

73. Carola Ureta Marín and Pedro Álvarez Caselli, *Luis Fernando Rojas: Obra gráfica, 1875– 1942*, LOM Ediciones, Santiago, 2014. Most of the information given here is drawn from their research, although gaps remain because relatively few traces of his life are available. See also the Memoria Chilena site: http://www.memoriachilena.gob.cl/602/w3-article-736.html.

74. The story is told in 'El dibujante Rojas', *El Peneca* (Santiago), 3:113, 16 Jan. 1911, 1–2, available on Memoria Chilena: http://www.memoriachilena.gob.cl/602/w3-article-98759 .html.

75. Exposición Internacional de Agricultura y Nacional de Industrias (Santiago, Chile), *Correo de la exposición*, Santiago de Chile, 1875–6.

76. Benjamín Vicuña Mackenna, *El album de la gloria de Chile*, Imprenta Cervantes, Santiago, 1883.

77. Cándido López, official artist attached to the Argentine campaign, who painted a series of fifty-eight panoramic scenes from the war, was also one of the country's first photographers.

78. Juan Antonio Bisama Cuevas, *Album gráfico militar de Chile: Campaña del Pacífico*, Sociedad Imprenta y Litografía Universo, Santiago, 1909. Most of these photographs were taken by a US American immigrant to Chile, Eduardo Spencer (see Memoria Chilena).

79. See Memoria Chilena: http://www.memoriachilena.gob.cl/602/w3-article-723.html.

80. R. Pérez Barredo, 'Legado de un genio olvidado', *Diario de Burgos*, 12 Apr. 2009.

81. Ibid.

82. Marilú Cerpa Moral, 'Manuel Moral y Vega, Fotógrafo y editor', *Acta herediana*, vol. 58, Apr.–Sept. 2016, 23–31.

83. Ibid., 31.

84. Argentina and Uruguay mark an annual 'Día del Canillita', when the story is always told of startled passers-by being urged to 'Buy *La República*!'. It is held on 7 Nov., the date of the death in 1910 of Uruguayan playwright Florencio Sánchez, whose one-act drama *Canillita* was a popular hit first in Rosario and then in Buenos Aires during the early twentieth century. Florencio Sánchez, *Canillita: Sainete en un acto*, Librería Teatral Apolo, Buenos Aires, 1915.

85. Pedro Elias Sarmiento, *La Escuela de Artes y Oficios de Santiago, tal como la ví y la conocí desde 1891 y 1901: Homenaje a su Centenario 1849–1949*, Imprenta Victoria, Valparaíso, 1949, 12–13.

Chapter Four: Knowledge Brokers: How Drawing Teachers Made Nations Possible

1. Jürgen Osterhammel, *The Transformation of the World: A Global History of the Nineteenth Century*, trans. Patrick Camiller, Princeton University Press, Princeton and Oxford, 2014.

2. Loraine Daston and Peter Galison, *Objectivity*, Zone Books, New York, 2007, 96–97.

3. Francisco Castañeda, 'Alocución, o arenga patriótica, que para la apertura de la nueva Academia de Dibuxo pronunció el dia diez de agosto de 1815 el ciudadano Fr. Francisco Castañeda' [*sic*], in Augusto E. Mallié, ed., *La Revolución de Mayo a través de los impresos de la época 1809–1815*, Comisión Nacional Ejecutiva del 150º Aniversario de la Revolución de Mayo, Buenos Aires, 1967, vol. 6, 371–85.

4. Manuel Belgrano, 'Medios generales de fomentar la agricultura, animar la industria y proteger el comercio en un país agricultor, Memoria', 15 July 1796, in his *Escritos económicos*, ed. Gregorio Weinberg, Editorial Raigal, Buenos Aires, 1954, 63–83; see also 'Industria', 21 Apr. 1810, ibid., 136. Camilo Henriquez, 'Escuela gratuita para la práctica del dibujo', 1815, reproduced in Gutiérrez, *Orígen y desarrollo*, 213–15.

5. For example, San Martín, as governor of Cuyo, supported a drawing school at the new secondary college in Mendoza; Juan Martín de Pueyrredón, former director of the United Provinces (1816–19) gave money to the drawing school at UBA; Martín Rodríguez, governor of Buenos Aires, contributed to the one at Colegio de la Unión.

6. *La Brújula* (Cusco), no. 4, 20 Feb. 1831, last page.

7. *Catálogo general de los productos nacionales y extrangeros* [*sic*] *presentados a la Exposición Nacional Argentina*, Córdoba, 1871; *Catálogo oficial de la Esposición Internacional de Chile*, Imprenta de la Librería del Mercurio, Santiago, 1875; *Catálogo de la Exposición Nacional de 1872*, Imprenta del Estado, Lima, 1872.

8. See Daniela Bleichmar, *Visible Empire: Botanical Expeditions and Visual Culture in the Hispanic Enlightenment*, University of Chicago Press, Chicago, 2012.

9. 'Mociones para la creación del cuerpo de ingenieros del ejército', *Aurora de Chile*, 1:45, 17 Dec. 1812.

10. Amunátegui, *Don Manuel de Salas*, I, 69–70, 82–3.

11. Maria Graham, *Journal of a Residence in Chile, during the Year 1822*, London, 1824, 178. See also Eugenio Pereira Salas, *Estudios sobre la historia del arte en el Chile republicano*, Ediciones de la Universidad de Chile, Santiago, 1992; Alexandra Kennedy, 'Circuitos artísticos interregionales de Quito a Chile: Siglos XVIII y XIX', *Revista Histórica* (Instituto de Historia, Pontificia Universidad Católica, Santiago), no. 31 (1998), 87–111.

12. Pedro Gjurinovic Canevaro, 'Cortés: Dibujante botánico', *Boletín del Instituto Riva-Agüero* (Lima), no. 16 (1989), 235–43, esp. 243.

13. Actas del Consulado, 30 Sept. 1819, cited in Rodolfo Trostiné, *La enseñanza del dibujo en Buenos Aires desde sus orígenes hasta 1850*, Ministerio de Educación / Universidad de Buenos Aires, Buenos Aires, 1950, 40–41.

14. Reginaldo de la Cruz Saldaña Retamar, *Rasgos biográficos de Manuel Núñez de Ibarra*, Corrientes, 1913.

15. *Gazeta de Buenos Aires*, 21 Apr. 1819, cited in Rodolfo Trostiné, *La pintura en las Provincias Argentinas: Siglo xix*, Santa Fe, 1950.

16. Rodolfo Trostiné, *El grabador correntino Manuel Pablo Núñez de Ibarra (1782–1862)*, Talleres Gráficos San Pablo, Buenos Aires, 1953, 42–43, 46–48.

17. Miguel Luis Amunátegui inveighed against *quiteño* art in his article 'Apuntes sobre lo que han sido las Bellas Artes en Chile', *Revista de Santiago*, no. 3 (1849), 37–47.

18. Valentina Ripamonti, 'Academia de Pintura en Chile: sus momentos previos', *Intus-Legere Historia* (Santiago), 4:1 (2010), 127–53, esp. 139.

19. Daston and Galison, *Objectivity*, 100.

20. D. F. Sarmiento, *El Progreso*, 16 Apr. 1844, cited in Domingo Amunátegui Solar, *El Instituto Nacional bajo los rectorados de don Manuel Montt, don Francisco Puente i don Antonio Varas (1835–1845)*, Imprenta Cervantes, Santiago, 1891, 461–62; A. Bouillon, *Principios de dibujo lineal*, trans. José Zegers, Imprenta de Julio Belín, Santiago, 1853 (no illustrations).

21. Daston and Gallison, *Objectivity*, 29.

22. Samuel Taylor Coleridge, 'On Poesy or Art' (1818), in Henry Nelson Coleridge, ed., *The Literary Remains of Samuel Taylor Coleridge*, W. Pickering, London, vol. 1, 1836, 216–30.

23. 'Ciencias: Discurso pronunciado al empezar sus tareas la Sociedad de Ciencias Físicas y Matemáticas establecida en esta ciudad', given 17 Apr. 1822, in *La Abeja Argentina* (Buenos Aires),

no. 4, 15 July 1822, 141–44. Facsimile in Senado de la Nación, *Biblioteca de Mayo: Colección de Obras y Documentos para la Historia Argentina, tomo vi, Literatura*, Buenos Aires, 1960, 5343–45.

24. 'Ciencias. Concluye el discurso suspendido en el numero sexto', *La Abeja Argentina*, no. 9, 15 Dec. 1822, 356–57; facs. edn., 5489.

25. Ibid., 358, facs. edn., 5490–91.

26. On the variety of practices of mimesis, see Christopher Prendergast, 'The Order of Mimesis: Poison, Nausea, Health', in his *Order of Mimesis*, Cambridge University Press, Cambridge, 1986, 1–23; Michael Taussig, *Mimesis and Alterity*, Routledge, New York and London, 1993; and, in relation to colonialism, Homi Bhabha, 'Of Mimicry and Man: The Ambivalence of Colonial Discourse', *October* (MIT Press), no. 28 (Spring 1984), 125–33; and his 'Signs Taken for Wonders: Questions of Ambivalence and Authority under a Tree Outside Delhi', *Critical Inquiry* (University of Chicago Press), 12:1 (Autumn 1985), 144–65.

27. Walter Benjamin, 'On the Mimetic Faculty' (1933), in *One Way Street, and Other Writings*, 160–63.

28. Trostiné, *La enseñanza del dibujo*, 76–78.

29. Pablo Caccianiga, 'Informe del catedrático Pablo Caccianiga sobre el estado y posibilidades de progreso de los estudios de dibujo en la Universidad de Buenos Aires, 1828', in Trostiné, *La enseñanza*, 93–94.

30. Alejandro Ciccarelli, *Discurso pronunciado en la inauguración de la Academia de Pintura*, Imprenta Chilena, Santiago, 1849.

31. Vicente Grez, Antonio Smith, *(Historia del paisaje en Chile)*, Tipográfica de La Época, Santiago, 1882, 70.

32. For a celebrated statement of the universalist outlook from Argentina, see Eduardo Schiaffino, 'La evolución del gusto artístico en Buenos Aires', *La Nación*, centenary special edition, 25 May 1910, 187–203. Schiaffino's article is also reproduced, with Malharro's response, 'El movimiento artístico y estético en 1910', in Rolando Martínez Mendoza and José Luis Petris, eds., *Entre el arte en la Argentina y el arte argentino: Los artículos para el Centenario de Martín A. Malharro y Eduardo Schiaffino*, Prometeo, Buenos Aires, 2016. For Chilean debates, see *El taller ilustrado* (Santiago), 1885–89, edited by sculptor José Miguel Blanco.

33. Martín Malharro, 'Del Pasado: Páginas de un libro inédito', *Athinae* (Buenos Aires), 2:15–16 (Nov.–Dec. 1909).

34. Laura Malosetti Costa, ed., *Cuadros de viaje: Artistas argentinos en Europa y Estados Unidos, 1880–1910*, Fondo de Cultura Economica, Buenos Aires, 2008, 36.

35. Martín Malharro, *Los cursos normales del dibujo y las veracidades de un documento oficial*, Imprenta de obras de E. Spinelli, Buenos Aires, 1909 (extract from *Revista de la Educación Física*, no. 2, Agosto de 1909), 8–9.

36. The key text was Ricardo Rojas, *La restauración nacionalista* (1909), A. Peña Lillo, Buenos Aires, 3rd edn., 1971.

37. Malharro, 'El dibujo y la educación estética en la escuela primaria y en la enseñanza secundaria', 1910, in República Argentina, *Censo general de educación levantado el 23 de mayo de 1909 durante la presidencia de Dr José Figueroa Alcorta*, ed. Alberto B. Martínez, Talleres de Publicaciones de la Oficina Meteorológica Argentina, 3 vols., 1910, vol. 2, 291–320, esp. 291–93.

38. Malharro, 'El dibujo', 293.

39. Malharro, 'El dibujo', 312.

40. Martín Malharro, 'Del patrioterismo en el arte' (1903), in Malosetti Costa, ed., *Cuadros de viaje,* 252–56.

41. Malharro, 'Pintura y escultura: Reflexiones sobre arte nacional' (1903), in Malosetti Costa, *Cuadros de viaje,* 245–51, esp. 248.

42. Malharro, 'El dibujo', 302.

43. Malharro, 'El dibujo', 297.

44. Juan Francisco González, 'La enseñanza del dibujo', *Conferencia dada en el Salon de Honor de la Universidad de Chile,* Nov. 1906, 77–86. See also Wenceslao Díaz Navarrete, ed., *Juan F. González: Cartas y otros documentos de su época,* RIL Editores, Santiago, 2004.

45. González, 'La enseñanza', 77–78.

46. González, 'La enseñanza', 80.

47. González, 'La enseñanza', 83.

48. González, 'La enseñanza', 84.

49. Gerardo Seguel, *Fisonomía del mundo infantil: El dibujo en la educación,* Imprenta El Esfuerzo, Santiago, 1929, 11–12.

50. Abel Gutierrez, *Dibujos indígenas de Chile: Para estudiantes, profesores y arquitectos, que quieran poner en sus trabajos el sello de las culturas indígenas de América,* Imprenta Universitaria, Santiago, 1929.

51. Natalia Majluf and Luis Eduardo Wuffenden, *Elena Izcué: El arte precolombino en la vida moderna,* Museo de Arte de Lima, Lima, 1999, 17.

52. Majluf and Wuffenden, *Elena Izcué,* 23.

53. Majluf and Wuffenden, *Elena Izcué,* 17.

54. Elvira García y García, *La mujer peruana a través de los siglos,* Lima, 1925, vol. 2, 511, 525.

55. Elena Izcué, 'El dibujo en la escuela primaria', *La Escuela Moderna: Revista Mensual de Pedagogía,* Lima, 4:31, Mar. 1914, 30–33, in Majluf and Wuffenden, *Elena Izcué,* 308–9.

56. Elena Izcué, *El Arte Peruano en la Escuela, Cuaderno I,* Excelsior, Paris, c. 1924, quotation in 'Advertencia' (no page numbers).

57. Natalia Majluf and Luis Eduardo Wuffenden, 'Elena Izcué, L'art précolombien dans la vie moderne', in *Elena Izcué: Lima-Paris, années 30,* Musée du quai Branly, Flammarion, Paris, 2008, 12–13.

58. *La Prensa,* 9 Aug. 1921, evening edition, 1; Majluf and Wuffenden, *Elena Izcué,* 69.

59. Izcué, *El Arte Peruano,* 'Prólogo'.

60. Majluf and Wuffenden, 'Elena Izcué, L'art précolombien', 22.

61. Theodor W. Adorno and Max Horkheimer, *Dialectic of Enlightenment,* trans. John Cumming, Allen Lane, London, 1979; Adorno, *Aesthetic Theory,* Bloomsbury Academic Press, London, 2013.

62. Ana Mae Barbosa, 'Gerardo Seguel, poeta e professor de Arte e Desenho', *Consejo Latinoamericano de Educación por el Arte,* 1:0 [*sic*], Jan.–June 2015.

Chapter Five: Touchstones of Knowledge

1. Allen Woll, *A Functional Past: The Uses of History in Nineteenth-Century Chile,* Louisiana State University Press, Baton Rouge, 1982, 2.

2. *Borges, Director,* 23–24.

3. The German philosopher Ernst Cassirer (1874–1935) elaborated the idea of 'the Enlightenment' as a coherent body of ideas formulated in certain European countries during the eighteenth century in his *Philosophie der Aufklärung*, 1932, trans. Fritz C. A. Koelin and James P. Pettegrove as *The Philosophy of the Enlightenment*, Princeton University Press, Princeton NJ, 1951.

4. References to the 'core' European countries, often what is actually meant by 'Europe', usually allude to France, Germany, Britain and the Benelux countries. Switzerland, at least the French-speaking part, is sometimes included, as is Scandinavia (and, less often, Italy, or more accurately, certain Italian cities or states).

5. Key works in the development of these debates were Felicity A. Nussbaum, ed., *The Global Eighteenth Century*, Johns Hopkins University Press, Baltimore, 2003; Charles W. J. Withers, *Placing the Enlightenment: Thinking Geographically about the Age of Reason*, University of Chicago Press, Chicago and London, 2007; Richard Butterwick, Simon Davies and Gabriel Sánchez Espinosa, eds., *Peripheries of the Enlightenment*, Voltaire Foundation, Oxford, 2008; and Daniel Carey and Lynn Festa, eds., *Postcolonial Enlightenment: Eighteenth-Century Colonialism and Postcolonial Theory*, Oxford University Press, New York, 2009. The historiography in English, French and German is summarised in Sebastian Conrad, 'Enlightenment in Global History: A Historiographical Critique', *American Historical Review*, 117:4 (Oct. 2012), 999–1027.

6. José Carlos Chiaramonte, ed., *Pensamiento de la Ilustración: Economía y sociedad iberoamericanas en el siglo XVIII*, Biblioteca Ayacucho, Caracas, 1979; David Brading, *The First America: The Spanish Monarchy, Creole Patriots and the Liberal State, 1492–1867*, Cambridge University Press, Cambridge and New York, 1991; Diana Soto-Arango, Miguel Ángel Puig-Samper and Luis Carlos Arboleda, eds., *La Ilustración en la América colonial*, Consejo Superior de Investigaciones, Madrid, 1995, and their collection *Recepción y difusión de textos ilustrados*, Colección Actas Távara, Madrid, 2003; Jorge Cañizares Esguerra, *How to Write the History of the New World: Histories, Epistemologies, Identities in the Eighteenth-Century Atlantic World*, Stanford University Press, Stanford CA, 2001; Margarita Eva Rodríguez García, *Criollismo y patria en la Lima ilustrada (1732–1795)*, Miño y Dávila Editores, Madrid and Buenos Aires, 2006; Neil Safier, *Measuring the New World: Enlightenment Societies and South America*, University of Chicago Press, Chicago, 2008; Gabriel Paquette, ed., *Enlightened Reform in Southern Europe and Its Atlantic Colonies, c. 1750–1830*, Ashgate, Farnham UK, 2009; Karen Stolley, *Domesticating Empire: Enlightenment in Spanish America*, Vanderbilt University Press, Nashville, 2013; and Bianca Premo, *The Enlightenment on Trial: Ordinary Litigants and Colonialism in the Spanish Empire*, Oxford University Press, New York, 2017. For a critical review of the literature, see Roberto Breña and Gabriel Torres Puga, 'Enlightenment and Counter-Enlightenment in Spanish America: Debating Historiographic Categories', *International Journal for History, Culture and Modernity*, no. 7, May 2019, online at http://doi.org/10.18352/hcm.562. The historiography on the Iberian Americas still tends to be marginalised in debates about global enlightenment.

7. Omar R. Regalado Fernández, 'Ciencia hecha en América Latina', *Mito, Revista Cultural*, no. 19, Mar. 2015. http://revistamito.com/ciencia-hecha-en-America-Latina. The new element was called *eritronio*, later known as *valadio*.

8. These societies began in 1775, with the foundation of the Real Sociedad de los Amigos del País in Madrid (earlier versions dating back to 1763 were wholly private associations). They spread throughout Spain and the colonies: Manila 1781; Santiago de Cuba 1787; Mompox, Nueva Granada 1789; Lima 1790 (Sociedad de Amantes del País, which produced the *Mercurio Peruano*); Quito 1791; Havana 1793; Guatemala 1795. For context and an overview, see Gabriel

Paquette, *Enlightenment, Governance and Reform in Spain and Its Empire, 1759–1808*, Palgrave, New York and London, 2008, esp. 142–45. For detailed case studies: Manuel Rubio Sánchez, *Historia de la Sociedad Económica de Amigos del País*, Editorial Académico Centroamericana, 1981; *El Humanismo ilustrado ecuatoriano de la segunda mitad del siglo XVIII*, Banco Central del Ecuador and Corporación Editora Nacional, 2 vols., 1984; Izaskun Álvarez Cuartero, *Memorias de la Ilustración: Las Sociedades Económicas de Amigos del País en Cuba (1783–1832)*, Real Sociedad Bascongada de los Amigos del País, Madrid, 2000; Lucas Mattei Rodríguez, *La Sociedad Económica de Amigos del País de Puerto Rico: Su historia natural*, Puerto Rico, 2015; and F. Lafit, 'Crónica de una frustración ilustrada: Los proyectos de los "Amigos del País" en el Río de la Plata tardo-colonial', *Cuadernos de Historia* (Santiago), no. 48 (June 2018), online version: http://dx .doi.org/10.4067/S0719-12432018000100033.

9. The phrase was suggested to him as a title by Ángel Rama: José Carlos Chiaramonte, *La Ilustración en el Río de la Plata* (1989), Editorial Sudamericana, Buenos Aires, 2007, 10. See also J. C. Chiaramonte, *Fundamentos intelectuales y políticos de las independencias: Notas para una nueva historia intelectual de Iberoamérica*, Teseo, Buenos Aires, 2010.

10. For example, the report of Spain's expedition of the 1860s: Manuel Almagro, *La Comisión Científica del Pacífico: Viaje por Sudamérica y recorrido del Amazonas 1862–1866*, with a study by Lily Litvak, Laertes Ediciones, Barcelona, 1984.

11. Moreno, *Doctrina democrática*, 178.

12. A notorious example was the execution by firing squad of Francisco José de Caldas (1771–1816), the first director of the Observatory at Bogotá.

13. *Primeras constituciones*, 447.

14. Constitution of Guatemala (1825, título 4, sección 2, art. 94, clause 8), *Primeras constituciones*, 149.

15. Constitution of Bolivia (1826, título 11, capítulo único, art. 155), *Primeras constituciones*, 362.

16. Constitution of Ecuador (1830, título 8, art. 62), *Primeras constituciones*, 376.

17. Alfredo Opisso, *Historia de la España y de las Repúblicas latino-americanas, tomo xxii*, Casa Editorial Gallach, Barcelona, c. 1920, 219–20.

18. Loyalist publications, like their *independentista* rivals, advocated general enlightenment—e.g., the 'Prospecto' of Viva el Rey. *Gazeta del Gobierno de Chile* (first issue, 1814 [no specific date]) called for wise works to 'enlighten the peoples' (*ilustrar a los pueblos*) and dissipate 'the thick fog' spread by the pro-independence journals *Aurora de Chile* and *El Monitor Araucano*.

19. Camilo Henríquez, 'Nociones fundamentales sobre los derechos de los pueblos', *Aurora de Chile*, 1:1, 13 Feb. 1812, in *Escritos políticos*, 60–65, quotation at 64.

20. Andrés Bello, 'Sobre los fines de la educación y los medios para difundirla' (1836), in María José López M. and José Santos Herceg, eds., *Escritos republicanos: Selección de escritos políticos del siglo XIX*, Lom Ediciones, Santiago, 2011, 82–88, esp. 83.

21. The Constitution of the United Provinces in South America, later Argentina (1819, capítulo 4, art. 42), specified that one of the responsibilities of the legislature was 'formar planes uniformes de educación pública' (to draw up uniform plans for public education), *Primeras constituciones*, 437. Chile (1818, capítulo 6, art. 2) specified: 'Los cabildos deberán fomentar el adelantamiento de la población, industria, educación de la juventud' (the town councils should promote the advancement of the population, industry, education of the young), *Primeras constituciones*, 427. Peru's Constitution (1823, sección 3, capítulo 3, 'Educación pública', art. 181 and

185), referred to 'instrucción' as 'una necesidad común' (a common necessity) to be supervised by a Dirección General de Estudios, formed of 'personas de conocida instrucción' (individuals known to be well educated), in *Primeras constituciones*, 336.

22. Esteban Echeverría, *Dogma socialista de la Asociación de Mayo*, Imprenta del Nacional, Montevideo, 1846, 3.

23. Recent research on various areas of the Americas has uncovered more literacy in the countryside than is compatible with any straightforward mapping of written culture onto urban areas, hence the term *campo letrado* (lettered countryside). See William E. French, *The Heart in the Glass Jar: Love Letters, Bodies, and the Law in Mexico*, University of Nebraska Press, 2015, esp. section 2, 'The Lettered Countryside', 89–172; Florencia Mallon, ed., *Decolonizing Native Histories: Collaboration, Knowledge, and Language in the Americas*, Duke University Press, 2012, esp. Mallon's introduction; Joanne Rappaport and Tom Cummins, *Beyond the Lettered City: Indigenous Literacies in the Andes*, 2012; Frank Salomon and Mercedes Niño-Murcía, *The Lettered Mountain: A Peruvian Village's Way with Writing*, 2011; Kathryn Sampeck, 'El campo letrado: reflexiones sobre la lectura y la escritura en regiones mayas de Mesoamérica', *Mesoamérica* (Guatemala), 34:55 (2013), 191–204.

24. Nicola Miller, *In the Shadow of the State*, Verso, London, 1989, esp. 96–114; Federico Neiburg and Mariano Plotkin, eds., *Intelectuales y expertos: La constitución del conocimiento social en la Argentina*, Paidós, Buenos Aires, 2004; Carlos Altamirano, ed., *Historia de los intelectuales en America Latina*, Katz Editores, Buenos Aires, vol. 1, 2008 and vol. 2, 2010.

25. Real Academia Española, *Diccionario de la lengua española*, 11th edn., Madrid, 1869.

26. See the pioneering study by Véronique Hébrard, *Le Venezuela indépendant: Une nation par le discours (1808–1830)*, l'Harmattan, Paris, 1996; translated as *Venezuela Independiente: Una nación al través del discurso (1808–1830)*, Vervuert/Iberoamericana, Frankfurt/Madrid, 2012.

27. The Iberconceptos project worked on 'opinión pública', but important though this is, the focus upon this phrase and its limitations has distracted attention from the ubiquity of the broader notion of 'the public'. Nicola Miller, 'Beyond the Nation: The Idea of the Public in Nineteenth-Century Latin American HIstory', *Bulletin of Hispanic Studies* (Liverpool University Press), no. 84 (2007), 9–24. François-Xavier Guerra and Annick Lempérière, *Los espacios públicos en Iberoamérica: Ambigüedades y problemas*, Fondo de Cultura Económica, Mexico City, 1998.

28. *Gazeta de Literatura de México* (1788–95); *Mercurio Peruano* (Lima, 1790–95); *La Gazeta de Guatemala* (1797–1816); *El Telégrafo mercantil, rural, político, económico e historiográfico del Río de la Plata* (Buenos Aires, 1801–2) and *El Semanario de Agricultura, Industria y Comercio* (Buenos Aires, 1803–6); *Semanario del Nuevo Reino de Granada* (Bogotá, 1808–10). The *Mercurio Peruano* was reprinted in the 1860s: *Biblioteca Peruana de Historia, Ciencias y Literatura. Colección de escritos* [...] *de los más acreditados autores Peruanos por M. A. Fuentes*, Sociedad Académica de Amantes de Lima, Lima, 1861–64.

29. Armando Martínez Garnica et al., eds., *Joaquín Camacho: De lector ilustrado a publicista republicano (1807–1815)*, Universidad Externado de Colombia, Bogotá, 2011, 24.

30. Vicente Fidel López, *La gran semana de 1810 (Crónica de la revolución de Mayo)*, Librería del Colegio, Buenos Aires, 1966, 35.

31. Notable examples included Juana Manso and Juana Manuela Gorriti, from Argentina; Martina Barros Borgoño, from Chile; and Mercedes Cabello, Teresa González de Fanning and

Clorinda Matto de Turner, from Peru. See Francesca Denegri, *El abanico y la cigarrera: La primera generación de ilustradas en el Perú*, Instituto de Estudios Peruanos, Lima, 1996; and Susanna Regazzoni, ed., *Antología de escritoras hispanoamericanas del siglo XIX*, Editorial Cátedra, Madrid, 2012.

32. Andrés Bello, 'Discurso pronunciado en la instalacion de la Universidad de Chile', in *Escritos republicanos*, 89–102, esp. 99. Here again is the problem that the plural Spanish *conocimientos* can only be idiomatically translated as a singular, but that in itself is to make monolithic an idea configured as multiple.

33. J. V. Lastarria, 'Discurso inaugural de la Sociedad Literaria' (1842), in *Escritos republicanos*, 119–33, esp. 119.

34. *La Ilustración Argentina: museo de familias*, Imprenta Americana, Buenos Aires, 1853–4.

35. Juana Manso, 'Emancipación moral de la mujer', *La Ilustración Argentina*, no. 2, 13 Dec. 1853, 17–18.

36. Myriam Southwell, 'Juana P. Manso (1819–1875)', *Prospects*, 35:1 (Mar. 2005), 7.

37. Benito Hortelano, *Memorias* (1860), Espasa-Calpe, Madrid, 1936, 237.

38. *El Nacional* (Buenos Aires, 1852–98) was founded by Dalmacio Vélez Sarsfield; the main contributors were Sarmiento, Alberdi, Mitre, Nicolás Avellaneda, Vicente Fidel López and Miguel Cané.

39. *La Ilustración argentina*, no. 6, 15 Jan. 1854, 85.

40. 'Amigos falsos de la libertad', *La Ilustración argentina*, no. 6, 15 Jan. 1854, 81–83, esp. 82.

41. 'Manual de cocinero y cocinera: Varias clases de sopas', *La Ilustración argentina*, no. 5, 9 Jan. 1854, 80.

42. 'Sección recreativa', *La Ilustración argentina*, 2a época, no. 1, 11 Dec. 1853, 12–13.

43. 'El Si y No verdaderamente democrático', *La Ilustración argentina*, no. 7, 22 Jan. 1854, 100–104.

44. Juan Espinosa, *Diccionario para el pueblo: Republicano, democrático, moral, político y filosófico*, Imprenta del Pueblo, Lima, 1855. See also the modern edition: Juan Espinosa, *Diccionario republicano*, ed. Carmen McEvoy, Pontificia Universidad Católica del Perú, Instituto Riva-Agüero and the University of the South (Sewanee), Lima, 2001.

45. Espinosa, *Diccionario*, 1855, 367.

46. Espinosa, *Diccionario*, 1855, 368–69.

47. McEvoy, 'Estudio preliminar', in Espinosa, *Diccionario*, 2001, 21–100, esp. 96–99.

48. Espinosa, *Diccionario*, 1855, 369.

49. Espinosa, 'Advertencia' *Diccionario*, 1855.

50. Espinosa, *Diccionario*, 388.

51. Espinosa, *Diccionario*, 447–49.

52. McEvoy, 'Estudio preliminar', esp. 88.

53. A sample from national library catalogues—Argentina: *La Ilustración argentina*, 1881–88; *La Ilustración infantil*, Buenos Aires, 1886; *La Ilustración popular*, Buenos Aires and Rosario, 1891; *El Hogar: Ilustración seminal argentina*, Buenos Aires, 1904–1963. Chile: *La Ilustración*, Valparaíso, 1871; *La Ilustración tipográfica*, Valparaíso, 1887; *La Ilustración*, Temuco, 1894; *La Ilustración militar*, 1899–1901; *La Ilustración*, Santiago, 1896 and 1899–1905; *La Ilustración obrera*, Santiago, 1910; *La Ilustración popular*, Santiago, 1912; *La Ilustración*, Antofagasta, 1923–4. Peru (all published in Lima): *El Faro*

peruano: Periódico de ilustración popular, 1866; *El Peru Ilustrado*, 1887–92; *Ilustración Peruana*, 1909–13; *Ilustración Obrera*, 1916–18 (a government-sponsored publication).

54. *El Plata ilustrado* (1871?–72); *Tit-Bits, revista argentina ilustrada de todo lo más interesante, útil y amenos de los libros*, 1909–13, 1919–57.

55. *La Ilustración Americana: Literatura, artes y ciencias*, Lima, 1890; *La Ilustración sud-americana*, Lima, 1891, and Buenos Aires, 1892.

56. Espinosa, *Diccionario*, 1855, 588.

57. Francisco Bilbao, 'El gobierno de la libertad a los electores' (1855), *Escritos republicanos*, 171–219, esp. 189.

58. Bilbao, 'El gobierno', 192.

59. Enrique Amador Fuenzalida, *Galería contemporánea de hombres notables de Chile (1850–1901)*, Imprenta del Universo de Guillermo Helfmann, Valparaíso, 1901, 25, referring to Luis Barros Borgoño.

60. Quotation from 'Acta de la Federación de las Provincias Unidas de la Nueva Granada' (1811, título 8, art. 24), *Primeras constituciones*, 268. On the general point, see Camilo Henríquez, 'De las provincias revolucionadas de América' (1812), *Escritos republicanos*, 54–59, where he writes about the ideal of 'las naciones cultas'.

Chapter Six: Languages: Universal, National and Regional

1. DiPerú, *Diccionario de Peruanismos*, 2016. For the quotation, see https://andina.pe /agencia/noticia-academia-peruana-de-lengua-presenta-nuevo-diccionario-peruanismos -625474.aspx.

2. Fundéu BBVA (Madrid), 'La Academia Chilena de la Lengua lanza un diccionario sobre el uso actual del español en Chile', 3 Sept. 2010, quotations by the director of the Chilean Academy, Alfredo Matus.

3. Ezequiel Viéitiez, 'Tercera edición del diccionario del habla de los argentinos', *Clarín* (Buenos Aires), 9 Nov. 2016: https://www.clarin.com/cultura/carpetazo-palabras-hicimos -populares_o_HyViFJb-g.html.

4. This specific phrase is from the *reglamento* of the Chilean branch: https://www.asale.org /academias/academia-chilena-de-la-lengua?qt-tab=0. Information on all the academies can be found on this site of the Asociación de Academias de la Lengua Española.

5. Rama, *La ciudad letrada*, 82.

6. 'Una página gramatical. Datos suministrados en clase a los alumnos', *Escuela de Artes y Oficios de la Nación, 1924—17 de septiembre—1934*, Mercedes, Buenos Aires province, n.d. (probably 1934), 9th page (no numbers).

7. Fidelis Pastor del Solar, *Reparos al Diccionario de Chilenismos de señor don Zorobabel Rodríguez*, Imprenta de F. Schrebler, Santiago, 1876, 88, 120, 59.

8. M. Calandrelli, *Informaciones Gramaticales y Filológicas de La Prensa*, L. J. Rosso, Buenos Aires, 2nd edn., 1919, 1, 195, 175, 159.

9. Joan Rubin, *National Bilingualism in Paraguay*, Mouton, The Hague and Paris, 1968; Jinny K. Chol, 'Bilingualism in Paraguay: Forty Years after Rubin's Study', *Journal of Multilingual and Multicultural Development*, 26:3 (May 2005), 233–48.

10. In Peru, Quechua was made an official language in 1975, Aymara and other indigenous languages in relevant departments in the 1993 Constitution. Indigenous languages were given constitutional recognition in 2006 in Ecuador and in 2009 in Bolivia. Mexico does not specify an official language, but in 2003 a constitutional amendment granted public status to indigenous languages.

11. César Vallejo, 'Poem xxxii, *Trilce*' (1922) in his *Sus mejores obras*, Fondo de Cultura Popular, Lima, 1971, 116.

12. On Spanish, see José María Rodríguez-García, *The City of Translation: Poetry and Ideology in Nineteenth-Century Colombia*, Palgrave Macmillan, Basingstoke, 2010; José del Valle and Luis Gabriel Stheeman, *The Battle over Spanish between 1800 and 2000: Language Ideologies and Hispanic Intellectuals*, Routledge, London, 2002. On indigenous languages: Alan Durston and Bruce Mannheim, eds., *Indigenous Languages, Politics, and Authority in Latin America: Historical and Ethnographic Perspectives*, University of Notre Dame Press, Indiana, 2018.

13. Malcolm Deas, *Del poder y la gramática, y otros ensayos sobre historia, política y literatura colombianas*, Tercer Mundo, Bogotá, 1993; and Iván Jaksič, *Scholarship and Nation-Building in Nineteenth-Century Latin America*, Cambridge University Press, New York, 2001.

14. Rodolfo Lenz, '¿Para qué estudiamos gramática?', Imprenta Cervantes, Santiago, 1912.

15. Rodolfo Lenz, *Diccionario etimológico de las voces chilenas derivadas de lenguas indígenas* (1910), Universidad de Chile, Santiago (1980?).

16. Simón Rodríguez, *Sociedades americanas* (1828), in *Obras completas*, Universidad Simón Rodríguez, Caracas, 2 vols, 1975, vol. 1, 260–412; Rama, *La ciudad letrada*, 61–67; Nicola Miller, 'The "Immoral Educator": Race, Gender and Citizenship in Simón Rodríguez's Programme for Popular Education', *Hispanic Research Journal*, 7:1 (Mar. 2006), 11–20.

17. Jorge Cañizares Esguerra, seminar at the Institute of Latin American Studies, University of London, 12 May 2016.

18. Andrés Bello, 'Prologue, Grammar of the Spanish Language' (1847), in Iván Jaksič, ed. *Selected Writings of Andrés Bello*, trans. Frances M. López-Morillas, 96–105, esp. 101.

19. D. F. Sarmiento, *Memoria sobre ortografía Americana leída a la Facultad de Humanidades*, Imprenta La Opinión, Santiago, 1843.

20. Marcos Sastre, *Ortografía completa*, Imprenta de la Revista, Buenos Aires, vol. 1, 1855, vol. 2, 1856, quotation 13, original emphasis.

21. Sastre, *Ortografía*, 12.

22. Sastre, *Ortografía*, 18–20.

23. Sastre, *Ortografía*, 18.

24. Roque Barcia, *Prólogo del primer diccionario general etimológico de la lengua Española*, Tipografía de A. Lahure, Paris, 1878, 9.

25. Letter from E. H. Roque to Vicente Fidel López, Córdoba, 31 Aug. 1888, Archivo Los López, Série Vicente Fidel López, 5085.

26. He mentioned Prudence Boissière, *Dictionnaire analogique de la langue française: Répertoire complet des mots par les idées et des idées par les mots*, Paris, 1885; and Giacinto Carena, *Vocabolario Italiano d'Arti e mestieri*, Napoli, 1859.

27. J. García Icazbalceta, 'Advertencia', *Apuntes para un catálogo de escritores en lenguas indígenas de America*, 1866.

28. Museo Mitre, *Catálogo razonado de la sección Lenguas americanas*, vol. 1, Imprenta de Coni Hermanos, Buenos Aires, 1909, xvii–xviii.

29. For more on Pedro de Angelis: http://bndigital.bn.br/projetos/angelis/projeto.html.

30. Archivo Los López, Série Vicente Fidel López, 2380, 5482, 5484, 5486, 5488 for letters discussing Quechua grammars, vocabularies, almanacs and *quipus*. Museo Mitre, *Catálogo razonado*, vii.

31. Museo Mitre, *Catálogo razonado*, ix, xx.

32. Samuel Lafone Quevedo, letter to Vicente Fidel López, Catamarca, 22 May 1886, Archivo Los López, Série Vicente Fidel López, 5061.

33. Samuel Lafone Quevedo, *Londres y Catamarca*, Imprenta y Librería de Mayo, Buenos Aires, xii.

34. Lafone Quevedo, *Londres y Catamarca*, 44.

35. Lafone Quevedo, *La lengua Vilela ó Chulupi: Estudio de filología Chaco-argentina fundado sobre los trabajos Hervás, Adelung y Pelleschi*, Imprenta Roma, Buenos Aires, 1895. The linguistic scholars referred to in the title were the Spanish Jesuit Lorenzo Hervás y Panduro (1735–1809); the German Johann Christoph Adelung (1732–1806); and the Italian-born Giovanni Pelleschi (1845–1922), who migrated aged twenty-eight to Argentina, where he worked as an engineer. Lafone Quevedo was fascinated by the indigenous vocabulary Pelleschi recorded during an eight-month journey of exploration to the Chaco, his account of which was published in the *Boletín del Instituto Geográfico Argentino*.

36. Martinus Dobrizhoffer, *Historia de Abiponibus*, Vienna, 1784, upon which Lafone Quevedo later drew more extensively in his *Lenguas Argentinas: Idioma Abipón; Ensayo fundado sobre el "De Abiponibus" de Dobrizhoffer y los manuscritos del Padre J. Brigniel, S.J., con introducción, mapa*, etc., Buenos Aires, 1896; José Jolis, *Saggio sulla storia naturale della Provincia del Gran Chaco*, Faenza, 1789; Félix de Azara, *Descripción é historia del Paraguay y del Río de la Plata*, Obra póstuma, Madrid, 1847; Gregorio Funes, *Ensayo de la Historia civil del Paraguay, Buenos Aires y Tucumán*, Buenos Aires, 1816, which was reissued in 1856.

37. Lafone Quevedo, *Londres y Catamarca*, vi–vii.

38. Lafone Quevedo, *La lengua Vilela*, 43. Brian Switek, 'DNA shows how the sweet potato crossed the sea', *Nature*, 21 Jan. 2013: https://www.nature.com/news/dna-shows-how-the-sweet-potato-crossed-the-sea-1.12257.

39. Lafone Quevedo, *La lengua Vilela*, 43.

40. Lafone Quevedo, *La lengua Vilela*, 80.

41. Lafone Quevedo, *La lengua Vilela*, 80; see also his *Londres y Catamarca*, xi.

42. Lafone Quevedo, *La lengua Vilela*, 80, 61.

43. Lafone Quevedo, *La lengua Vilela*, 80.

44. *Escritores chilenos*, year 10, no. 85: https://www.elfortindelestrecho.cl/hoja-amarilla/escritores-de-chile/escritores-chilenos-daniel-barros-grez-18341904/.

45. Mar Campos Souto, 'El Diccionario filológico comparado de la lengua castellana de Matías Calandrelli', *Revista de Investigación Lingüística*, no. 11 (2008), 45–64.

46. Alberto Navarro Viola, 'Diccionario filológico comparado de la lengua castellana', *Anuario bibliográfico de la República Argentina* (Buenos Aires), vol. 2 (1880), 157–74. Navarro Viola later judged Calandrelli's work to be far superior to that of the Spaniard Roque Barcia, which he said was ridden with elementary errors: Alberto Navarro Viola, *Juicio crítico del Diccionario filológico-comparado de la lengua castellana*, Imprenta de Martín Biedma, Buenos Aires, 1884, esp. 36.

47. Daniel Barros Grez, 'A propósito de una obra maestra', *Revista de Artes y Letras* (Santiago), vol. 4, 1885, 126–48, 277–92, 388–403, 426–40, quotation at 282.

48. Barros Grez, 'A propósito', 143.

49. Barros Grez, 'A propósito', 134.

50. Daniel Barros Grez, *Notes on the Prehistoric, Pictographic, Gerographic Writings and Geroplasts of the Ancient Peoples of the Southern Hemisphere of the New World*, trans. William Bartlett-Calvert, Imprenta del Universo, Valparaíso, 1903, 12, 28. The translator taught history, geography and languages at the Liceo de Quillota in central Chile.

51. Barros Grez, *Notes*, 6.

52. Barros Grez, *Notes*, 24.

53. Barros Grez, *Notes*, 19–20, 26.

54. Barros Grez, 'Los Jeroglíficos de la piedra de la Batalla. Carta a José Toribio Medina', *Actes de la Société Scientifique du Chili: Notes et mémoires*, vol. 3, 1893, 14–25, esp. 24. Barros Grez refers to ch. 4 of José Toribio Medina, *Los aboríjenes de Chile*, Gutenberg, Santiago, 1882.

55. Barros Grez, 'Los Jeroglíficos', 24.

56. Eduardo de la Barra, *Las palabras compuestas son conservadores: Estudios etimolójicos*, Imprenta Cervantes, Santiago, 1897, 12.

57. Barros Grez, 'A propósito', 129.

58. Benjamin, 'Unpacking my library', *Illuminations*, 60.

59. David Carlos Rengifo Carpio, *El reestreño de la Opera Ollanta, Lima 1920*, UNMSM, Lima, 2014, 14. The opera was by José Valle Riestra.

60. Mariano Eduardo de Rivero and Juan Diego von Tschudi [*sic*], *Antigüedades peruanas*, Imprenta Imperial de la Corte y del Estado, Vienna, 1851, iv.

61. Rivero, *Antigüedades peruanas*, v–vi.

62. Rivero, *Antigüedades peruanas*, vii.

63. Rivero, *Antigüedades peruanas*, v.

64. Johann Jakob von Tschudi, *Die Kechua-Sprache*, Vienna, 1853; *Ollanta: Ein altperuanisches Drama aus der Kechuasprache*, Vienna, 1857.

65. 'Prospecto', *Museo Erudito* (Cusco), 1:1, 15 Mar. 1837, 1–2; 'Antigüedades', 1:1, 2–3; 1:2, 1–2; and 1:3, 1–2, an article originally in *Mercurio Peruano*, 17 Mar. 1791.

66. Later, Tschudi stated rather defensively that he had heard about the material in *Museo Erudito* but had been unable to obtain a copy. According to Jorge Basadre, Tschudi later revised his translation, drawing upon another ms. from La Paz, sent to him by a businessman of Arequipa, plus the work of Barranca, Fernández Nodal and Markham, and published it—in German—with a commentary and documents. Jorge Basadre, *Introducción a las bases documentales para la historia de la República del Perú, con algunas reflexiones*, P. L. Villanueva, Lima, 2 vols., 1971, vol. 1, 467, entry 6212. Tschudi, *Ollanta: Ein altperuanisches Drama aus der Kechuasprache*, 167–384.

67. *Museo Erudito*, 1:3, 1.

68. Clements R. Markham, *Cuzco: A Journey to the Ancient Capital of Peru*, Chapman and Hall, London, 1856; and his *Ollanta: An Ancient Ynca Drama, translated from the original Quichua*, Trübner & Co., London, 1871. See also Peter Blanchard, ed., *Markham in Peru: The Travels of Clements R. Markham, 1852–1853*, University of Texas Press, Austin, 1991.

69. Sarah Castro-Klarén, 'The Ruins of the Present: Cuzco Evoked', in Michael J. Lazzara and Vicky Unruh, eds., *Telling Ruins in Latin America*, Palgrave Macmillan, New York, 2009, 77–86, esp. 85.

70. José S. Barranca, *Ollanta, ó sea, La severidad de un padre y la clemencia de un rey*, Imprenta Liberal, Lima, 1868, v.

71. Barranca, *Ollanta*, xii.

72. Alan Durston, 'Quechua Political Literature', in Paul Heggarty and Adrian J. Pearce, eds., *History and Language in the Andes*, Springer, 2011, 165–86, esp. 174–75. The official grammar was José de Anchorena, *Gramática quechua ó del idioma del imperio de los incas*, Imprenta del Estado, Lima, 1874, 174–75.

73. Barranca, *Ollanta*, vi.

74. Barranca, *Ollanta*, 77.

75. Barranca, *Ollanta*, 57n20, citing Markham, *Ollanta*, 124n28.

76. Markham, *Ollanta*, 29; Barranca, *Ollanta*, 6.

77. Barranca, *Ollanta*, xiii.

78. Barranca, *Ollanta*, 63n34.

79. Little is known about Fernández Nodal's life. The catalogue of the Lilly Library, at Indiana University, where his papers are held, gives 1822 as the year of his birth, but the date of his death is unknown. For a brief biography, see Biblioteca Virtual de la Filología Española: https://bvfe .es/component/mtree/autor/9727-fernandez-nodal-jose.html.

80. His papers contain drafts of an Aymara dictionary and grammar, as well as material on Quechua. Lilly Library Manuscript Collections, Indiana University, Bloomington.

81. José Fernández Nodal, *Elementos de gramática quichua ó idioma de los Yncas*, La Redentora, Sociedad de Filántropos para mejorar la suerte de los Aboríjenes Peruanos, Cuzco, 1872. On flaws in Anchorena's Quechua, see Durston, 'Quechua Political Literature', 177–78.

82. José Fernández Nodal, *Los vínculos de Ollanta y Cusi-Kcuyllor: Drama en Quichua*, Trübner, London, 1874.

83. Raúl Porras Barrenechea thought so: 'A propósito de una biografía de Gabino Pacheco Zegarra', *Los Andes*, 27 Dec. 2009. http://www.losandes.com.pe/oweb/Sociedad/20091227 /31336.html.

84. *Congrès internationale des Américanistes: Compte-rendu de la première session Nancy—1875*, Maisonneuve, Paris, 1875, 301.

85. Victor Henry, *Le Quichua, est-il une langue aryenne? Examen critique du livre de D. V.-F. López*, Imprimerie G. Grépin-Leblond, Nancy, 1878.

86. Comments made at Congress 29, New York, 1949, cited in Juan Comas, *Cien años de Congresos Internacionales de Americanistas*, UNAM, Mexico City, 1974, 15.

87. 'Note de M. Foucaux' in *Congrès internationale* [...] *Nancy*, 131–34.

88. Comas, *Cien años de Congresos*, 16.

Chapter Seven: Making Natural Nations

1. Earle, *Return of the Native*, 10.

2. Constitution of Peru (1823, sección I, capítulo II, art. 6), in *Primeras constituciones*, 314.

3. Jujuy seceded from Salta in 1834 to take it to the fourteen provinces mentioned in the 1853 Constitution. In 1862 the lands beyond the frontier were declared national territories, but were not made provinces until the 1950s or, in the case of Tierra del Fuego, 1990.

4. This pithy declaration was widely cited. The full quotation brings out Alberdi's view of nationhood as an outcome of interactions, both material and moral, between a population and its territory: 'The *patria* is liberty, order, wealth, civilisation, organised on the native soil, under its insignia and in its name'. J. B. Alberdi, *Bases y puntos de partida para la organización de la República Argentina* (1852), Francisco Cruz, Buenos Aires, 1914.

5. *Constitución de la República de Chile*, Imprenta de La Opinión, Santiago, 1833.

6. P. M. Barber, '"Riches for the Geography of America and Spain": Felipe Bauzá and his Topographical Collections, 1789–1848', *British Library Journal*, 12:1 (Spring 1986), 28–57.

7. Alicia N. Lahourcade, *Ingeniero Felipe Senillosa: Una vida positiva al servicio del país*, Ministro de Economía de la Provincia de Buenos Aires, 1997, 45.

8. Key texts include Richard Drayton, *Nature's Government: Science, Imperial Britain, and the 'Improvement' of the World*, Yale University Press, New Haven and London, 2000; Roy MacLeod, ed., *Nature and Empire: Science and the Colonial Enterprise*, University of Chicago Press, Chicago, 2000; Tony Ballantyne, ed., *Science, Empire and the European Exploration of the Pacific*, Ashgate, Aldershot UK, 2004; *Journal of Postcolonial Studies*, 12:4, issue on 'Science, colonialism, postcolonialism', 2009; Moritz von Brescius, *German Science in the Age of Empire*, Cambridge University Press, Cambridge and New York, 2019.

9. Marcelo Montserrat, ed., *La ciencia en la Argentina entre siglos: Textos, contextos e instituciones*, Ediciones Manantial, Buenos Aires, 2000; Irina Podgorny and María Margaret Lopes, *El desierto en una vitrine: Museos e historia natural en la Argentina (1810–1890)*, LIMUSA, México DF, 2008; Máximo Farro, *La formación del Museo de La Plata: Coleccionistas, comerciantes, estudiosos y naturalistas viajeros a fines del siglo xix*, Prohistoria ediciones, Rosario, 2009; and Patience Schell, *The Sociable Sciences: Darwin and His Contemporaries in Chile*, Palgrave Macmillan, New York, 2013.

10. For example, Manuel Villavicencio's major, pioneering work *Geografía de la República del Ecuador*, published in New York in 1858, was written during his ten years as an administrator in Oriente province.

11. José María Córdova y Urrutia, *Estadística* [. . .] *del departamento de Lima*, Imprenta de Instrucción Primaria, Lima, 1839, 6.

12. Irina Podgorny, 'Travelling Museums and Itinerant Collections in Nineteenth-Century Latin America', *Museum History Journal*, 6:2 (July 2013), 127–46.

13. Manuel Almagro, *Breve descripción de los viajes hecho en América por la Comisión Científica enviada por el Gobierno*, Imprenta de M. Rivadeneyra, Madrid, 1866; see also Almagro, La Comisión Científica.

14. 'Don Andrés Bello y el cultivo de las dalias en los jardines de San Miguel del Norte (Una carta original)', *Revista de Artes y Letras* (Santiago), vol. 2, year 1, no. 9 (15 Nov. 1884), 190–91.

15. On the British empire: Drayton, *Nature's Government*; on the Spanish empire: Cañizares Esguerra, *Nature, Empire, and Nation*.

16. Federico Philippi, *Los jardines botánicos*, Imprenta Nacional, Santiago, 1878, 4.

17. Becerra and Saldivia, *El Mercurio de Valparaíso*, 14

18. Mario Berríos C. and Zenobio Saldivia M., 'La construcción de un concepto de ciencia en Chile: Manuel de Salas and Claudio Gay', *Revista de Sociología*, 8 (1993), 131–36, esp. 135.

19. Claudio Gay, *Historia física y política de Chile: Botánica*, vol. 1, Paris, en casa del autor, and Chile, Museo de Historia Natural de Santiago, 1845, 11.

20. Antonio Raimondi, *El Perú* (1874–1913), facs. edn. Editores Técnicos Asociados, Lima, 5 vols., 1983, vol. 1, 420, 421, cited in Mariano F. Paz Soldán, *Diccionario geográfico estadístico del Perú*, Imprenta del Estado, Lima, 1877, xxix.

21. The first issue of *Anales Científicos Argentinos* (Buenos Aires), 1:1–5 (May–Sept. 1874), 31, invited anyone who wanted 'to contribute to the scientific progress of the country' to send material.

22. Examples include: Ignacio Domeyko, 'Apéndice: Instrucciones para observaciones meteorolójicas en Chile', *Anales de la Universidad de Chile*, 43, Jan. 1870, 397–414; and Francisco Latzina, *Instrucciones para observaciones meteorológicas*, Imprenta de J. Peuser, Buenos Aires, 1882.

23. Emilio Romero, 'Fines y alcances de las jornadas de geografía nacional', broadcast by Radio Nacional del Perú, in Sociedad Geográfica de Lima, *Primeras jornadas de geografía nacional*, 18–26 Feb. 1949, Lima, 1949, 17–20, esp. 18.

24. Mateo Paz Soldán, *Geografía del Perú, obra póstuma de D. D. M. P. S., corregida y aumentada por M. F. Paz Soldán*, Paris, 1862, 1863, also published in French (see note 27); Mariano Felipe Paz Soldán, *Atlas geográfico del Perú*, Paris, 1865, also published in French. Mariano Felipe Paz Soldán, *Diccionario geográfico estadístico del Perú*, Imprenta del Estado, Lima, 1877. Mariano's son Carlos issued a revised version of his father's atlas, *Nuevo atlas geográfico del Perú: Obra póstuma*, J. Gatland, Lima, 1887; and his own adaptation for schools: *Atlas geográfico escolar del Perú*, 1887, reprinted 1895.

25. José Pareja Paz Soldán, *Mariano F. Paz Soldán*, Biblioteca Hombres del Perú, no. 26, Editorial universitaria, Lima, 1965.

26. Manuel Moreyra Paz Soldán, *Manuel Rouaud y Paz Soldán y la exploración al río Yavari en 1866*, Lima, 1970, 5.

27. Mateo Paz Soldán, *Tratado elemental de astronomia teórica y práctica*, Imprenta de Crapelet, Paris, 1848. For biographical information, see Manuel-Nicolas Corpancho, 'Notice biographique', in *Géographie du Pérou: Oeuvre posthume de D. D. Mateo Paz Soldán corrigée et augmentée par son frère le D. D. Mariano Felipe Paz Soldan*, trans. P. Arsène Moqueron with Manuel Rouaud y Paz Soldán, Librairie de Firmin Didot Frères, Fils et Cie, Paris, 1863.

28. 'Avertissement de l'Éditeur', *Géographie du Perou*, xviii.

29. 'Biblioteca geográfica del Perú', appendix 3 of M. F. Paz Soldán, *Diccionario geográfico*, 1056–77.

30. For example, Jervasio Álvarez, *Guía histórica y cronolójica y eclesiástica del Departamento de Ayacucho para el año 1847*, Imprenta Libre de Bernabé Parra, Lima, 1847; José Domingo Choquehuanca, *Ensayo de Estadística completa de los ramos económico políticos de la Provincia de Azángaro en el departamento de Puno*, Imprenta de M. Corral, Lima, 1833; Fuentes, *Estadística de Lima*.

31. Pareja Paz Soldán, *Mariano F. Paz Soldán*, 75.

32. M. F. Paz Soldán, *Diccionario geográfico*, xii, xiv.

33. M. F. Paz Soldán, *Diccionario geográfico*, xii.

34. M. F. Paz Soldán, *Diccionario geográfico*, ix.

35. Letter from Pedro Hogsgaard to Antonio Raimondi, Tucupilla, 1 July 1874, in Mariano Felipe Paz Soldán, *Verdaderos límites entre el Perú y Bolivia*, Imprenta Liberal, Lima, 1878, 70.

36. M. F. Paz Soldán, *Diccionario geográfico*, vi.

37. After a series of unsuccessful attempts (1848, 1853, 1861) regular production of statistics was sustained from 1876 to 1940 by the Dirección de Estadística based at the Ministry of Finance and Trade. A separate Instituto Nacional de Estadística was created by the reformist military government in 1975.

38. José de la Riva Agüero y Osma, *La historia en el Perú*, Imprenta Nacional de Federico Barrionuevo, Lima, 1910, 453–538. Riva Agüero's doctoral thesis became notorious for criticising almost all of his predecessors.

39. Cited in Pareja Paz Soldán, *Mariano F. Paz Soldán*, 108.

40. Pareja Paz Soldán, *Mariano F. Paz Soldán*, 116.

41. Alberto Jochamonitz, 'Situación de Antonio Raimondi en la geografía nacional', in Sociedad Geográfica de Lima, *Primeras jornadas de geografía nacional*, 18–26 Feb. 1949, Lima, 1949, 136–51, 139.

42. Antonio Raimondi, *Mapa del Perú* (1888), H. Barrère, Paris, 1900.

43. Pablo Patrón, *Observaciones sobre la obra 'El Perú' del señor Antonio Raimondi*, Imprenta de Masias Hermanos, Lima, 1878.

44. *Revista Peruana*, vol. 1 (1879), 137.

45. Manuel Rouaud y Paz Soldán, *Dos ilustres sabios vindicados*, Imprenta A. Alfaro y Ca, Lima, 1868. Desjardins's reviews were first published in the *Bulletin de la Société Géographique de Paris*, Apr.–May 1863.

46. Antoine Émile Ernest Desjardins, *Le Pérou avant la conquête espagnole, d'après les principaux historiens originaux et quelques documents inédits sur les antiquités de ce pays*, Paris, 1858.

47. Desjardins in Rouaud y Paz Soldán, *Dos ilustres sabios*, 10–11.

48. Desjardins in Rouaud y Paz Soldán, *Dos ilustres sabios*, 14, citing pages 169, 173.

49. Desjardins in Rouaud y Paz Soldán, *Dos ilustres sabios*, 15.

50. Rouaud, *Dos ilustres sabios*, 19–23. Antonio Raimondi, *Apuntes sobre la provincial litoral de Loreto*, Lima, 1862.

51. La Condamine's map, with an account of his voyage, was first published by the Académie de Sciences in 1745. For a modern edition, see Hélène Patris, ed. *Voyage sur l'Amazone*, La Découverte, Paris, 2004.

52. Rouaud, *Dos ilustres sabios*, 12.

53. Desjardins attended the literary salon run by the emperor's childhood companion Madame Hortense Cornu.

54. The term 'knowledgeable entrepreneurs' is borrowed from Margaret C. Jacob, *The First Knowledge Economy: Human Capital and the European Economy, 1750–1850*, Cambridge University Press, Cambridge 2014.

55. 'Domingo Olivera Barona, Creador del Rambouillet argentino', http://studylib.es/, accessed 17 Apr. 2018.

56. Eduardo Olivera, 'Juicio económico sobre el porvenir de la especulación del ganado lanar en el Río de la Plata', 30 Apr. 1859, in Daniel Perez Mendoza, *Manual del pastor*, P. Lastarria y Ca, Montevideo, 1863.

57. Eduardo Olivera, *Estudios y viages agrícolas en Francia, Alemania, Holanda y Bélgica*, Imprenta del Porvenir, Buenos Aires, 4 vols., 1879, vol. 1, 14.

58. *Anales de la Sociedad Rural Argentina*, Imprenta Americana, Buenos Aires, 1:1 (1866), 1.

59. Olivera, *Estudios y viages*, vol. 1, 189.

60. Olivera, *Estudios*, vol. 2, 11; vol. 3, ix.

61. Tulio Halperín Donghi, *José Hernández y sus mundos*, Editorial Sudamericana, Buenos Aires, 1985, 223–35.

62. Olivera, *Estudios*, vol. 3, xiv; *Anales de la Sociedad Rural Argentina*, Imp. Americana, Buenos Aires, 1:1, 30 Sept. 1866, 6.

63. Perez Mendoza, *Manual del pastor*.

64. The Mexican Geographical Society, founded in 1833 by then president Valentín Gómez Farías, was the first such learned society in the Americas and only the fifth in the world, after Paris 1821, Berlin 1827, London 1830 and Bombay 1831. A geographical society was started in Chile in 1839, but it was short-lived and not revived until 1911. The widely admired Instituto Histórico e Geográfico Brasileiro, an initiative of the Sociedade Auxiliadora da Indústria Nacional, dates back to 1838. The Sociedade de Geografia do Rio de Janeiro was founded in 1883. Most of the other countries of the Americas, including the United States (1888), followed suit during the late nineteenth century.

65. *Boletín de la Sociedad Geográfica de Lima* (Imprenta Liberal, Lima), 1:1 (15 Apr. 1891), 2.

66. *Boletín de la SGL*, 1:1, 6.

67. *Boletín de la SGL*, 1:1, 39–40, lists fifty-seven members plus the twenty or so on the Consejo Directivo. From 1891 the SGL encouraged the foundation of departmental societies, known as Clubes Andinos; there were eleven of them by 1913, although I could not find any information about how active any of them were.

68. *Boletín de la SGL*, 1:1, 2.

69. Luis Carranza, in *Boletín de la SGL*, 1:1, 8.

70. *Estatutos y reglamento interior de la Sociedad Geográfica de Lima*, Libreria e Imprenta Gil, Lima, 1897. Enrique de las Casas, 'La Sociedad Geográfica de Lima', in *Primeras jornadas*, 57–61, 59.

71. Jens Andermann, 'Argentine Literature and the "Conquest of the Desert", 1872–1896', http://www.bbk.ac.uk/ibamuseum/texts/Andermann02.htm#top. The Roca government sent a scientific expedition: Informe oficial de la comisión científica agregada al Estado Mayor General de la Expedición al Río Negro, Patagonia, Buenos Aires, 1881. Further evidence of the extent to which science was deployed to justify conquest can be found in Nora Siegrist de Gentile and María Haydée Martín, *Geopolítica, ciencia y técnica a través de la campaña del desierto*, Editorial Universitaria de Buenos Aires, Buenos Aires, 1981. For an overview of later historiography, see Pilar Pérez, 'Historia y silencio: La Conquista del Desierto como genocidio no-narrado', *Corpus* (Archivos virtuales de la alteridad Americana), 1:2 (July–Dec. 2011): https://journals.openedition.org/corpusarchivos/1157.

72. For a summary with bibliography, see Laura Blanco and Vanesa Gaido, 'La Antropología bajo la lupa del Grupo GUIAS y de Marcelo Valko', *Mito, Revista Cultural*, 2014, http://revistamito.com/la-antrolopogia-bajo-la-lupa-de-la-antropologia (accessed 8 Nov. 2018). Key works are O. Bayer, D. Lenton et al., *La crueldad argentina: Julio A. Roca y el genocidio de los pueblos originarios*, Ediciones El Tugurio, Buenos Aires, 2010; and Marcelo Valko, *Pedagogía de*

la desmemoria: Crónicas y estrategias del genocidio invisible, Ediciones Madres de Plaza de Mayo, Buenos Aires, 2010.

73. Estanislao Zeballos, *La conquista de quince mil leguas* (1878), Círculo Militar, Dirección y Administración, Buenos Aires, 1931. See also the more recent edition *La conquista de quince mil leguas: Ensayo para la ocupación definitiva de la Patagonia (1878)*, Ediciones Continente, Buenos Aires, 2008.

74. 'Ramón Lista, el hombre enamorado de los tehuelches', *Clarín* (Buenos Aires), 12 May 2001: https://www.clarin.com/sociedad/ramon-lista-hombre-enamorado-tehuelches_o_S13GozdlAYg.html.

75. Paraná 1869; Tucumán 1873; Concepción and City of Buenos Aires, 1874.

76. Susana I. Curto et al., 'La Fundación de GÆA Sociedad Argentina de Estudios Geográficos—1922', *Boletín de GEA* [*sic*], no. 126, 2008, 1–20.

77. Curto, 'La fundación', 12.

78. On her life, see Susana I. Curto and Marcelo E. Lascano, 'Elina González Acha de Correa Morales, intelectual y académica', Academia Nacional de Geografía, *Anales Año 2014*, Buenos Aires, no. 35, 2015, 27–70. For a bibliography, including unfinished works: *Dos semblanzas, dos bibliografías: Elina González Acha de Correa Morales y Francisco de Aparicio*, Fundación Francisco de Aparicio, Buenos Aires, 1977, 19–22.

79. Curto, 'La fundación', 16.

80. Elina González Acha de Correa Morales, 'Nomenclature géographique argentine', in A. de Claparède (ed.), *Neuvième Congrès International de Géographie, Genève, 27 juillet—6 août 1908*, Geneva, 1908, 463–469.

81. Curto and Lascano, 'Elina González Acha . . .', found a copy of her application in 1897 but no record of the IGA's response; her name was, however, listed among members a few years later.

82. Benjamín Vicuña Mackenna, 'Informe universitario sobre la Geografía de don Gonzalo de la Cruz', *Anales de la Universidad de Chile*, vol. 52 (1877), 774–85.

83. José Ignacio Vergara, *Informe presentado al Ministerio de Instrucción Pública por el Director del Observatorio Astronómico*, Imprenta de La Época, Santiago, 1883, 4–6. In this report, Vergara was urging the Chilean government to support the fixing of Greenwich as the international meridian.

84. Ignacio Domeyko, *Araucanía y sus habitantes, recuerdos de un viaje hecho en 1845*, Santiago, 1845. See also Rafael Sagredo Baeza, *La ruta de los naturalistas: Las huellas de Gay, Domeyko y Philippi*, Patrimonio Cultural de Chile, Santiago, 2012. Naval officer Francisco Vidal Gormaz made numerous hydrographical studies of southern Chile, for example: *Plano de la Costa Araucana que comprende desde la Punta Cauten hasta la Punta Chanchan, levantado por el Teniente 1º de Marina Dn. F. Vidal Gormaz en 1866 i 1867*, Lit. Cadot i Brandt, Santiago, 1867.

85. Francisco J. San Román, *El mapa geográfico del Desierto y Cordilleras de Atacama*, Santiago, 1890; *Desierto y cordilleras de Atacama*, Santiago, 1896. San Román also studied one of the area's native languages: *La lengua Cunza de los naturales de Atacama*, Impr. Gutenberg, Santiago, 1890.

86. Alberto Edwards, 'Un nuevo mapa de Chile', *Revista Chilena de Historia y Geografía*, 1:1, 1911, 49–70, 52n1.

87. Edwards, 'Un nuevo mapa', 53.

88. Comisión Chilena de Límites, *Mapas de la Rejión Andina*, Santiago, 1906–12; Álvaro Donoso, *Demarcación de la línea de frontera en la parte sur del territorio: Trabajos de la Quinta Sub-Comisión Chilena de Límites con la República Arjentina*, Oficina de Límites, Santiago, 1906.

89. Luis Risopatrón, 'Principales errores y deficiencias del mapa de Chile confeccionado por la ex Oficina de Mensura de Tierras', *Revista Chilena de Historia y Geografía*, no. 26 (1917), 4, 16–46.

90. 'Dos palabras', *Revista Chilena de Historia y Geografía*, 1:1 (1911), 5.

91. *Revista Chilena de Historia y Geografía: Número especial en el Centenario de su Fundación*, 2011, 14–16.

92. C. L. [*sic*], 'Patria en América', *Revista Peruana*, vol. 1, 1879, 219–20.

93. David Harvey, *The Ways of the World*, Profile Books, London, 2017, 6.

94. Nancy P. Appelbaum, *Mapping the Country of Regions: The Chorographic Commission of Nineteenth-Century Colombia*, University of North Carolina Press, Chapel Hill, 2016.

Chapter Eight: Not the 'Dismal Science' but the 'Lifeless' One: Critiques of Classical Political Economy in Latin America

1. Raúl Prebisch, *The Economic Development of Latin America and Its Principal Problems*, United Nations Department of Economic Affairs, Lake Success, 1950; Joseph Love, 'Raúl Prebisch and the Origins of the Doctrine of Unequal Exchange', *Latin American Research Review* (Latin American Studies Association), 15:3 (1980), 45–72; Edgar J. Dosman, *The Life and Times of Raúl Prebisch, 1901–1986*, McGill-Queen's University Press, Montreal and London, 2008.

2. Verónica Montecinos and John Markoff note that CPE was 'widely propagated since the mid-nineteenth century', in their chapter 'From the Power of Economic Ideas to the Power of Economists', in Centeno and López-Alves, *The Other Mirror*, 105–52, 111.

3. Joseph Love and Nils Jacobsen, eds., *Guiding the Invisible Hand: Economic Liberalism and the State in Latin American History*, Praeger, New York and London, 1988, 27. For recent studies of industrialisation in Argentina, see Fernando Rocchi, *Chimneys in the Desert: Industrialization during the Export Boom Years, 1870–1930*, Stanford University Press, Stanford CA, 2006; and Yovanna Pineda, *Industrial Development in a Frontier Economy: The Industrialization of Argentina, 1890–1930*, Stanford University Press, Stanford CA, 2009.

4. John H. Coatsworth and Jeffrey G. Williamson, 'Always Protectionist? Latin American Tariffs from Independence to the Great Depression', *Journal of Latin American Studies* (Cambridge University Press), 36:2, May 2004, 205–32.

5. *El Monitor Araucano*, 26 Oct. 1813, in *Colección de historiadores*, xxvii, 150.

6. The first Latin American *cátedra* (chair) of political economy was established at the newly founded UBA in 1823, although it was closed in 1831; in Chile, the subject was taught at the Instituto Nacional from its foundation and at the Universidad de Chile from 1856, when Frenchman Courcelle-Seneuille was invited to occupy a dedicated chair; in Peru, a chair was created at the Universidad Mayor de San Marcos in 1875, filled by Paul Pradier-Fodéré. In comparison, Harvard and Yale founded chairs of political economy in 1872.

7. On encyclopedias, see Jesús Astigarraga and Juan Zabalza, 'The Popularization of Political Economy in Spain and Latin America through Encyclopedias, 1887–1930', *Journal of History of Economic Thought*, 34:2 (June 2012), 219–42.

8. Undergraduate degrees in economics or economic sciences began in most Latin American countries in the twentieth century as was the case elsewhere.

9. Emma Rothschild, 'Political Economy', in Gareth Stedman Jones and Gregory Claeys, eds., *Cambridge History of Nineteenth-Century Political Thought*, Cambridge University Press, 2011, 748–79, esp. 751.

10. As Victor Bulmer-Thomas has argued, the distinction is not always sufficiently appreciated. Victor Bulmer-Thomas, 'Freedom to Trade, Free Trade and Laissez-Faire: Latin American Approaches to Economic Liberalism in the Nineteenth Century', lecture, 6 June 2012, Senate House, London (unpublished). https://sas-space.sas.ac.uk/4278/1/LIA%2C_Freedom_to _Trade%2C_Bulmer-Thomas%2C_06.06.12.pdf.

11. Domingo Morel, 'Ensayo sobre el desarrollo de la riqueza en Chile' (1870), extracts in Sergio Villalobos R. and Rafael Sagredo Baeza, eds., *Ensayistas proteccionistas del siglo xix*, DIBAM, Santiago, 1993, 272.

12. Esteban Echeverría, 'Segunda lectura' (1837), *Obras completas*, Imprenta y Librería de Mayo, Buenos Aires, 5 vols., 1870–74, vol. 5, 1874, 337–52, esp. 348.

13. There are echoes of Rousseau here. His essay on political economy from *L'Encyclopédie* was translated into Spanish, anonymously, by friar Diego Padilla (1751–1829), in Bogotá. This text is available in Oreste Popescu, *Un tratado de economía política en Santafé de Bogotá en 1810: El enigma de Fray Diego Padilla*, Librería de la Academia Colombiana de Historia, Bogotá, 1968, 59–95.

14. 'Decreto del Poder Ejecutivo de la Provincia de Buenos Aires: Organiza la cátedra de Economía Política en la Universidad' (28 Nov. 1823), in Sergio Bagú, *El plan económico del grupo rivadaviano, 1811–1827*, Universidad Nacional del Litoral, Rosario, 1966, 236–37.

15. Manuel Fernández López, *Economía y economistas argentinos: 1600–2000*, Fondo Editorial Consejo, Buenos Aires, 2007, 83–84.

16. Echeverría, 'Segunda lectura', 347; Bello, 'Discurso', in *Escritos republicanos*, 97.

17. Espinosa, *Diccionario*, 397.

18. Patrick Chorley, *Oil, Silk and Enlightenment: Economic Problems in Nineteenth-Century Naples*, Istituto Italiano per gli studi storici, Napoli, 1965, 9.

19. Jean-Baptiste Say, *Tratado de economía política, o exposición sencilla del modo con que se forman, se distribuyen y se consumen las riquezas*, Editorial Villalpando, Madrid, 1821. Say revised his work over six editions (1803–29), most of which were translated into Spanish. This 1821 version of the fourth edition (1819) is the one that appears most frequently in Latin American library catalogues.

20. Richard Whatmore made a case for this interpretation of Say in his *Republicanism and the French Revolution: An Intellectual History of Jean-Baptiste Say's Political Economy*, Oxford University Press, New York and Oxford, 2000.

21. Jean-Baptiste Say, *Catecismo de economía política, o instrucción familiar*, Madrid, 1822.

22. Quezada, 'Introducción', 93n1.

23. *Principios de la ciencia económica-política*, trans. Manuel Belgrano, Real Imprenta de los Niños Expósitos, Buenos Aires, 1796.

24. Antonio Scialoja was one of the first and most prolific thinkers in the school of social economy: see his *I principii della economia sociale*, Napoli, 1848, translated into French as *Les Principes de l'économie sociale exposés selon l'ordre logique des idées*, trans. H. Devillers, Paris, 1844. Pinoli's 'Curso de Economía Política Ecléctica' was not published; the ms. is available on www.ciencias.org.ar. See also the biographical note: Manuel Fernández López, 'Clemente Pinoli', *Página 12* (Buenos Aires), 23 Feb. 2004: http://www.pagina12.com.ar/diario/suplementos/cash /2-1198-2004-02-23.html, accessed 30 Aug. 2018.

25. Manuel Colmeiro, *Principios de economía política*, Madrid, 2nd edn., 1865.

26. M. A. Fuentes translated Pradier-Fodéré's work while in Paris in the late 1850s, adding his own essay elucidating how the French author's ideas might be adapted to Peru. Paul Pradier-Fodéré, *Compendio de derecho político y economía social: Con un apéndice original sobre algunos puntos del derecho político del Perú*, trans. M. A. Fuentes (1861), Librería central de F. Bailly, Lima, 3rd edn., 1870.

27. Nicolás Avellaneda, *Estudio sobre las leyes de tierras públicas* (1865), Librería La Facultad, de Juan Roldán, 1915; and review by Vicente Quesada, *Revista de Buenos Aires*, 2:25, May 1865, 463 and 469. Juan B. Alberdi, *Sistema económico y rentístico de la Confederación Argentina según la Constitución de 1853*, Imprenta y Librería del Mercurio, Valparaíso, 1854.

28. J. B. Alberdi, *Fragmento preliminar al Estudio del Derecho*, Imprenta de la Libertad, Buenos Aires, 1837, 43–47.

29. Ricardo D. Salvatore, 'The Strength of Markets in Latin America's Sociopolitical Discourse, 1750–1850', *Latin American Perspectives* (SAGE Publications), 26:1 (Jan. 1999), 22–43.

30. Paul Gootenberg, *Imagining Development: Economic Ideas in Peru's 'Fictitious Prosperity' of Guano, 1840–1880*, University of California Press, Berkeley, 1993; Edward Shawcross, *France, Mexico and Informal Empire in Latin America, 1820–1867*, Palgrave Macmillan, 2018, esp. 159–71; José Carlos Chiaramonte, *Nacionalismo y liberalismo económicos en Argentina 1860–1880*, Ediciones Solar, Buenos Aires, 1971.

31. Sergio Villalobos R. and Rafael Sagredo Baeza, eds., *Ensayistas proteccionistas del siglo xix*, DIBAM, Santiago, 1993; Tomás Buch and Carlos E. Solivérez, *De los quipus a los satélites: Historia de la tecnología en la Argentina*, Universidad Nacional de Quilmes Editorial, Bernal, Argentina, 2011, ch. 5, 'El debate sin fin'.

32. Víctor Fidel López, *Prontuario del curso de economía política*, Imprenta de Mayo, Buenos Aires, 1874, 9.

33. Also, at UBA, the Italian professor Pinoli had been disseminating alternative views since 1854.

34. Antonio P. Castro, *Nueva historia de Urquiza: Industrial, comerciante y ganadero*, Buenos Aires, 4th edn, 1953, esp. 74–76, which lists forty investments. See also Ana María Barreto Constantín, *Urquiza: Estadista y empresario*, Dunken, Buenos Aires, 2013.

35. 'Visionario en tiempos difíciles', *La Gaceta* (Tucuman), 15 Apr. 2012. See also Antonio Castro, *El general Urquiza, con Baltasar Aguirre, funda en 1858 un ingenio azucarero en Tucumán*, Buenos Aires, 1945.

36. López, *Prontuario*, 10.

37. Aurora Gómez-Galvarriato and Jeffrey G. Williamson, 'Was It Prices, Productivity or Policy? Latin American Industrialisation after 1870', *Journal of Latin American Studies*, 41:4 (Nov. 2009), 663–94, esp. 669.

38. Emilio de Alvear, 'Reforma económica', *Revista de Buenos Aires*, year 8, no. 81 (Jan. 1870), 247–58, 417–33, 593–606.

39. Juan Copello and Luis Petriconi, *Estudios sobre la independencia económica del Perú*, El Nacional, Lima, 1876; Gootenberg, *Imagining Development*, 164.

40. José Antonio Terry, *La crisis: 1885–1892 sistema bancario*, M. Biedma, Buenos Aires, 1893.

41. Terry, *La crisis*, cited in *Centenario del d. José Antonio Terry: Discursos pronunciados en su homenaje*, Buenos Aires, 1946, 39.

42. Charles A. Jones, 'Liberalism, Nationalism and Transnationalism in the Works and Life of Vicente Fidel López (1815–1903)', *Revista Complutense de Historia de América*, no. 39 (2013), 39–57, 55.

43. Andrés Asiain, Rodrigo López and Nicolás Zeolla, 'Análisis del plan de estudios de la carrera económica. Historia y propuesta' (2011?), online at https://studylib.es/doc/187601/historia-de-los-planes-de-estudio, accessed 27 Nov. 2019, quotation (no page numbers): 'las principales líneas de Economía Política eran trazadas desde Londres'.

44. Marcial Martínez, *La cuestión económica: Cartas relativas á la materia*, La Unión, Santiago, 1886.

45. *Boletín de la Sociedad de Fomento Fabril* (Santiago), 1:1, 5 Jan. 1884, 4.

46. 'Informe de la Sociedad Fomento Fabril, no. 59, 7 de noviembre de 1892', *Boletín de la Sociedad Fomento Fabril*, 9:11, Nov. 1892, 506–11, 507; Jorge Gilbert Ceballos, *Chile país del vino: Historia de la industria vitivinícola, 1492–2014*, Edit. Universitaria, 2014, 92.

47. Manuel Arístides Zañartu, *Luis Rios, o una conversión al proteccionismo*, Imprenta Cervantes, Santiago, 1884. Martineau's novels were translated into Spanish in 1836, in Madrid, and frequently appeared in South American booksellers' catalogues.

48. Zorobabel Rodríguez, 'Luis Rios por Miguel [sic] A. Zañartu', *Revista de Artes y Letras*, 1:1, 1884, 136–54, quotation 142.

49. Virgilio Figueroa, *Diccionario histórico y biográfico de Chile (1800–1930)*, 5 vols., Santiago, 1925–31, vol. 5, 1931, 1112.

50. In Argentina, the famous Unión Industrial Argentina, founded in 1887, started out as the Club Industrial Argentino in 1875, when it also began to publish *El Industrial* (Buenos Aires, 1875?–1883). In Santiago the main publications were *La Industria chilena* (1875–77) and the long-lasting *Boletín de la Sociedad de Fomento Fabril* (1884–1935); the BNCh catalogue lists over twenty other publications on industry, published throughout the country from the 1870s to the 1920s, including some that lasted several years (1882–91 in Iquique; 1903–10 in Yumbel, Bío-Bío). In Peru, the Sociedad Nacional de Industrias launched *La Industria* in 1897.

51. Can it be a coincidence that the British Library, despite its extensive holdings of nineteenth-century Argentine material, has almost nothing on the societies and events related to industrialisation there?

52. Juan Eduardo Vargas, *La Sociedad de Fomento Fabril 1883–1928*, Ediciones Historia, Santiago, 1976, 11, 12. *Catálogo de la Exposición Permanente y Museo Industrial de la Sociedad de Fomento Fabril*, Imprenta Barcelona, Santiago, 1904.

53. *Anuario Estadístico de la República de Chile*, Dirección General de Estadística, Santiago, vol. 1: 1848–58, 1860, and annually thereafter.

54. Alejandro A. Bunge, *Los problemas económicas del presente*, Buenos Aires, 1920, 2.

55. Dosman, *Life and Times of Raúl Prebisch*, 30.

56. *Anales de la Hacienda Pública del Perú*, ed. Emilio Dancuart and J. M. Rodríguez, Ministerio de Hacienda y Comercio, Lima, 24 vols., 1902–26.

57. Carlos Contreras Carranza, 'El nacional liberalismo del economista peruano José Manuel Rodríguez, 1857–1936', *América Latina en la Historia Económica*, 23:1, Jan.–Apr. 2016, 41–67.

58. Contreras Carranza, 'El nacional liberalismo', 43.

59. Guillermo Subercaseaux, '¿Qué es Economía Social?', *Anales de la Universidad de Chile*, no. 136 (Jan.–Feb. 1915), 729–40, sesp. 729.

60. Armando Quezada, 'Introducción al estudio de la Economía Política', *Anales de la Universidad de Chile*, no. 117 (July–Dec. 1905), 75–94, esp. 85n2.

61. Armando Quezada, 'La economía social', *Anales de la Universidad de Chile*, no. 117 (July–Dec. 1905), 225–304, esp. 228.

62. Quezada, 'La economía social', 304.

63. Patricio Silva, 'Pablo Ramírez: A Political Technocrat Avant-la-Lettre', in Miguel A. Centeno and Patricio Silva, eds., *The Politics of Expertise in Latin America*, Macmillan, Basingstoke, UK, 1998, 52–76.

64. His work was published as Malaquías Concha, *La lucha económica*, Imprenta Cervantes, Santiago, 1910.

65. Concha, *La lucha económica*, 55.

66. Concha, *La lucha económica*, 73.

67. Concha, *La lucha económica*, 63, 78.

68. Concha, *La lucha económica*, 63, 111–12. See also Malaquías Concha, *Cartilla de educación cívica: Elementos de derecho publico y economía política para uso de las Escuelas superiores y Normales de la República*, Imprenta Cervantes, Santiago, 1905, with further editions in 1909, 1920, 1923 and 1924.

69. Gómez-Galvarriato and Williamson, 'Was It Prices?'. Their findings relate mainly to Mexico, Brazil, Chile and Venezuela.

70. 'Latin America's Keynes', *Economist*, 5 Mar. 2009. On the Nobel Prize, see Dosman, *Life and Times of Raúl Prebisch*, 485.

Chapter Nine: Infrastructure: Engineering Sovereignty

1. Data for all Latin American countries can be found in Jesús Sanz Fernández, ed., *Historia de los ferrocarriles de Iberoamérica (1837–1995)*, Ministerio de Fomento, Madrid, 1998. In Chile the state was responsible for two-thirds of the whole network: Santiago Marín Vicuña, *Los ferrocarriles de Chile*, Imprenta Cervantes, Santiago, 1909, 125. On Argentina, see Mario J. López and Jorge E. Waddell, eds., *Nueva historia del ferrocarril en la Argentina, 150 años de política ferroviaria*, Ediciones Lumière, Buenos Aires, 2007; on Peru, Alejandro Salinas Sánchez, *Ferrocarriles e imaginario modernista en el Perú y México, 1860–1890*, Universidad Nacional Mayor de San Marcos, Lima, 2010. Financing was a different matter: most of that did come from overseas, although again the picture is mixed during the early stages: see Colin Lewis, '"Anglo-criollo" Rather Than British: Early Investments in Argentinian Railways and Utilities', in Jorge Schvarzer, Andres Regalsky and Teresita Gómez, eds., *Estudios sobre la Historia de los Ferrocarriles Argentinos (1857–1940)*, Facultad de Ciencias Económicas, UBA, Buenos Aires, 2003, 223–39;

and S. A. Palermo, 'Del Parlamento al Ministerio de Obras Públicas: La construcción de los Ferrocarriles del Estado en Argentina, 1862–1916', *Desarrollo económico*, 46:182 (July–Sept. 2006), 215–43.

2. Francisco Alvarado Ortiz, Enrique Higginson and Joaquín Soroa, 'Informe al ministro', 22 Mar. 1869, document 9 in *Representación documentada del Comercio del Callao y Lima al Congreso de 1870 sobre el Contrato muelle-dársena*, Imprenta Liberal, Lima, 1870, 42–5. On Prentice, see: http://elmisteriodelpasado.blogspot.co.uk/2010/08/alexander-prentice.html, accessed 27 Nov. 2019.

3. *Informe de la Comandancia General de Marina en la primitiva propuesta, esencialmente modificada, en resolución de 7 de mayo de 1869, convocando licitadores*, Callao, 26 Feb 1868, reproduced in *Muelle darsena: Refutación del folleto de los agentes y comerciantes del Callao por Templeman y Bergmann*, Tipografía de 'El Comercio', Lima, 1870 (no page numbers). There is little information available about Rivadeneira, except that he later wrote an indictment of French involvement in guano production: *Breves observaciones sobre los derechos de Cochet y Landreau a propósito de la Gran Compañía Americana destinada a esplotar el Perú*, Imprenta de la Patria, Valparaíso, 1882. Ventura Sánchez had spent time in California during the gold rush; during the early 1860s he had bid unsuccessfully for state support to construct privately run port facilities at Valparaíso. Pedro Sapunar Perić, 'Monografia de las obras portuarias de Valparaíso', https://revistamarina.cl/revistas/1986/3/sapunar.pdf.

4. 'Vista Fiscal pedida por el Supremo Gobierno', 29 Sept. 1868, *Representación documentada*, 6–14, esp. 7.

5. It has been argued that the deal was speculative from the start and that Templeman and Bergmann bribed government ministers to secure the contract in order to sell it on to a European enterprise (Alfonso W. Quiroz, *Historia de la corrupción en el Perú*, IEP / Instituto de Defensa Legal, Lima, 2013). Even so, they still had to persuade enough members of Congress to support it in the context of a hostile press, so the terms in which this very public dispute was conducted are significant.

6. Jorge Basadre, *Historia de la República del Perú*, 3rd edn. in 2 vols., Lima, 1946, vol. 2, 218.

7. *El Comercio*, 21 Apr. 1897, in *Resumen de los principales documentos sobre el contrato muelle dársena por Templeman y Bergmann y Ca*, Imprenta del Heraldo de Lima, Lima, 1870, 23–25.

8. 'Informe que presenta á la consideración del Congreso y del Gobierno el ex-Director General de Obras Públicas, Don Mariano Felipe Paz-Soldán', *Representación documentada*, 17–39.

9. Ibid., 20.

10. Ibid., 21.

11. Ibid., 23.

12. Ibid., 23.

13. Ibid., 29.

14. Ibid., 27.

15. Ibid., 33–34.

16. Ibid., 27.

17. *Representación documentada*, iv.

18. This was not surprising, given their lack of specialist knowledge in the field: the first, Federico Hohagen, was known for his topographical work (an important map of Cusco) but

was no expert in port installations; the second, Mario Alleón, was briefly appointed chief engineer of the works that began in 1870: 'Medal commemorating the improved harbour works at Callao', 6 June 1870, National Maritime Museum, Greenwich, London: http://collections.rmg .co.uk/collections/objects/39977.html, accessed May 2017.

19. Paz Soldán, 'Informe', 37.

20. 'Breve analisis de las principales bases del contrato', in *Resumen de los principales documentos*, 22.

21. *Muelle dársena: Refutación del folleto de los agentes y comercios del Callao por Templeman y Bergmann*, Tipografía de 'El Comercio', Lima, 1870, 34–35.

22. *Muelle dársena: Refutación*, 3ff.

23. Jorge Basadre, *Historia de la República del Perú*, 5th edn. in 5 vols., Ediciones Historia, Lima, 1961, vol. 4, 1821–22. Peru, Cuerpo de Ingenieros y Arquitectos del Estado, *Memoria sobre las Obras Públicas del Perú presentada al Supremo Gobierno*, Imprenta liberal de 'El Correo del Perú', Lima, 1874.

24. *Muelle dársena: Refutación*, 1–2, 27–28.

25. *El Perú Ilustrado*, 1:3, 28 May 1887, 2–3.

26. An earlier version of this section was published in Nicola Miller, 'Republics of Knowledge: Interpreting the World from Latin America', in T. Hauswedell, A. Körner and U. Tiedau, eds., *Remapping Centres and Peripheries*, UCL Press, London, 2019, 77–93, 87–90.

27. On the reaction to Bateman's plans, see Hernán Huergo, *Luis A. Huergo y la cuestión puerto*, Editorial Dunken, Buenos Aires, 2013, 33–34.

28. H. Huergo, *Luis A. Huergo*, 34. For primary materials, see *Documentos relativos a la Cuestión Obras del Puerto de Buenos Aires e Informe del Injeniero J. F. Bateman*, Buenos Aires, 1870.

29. Luis A. Huergo, *Los intereses argentinos en el Puerto de Buenos Aires*, Buenos Aires, 1873.

30. Quotation from *La Prensa*, cited in H. Huergo, *Luis A. Huergo*, 37.

31. Martha Mayorano, *Un ingeniero, un puerto: Luis A. Huergo, primer ingeniero argentino*, Editorial COGTAL, Buenos Aires, 1992, 208.

32. H. Huergo, *Luis A. Huergo*, 55.

33. Asamblea de Ingenieros, 'Informe de la Comisión y Resolución de la Asamblea', 30 Mar. 1886, in Luis A. Huergo, *Examen de la propuesta y proyecto del puerto del Sr Eduardo Madero, discusión franca*, Imprenta de M. Biedma, Buenos Aires, 1886, 189–91. For an indication of Madero's perspective, see his *Historia del Puerto de Buenos Aires* (1892, 1902), 3rd edn., Buenos Aires, 1939.

34. H. Huergo, *Luis A. Huergo*, 61.

35. H. Huergo, *Luis A. Huergo*, 76–77.

36. H. Huergo, *Luis A. Huergo*, 42.

37. H. Huergo, *Luis A. Huergo*, 67–68; see also José Isaacson, *Luis Augusto Huergo: Primer ingeniero argentino; Ciencia y técnica en el proceso cultural del Río de la Plata*, Academia Nacional de Ingeniería, Buenos Aires, 1993.

38. Charles Tellier, *Histoire d'une invention moderne: Le frigorifique*, Librairie Charles Delagrave, Paris, 1910, 78.

39. Tellier, *Histoire*, 377.

40. Tellier, *Histoire*, 76–77.

41. Tellier, *Histoire*, 77.

42. Ramón Carcano, in Pedro Bergès, *Los iniciadores de la industria frigorífica: Los méritos respectivos de Lecocq, Harrison, Carré, Tellier y Mort-Nicolle*, Buenos Aires, 1919, 7–8.

43. Carcano, in Bergès, *Los iniciadores*, 8.

44. Gastón A. Nin, *Federico Nin Reyes y el génesis de la industria frigorífica: A propósito de una errónea afirmación histórica del doctor Ramón J. Carcano*, C. García, Montevideo, 1919.

45. Lacoste, *El ferrocarril trasandino*, 94.

46. D. F. Sarmiento, 'El Ferrocarril interoceánico', *El Nacional*, 14 Dec. 1871, in *Obras de Domingo Faustino Sarmiento*, Imprenta Mariano Moreno, Buenos Aires, vol. 42, 43–48, quotation at 45; letter to Governor Emilio Castro, 15 June 1871, 'Papeles del Presidente', in *Obras*, vol. 51, 130.

47. D. F. Sarmiento, letter to Manuel Montt, Oct. 1872 (no exact date), *Obras*, vol. 51, 225. He also admired and trusted the Clarks, to whom he was distantly related through their mother.

48. Emilio Rosetti, *Informe sobre la practicabilidad de un ferrocarril trasandino en dirección al paso llamado del Planchón, en el sur de la provincia de Mendoza*, Imprenta del Siglo, Buenos Aires, 1870; Robert Crawford, *Across the Pampas and the Andes*, Longmans, Green & Co., 1884.

49. Argentina, Cámara Nacional de Diputados, *Diario de sesiones*, 18 Sept. 1873, 1164–65.

50. Arturo Titus, 'Apuntes para una monografía de los Ferrocarriles Particulares de Chile', *Anales del Instituto de Ingenieros de Chile*, 10:7 (July 1910), 287–303, esp. 290.

51. Titus, 'Apuntes', 290.

52. Biblioteca del Congreso Nacional de Chile (BCN), *Diarios de Sesiones e Intervenciones Parlamentarias* (available online at https://www.bcn.cl/historiapolitica/corporaciones/index .html); 'Senado, Sesión 12, Extraordinaria, en 4 de noviembre de 1872', 47.

53. BCN, *Diarios de Sesiones*, 'Cámara de Diputados, Sesión 38, en 16 de diciembre de 1875', 689.

54. BCN, *Diarios de Sesiones*, 'Cámara de Diputados, Sesión 37, Extraordinaria, en 25 de enero de 1897', 620.

55. Ibid., 620.

56. Ibid., 625–26; BCN, *Diarios*, 'Cámara de Diputados, Sesión 38, en 26 de enero de 1897', 643.

57. Ibid., 642.

58. Federico Torrico, *Exposición a S. E. el Presidente sobre la conveniencia de modificar el contrato celebrada para la construcción del Ferro-carril de Arequipa, y examen crítico de este documento*, Imprenta Liberal, Lima, 1868.

59. 'Breve analisis', in *Resumen de los principales documentos*, 22.

60. *Exposición de la empresa muelle y dársena del Callao, ante la Honorable Cámara de Senadores en 21 de agosto de 1886*, Imprenta del Muelle y Dársena, Callao, 1886, 12.

61. Luis Huergo, 'Petróleo de Comodoro Rivadavia', Memorandum de la Dirección General relativo a la explotación futura de los yacimientos del Petróleo de Comodoro Rivadavia, Acta del 8 de abril de 1913, 19–21, in José Isaacson, *Luis Augusto Huergo: Primer ingeniero argentino; Ciencia y técnica en el proceso cultural del Río de la Plata*, Academia Nacional de Ingeniería, Buenos Aires, 1993, 218.

Chapter Ten: Education for Citizenship: Beyond Morality and Patriotism

1. For Peru, the visibility of discussion about popular education in independence-era periodicals has been charted by Daniel Moran and María Aguirre, *La educación popular en los tiempos de la independencia*, Grupo Gráfico del Piero, Lima, 2011. My less systematic surveys of the periodicals of Argentina and Chile indicated a similarly high level of interest.

2. 'Pueblo: ilustrate, ilustrate, conoceras por ti mismo las farsas y las comedias sin necesidad de censores' [*sic*], *La Abeja Republicana* (Lima), no. 31, 17 Nov. 1822.

3. *El Satélite del Peruano*, Feb. 1812, cited in Moran and Aguirre, *La educación popular*, 28. A *pardo* was a person of mixed race, usually Black and indigenous (although the term had a range of meanings in different contexts).

4. Moran and Aguirre, *La educación popular*, 28–29; Noemí Goldman, 'Morenismo y los derechos naturales en el Río de la Plata', in Leopoldo Zea, ed., *América Latina ante la Revolución francesa*, UNAM, Mexico City, 1993, 151–67. See also her biography: *Mariano Moreno: De reformista a insurgente*, Edhasa, Buenos Aires, 2016.

5. Sección 3, capítulo 3, art. 181, in *Primeras constituciones*, 336.

6. See Adriana Puiggrós, *De Simón Rodríguez a Paulo Freire: Educación para la integración Iberoamericana*, Ediciones Colihue, Buenos Aires, 2011; and Jacob Kornbeck and Xavier Úcar, eds., *Latin American Social Pedagogy: Relaying Concepts, Values and Methods between Europe and the Americas*, EHV Academicpress, Bremen, 2015.

7. Domingo Amunátegui Solar, *El sistema de Lancaster en Chile i en otros paises sud-americanos*, Imprenta Cervantes, Santiago, 1895.

8. Letter from Vicente Fidel López to Félix Frías in Paris, Buenos Aires, 1 July 1852. AGN, Archivo Los López, 4289 L2368.

9. Fernando Villagrán, *Simón Rodríguez: Las razones de la educación pública; Reflexiones del educador americano que vence el paso de los siglos*, Editorial Catalonia, Santiago, 2011; Magaldy Téllez, Norah Gamboa and Olady Agudelo, eds., *Simón Rodríguez: Resonancias de su vida y obra en nuestros tiempos*, Fondo Editorial Fundarte, Caracas, 2018.

10. Key works include A. Rumazo González, *Simón Rodríguez: Maestro de América*, Universidad Experimental Simón Rodríguez, Caracas, 1976; J. A. Lasheras, *Simón Rodríguez: Maestro ilustrado y político socialista*, Universidad Nacional Experimental Simón Rodríguez, Caracas, 2004; Ronald Briggs, *Tropes of Enlightenment in the Age of Bolívar: Simón Rodríguez and the American Essay at Revolution*, Vanderbilt University Press, Nashville, 2010; Carla Wainsztok, *Simón Rodríguez y las pedagogias emancipadoras en Nuestra América*, Editorial Primero de Mayo, Montevideo, 2012.

11. Key works on my country case studies are Adriana Puiggrós, *Qué pasó en la educación Argentina: Breve historia desde la conquista hasta el presente*, Galerna, Buenos Aires, 2003; Sol Serrano, with Macarena Ponce de León, Francisca Rengifo and Rodrigo Mayorga, *Historia de la educación en Chile (1810–2010)*, Taurus, Santiago, vols. 1 and 2, 2012; vol. 3, 2018; Antonio Espinoza, *Education and the State in Modern Peru: Primary Schooling in Lima, 1821–c.1921*, Palgrave Macmillan, New York, 2013.

12. In 1860 there were 486 primary schools; in 1900 1,547 schools. A further 263 schools were built during 1901–15, which made a total of 1,810 schools for a population of just over 3.52 million

in 1915 (that is, a school for every 1,945 inhabitants). Chile, Archivo Nacional, 'Creación de escuelas en Chile (1860–1920)': http://archivonacional.gob.cl/sitio/Contenido/Colecciones-digitales/8098:Creacion-de-Escuelas-en-Chile-1860-1920.

13. See Carla Aubry, Michael Geiss, Veronika Magyar-Haas and Jürgen Oelkers, eds., *Education and the State: International Perspectives on a Changing Relationship*, Routledge, London, 2014.

14. On Argentina, see especially *La Nación*, centenary supplement, May 1910; and *La República Argentina en su Primer Centenario, 1810–1910*, facs. edn., Biblioteca Nacional, Buenos Aires, 2010 (a collection of photographs). On Chile: *El Santiago del Centenario visto por 'El Mercurio' 1900–1910*, El Mercurio / Aguilar, Santiago, 2006; and Édouard Poirier, *Chile en 1910: Edición del Centenario de la Independencia*, Santiago, 1910. On Peru: 'Programa de las fiestas del Centenario', in Ministerio de Relaciones Exteriores del Perú, *Discursos y Documentos Oficiales en las fiestas realizadas en Lima celebrando el Primer Centenario de la Independencia*, Imprenta Torres Aguirre, Lima, 1822, lxvii–lxix.

15. Gabriela Mistral, 'A guisa de prólogo', in Julio R. Barcos, *Como educa el estado a tu hijo*, Editorial Acción, Buenos Aires, 2nd edn., 1928, 12.

16. Notable examples include, in Argentina: Félix Martín de Herrera, *Curso sumario de filosofía moral: Extracto de las lecciones dadas en la escuela normal*, Imprenta de M. Biedma, Buenos Aires, 1888; in Chile: José Bernardo Suárez, *Compendio de moral i urbanidad, arreglado para uso de las escuelas primarias*, Imprenta y Litografía de los Tiempos, Talca, 2nd edn., 1890.

17. Reglamento para las Escuelas Primarias de los Cuerpos del Ejército, Santiago, 1906; and Francisco J. Quevedo, *Libro de lectura: Para las escuelas del Ejército, tomo I*, Santiago, 1915. The quotation is from Prussian officer Emilio Körner (1846–1920), who spent twenty-five years in Chile from 1885 onwards. Emilio Körner, 'El desarrollo histórico del Ejército chileno', in Carlos Maldonado and Patricio Quiroga, *El prusianismo en las Fuerzas Armadas chilenas (1885–1945): Un estudio histórico*, Documentas, Santiago, 1988, 210.

18. República Argentina, *Cartilla militar*, Talleres Gráficos Solá y Franco, Buenos Aires, 1907. In Peru, however, even though conscription was introduced partially in 1898 and fully in 1912, problems of language made it far harder to teach conscripts successfully: see Eduardo Toche, 'Servicio militar y la construcción nacional: Notas sobre el origen de la institución', *Investigaciones Sociales* (Lima), 9:14 (2005), 395–409.

19. Gabriela Ossenbach and Miguel Somoza, eds., *Los manuales escolares como fuente para la historia de la educación en América Latina*, Universidad Nacional de Educación a Distancia, Madrid, 2001.

20. Marta Elena Samatán, *Autodidactos: Los que aprendieron sin maestros*, Libros del Caminante, Buenos Aires, 1965.

21. Juana Manso, *Informe sobre las escuelas infantiles para ambos sexos por el año de 1869*, Imprenta Americana, Buenos Aires, 1870, 9.

22. Manso, *Informe*, 13.

23. Manso, *Informe*, 14, 7; *Curso graduado de instrucción en las escuelas públicas de Chicago: Para servir de modelo a las de la República Argentina*, trans. Juana Manso, Imprenta Americana, Buenos Aires, 1869, 7.

24. *Curso graduado*, 7, 10.

25. *Curso graduado*, 7.

26. Juana P. Manso de Noronha, *La Revolución de Mayo 1810: Drama histórico*, Imprenta de Mayo, 1864.

27. Graciela Morgade and Mabel Bellucci, *Mujeres en la educación: Género y docencia en Argentina, 1870–1930*, Miño y Dávila Editores, Buenos Aires, 1997.

28. Rosa Vera Peñaloza, *Pensamiento vivo de Rosario Vera Peñaloza*, Universidad Nacional Del Litoral, Santa Fe, Argentina, 1954.

29. An online database of primary sources for the popular libraries is under construction: http://www.conabip.gov.ar.

30. A catalogue of this library is available in *Memoria del Décimo Cuarto Directorio a la Asamblea General . . . 9 de Julio de 1871*, Sociedad Tipográfica Bonaerense, Buenos Aires, 1871, 49–80. A total of 721 books were listed, divided as follows, with the categories translated exactly (although they were not rigorously observed—for example, printing manuals appeared under 'biographies'): 'history 118; history, geography and statistics 60; biographies 14; exact, physical and natural sciences 54; philosophy, religion and education 107; politics, administration, colonisation, public works 126; literary studies, novels, poems, travels 91; law, political economy 13; industry, arts, commerce, agriculture 22; periodicals, dictionaries, etc. 68; regulations of associations, etc. 48', 80. Of these books, 537 were in Spanish, 121 in French, 43 in English, 8 in Latin, 6 in Portuguese, 3 in Italian and 3 in German, 80. Victory y Suárez also started the first left-wing publishing company in Buenos Aires: see the conference paper by Horacio Tarcus, 'La Biblioteca Popular de Bartolomé Victory y Suárez, primera editorial de la izquierda argentina', Universidad Nacional de La Plata, 2012: http://sedici.unlp.edu.ar/handle/10915/29407. See also Silvia Badoza, 'Typographical Workers and their Mutualist Experience: The Case of the Sociedad Tipográfica Bonaerense, 1857–80', in Jeremy Adelman, ed., *Essays in Argentine Labour History, 1870–1930*, Palgrave Macmillan, UK, 1992, 72–90.

31. Leandro H. Gutiérrez and Luis Alberto Romero, 'Barrio Societies, Libraries and Culture in the Popular Sectors of Buenos Aires in the Inter-war Period', in Adelman, *Essays*, 217–34, esp. 223.

32. On the early period, see María Elsa Rubio Araya, *Ni caridad privada ni paternalismo estatal: artesanos y educación, Santiago, 1850–1862*, Santiago, 2003.

33. Julio C. Jobet, 'Notas en torno a Santiago Arcos, Fermín Vivaceta, Alejando Escobar y Luis Emilio Recabarren', *Occidente* (Santiago), no. 236 (May 1972), 53–60, esp. 55.

34. Arturo Blanco, *Vida y obras del arquitecto Don Fermín Vivaceta*, Santiago, 1924, 16–17. Vivaceta gave free classes to workers at the Instituto Nacional, then later, at the request of Benjamín Vicuña Mackenna, at a Santiago school.

35. Eduardo Devés Valdés, 'Orígenes del socialismo chileno: Fermín Vivaceta y el mutualismo', *Cuadernos hispanoamericanos* (Madrid), no. 453 (Mar. 1988), 31–48.

36. Blanco, *Vida y obras*, 20–21.

37. Blanco, *Vida y obras*, 21.

38. 'Buzón. Programa del Partido Republicano', *El Taller* (Santiago), 12, 14 and 15 Feb. 1879, cited in Sergio Grez Tozo, *De la 'regeneración del pueblo' a la huelga general: Génesis y evolución histórica del movimiento popular en Chile (1810–1890)*, DIBAM, Santiago, 1997, 510.

39. Eloísa Díaz, 'Reorganización del Servicio Médico Escolar', *Primer Congreso Médico Latino-Americano, Santiago de Chile, 1e al 9 de enero de 1901, Actas y Trabajos*, 3 vols., Imprenta Barcelona, Santiago, 1902, vol. 2, 113–24.

40. Eloísa Díaz, *Breves observaciones sobre la aparición de la pubertad en la mujer chilena*, Imprenta Nacional, Santiago, 1888; and *La alimentación de los niños pobres en las escuelas públicas*, Imprenta, Litografía y Encuadernación Barcelona, Santiago, 1906. She also gave well-received papers on school hygiene at the Congreso Médico Latinoamericano in Santiago in 1901 and in Buenos Aires four years later.

41. *Resumen de las discusiones, actas i memorias presentados al Primer Congreso Pedagójico*, ed. J. Abelardo Núñez, Imprenta Nacional, Santiago, 1890.

42. Amanda Labarca, *Historia de la enseñanza*, Imprenta Universitaria, Santiago, 1939, 236. See also María Loreto Egaña Baraona, *La educación primaria popular en el siglo xx en Chile: Una práctica de política estatal*, DIBAM, Santiago, 2000.

43. *Congreso Nacional de Enseñanza Secundaria*, Imprenta Universitaria, Santiago, 2 vols., 1912–13.

44. 'Creación de Escuelas en Chile (1860–1920): Enseñanza técnica: educación para el trabajo?', Archivo Nacional de Chile: https://www.archivonacional.gob.cl/616/w3-article-8101 .html?_noredirect=1, accessed 17 Dec. 2019.

45. The arguments in Barcos, *Como educa el estado*, 1928, can be traced in many of his earlier writings: for a survey, including some of Barcos's articles, see Dora Barrancos, *Anarquismo, educación y costumbres en la Argentina del principios del siglo*, Editorial Contrapunto, Buenos Aires, 1990, 71–82.

46. Humberto Tejera, *Maestros indoiberos*, Ediciones Minerva, Mexico, 1944, 81–90, 86.

47. Luis E. Recabarren, 'Ricos y pobres' (1910), in *Obras*, Casa de las Américas, Havana, 1976, 57–99, esp. 63.

48. Luis E. Recabarren, 'Las dos fuerzas', *El Socialista*, Valparaíso, 9 Oct. 1915, in Ximena Cruzat and Eduardo Devés, eds., *Escritos de prensa*, Editorial Nuestra América, Santiago, 1986, vol. 3 (1914–18), 170.

49. Recabarren, 'Las dos fuerzas', 171.

50. Luis E. Recabarren, 'La civilización europea', *El Despertar*, Iquique, 30 Aug. 1914, in his *Escritos de prensa*, vol. 3, 47–48; 'Qué es el socialismo?', *La Aurora*, Taltal, 13 Oct. 1916, *Escritos de prensa*, vol. 3, 124; and 'Un fondo para alimentar la cultura popular', *La Federación Obrera*, Santiago, 21 Nov. 1921, *Escritos de prensa*, vol. 4 (1919–24).

51. Luis E. Recabarren, *Escritos de prensa*, vol. 4. See also María Alicia Vetter and John D. Holst, 'A Pedagogy for Power: Antonio Gramsci and Luis Emilio Recabarren on the Educational Role of Working-Class Organizations', in Nicola Pizzolato and John D. Holst, eds., *Antonio Gramsci: A Pedagogy to Change the World*, Springer International, Switzerland, 2017.

52. Manuel González Prada founded *Los Parias* (1904–10).

53. Guillermo Sánchez Ortiz, *La prensa obrera 1900–1930 (Análisis de El Obrero Textil)*, Ediciones Barricada, Lima, 1987, 14.

54. Sánchez Ortiz, *La prensa obrera*, 7, 28.

55. Sánchez Ortiz, *La prensa obrera*, 25–26.

56. See the account by Delfín Lévano in César Lévano La Rosa and Luis Tejada Ripalda, eds., *La utopía libertaria en el Perú*, Fondo Editorial del Congreso del Perú, Lima, 2006, 491–93.

57. The first workers' congress of 1921, held to celebrate a successful struggle for an eight-hour day, listed representatives from a range of workers' libraries and cultural organisations. Wilfredo

Kapsoli, *Mariátegui y los congresos obreros*, Biblioteca Amauta, Lima, 1980, 29–31. Near Cuzco, in the southern province of Sicuani, there was a Biblioteca El Ayllu, which was visited by José María Arguedas when he was teaching in a local school, and later by Neruda.

58. Lévano La Rosa and Tejada Ripalda, *La utopía libertaria*, is a 670-page collection of speeches and articles by two leaders of the bakers' union, father and son Manuel and Delfín Lévano.

59. Delfin Lévano, 'La instrucción fiscal', *La Protesta* (Lima), 4:40, Jan. 1915, in Lévano La Rosa, *La utopía libertarian*, 662.

60. 'Discurso de Delfín Levano ante los campesinos de Hualmay, Huacho (28.2.1921) Labor educativa', in Lévano La Rosa, *La utopía libertarian*, 666.

61. Delfin Lévano, 'Discurso', 667–68.

62. Octavo Carbajo, 'Los agentes de la burguesía en acción', *El Obrero Textil*, year 5, no. 58 (Apr. 1924), 4, cited in Sánchez Ortiz, *La prensa*, 105–6.

63. Delfín Lévano, 'Conferencia dada en la velada literario-musical y teatral organizada por el Centro Musical Obrero', Lima, 31 (no month given) 1924, ms. from the archive of César Levano, in Lévano La Rosa, *La utopía*, 506–10, esp, 507.

64. Lévano, 'Conferencia', 508.

65. Kapsoli, *Mariátegui*, 25.

66. José Carlos Mariátegui, *El alma matinal y otras estaciones del hombre de hoy* (1925), *Obras completas*, vol. 3, Editorial Amauta, Lima, 1950, is probably the key text for understanding Mariátegui's philosophy of culture in revolution, although he wrote about the relationship between culture and politics consistently from his early days as a journalist in Lima. See Nicola Miller, *Reinventing Modernity in Latin America: Intellectuals Imagine the Future, 1900–1930*, Palgrave Macmillan, New York, 2008, ch. 5, 'A Vital Form of Public Space: Mariátegui's Revolution in Modernity', 143–86.

67. Roberto MacLean y Estenós, *Sociología educacional del Perú*, Librería e Imprenta Gil, Lima, 1944, 340–60. The situation was dire throughout the country, with school places available for only 40 per cent of children, high rates of absenteeism among those enrolled and poor levels of literacy even among those who attended.

68. José Antonio Encinas, *Un ensayo de escuela nueva en el Perú*, Imprenta Minerva, Lima, 1932, 15.

69. On indigenous mobilisations, see Nils Jacobsen, *Mirages of Transition: The Peruvian Altiplano, 1780–1930*, University of California Press, Berkeley, 1993; and Brooke Larson, *Trials of Nation Making: Liberalism, Race and Ethnicity in the Andes, 1810–1910*, Cambridge University Press, New York, 2004.

70. Encinas, *Un ensayo*, 87–90.

71. Churata, 'Prólogo', in Encinas, *Un ensayo*, iv–v.

72. Encinas, *Un ensayo*, 112.

73. The reference was presumably to E. A. Sheldon, *Lecciones de cosas, en séries graduados, con nociones de objetos comunes*, D. Appleton & Compañía, New York, 1888, which was widely distributed throughout Spanish America in Appleton's series Biblioteca del Maestro.

74. Encinas, *Un ensayo*, 118.

75. Encinas, *Un ensayo*, 133.

76. Encinas, *Un ensayo*, 85–86.

77. David Ruelas Vargas, 'La Escuela Rural de Utawilaya y los adventistas en el Altiplano Puneño, 1898–1920: Precursora de la educación rural indígena peruana y Latinoamericana', *Revista Historia de la Educación Latinoamericana*, 19:29 (Sept. 2017), 67–87.

78. Gamaliel Churata (Arturo Peralta), 'Prólogo', Encinas, *Un ensayo*, vii.

79. Encinas, *Un ensayo*, 11.

80. Encinas, *Un ensayo*, 23.

81. Encinas, *Un ensayo*, 123.

82. Encinas, 'Nota preliminar', *Un ensayo*.

83. José A. Encinas, 'Algunas consideraciones sobre la educación del indio en el Peru', *Amauta* (Lima), 32 (Aug.–Sept. 1930), 75–79, esp. 78.

84. For the main dispute, see Alejandro Deustua, 'La ley de Instrucción. Carta dirigida al Dr. Manuel V. Villarán, Roma, Diciembre 5 de 1910', in *La idea de la universidad en el Perú*, Universidad Ricardo Palma, Lima, 1994, 43–50; and Manuel V. Villarán, 'Discurso', *III Congreso Internacional de Estudiantes Americanos, Lima, July 1912*, in ibid., 51–60.

85. Cited in Juan Carlos Zapata Ancajima, *Pensadores de la educación peruana del siglo xx*, Universidad Nacional de Piura, Piura, 2007, 33.

86. Encinas, *Un ensayo*, 90.

87. Encinas, *Un ensayo*, 118.

88. José A. Encinas in *Boletín Titikaka* (Puno), Sept. 1926, no. 2, 2, in Dante Callo Cuno, ed., *Boletín Titikaka: Edición facsimilar*, Universidad Nacional de San Agustín, Arequipa, 2004, 12.

89. Encinas, 'Algunas consideraciones'. For Churata's view that the right education policy was dependent on 'a thorough shaking up of property relations and the revaluation of the *ayllu*', see his prologue to Encinas's *Un ensayo*, x. For José Carlos Mariátegui, see his *Siete ensayos de interpretación de la realidad peruana* (1928), Biblioteca Ayacucho, Caracas, 1979, esp. 'El problema del indio'.

90. Encinas, 'Algunas consideraciones', 77.

91. Encinas, *Un ensayo*, 4.

92. José A. Encinas, *Contribución a una Legislación tutelar indígena*, C. F. Southwell, Lima, 1918.

93. 'Bases de la Asociación Pro-Indígena' (1910), cited in Katalin Jancsó, 'La asociación proindígena—en las fuentes del archivo Pedro Zulen', *Acta Hispanica* (Szeged), 12 (2007), 129–42, esp. 132–33, online at: http://acta.bibl.u-szeged.hu/616/1/hisp_012_129-142.pdf.

94. República peruana, *Ley orgánica de enseñanza, promulgada por el poder ejecutivo en cumplimiento de la ley no. 4004*, Imprenta Americana, Lima, 1920.

95. *El Oprimido*, vol. 2:33 (Jan. 1909), 4. In 1908, *El Oprimido* listed its exchanges of periodicals from Chile, Bolivia, Argentina, Uruguay, Brazil, Spain, France and Florida.

Conclusion

1. On politics, see especially Miguel A. Centeno and Agustín E. Ferraro, eds., *State and Nation Making in Latin America and Spain: Republics of the Possible*, Cambridge University Press, New York, 2013; James E. Sanders, *The Vanguard of the Atlantic World: Creating Modernity, Nation, and Democracy in Nineteenth-Century Latin America*, Duke University Press, Durham NC, 2014; and Hilda Sabato, *Republics of the New World: The Revolutionary Political Experiment in*

Nineteenth-Century Latin America, Princeton University Press, Princeton, 2018. On economic development, see Edward Beatty, *Technology and the Search for Progress in Modern Mexico*, University of California Press, Berkeley CA, 2015; and Teresa Cribelli, *Industrial Forests and Mechanical Marvels: Modernization in Nineteenth-Century Brazil*, Cambridge University Press, New York, 2016.

2. José Ignacio Vergara, *Informe presentado al Ministerio de Instrucción Pública por el Director del Observatorio Astronómico*, Imprenta de La Época, Santiago, 1883, 4–5.

3. See Karen Ordahl Kupperman's characterisation of the colonial North American seaboard, in her *Atlantic in World History*, Oxford University Press, New York, 2012.

4. Manuel V. Villarán, 'La educación nacional y la influencia extranjera' (thesis, 1908), cited in Mariátegui, *Siete ensayos*, 76.

5. Museo de Ciencias Naturales y Antropológicas Juan Cornelio Moyano. Moyano was the governor who supported Mendoza's first Museo de Historia Natural, which opened in 1858 but was ruined in the earthquake three years later.

6. 'Los medios de comunicación: De la primera imprenta a los multimedios', http://www .mendoza.edu.ar, Progama 21.

7. Roig, Lacoste and Satlari, eds., *Mendoza, cultura y economía*, 534.

8. For an account of the strike and three of its leaders, Rosario Sansano, Angélica Mendoza and Florencia Fossatti, see http://www.unidiversidad.com.ar/maestras-rebeldes-sediciosas-y -temerarias.

SELECT BIBLIOGRAPHY

My aim here is to offer suggestions for further reading to anyone interested in learning more about the history of knowledge and how it has been thought about in relation to Latin America. A full bibliography would run to many pages, so I've limited this one to books and selected them on the principle of approaches I found inspiring, in the hope that other readers will be drawn to follow some of these authors into this expanding and increasingly topical field of enquiry. Most of these works are comparative and/or transnational in scope: studies of individuals or specific places have been excluded unless they offer a more widely applicable way of thinking. The chronological focus is the nineteenth century, but many of these works also contain leads to material on the colonial period and on the twentieth century.

Acree, William Garrett, Jr., *Everyday Reading: Print Culture and Collective Identity in the Río de la Plata (1780–1910)*, Vanderbilt University Press, Nashville TN, 2011.

Aguirre, Carlos, and Carmen McEvoy, eds., *Intelectuales y poder: Ensayos en torno a la república de las letras en el Perú e Hispanoamérica (siglos xvi–xx)*, Instituto Francés de Estudios Andinos / Instituto Riva Agüero, Lima, 2008.

Aguirre Salvador, Rodolfo, ed., *Espacios de saber, espacios de poder: Iglesia, universidades y colegios en Hispanoamérica, siglos xvi–xix*, UNAM, México D. F., 2014.

Alonso, Paula, ed., *Construcciones impresas: Panfletos, diarios y revistas en la formación de los estados nacionales en América Latina, 1820–1920*, Fondo de Cultura Económica, México DF and Buenos Aires, 2004.

Altamirano, Carlos, director, *Historia de los intelectuales en América Latina, vol. I: La ciudad letrada, de la conquista al modernismo*, ed. Jorge Myers, Katz Editores, Buenos Aires, 2008.

Altschul, Nadia R., *Geographies of Philological Knowledge: Postcoloniality and the Transatlantic National Epic*, University of Chicago Press, Chicago, 2012.

Appelbaum, Nancy P., *Mapping the Country of Regions: The Chorographic Commission of Nineteenth-Century Colombia*, University of North Carolina Press, Chapel Hill, 2016.

Asúa, Miguel de, *La ciencia de Mayo: La cultura científica en el Río de la Plata, 1800–1820*, Fondo de Cultura Económica, Buenos Aires, 2010.

Bayly, C. A., *Empire and Information: Intelligence Gathering and Social Communication in India, 1780–1870*, Cambridge University Press, Cambridge and New York, 1996.

Becerra Riquelme, Silvia, and Zenobio Saldivia Maldonado, *El Mercurio de Valparaíso: Su rol de difusión de la ciencia y tecnología en el Chile decimonónico*, Bravo y Allende Editores, Chile, 2010.

Brice Heath, Shirley, *Telling Tongues: Language Policy in Mexico, Colony to Nation*, Columbia University Teachers College Publications, New York, 1972.

Brown, Richard D., *The Strength of a People: The Idea of an Informed Citizenry in America, 1650–1870*, University of North Carolina Press, Chapel Hill and London, 1996.

Buch, Tomás, and Carlos E. Solivérez, *De los quipus a los satélites: Historia de la tecnología en la Argentina*, Universidad Nacional de Quilmes Editorial, Bernal, Argentina, 2011.

Burke, Peter, *What is the History of Knowledge?*, Polity Press, Cambridge, 2016.

Burke, Peter, 'Writing the History of Knowledge in Brazil', *História, Ciências, Saúde-Manguinhos* (Rio de Janeiro), 25:3, July–Sept. 2018 (for bibliography on Brazil): http://dx.doi.org/10.1590/s0104-59702018000400014.

Cancino, Hugo, ed., *Los intelectuales latinoamericanos: Entre la modernidad y la tradición, siglos xix y xx*, Iberoamericana/Vervuert, Frankfurt, 2004.

Cañizares-Esguerra, Jorge, *Nature, Empire, and Nation: Explorations in the History of Science in the Iberian World*, Stanford University Press, Stanford CA, 2006.

Carrera, Magali, *Traveling from New Spain to Mexico: Mapping Practices of Nineteenth-Century Mexico*, Duke University Press, Durham NC, 2011.

Carreras, Sandra, and Katja Carrillo Zeiter, eds., *Las ciencias en la formación de las naciones americanas*, Iberoamericana/Vervuert, Madrid/Frankfurt, 2014.

Castro-Klarén, Sara, and John Charles Chasteen, eds., *Beyond Imagined Communities: Reading and Writing the Nation in Nineteenth-Century Latin America*, Woodrow Wilson Center Press, Washington DC, 2003.

Centeno, Miguel Angel, and Agustin E. Ferraro, eds., *State and Nation Making in Latin America and Spain: Republics of the Possible*, Cambridge University Press, New York, 2013.

Chiaramonte, José Carlos, *Fundamentos intelectuales y políticos de las independencias: Notas para una nueva historia intelectual de Iberoamérica*, Teseo, Buenos Aires, 2010.

Cid, Gabriel, *Pensar la revolución: Historia intelectual de la independencia chilena*, Ediciones Universidad Diego Portales, Santiago, 2019.

Cowie, Helen, *Conquering Nature in Spain and its Empire, 1750–1850*, Manchester University Press, Manchester, 2011.

Cueto, Marcos, and Steven Palmer, *Medicine and Public Health in Latin America: A History*, Cambridge University Press, New York, 2015.

Daston, Lorraine, and Peter Galison, *Objectivity*, Zone Books, New York, 2010.

Del Castillo, Lina, *Crafting a Republic for the World: Scientific, Geographic and Historiographic Inventions of Colombia*, University of Nebraska Press, Lincoln, 2018.

Del Valle, José, and Luis Gabriel Stheeman, *The Battle over Spanish between 1800 and 2000: Language Ideologies and Hispanic Intellectuals*, Routledge, London, 2002.

Denegri, Francesca, *El abanico y la cigarrera: La primera generación de ilustradas en el Perú*, Instituto de Estudios Peruanos, Lima, 1996.

Durston, Alan, and Bruce Mannheim, eds., *Indigenous Languages, Politics and Authority in Latin America: Historical and Ethnographic Perspectives*, University of Notre Dame Press, Indiana, 2018.

Dym, Jordana, and Karl Offen, eds., *Mapping Latin America: A Cartographic Reader*, University of Chicago Press, Chicago, 2011.

Earle, Rebecca, *The Return of the Native: Indians and Myth-Making in Spanish America, 1810–1930*, Duke University Press, Durham NC, 2007.

Espinoza, G. Antonio, *Education and the State in Modern Peru: Primary Schooling in Lima, 1821–c.1921*, Palgrave Macmillan, New York, 2013.

Farro, Máximo, *La formación del Museo de La Plata: Coleccionistas, comerciantes, estudiosos y naturalistas viajeros a fines del siglo xix*, Prohistoria Ediciones, Rosario, 2009.

Fernández-Sebastián, Javier, ed., *Diccionario político social del mundo iberoamericano, Tomo I, La era de las revoluciones*, Fundación Carolina / Sociedad de Conmemoración Estatal / Centro de Estudios Políticos y Constitucionales, Madrid, 2009; and *Tomo II, Los conceptos fundamentales, 1770–1870*, 2014.

Glave, Luis Miguel, ed., *Del pliego al periódico: Prensa, espacios públicos y construcción nacional Iberoamericana*, Fundación Mapfre Tavera, Madrid, 2003.

González Stephan, Beatriz, and Jens Andermann, eds., *Galerías del progreso: Museos, exposiciones y cultural visual en América Latina*, Beatriz Viterbo Editora, Rosario, 2006.

Goody, Jack, *The Theft of History*, Cambridge University Press, Cambridge and New York, 2006.

Gootenberg, Paul, *Imagining Development: Economic Ideas in Peru's 'Fictitious Prosperity' of Guano, 1840–1880*, University of California Press, Berkeley, 1993.

Guerra, François-Xavier and Annick Lempérière et al., *Los espacios públicos en Iberoamérica: Ambigüedades y problemas*, Fondo de Cultura Económica, Mexico City, 1998.

Heggarty, Paul, and Adrian J. Pearce, eds., *History and Language in the Andes*, Springer, 2011.

Jaksić, Iván, ed., *The Political Power of the Word: Press and Oratory in Nineteenth-Century Latin America*, Institute of Latin American Studies, London, 2002.

Jouve Martín, José R., *The Black Doctors of Colonial Lima: Science, Race, and Writing in Colonial and Early Republican Lima*, McGill-Queen's University Press, 2014.

Kohl, Philip L., Irina Podgorny and Stefanie Gänger, eds., *Nature and Antiquities: The Making of Archaeology in the Americas*, University of Arizona Press, Tucson, 2014.

Laird, Andrew, and Nicola Miller, eds., *Antiquities and Classical Traditions in Latin America*, Wiley, Oxford, 2018.

Lazzara, Michael J., and Vicky Unruh, eds., *Telling Ruins in Latin America*, Palgrave Macmillan, New York, 2009.

Lloyd, G. E. R., *The Ideals of Inquiry: An Ancient History*, Oxford University Press, Oxford, 2014.

McDonough, Kelly S., *The Learned Ones: Nahua Intellectuals in Postconquest Mexico*, University of Arizona Press, Tucson AZ, 2014.

Mallon, Florencia, ed., *Decolonizing Native Histories: Collaboration, Knowledge, and Language in the Americas*, Duke University Press, Durham NC, 2012.

Martínez Zuccardi, Soledad, *En busca de un campo cultural propio: Literatura, vida intelectual y revistas culturales en Tucumán (1904–1944)*, Corregidor, Buenos Aires, 2012.

Mignolo, Walter, *Local Histories / Global Designs: Coloniality, Subaltern Knowledges, and Border Thinking*, Princeton University Press, Princeton NJ, 2000, reissued with new preface, 2012.

Montserrat, Marcelo, ed., *La ciencia en la Argentina entre siglos: Textos, contextos e instituciones*, Ediciones Manantial, Buenos Aires, 2000.

Morán, Daniel, and María Aguirre, *Prensa política y educación popular en la independencia de América Latina*, no publisher identified, Lima, 2015.

Morgade, Graciela, ed., *Mujeres en la educación: Género y docencia en Argentina, 1870–1930*, Miño y Dávila Editores, Buenos Aires, 1997.

Ochoa Gautier, Ana María, *Aurality: Listening and Knowledge in Nineteenth-Century Colombia*, Duke University Press, Durham NC, 2014.

Ossenbach, Gabriela, and Miguel Somoza, eds., *Los manuales escolares como fuente para la historia de la educación en América Latina*, Universidad Nacional de Educación a Distancia, Madrid, 2001

Palti, Elias J., ed., *Mitos y realidad de la cultura política latinoamericana: Debates en IberoIdeas*, Prometeo Libros, Buenos Aires, 2010.

Paquette, Gabriel, ed., *Enlightened Reform in Southern Europe and its Atlantic Colonies, c. 1750–1830*, Ashgate, Farnham UK, 2009.

Parada, Alejandro E., *Cuando los lectores nos susurran: Libros, lecturas, bibliotecas, sociedad y prácticas editoriales en la Argentina*, Instituto de Investigaciones Bibliotecológicas, Universidad de Buenos Aires, Buenos Aires, 2007.

Peard, Julyan, *Race, Place and Medicine: The Idea of the Tropics in Nineteenth-Century Brazilian Medicine*, Duke University Press, Durham NC, 1999.

Plotkin, Mariano Ben, and Eduardo Zimmermann, eds., *Los saberes del Estado*, Edhasa, Buenos Aires, 2012.

Podgorny, Irina, and María Margaret Lopes, *El desierto en una vitrina: Museos e historia natural en la Argentina (1810–1890)*, LIMUSA, México DF, 2008.

Puiggrós, Adriana, et al., *La fábrica del conocimiento: Los saberes socialmente productivos en América Latina*, 2004.

Rama, Angel, *The Lettered City*, trans. John Charles Chasteen, Duke University Press, Durham NC, 1984.

Rappaport, Joanne, and T. Cummins, *Beyond the Lettered City: Indigenous Literacies in the Andes*, Duke University Press, Durham NC, 2012.

Rodríguez-García, José María, *The City of Translation: Poetry and Ideology in Nineteenth-Century Colombia*, 2010.

Roldán Vera, Eugenia, and Marcelo Caruso, eds., *Imported Modernity in Post-Colonial State Formation: The Appropriation of Political, Educational, and Cultural Models in Nineteenth-century Latin America*, Peter Lang, Frankfurt am Main, 2007.

Sagredo Baeza, Rafael, *Ciencia-mundo: Orden republicano, arte y nación en América*, Editorial Universitaria, Santiago, 2010.

Saldaña, Juan José, ed., *Science in Latin America: A History*, University of Texas Press, Austin, 2006.

Salomon, Frank, and Mercedes Niño-Murcia, *The Lettered Mountain: A Peruvian Village's Way with Writing*, Duke University Press, Durham NC, 2011.

Salvatore, Ricardo, *Disciplinary Conquest: US Scholars in South America, 1900–1945*, Duke University Press, Durham NC, 2016.

Santos, Boaventura de Sousa, *The End of the Cognitive Empire: The Coming of Age of Epistemologies of the South*, Duke University Press, Durham NC and London, 2018.

Schnell, Patience, *The Sociable Sciences: Darwin and His Contemporaries in Chile*, Palgrave Macmillan, New York, 2013.

Serrano, Sol, with Macarena Ponce de León, Francisca Rengifo and Rodrigo Mayorga, *Historia de la educación en Chile (1810–2010)*, Taurus, Santiago, vols. 1 and 2, 2012; vol. 3, 2018.

Servelli, Martín, *A través de la República: Corresponsales viajeros en la prensa porteña de entre siglos XIX–XX*, Prometeo, Buenos Aires, 2018.

Simon, Joshua, *The Ideology of Creole Revolution: Imperialism and Independence in American and Latin American Thought*, Cambridge University Press, Cambridge and New York, 2017.

Stuven, Ana María, *La seducción de un orden: Las elites y la construcción de Chile en las polémicas culturales y políticas del siglo xix*, Ediciones Universidad Católica de Chile, Santiago, 2000.

Subercaseaux, Bernardo, *Historia del libro en Chile (alma y cuerpo)*, LOM Ediciones, Santiago, 1993.

Thurner, Mark, ed., *The First Wave of Decolonization*, Routledge, London, 2019.

Thurner, Mark, and Andrés Guerrero, eds., *After Spanish Rule: Postcolonial Predicaments of the Americas*, Duke University Press, Durham NC, 2003.

Uribe-Uran, Victor M., *Honorable Lives: Lawyers, Family and Politics in Colombia, 1780–1850*, University of Pittsburgh Press, Pittsburgh PA, 2000.

Whipple, Pablo, *La gente decente de Lima y su resistencia al orden republicano: Jerarquías sociales, prensa y sistema judicial durante el siglo XIX*, Instituto de Estudios Peruanos, Lima, 2013.

INDEX

Academicism, critiques of, 92–93, 98, 116, 202–3

Adorno, Theodor, on mimesis, 100

Aguirre, Baltazar, 171

Aguirre y Tejada, Juan Luis de, 60

Alberdi, Juan Bautista, 49, 72, 143, 169, 262n38

Alcorta, Diego, 44–49

Alem, Leandro, 172

Allende, Juan Rafael, 77, 80

Alleón, Mario, 184

Almanacs, 56, 63, 68–69, 145

Alvear, Emilio de, 172–73

Amazon River, navigation of, 144, 152

Ameghino, Carlos, 254n68

Ameghino, Florentino, 157

Americanismo, 53, 117

Anderson, Benedict, 8, 12, 24, 37, 80, 218

Angelis, Pedro de, 130

Anti-colonialism, 11, 219, 221

Appelbaum, Nancy, 163

Araucanía (Chile), military occupation of, 75, 160

Arce, Mariano José de, 22

Archaeology, 98, 129, 162

Architecture, 82, 83, 205–6, 214; of national libraries, 30, 37; neo-classical, 29, 56, 87; teaching of, 41, 91, 206

Arequipa (Peru), 40, 148, 210

Argentina: agriculture in, 51–53, 154–55, 171; book trade in, 63–67, 70–72, 73–75; as case study, 11; Confederation of, 171; constitutions of, 48–49, 143, 260n21; drawing teaching in, 87, 93–95; education

in, 199, 201–5, 213; industrialisation in, 175–76; infrastructure in, 182–3, 187–190, 197 (*see also* Refrigerator ships, invention of; Transandine Railway); literacy in, 61; national library of, 16, 17, 19–21, 23, 27–29, 36, 37; philosophy in, 44–49; political economy in, 170–74; popular libraries in, 33; role of land in, 49–53, 152–55, 162; study of geography in, 156–59; study of language in, 130–32, 141; universities in, 39–41, 44, 57–58, 187, 232

Argerich, Cosme, 41–43

Arguedas, José María, 123, 285n57

Arielismo, 117

Aristides Zañartu, Manuel, 175

Artigas, José, 17

Asociación Pro-Indígena (Peru), 215

Astronomy, 103, 104, 145, 148, 160 *See also* Ephemerides

Atacama Desert, 77, 143, 195; mapping of, 160

Atlases: in Chile, 161; in Peru, 148–50

Australia, 160, 183, 191, 192

Authorship, invention of, 72–74

Autodidacticism, 57, 68, 84, 108, 110, 112, 114, 148, 151, 208, 216, 229; publishing for, 67–70; among women, 203

Avellaneda, Nicolás, 189, 201, 204, 262n38; on landownership, 169

Azamor y Ramírez, Manuel de, 23

Azara, Félix de, 131

Bachelet, Michelle, 32

Bacle, Andrea Macaire, 65–67

A NOTE ON THE TYPE

This book has been composed in Arno, an Old-style serif typeface in the
classic Venetian tradition, designed by Robert Slimbach at Adobe.